Mediated Communication

CURRENT COMMUNICATION

AN ADVANCED TEXT SERIES

Series Editor

Jesse G. Delia *University of Illinois*

VOLUMES IN THE SERIES

James A. Anderson and Timothy P. Meyer
Mediated Communication
A SOCIAL ACTION PERSPECTIVE

FORTHCOMING VOLUMES

Daniel J. O'Keefe
Persuasion: Theory and Research

Victoria O'Donnell
Analyzing Media: Making Meanings Out of Media

CURRENT COMMUNICATION is a series of advanced texts spanning the full range of the communication curriculum and including all the core areas of the field. Each volume in the series is a substantive, lucidly written book appropriate for use in advanced undergraduate and beginning graduate level courses. All the volumes survey current theories and concepts, research and critical literatures, and scholarly methods, but each does this within a distinctive and original framework that makes the material accessible to students while enhancing and shaping understanding of its area for professionals.

Mediated Communication

A Social Action Perspective

James A. Anderson

Timothy P. Meyer

SAGE PUBLICATIONS
The Publishers of Professional Social Science
Newbury Park Beverly Hills London New Delhi

For information address:

SAGE Publications, Inc.
2111 West Hillcrest Drive
Newbury Park, California 91320

SAGE Publications Inc.
275 South Beverly Drive
Beverly Hills
California 90212

SAGE Publications Ltd.
28 Banner Street
London EC1Y 8QE
England

SAGE PUBLICATIONS India Pvt. Ltd.
M-32 Market
Greater Kailash I
New Delhi 110 048 India

Printed in the United States of America

Library of Congress Cataloging-in-Publication Data

Anderson, James A. (James Arthur), 1939-
Mediated communication : a social action perspective / by James A. Anderson and Timothy P. Meyer.
p. cm. — (Current communication, an advanced text series ; v. 1)
Bibliography: p.
Includes index.
ISBN 0-8039-3050-X
1. Mass media—Influence. 2. Mass media—Research—Methodology. 3. Mass media—Social aspects. I. Meyer, Timothy P. II. Title. III. Series.
P94.A48 1988
302.2'34—dc19 88-23903
CIP

FIRST PRINTING 1988

Contents

Preface

WORK ON THIS BOOK BEGAN in the mid-1970s when we embarked on a program of ethnographic research focusing on media and the family. A series of publications written together, separately and with other colleagues followed. What we learned was that the old style theories which located the site of media effects in the individual and the source of those effects in the content were inadequate to the task of explaining the media and texts of mediated communication as they appeared in the lives we live. As we had written in support of the older theories (Anderson & Meyer, 1973), this redirection was truly a case of the empirical evidence sweeping away our preconceptions.

This book is based on the premise that theory in communication cannot be narrowly drawn. Any theory posed must account for the nature and practices of communication in its many forms and locations. In short, we do not believe that there is a useful mediated communication theory that is separate from an interpersonal or organizational communication theory. While there are obvious differences in forms and local practices, the course of our own lives organize these into a sensibility unity.

This book views any human life as a coconstruction between self and other. It is our fundamental axiom. This position may harbor some difficulties for the person who views human life as populated by separate individuals who in their mature state carry all the cognitive programming necessary for action.

Nearly as fundamental, the second axiom of this book is that meaning is an achievement of interpretation located in the time and place of its accomplishment and not something that is delivered by content. This axiom is in clear opposition to the conceptualization of meaning used whether acknowledged or not by the majority of media research studies.

These two axioms presented some difficulties for us in the writing of this book. First, we had to assume a model reader who would not come to either of these axioms naturally as the concepts of the autonomous individual and of content being a delivery system are well-entrenched. Second, the axioms collapse the foundation for the traditional concept of media effect itself by rejecting the linear flow of content as agent, exposure as mechanism, and individual behavior as effect.

Our solution to these problems (and in support of our belief of a useful unity of theory) was to step back from a close focus on the consequences of mediated communication and to attempt a wider view instead that would let the reader participate in the insights of our field experiences.

We begin in Chapter 1 about as far back as one can get by considering the nature of communication as the production of and participation in meaning, move to its performance in interpersonal relationships, and finally consider its performance in mediated communication sites. One of the characteristics discovered in this analysis is that mediated communication is composed of two relatively separate functions of production and reception. Chapter 2, therefore, takes up the nature of the production process by examining the market forces that shape the content commodity. Chapter 3 looks at the embedded qualities of that content as it is addressed by its audiences. Chapter 4 completes this overview by considering the methods and practices of everyday life that accommodate the media and their texts in our daily routines.

Chapter 5 starts Part II of the work that involves a journey in search of the effects of mediated communication. This chapter explores the theories that populate the literature and constitute the very notion of effect. Chapters 6 and 7 consider the researcher methodologies that, in concert with theory, generate the evidence that supports the explanations of effects. Because methods constitute the facts of these explanations, it is not possible to understand our present ideas about effects unless one has an understanding of these methods. Chapter 8 shows how theory and method come together to produce the knowledge claims that are what we know as the effects of the media. Chapter 8 ends our search for effects by providing the principles by which an effect can be recognized.

Finally Chapter 9 takes up the third part of the text by laying out the elements of Accommodation Theory—a description of the interpenetration of media, their texts, and our daily lives. The chapter begins with a condensation of the work accomplished in the first two parts, states the components of the theory, and finally considers the implications of it.

Each of the three parts of the book stand alone and stand in relation to the other two. While we have given one organization, another useful arrangement is to begin with Part II before returning to the beginning chapters. Each of the parts is also written as an extended essay. The chapter divisions represent a pause but not a full stop in the flow of content. The reader should anticipate returning to some of the themes introduced in an earlier chapter, as we regularly note.

This book is written for the advanced undergraduate, graduate student, and faculty colleague. It is not an introductory text. We are indebted to a broad literature that we have referenced in the bibliography, but in the main, have chosen not to cite in the body of the text, primarily in defense of a readable text. The knowledgeable reader will recognize our allusions and debts, the less knowledgeable reader will not be impeded by meaningless parenthetical names. We understand the limits of this solution and hope the benefits outweigh them.

Because we do have a multiple audience in mind, there are mixed levels in the writing. As helps, we have provided chapter précis; a glossary of words highlighted in the text, heading, and chapter summaries; and a device called "central ideas." The central ideas conclusion of all but the shortest sections that divide the chapters offers not a summary but a coalescence of the ideas of the section to provide another perspective on them. This perspective can be used as tool to reengage the ideas of the section. In short, the summaries summarize; the central ideas ending begins again. We hope the reader can use the central ideas to reflect on what has been read.

Because we believe that everyday life is the proper location of study, we have shared stories from our own lives with you. On occasion they are recognizably white, middle-class, and male. These stories appear because they are part of the action in which we perform and not from any sense of the proper order of things. The reader should be aware that had a woman, for example, written here, she would likely have different stories to tell that would incarnate the theoretical principles within them.

Over the years of its development, scores of people have made a contribution to this book. We need to take note of David Swanson whose painstaking comments were of high value. Other readers, too, gave of their time and insight: Robert Avery, Julie Brown, Susan Tyler Eastman, Aubrey Fisher, Susan Goodwin, Leonard Hawes, Karen Huck, Horace Newcomb, Alexis Olds, Malcolm Sillars, and Paul Traudt is an incomplete list. In the end, we dedicate this to our wives who suffered our struggles with a righteousness offering proper justice, and whose doubt and occasional derision drove us on.

We would also like to thank Gary Rosenberg and family for their generous financial support, which greatly facilitated the final stages of this book.

We are grateful to the following for permission to reprint portions of copyrighted material: The Salt Lake Tribune Corporation for R. Reno, *The Salt Lake Tribune*, 15 September, 1986, p. B-10; Broadcast Education Association for permission to adapt material from J. A. Anderson and R. K. Avery (1988) "The Concept of Effects: Recognizing our Personal Judgments," *Journal of Broadcasting and Electronic Media, 32*, pp. 359-366; Ablex Publishing Company of Norwood, New Jersey for T. Lindlof (Ed.) (1987) *Natural Audiences*.

Part I

The Perspective of Analysis

1

The Nature of Communication

BEN WALKED UP TO the table in the student union where Lynette was sitting reading a book. "Hi," he said. With that time-worn and well-practiced greeting, Ben initiated the process of creating an interaction we call communication. At this point, neither Ben nor Lynette have any knowledge of what this communication event will actually be. They do have a very good idea of the kinds of events it could be and an excellent notion of the ways in which any one of them might be achieved. After all, they are competent people having participated in conversations like these from a very early age. But neither can achieve any *communication* outcome alone. They must negotiate whatever outcome will be, together.

Let's consider Ben for a moment: He comes to this interaction carrying his understanding of the rules, customs, mores that govern his behavior as a male member of his society as interpreted through his own personality. He has his past history of events like these and of specific interactions with Lynette. His desired outcome may be as simple as merely sustaining an interaction for a given period of time before his next class or he may seek the most complex of human interactions.

Lynette for her side has her understanding of the rules, customs, mores that govern her behavior as a female member of her society as interpreted through her own personality. She has her past history of events like these and of specific interactions with Ben. By saying "Hi" so that she could hear, Ben has forced a communication situation on Lynette. No matter what she does (even if she totally ignores him) her actions will be interpreted as a response to that situation. She does, however, have an enormous range of possible responses including a quick dismissal ("Hi, Ben. Hey, I'm studying for a test next period. Can I talk to you later?") and the most complex of human interactions.

SYNOPSIS

It might seem strange to begin a book about mediated communication with an example of an interpersonal conversation. We do so because we are going to spend some time exploring interpersonal communication before turning our attention for the rest of the book to mediated communication. The reason we spend the time here with conversations is that, first, this form of communication is the most fundamental. It is necessary to establish some basic principles of interpersonal communication before we can move to mediated communication. Second, we believe that the ultimate form of human sense making is in the action surrounding human discourse. We come to understand the texts of mediated communication in the **social action** frames of everyday life in which conversation is so much a part.

This chapter has the responsibility of introducing us to the general character and terminology of a social action approach to communication. We begin with the baseline requirements for communication of any kind. We, then, make a most important move in separating the concepts of signification and meaning. This separation will allow us to understand how meaning is an achievement under some **local control** rather than a cognitive spasm.

The next major section considers communication as an interactive process. The point of this section is to show by examples the principles of communication in action. We follow these examples with an analysis of some characteristics of meaning. We introduce meaning as an interpretive performance that is emergent, prolific, and promiscuous.

We then begin the first of two sections, which, taken together, compare the characteristics of interpersonal communication—conversations—with the characteristics of mediated communication. Here we make the final turn from interpersonal to mediated communication. To help you find your way through what can be a confusion of ideas and terms, we have divided the chapter into three major partitions. After each of these partitions, we pause to list the major concepts that have been presented. These concepts are the building blocks for the next set of ideas. You should assure yourself of a reasonable understanding of them before going on. Don't forget to make use of the glossary for additional help.

THE FOUNDATIONS OF COMMUNICATION

What is required to communicate to another? In very simple terms three things are required: (a) a base of common experiences about which to communicate; (b) some system to reference that base; and (c) a relationship that enables the mutual accomplishment of meaning.[1] Let's look briefly at each:

EXPERIENTIAL BASE

The ability to communicate develops through a lifetime of shared history. It is easy in our American mythology to claim that we are all different—uniquely raised. In fact, however, there are powerful—and necessary for communication—mechanisms in place to ensure that we are very much alike. We begin with a common physiology subject to common physical forces—an irreducible and continually present communality, perhaps the primeval basis for communication. We are born into an ongoing social communication process. We are raised in adult/child and child/child relationships that do not simply appear, but are governed by larger institutions. As these relationships progress, they provide the members with a common history. As we learn to communicate, the strategies and performances of discourse are largely the same. We talk together, ask questions, get answers. We go to school together, do our social thing together, work together. We drive cars, call on the phone, read books, hear music, see movies, watch television. If we did not have this vast reservoir of common experience, we would not be able to communicate.[2]

A SYSTEM OF SIGNIFICATION

Signification is a term that comes to us from **semiotics**. It refers to the process of creating and maintaining signs. The **sign** is a general term used to describe anything that cognitively comes to stand for something else, whether a thing or an idea. Signs, then, would include words, pictures, **icons,** textures, odors, gestures, melodies—in short anything that is used to reference something else. The process of signification involves, first, the capacity to reference something outside of present experience, and then the manner in which, for example, certain sounds or pen strokes become a word. In more general terms, signification is the way in which one thing becomes a sign of another.

Some signs reside within **sign systems.** A sign system is a collection of signs within a system of signification that includes a set of rules for governing the relationships among its signs. The forms and conventions of the ballet or of cinematography can be seen as a sign system. The most powerful of signs exist within a **semiotic system.** A semiotic system is a reality-defining—some say reality-producing[3]—system of symbolic knowledge. Such systems approach completeness when members can ordinarily constitute the whole of their understanding within them. It is probable that only **language** approaches the nature of a complete semiotic system.[4]

SIGNIFICATION AND COMMUNICATION Signification starts with the capacity of the human mind to partition the ongoing flow of sensation into an understanding of time, space, essences, and relationships. The human consciousness first punctuates—sets boundaries within—the continuous movement of experience and then separately names the bounded experiences. This process of first perceiving a difference and then naming that difference is the process of signification.

It is obvious that human knowledge, if it is to extend beyond what is sensately present, requires some system of signification. That is, if the past, the future, the distant, the abstract are to exist, there must be signification systems to create and reference them. Similarly, it is obvious that communication, if it is to extend beyond the mutual, face-to-face performance of the present, requires *common* systems of signification.

The value of communication for the human species moved signification from the psychological cognitions of the individual into the sociological processes of language. Language is a common system of signification by which we understand and can exchange those understandings of ourselves and the world. Language is both method and product of the conventionalized agreements that form the fundamental social contract between people. The semiotic—the method of our joint understanding—and the community—the product of our common understandings—are mutually created in those agreements.

Semiotic systems, such as language, occur on the grand **sociological scale** and have grand procedures for ensuring acceptance and compliance with the contract. As many have pointed out, we are "born into" the contract. We are often well-grown before gaining the slightest recognition of the terms of this contract having been socialized into functioning naturally within those terms. The semiotic contract is a communal agreement that every member affirms in each usage. Change occurs within this overarching communal scale. The lone individual can neither institute nor resist this change.

Semiotic systems, while in time and place, are independent of the particular moment, the particular conditions, and the particular individuals surrounding an occurrence of their use. *It is this independence from the particular that distinguishes signifying from meaning.* Signifying occurs within a **semiotic community** in sociological time and space; meaning occurs within individuals at a given moment in given conditions. Competent members of a linguistic community all know what the signs of their language signify. What they mean, however, in a particular sentence spoken by one individual to another depends on the interpretation of that situation by those individuals. Meaning is a **sense making** act, not a delivered commodity.

Meaning is, however, dependent upon signification. That is, for symbolic meaning[5] to occur there must first be signification. Without signification, as we have argued, we have no greater world than that which is materially present at the moment. To have the greater world of the past, the future, the distant, the abstract, we must have some system of signs that will permit us to first represent (or create) and then to interpret, manipulate, relate, compare, contrast, and so on, ourselves, the world about us, and our ideas of both. Signification occurs in the representation (or creation) of our human reality; meaning occurs in the interpretation of that reality (always embedded in time, place, and condition).

SIGNIFYING AND MEANING The distinction that we make between signifying and meaning gives us a useful solution to the vexing problem of how the symbolic representations that we use in language, gesture, pictures, and so on have common references across large numbers of people, yet are capable of an infinite variety of meaningful interpretation. Stanislavski, for example, is reputed to have auditioned actors by asking them to come up with 40 different messages from the words "this evening" (Jakobson, in Innis, 1985, p. 151). While we might struggle with 40, we can certainly come up with several by varying the expressive tint of our presentation. Consequently, we find ourselves not being able to predict the meaning that the words "this evening" would be used to present, yet at the same time, as competent English-speaking members, we know to what the words "this evening" refer. This infinite variation of potential meaning coupled with a fixed reference appears to be a contradiction.

We break this apparent contradiction when we separate the process of the creation of signs from the use of those signs once created into the separate processes of signifying and meaning. To continue our example, the words "this evening" *signify* two ideas—the ideas of reference and of a time of day. "This" and "evening" exist as words because they signify those ideas—that is their ontology. What "this evening" *means*, however, is never fixed. Its meaning depends on an interpretation, which, in turn, depends on how that phrase is presented in a particular context to a particular audience. The concept here is analogous to taking a large rock and placing it in a living room, a garden, the middle of a road, and in a field of rocks. It is always the same rock, but its meaning changes radically as it is used in a particular place and viewed by particular individuals.

In later sections in this chapter, we will spend considerable time on the attributes of meaning. Let us spend just a few paragraphs to highlight the distinctions we are making. For a term so central to communication, the concept of *meaning* remains extremely vague and poorly developed.

It is, perhaps, easiest to consider what meaning is not. Meaning is not contained in a dictionary. Dictionary "meanings" are at best partial, highly conventionalized, descriptors of the signified. To say that a rock is "any relatively hard, naturally formed mass of mineral or petrified matter" (American Heritage Dictionary, p. 1123) doesn't help us understand Lionel Richie when he sings that he is "like a rock." As we have argued, the meaning of the word *rock* is dependent on the sign rock signifying the conceptualized rock, but any appearance of the word *rock* will always be interpreted according to the conditions of its presentation in relation to a particular meaning maker.

The commonalities and differences of our separate and shared experiences will be reflected in meaning as the site of that interpretation is in the individual consciousness. This emphasis on the individual is not to press a claim that each individual independently creates the meaning that a sentence has without reference to the sense making of any other. "Individual consciousnesses" are, after all, the product of the semiotic community—a claim we will more fully develop in Chapter 4.

We want to point out here that sense making is a set of acts like any other emanating from an individual. That it is practiced according to social rules, supervised by others, emerges in the interaction with others, and in general, is exquisitely responsive to **the Other** is not denied. At the same time, one cannot substitute an instantiated cultural meaning (perhaps, devised by academic elitists) for what are the sense-making performances of individuals. Nevertheless, *the meaning of a word embeds the sign in someone's ongoing experience.* We may know your class or your gender, but we may not presume the conclusion of your meaning. *Your* meaning becomes known only in the interaction between us.

In its fullness, then, only you can experience what a word means to you. Meaning, therefore, is as multidimensional as the experiential base of interpretation available to the meaning maker. The multidimensionality of meaning directs us to examine the thickness of meaning—the fact that meaning is always multiple and that this multiplicity is present for the meaning-maker. We are not talking about ambiguity—that words "carry" more than one meaning, making it difficult to determine which one is meant. We are pointing out that the meaning maker accomplishes the task of sense making in a number of interpretive contexts, all of which result in different, perhaps even radically different, meanings that coexist for the individual. We seem to deal with this multiplicity in our **quotidian** endeavors without great effort.

Consider for example, our large rock in the middle of the road. For the flatlander driving in the mountains for the first time, it represents a serious danger; for the experienced hill driver, it is a commonplace; for the backpacker looking down from the trail on the action on the road, it may be a source of some devilish amusement. Now roll all those meanings into the consciousness of the backpacker who says to herself: "Boy, I can remember when I first came here, a rock like that would scare me to death, now I just whip around them. Still, somebody is going to be awfully surprised when they come around that curve." On which of these meanings does she act? Does she sit to await what happens (her amusement)? Does she walk on (the rock poses no real danger)? Does she call the authorities (it could badly scare someone into a fatal error)? All of these actions can be justified from the multiple meanings that are available to her. Note that there is no ambiguity here; there is a multiplicity of layered meanings and, therefore, uncertainty as to the outcome.

Signification frees us from the here and now. It permits us a knowledge of extended time and space. When we hold that signification in common, we create a method of exchange. Any given exchange, however, returns us to the here and now. We must have a system of common signs to communicate, but their meaning (not what they signify) can be realized only in the conditions of their presentation.

THE RELATIONSHIP

The third and final fundamental of communication is the relationship. Communication requires the cooperative effort of all **communicants.** To attain any mutual accomplishment of meaning, communicants must recognize the intent to communicate, grant the effort to find the means of exchange, work to develop some common meaning for the content that is exchanged, and make their performance sensible within that common meaning.

Before analyzing these requirements, a warning flag should be raised concerning the previous sentence. While perhaps reasonable on the face of it, it is full of great glosses and yawning traps. Not the least of these is in the phrase the "mutual accomplishment of meaning." Communication in its strictest sense involves some common achievement of meaning—a common idea held in more than one consciousness as a result of the intent, however vague, to achieve that mutuality. But accomplishments can be large or small, and efforts may fail as well as succeed. What we expect in a passing greeting is not the same as our expectations for a late night, brandied, soul search with a good friend. One can accomplish the mutual meaning of a passing greeting with some ease because not much needs to get done. Greetings are well-practiced performances. A soul search is not. Neither communicant may have a clear idea of what meanings are to be meant. Their performance may be better seen as the joint creation of (rather than exchange of) meanings that may continue to emerge for each of them long after the conversation ceases. Meaning is not a package to be delivered; it is an accomplishment. In communication, it is a mutual accomplishment.

There is a great range of improvisation and invention in the relationship that enables communication. An analysis such as this one can fix only some rather artificial reference points by which we can partially examine the terms of that relationship. This analysis examines it under the four headings that follow.

INTENT TO COMMUNICATE It is our claim that the valid act of communication is to mutually establish a common meaning—we are working hard here to have you understand what we mean in this essay. We initiate this effort by the intent to accomplish a meaning we can hold in common. (We are not writing simply to accomplish a conventional form or to create a text that may be meaningful in some way to others, but to discover what our ideas can mean in relationship to you, although we may never find this out.) This intent establishes the necessary relationship in which the communicants are identified, and the rule that communication is what is being accomplished is set in place. While it is true that everything one does can be interpreted by another, not everything being done involves the mutual achievement of meaning (which is our *raison d'ètre* of communication). The person who "reads" the outfit of another and says, "I see that you are a jogger; that says a lot to me about you," knows only his or her own meanings and references an act of interpretation rather than communication. And, of course, one can give a performance with little concern of what it means to another—the performance being its own reward. In short, neither every meaningful event nor every discursive performance is necessarily an act of communication. Human communication, then, is identified by the intent to achieve meaning.

MEANS OF ACCOMPLISHMENT Much of the means of communication is established on the sociological level (e. g., the signification process) and is beyond the control, although often within the choice, of the individual. Many of the circumstances that govern the success of communication can be manipulated. We communicate within a form—conversations, letters, textbooks; using systems of signs—words, images, gestures, pictures; in a relationship—friend to friend, teacher to student, performer to audience; within a context of time, space, and performance. The characteristics of *form, code, relationship, context,* and *content* create the arena of available choice in communicating meaning. Each of these characteristics separately and in combination matter in the mutual exchange of meaning. The analysis of any communication requires their consideration.

THE WORK OF MUTUAL ACCOMPLISHMENT The choices that we make, however, carry no guarantees as to the meaning another will make of them. The work of an honest mutual exchange involves, for each, a commitment to discover the meaning intended and the effort to supervise the meaning construction of the other. It seems clear that we can best accomplish this work in face-to-face conversation—at least, we have the best opportunities there. In mediated communication such as this book, we will probably have no opportunity to discover the sense that you make of what we write. If you are reading this book as part of a class, our intended meaning may be less important than the interpretation provided by the instructor. Our own process of writing is conflicted as we are presumably communicating with students but must, in fact, capture the imagination of our colleagues—a much different audience. We shall see in later sections that the impediments to the work of mutual exchange within mediated communication create a far different communication situation. Nevertheless, we will, and have already, interacted extensively in person and through texts to accomplish an understanding of "what we mean" in this text. Our understanding (yes, we're talking as the authors here) will grow as others comment, reflect, and use this text. Our understanding will grow because no one can anticipate the full potential of any communication performance.

SENSIBLE PERFORMANCES It is clear that communication can never be understood by the words alone. Communication is always a performance of social action. It is the performance that provides the interpretive frame of the content. That is, *I* understand what *you* are saying because of what *we* are doing. Consider an act of self-disclosure conducted in a singles bar, and another conducted at the breakfast table, lingering over a cup of coffee. The words may be the same but it's difficult to suppose that the intended meaning and the meaningful consequences would be the same. Now presume that we were to import the breakfast-table performance into the singles-bar context. There would be confusion, maybe claims of playacting—the breakfast-table performance would not be clearly sensible in that context. The questions would always remain: "Why are you doing a breakfast-table performance in this singles bar? How does that make sense?"

In a similar manner, we will argue that mediated communication has its sensible performances. Simply contrast the reading of a romance novel as an assignment in a popular culture class and as the way to spend an hour or two. The text is the same, but little else. These two performances provide radically different frames of interpretation. As in interpersonal communication, mediated communication performances can be highly conventionalized—that is, governed by widely accepted rules (e.g., attending the theater)—but, the presence of household (the various forms of television) and, now, personal (computers, tape players) media give rise to interpretive frames whose social action is determined in much smaller spheres. That fact that interpretive frames can develop on the individual level dispels the view of the mass audience. We may all play the same tape, but we don't hear the same music.

SUMMARY

It was, perhaps, any of genes, procreation, food, or shelter that brought us initially together. Now we humans are inextricably bound in relationships to the extent that we may fail to see the special requirements that communication demands. In our well-practiced performances, we easily assume the intent to communicate; the means of accomplishing meaning are simply there before us; we are often careless of the work of that achievement; and our actions are without reflection. Nonetheless, our social fabric is dependent on these elements. As a society and as individuals, we commit extensive resources to accomplish them.

The three fundamental requirements of communication are common experiences, shared signification, and a relationship in which to accomplish the mutual achievement of meaning. To solve the problem of communication with an alien, we must first discover what we can do together, find a common means to refer to that doing, and in the process develop a relationship that permits our achievement. Without the common experience of sound, there would have been no music, and no connection of any kind would have been possible in that cinematic encounter.

In the next section, we move from the static examination of these fundamentals to an examination of the interactive nature of communication. Interaction is social action, and it is in social action that meaning appears. Meaning is *not* the *product* of communication. Communication is a process by which we can achieve meaning. We have much to say about meaning. To begin our study of it, we first consider the interactive nature of communication.

CENTRAL IDEAS: THE FOUNDATIONS OF COMMUNICATION

1. Communication requires a common experiential base, a system of signification, and a relationship that enables the mutual accomplishment of meaning.
2. We are born into a living system that guarantees a vast reservoir of face-to-face experiences that we can jointly reference.
3. Signification involves the cognitive creation of a concept and indexing it with a sign. It is not meaning. With the advent of language, both concepts and signs have communal rather than individual ownership in the semiotic community.
4. Meaning is the product of the interpretation of a sign in some ongoing experience. It is the sense of the sign to an interpreter in a particular circumstance.
5. The relationship of accomplishment implies an intent to communicate, the means of a mutual accomplishment of meaning, and the work of that achievement in sensible performances.

SOME CHARACTERISTICS OF MEANING

Communication cannot be accomplished in a single act. Our writing of those words communicates nothing until they are read by you. This simple little notion tells us a lot about the concept of communication. It tells us that the communication event is dependent on all the members involved. What the speaker says, the writer writes, the cinematographer photographs is not sufficient for our understanding of what was communicated. We must also know what the listener hears, the reader reads, and the viewer sees. The angry mother may claim, "You know, I told you not to do that!" She may remember the exact words that she said, but she can only guess at what was heard and the interpretation given. She will justify her anger on the mistaken notion that what she said guaranteed that the prohibition was understood. A student handing in a late paper saying, "I know the syllabus says that late papers are not accepted, but I was sick last week and couldn't get it done," understands that the words, *late papers are not accepted,* may not mean exactly that. This student may know from past experience that teachers often accept papers delayed for a good reason. For this student, the words, *late papers are not accepted* actually read, *late papers are not accepted but not all delayed papers are late.* For another student, without this past experience, the words may read as an absolute prohibition based on time. These are two very different sense-making events surrounding the same phrase in a syllabus.

Communication, then, occurs within an interactive process. *Process* is one of those wonderfully malleable words whose meaning can take many shapes. In a simple form, it can refer to an event of connected steps occurring over time. In the communication discipline, it is generally used to describe the communication event as one that has elements interacting in highly variable conditions. That is to say that the requirements for getting from step one to any other step can be met in diverse ways. The consequence of such a process is that no step can be predicted by what has preceded it, and any possible outcome is equally likely from any given starting point. We use the term *interactive* to describe this process to highlight the fact that each element in the process functions in reference to all the others. Communication, therefore, occurs in the particular relationship of its elements. A communication event is a holism whose outcome cannot be determined by merely considering the content that is presented.

We have begun to create an argument here that is contrary to much of our informal and some of our scientific thinking on communication. Our argument is centered on the concept of meaning—how it is created, what are its characteristics and the like. In the sections that follow we first present a conversational example of the complexities involved in the mutual achievement of meaning and then introduce four notions about meaning: that meaning is (a) the product of sense-making performances embedded in interpretive frames of action and that meaning-making is (b) an ongoing process, (c) inevitable, and (d) incessant.

THE ACHIEVEMENT OF MEANING: A CONVERSATIONAL EXAMPLE

The interactive nature of communication means that we cannot know what *communication*—the mutual accomplishment of meaning—occurred until after the fact. But even then what is known and who knows it is problematic. Consider this bit of dialogue taken from an actual conversation between a child and her father.

(1) C: "Daddy, let me see Fuzzy Bear."
(2) F: "MmHm, you know I bought that bear for your mommy . . . when we were in college."

(3) C: "I know I can't keep it."
(4) F: "MmHm."
(5) C: "I wish I could keep it . . . for my other dolls."
(6) F: "Yeah."

As we begin this analysis let's make explicit some of the terms of the ordinary contract that permits interpersonal conversations: (1) the members are making a valid effort to communicate something (signifying a common experiential base with the intent to exchange); (2) unless specifically noted, each turn of talk is in reference to the turns that precede it; (3) not everything has to be stated explicitly—each member can use a commonly held body of knowledge concerning the subject matter of the conversation.

Using these terms, we can briefly analyze this conversation in order to demonstrate some principles of communication. The first turn appears to be a simple enough request, but the verb "see" is deeply ambiguous to us who cannot know the context in which it was uttered. "Let me see" can easily mean, "Take the bear out of the box and show it to me," or, "Take the bear down from the shelf and hold it in front of me"; or "Hand me the bear and let me hold it"; but it probably does not mean, "Take the blindfold off of my eyes that I may see the bear." For the father and child in this conversation, the word *see* seems to pose little problem. They have the context before them and can further index whatever rules may govern the seeing of Fuzzy Bear. In fact, the father may be commenting on those rules when he reminds the child of a special characteristic of this toy, "I bought that bear for your mommy."

We have a much better understanding of both turn 1 and turn 2 when the child in turn 3 ignores what textually could be a straight expositional statement by the father, and responds with her reference to the rules. We now understand the child's first turn to mean, "Let me hold Fuzzy Bear," or, "Let me play with Fuzzy Bear," or even, "Let me have Fuzzy Bear for my own." We can also assume that the father in turn 2 was not simply describing the bear but was indeed indexing a rule known to both parties, perhaps to preclude the child from making a request to keep the toy. In his turn 4, the father may be affirming the rule and the child's understanding of it, or may be only filling his turn as required. Turn 5 appears to reveal the entire conversation to us. The toy is a desired object for the child, not simply something pleasant to look at or to hold. Was the child's purpose from the beginning to gain possession of the toy? Perhaps not, but that would be a most favored outcome. In turn 5, then, the child may be acknowledging her initial meaning of wanting to keep the bear and now reinitiating the request in a polite, indirect manner. The indirectness of the request may be an attempt to deflect any judgment about herself by placing the reason for the request outside of her. Turn six could be an agreement to the request, but more likely, it is an oral shorthand by which the father shows that he recognizes the child's gambit and again refuses, as in "Yeah, I know you want the bear, but you can't have it. It belongs to mommy."

The analyst who provided this explanation of this conversation would not claim that it is the only explanation of the meanings revealed in the interaction, just that it is a plausible or probable explanation. In the final analysis, the analyst cannot know what this conversation meant to the child and her father individually and together. The analyst can explicate only what the conversation meant to the analyst. You may arrive at a different interpretation. Our understanding of any communication is always probabilistic because content does not speak for itself. It interacts with its receiver in a process of interpretation.

We can show this interpretive interaction in the critical analysis of our conversation by pointing out that the explanation depends on the claim made about turn 2—that this turn indexes a *rule* about the toy and is not just descriptive. The "rule" interpretation permits us to understand turn 6 as a refusal. Take away the idea of a rule and the father's "Yeah" could now stand for, "Yeah, you can keep it." Is the claim about the presence of a rule correct? We can't know, but with the rule the whole conversation better fits the terms of the interpersonal contract that we noted in the beginning of this analysis. That better fit makes the rule interpretation more likely and, therefore, more reasonable, but certainly not absolute.

It has taken us these several paragraphs to analyze minimally a conversation of five turns. That conversation that was easily managed by a very young child left us in doubt as to its interpretation. It is clear that whatever meanings were held by the conversationalists, they were not in the words but in the ongoing interpretive processes at work.

THE INTERPRETIVE PROCESSES OF MEANING

Outcomes of communication events, we would claim, are the result of the ongoing interactions between communicants, content, and context within the interpretive performances of some ongoing action. These interactions form a **semantic frame**—a system of interpretation that defines relationships between signs and meanings—in which the construction of meaning gets done. The significance of this last statement is that for any given piece of content—a television program, a newspaper article, a turn in a conversation—there is no single, true meaning that can be derived from the content itself. The first principle of meaning is that meanings are *not delivered* in content but are *constructed* within the semantic frame in which the content appears and is a part. This principle changes the question of "What is the meaning of this sentence?" to "What meanings are likely to appear given the particular sentence, communicants, and context involved in the action of a given scene?" The authors would hold that there are many valid meanings for any unit of content. The construction of meaning is governed by the system of constraints embodied in the interaction between communicants, content, and context as they participate in some ongoing action. Let's consider each of these just for a moment.

COMMUNICANTS Communicants exist in a relationship—friend to friend, competitor to competitor, parent to child, stranger to stranger. That relationship may be in the progress of a first meeting or well practiced in an extensive history. For example, consider a graduate-level class that a professor might teach. She walks into the classroom to see 15 students enrolled. Three of those students she has never met; the others she knows by name. Of the 12, 8 have taken other classes with her; 5 of the 8 have been in the program for 3 years and have done research together, played softball together, shared a variety of social gatherings and so on—perhaps, you get the picture. In terms of meaning, whatever words that professor chooses, she cannot "say" the same thing to each of those students; the relationship between them, with its components of status, power, rights, responsibilities, freedom, autonomy, credibility, and trust, is part of the system by which those words will be interpreted both by her in the production of her conversational turn and by the students as they make sense of what was said.

In addition to the relationship between communicants, each communicant has a presence and performance skills. This presence and these skills cannot be discounted in the construction process. There have been a number of studies showing the effects of stature, features, fashion, vocal quality, articulation, and the like, on the meanings a message will have.

CONTENT Traditionally content has held the primary position as the determinant of meaning. While lessening its importance, we would want to emphasize that meaning is constrained by the content presented. That is, a given image, sentence, or any piece of content limits the meanings that can be competently constructed from it. These limits are like the limits imposed in the phrase, "All the numbers between 1 and 2." Now we know that there is an infinite number of numbers between 1 and 2 (e.g., 1.000 . . . 00001, 1.000 . . . 00002); however, there is no 3. In a like manner there is a large number of interpretations that can be given to any content, but there is an even larger number that can't. It's this larger number that makes communication work. The net worth of this discussion is that even in holding communicants and context constant, the interpretation that will arise and in which content it will be made sensible remains probabilistic. What one of us makes of a television program may not be what you make of that same program. Not because we see different images, but because we make valid sense of those images in different ways.

There is one last cautionary note before we leave the discussion of content. In examining a communication event, the analyst must be very careful to identify all of the content. The spoken word, the written sentence, the televised image, are all embedded in a performance that surrounds their presentation and reception. A conversation is not the words, but the performance of a social action called conversing. The words as performed form the text of the content. If one is to understand the meaning of a conversation *for the communicants*, the entire text must be examined. You can see why we are so severely limited in understanding the Fuzzy Bear conversation: We have only the verbal text; we have none of the performance (or little of the relationship and other context). As we shall see, the question of content is similarly problematic when considering mediated communication. The reception of media content is also embedded in a performance—the characteristic methods and practices by which we use the media. Again, to understand the meaning of participation in mediated communication *for the audience member*, one must examine the entire text. Analyses that claim to explicate the meaning of a communication event for the participants on the basis of a symbolic text alone are necessarily suspect.

CONTEXT Communication scholars have had a difficult time in getting a firm grasp on the slippery notion of context. We don't expect to be entirely successful either. One of the problems is that the separation of context from content is an artificial or analytical one. Content cannot occur except within some context; they are, therefore, separable only in abstract analysis and not in actual fact. The consequence is that what is content and what is context is always problematic.

We will use context as analogous to a **scene** in which a performance of content is given. The scene is our basic unit of context. The scene is a semantic frame that contains the rules that enable some and disable other meaning constructions. The scene of a cocktail party, the scene of a family discussion, the scene of an all-male fishing trip, the scene of the women's room in a singles bar, the scene of the classroom, all evoke images of circumstances in which kinds of conversations will occur and particular meanings will be applied to the content of those conversations. (Just consider how sexual relationships would be discussed in each of those scenes.) The scene provides a format in which sense making will progress. A format guides the performance of the communication event, establishes priorities of significance and orders the likelihood of interpretations.

It is our claim, then, that context is a powerful influence in the construction of meaning. Yet most media studies ignore context altogether using only the symbolic text as the basis of the analysis. Such studies use the presence or absence of exposure to content as the sole basis of their explanation of the outcomes. The consequences of this neglect are considered in some detail in the chapter essays that follow.

INTERPRETIVE PERFORMANCES

Earlier in this chapter we distinguished between signification and meaning. Now, we use the concept of interpretive performances to underline that distinction. Signification, we argued, was a cognitive act involving the creation of a concept transcending experience and referencing that concept with a sign. Meaning, however, is the product of interpretive performances by which the sign(s) are made sensible in some ongoing action. Meaning is not a capturable cognitive state that can be evoked when the right buttons are pushed. Meaning is the creation of an interpreter who is guided by a history of repeated, supervised, practiced performances of sense making. Sense making is a performance in that it involves some directed and connected series of acts rather than an autonomic function. It is **historicized:** When and where interpretation takes place matters as to the nature of the performance. It is **improvisational** rather than **determined** in that there is space for variation and **innovation.** The improvisational nature of sense making means that the performance is under some local control—in part, a consequence of the individual interpreter, albeit socially implicated and ideologically constrained. The outcome is uncertain, although, if competent, the performance will be appropriate to the boundaries of the communication scene in which communicants, content, context, intent, and so on interact. (If incompetent, it will be marked as such by the other communicants.) Sense making, therefore, is a recognizable improvisation on the thematics of the communication scene. Any given sense-making performance is a **partial representation** of the set of competent interpretations—a set whose own boundaries are open to change through the innovation of improvisation. *The question of what does this mean, then, always results in a local and partial answer.* It means X to Y at that moment.

As a performance, sense making occurs in time and place as a scene unfolds in reference to the other and as a consequence of a particular actor. Each sense-making performance, then, has it own ends in the **empowerment** of the sense maker (interpretations make sense in—are appropriate to—the action-realm of the interpreter). Empowerment describes the method by which the premises of action are created and maintained. It is the method by which the **pragmatics** of communication are accomplished. These premises are the manner by which one understands the world or any part of it, and contain the alternatives of what can and cannot be done.

For example, it is the **natural attitude** of critical, scientific, and commonsense knowledge to assume that a meaning that can be constructed for a piece of content is the meaning for all who encounter it. Criticism is rendered, experiments designed, textbooks written from the belief that one interpretation is correct and should be operant for all. Such statements are merely claims that enable the critical, scientific, or commonsense argument that will follow.

Consequently, claims of meaning can be seen back through the lens of some response. We replace the question: "What is the meaning of X," with the question: "What is the meaning of X for action Y." The "meaning for" reconceptualization also helps us to understand the idea of layers of meaning. The meaning of something depends on the actions to be taken. The meaning of a television commercial is quite different in a social criticism class, in a researcher's laboratory, and in a family's living room. The differences occur, in part, because that content gets accommodated within very different response motives. Nevertheless, we can hold the potential of all those meanings simultaneously shifting with little effort as we move from scene to scene.

The improvisational nature of sense making in no way suggests chaos. Each of us is well-practiced in our improvisational interpretations of everyday content. Further, these improvisations have a history of and continue to be supervised both interpersonally and institutionally. There is little **improvisational space** and a lesser value to innovation in many interpersonal communication situations. Saying "pass the salt" at the dinner table will usually get you the salt shaker. On the other hand, much of what we call mediated communication presents **open texts** with poor or no supervision of sense making—conditions that seem to give considerable improvisational space and may well call for innovation. It is an error of great magnitude to confuse the regularity of our interpretive performances as supporting a claim that no improvisation occurs. The questions of what grants improvisational space and when is innovation valued are not attempted here, but their answers are certainly worthy of study.

SUMMARY—INTERPRETIVE PROCESSES OF MEANING

We have suggested a scenic view of communication in which communicants, content, context, intent, and so on interact as a set of constraints within which an improvisational performance of sense making by an interpreter is enacted. Communication scenes are culturally formatted, performances are located in routinized social action, and interpretation may be directly supervised, all of which guide our sense making by limiting improvisational space and controlling innovation. Any meaning, however, is a local and partial representation of the socially embedded sense-making performances that can be given. Such performances have a depth and complexity and are implicated in the empowerment of the interpreter. Finally, to emphasize the central theme of this section, meaning is not a fixed characteristic of content or a determined, cognitive reflex. Meaning is the product of interpretation.

MEANINGS AS EMERGENT

The next precept is that meanings are emergent, not static. That is, our interpretive construction of meaning does not end with our first understanding. We are always open to the process of reconceptualizing what is occurring in the communication act. Grant that the interpretation given to the conversation between father and child is appropriate. Then *from that interpretive stance,* the full meaning of the child's first turn ("Daddy, let me see Fuzzy Bear.") is not actualized until turn 5 ("I wish I could keep it"). Her first turn was the initial statement in what was intended to be a request to gain possession of the stuffed animal. That meaning is not a very likely one given turn 1 alone. The request nature of the turn becomes more clear in turn 3 and is explicitly stated in turn 5. That is to say, the meaning of turn 1 emerges *for us as well as for her* as the conversation progresses. We can say that the content of turn 1 is very plastic. It can be shaped into a number of meanings depending on how the rest of the conversation progresses. It is, for example, quite possible that the request character of that first turn would never have been made explicit had the father's first turn been a direct denial ("No, you cannot have Fuzzy Bear."). The potential request meaning of the child's first turn would not change as a consequence; it simply would not emerge. The turn would remain ambiguous until further interpreted ("But I just want to see it.").

Meanings can emerge long after the moments of production of the content. Our example of the student gaining acceptance of a late paper despite a written prohibition demonstrates this notion. It also shows how different meanings emerge in different contexts. Sure of her position at the time of writing the syllabus, the instructor finds it indefensible when faced with a distraught student. Does she or does she not mean that late papers are not accepted? The answer is yes to both in our example. For the student without an "acceptable" excuse, she can point to the rule in refusing the paper. For the student with an acceptable excuse, she can reference the practices of other teachers and say that the rule is not absolute. For the student who finished his paper while ill, no late papers are to be accepted. For our exemplar student, late papers will possibly be accepted. But then, we all know what "late papers are not accepted" means.

The idea of emergent meanings has a great deal of significance when studying the mass media. We have already seen that one cannot unequivocally state that a unit of content has a given meaning for all because we individually make sense out of the content we receive. Now we are prohibited from saying that for a given individual we can find one meaning for some content that will be constant over time and conditions. It's not so much that meanings change, but that different circumstances allow different meaning constructions to emerge. For example, the claims of product quality made in a commercial may be the object of derision and rejection in a class on television literacy and still be the basis of product selection at the store. There is no conflict because each meaning emerges and is sensible in its appropriate setting. It clearly is not useful to reject the claims at the store or to accept them in the classroom.

One can also demonstrate the process nature of the communication event within this conversation by asking, "When did it start," and, "When did it end?" Although the conversation content begins with the first turn of talk, the communication event involved in it begins long before as part of the history that the child and father have with Fuzzy Bear and the rules surrounding it. Not one of the turns is understandable without that history. In our analysis, we have to develop a history (and a context) to make those turns sensible.[6] And again, although the conversation ends with the father's "Yeah," what is communicated about the bear and the child's relation to it will continue to emerge in future conversations. Both father and daughter will stay tuned.

THE PROLIFICACY OF MEANING

That meanings are emergent and not static leads us to the prolificacy of meaning. We are prolific in our constructions of meaning. Each time we engage living content a new meaning, at least in some respects, emerges.[7] The process of engagement builds a history of our own meaning constructions that in turn become part of the context for further interpretations. What something means, then, depends on the time and conditions of that question. Are we suggesting that nothing can have the same meaning from time to time? In a way, yes, but not for iconoclastic ends. The prolificacy of meaning is like a spreading plant—the parent remains even as the offspring grows. Living content has the capacity to engage the interpretive process again and again, which adds to the complexity of the understanding we have for that content. Nevertheless, we don't necessarily act on or respond to that complexity. Our relationship with the other communicants and the context of the communication is likely to direct a practiced response. In short, we develop strategies of interpretation appropriate to a given relationship and context. Presented with a "Hi, how are ya?" We give them the practiced response "Fine, how 'bout yourself?" That practiced strategy eliminates the motive for a deep engagement of the interpretive process.

On the other hand, should we respond with something like: "Have you ever thought about what 'Hi, how are you?' actually means?" we might get a return like, "Hold it. I was only trying to give you a number three verbal touching, and now you've gone crazy on me." And the speaker might follow with "I don't have time for this." Or "Let's talk about what you want." The first speaker offers the opportunity for a brief encounter. The second counters with an innovation that the first acknowledges, interprets as a request for something more, and then either refuses or accepts.

In our two examples of a greeting, there is little interpretive work done or demanded in the first. In the second, there is considerably more demand and effort. The concept of the prolificacy of meaning recognizes the potential for that difference.

MEANING AS PROMISCUOUS

Human beings are incessant meaning makers. We make sense of our ongoing world in whatever way that we can. Meaning is open to us all. Again we need to set aside the concept of "the" meaning of something and consider the range of meanings that are probable within a given system of constraints. Let us pose this scenario: Three people are standing in a hall conversing. Two of the three are close friends and the third is an acquaintance of each of the friends. The two friends are arguing; the acquaintance tries to play peacemaker and both friends reject the efforts saying, "You just don't understand." The acquaintance wanders off muttering, "It's those two that don't understand. They don't understand the game they are playing on one another. But if they don't want my help . . ."

All three people in this scenario have a very clear understanding of what is going on. Each understanding, however, is drawn from its own perspective. We, too, from our overview stance, have a very clear understanding of what is going on, but it too is possible only from our perspective. So which is the true story? Very likely they all are. That is, each interpretation is a valid interpretation given the particular perspective of the sense maker. Further, each interpretation is the appropriate interpretation given the relationship and context the individuals are in. It would not do for one of the friends to adopt the metaperspective of one of us analysts. Such would be a violation of the contract that the friends are operating under. A likely response would be, "I'm talking to you about serious matters and all you can give me is that communication psychobabble!"

The concept of the promiscuity of meaning is that meaning is open to us all, but not every meaning is equally available. Meaning is accomplished from a given perspective. We all have a meaning for the scenario. Each of the meanings is a valid one. In all likelihood, however, we will ignore all other interpretations and act out of our own. Further, we are likely to interpret the acts of others as coming from that same interpretation (ours) unless forcibly redirected. Meaning may be everywhere, but the meanings of a communication event are processed within the separate acts of interpretation appropriate to the perspective of the meaning maker.

If we reflect on the promiscuity of meaning, we begin to see the complexity of the task of understanding even a simple conversation: Not only is the meaning of the conversation continually emerging and propagating, but there are also at least three separate interpretive stances involved in any conversation, the two held by the coproducers and the stance used to approach the resultant content itself. For example, an analyst of the Fuzzy Bear conversation can interpret only the available content within an analytical context. He or she cannot approach the meanings that are held by the child or those held by the father because their meanings are uniquely the product of their conversation.

We can easily express the concept of the three meaningful perspectives in terms of a conversational turn between Ben and Lynette. In a turn of talk that, say, Lynette initiates, there is first the meaning that Lynette intends to express; there is the meaning that Ben produces in his

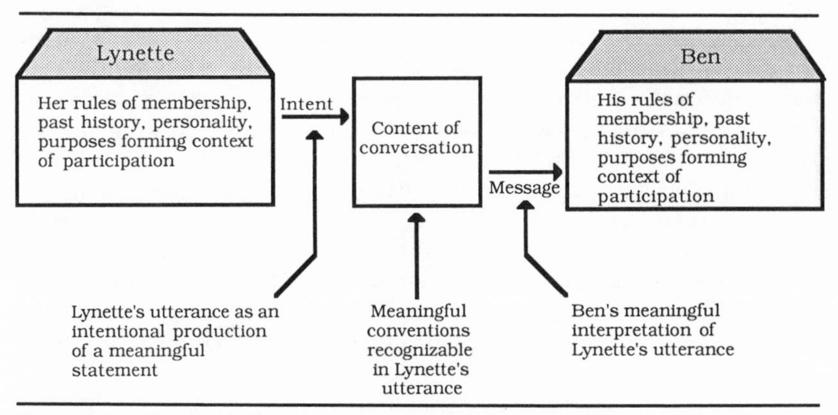

Figure 1.1 Three meanings in an utterance of conversation.

interpretation of Lynette's utterance; and there is the meaning that the content—the words in their particular arrangement—invoke within the conventions of analysis, that is, what we sometimes call the **literal meaning** (see Figure 1.1). These conventional meanings are interpretive strategies that have been institutionalized. We spend years in school learning and performing such conventions. Consider the problem of interpreting the traditional, "See Spot run." By the end of the third or fourth week, we all knew not to run to the window to look. Actually none of us thought of running to the window to look because it was not part of the classroom performance. That is our point: Literal meanings are the product of a conventionalized interpretive performance—a performance academic institutions teach well. These institutionalized interpretations are simply one more layer in the many layers of meaning we can construct.

Any content with its signs and symbols has a potential for meaning. Individual meanings can be constructed from this content accounting for the representations that the signs and symbols carry within a particular interpretive performance. As we have already seen, interesting things "happen" to the content of a conversation when viewed by someone unknowing of the speaker and the listener. The words lose their special meanings derived from the joint history of speaker, listener, and subject. Now outside the context of that conversation but inside his or her own, the reader is less responsible for determining the meaning intended by the producer. There is less constraint on the meanings the reader can construct. If you, for example, are reading this text for your own purposes, you might have little concern for what we meant to say, being interested mainly in the meanings that you derive for your purposes. As we noted, if you are reading it as a text in a classroom, you are probably more concerned as to the sense made of this work by the instructor than what we actually meant. We as the authors of this text can know (more or less) what we intend to say, but even though we use the conventions of this form as a guide, we can only guess at how you, the reader, will interpret what we wrote. You as the reader can know (more or less) what the words mean to you, but can only guess at what we intended to say and at what some other reader (like the instructor) will understand. There are clear implications for the social impact of mediated communication (like this book) in all this. The remaining chapters will spend a good deal of time making them explicit. For now, in the next two major sections, we will draw the implications of our analysis of communication, signification, and meaning, first, to the situation of interpersonal conversations and then to mediated communication scenes.

CENTRAL IDEAS OF SECTION II: SOME CHARACTERISTICS OF MEANING

1. Communication is an interactive process in which communicants, content, and scene are all referenced and must be accounted for in sense-making performances.
2. Sense making in communication is an improvisational performance of interpretation under the local control of the interpreter that results in what is always a partial representation of the interpretations of that communication scene.
3. The interpretations of sense making empower the premises of action of the interpreter that form his or her natural attitude about self and the world.
4. Sense making is an ongoing process in which meanings emerge in layers of time and circumstance.
5. The development of one meaning does not preclude the development of others. We are prolific in our sense making, developing a depth and complexity of meaning.
6. Sense making is open to us all and can proceed from any perspective, but different perspectives result in different meanings.
7. Literal meanings are the product of practiced, conventionalized strategies of interpretation.

SOME CHARACTERISTICS OF CONVERSATIONS

It is relatively easy when considering the processually embedded, emergent, prolific, and promiscuous nature of meaning to wonder how communication can effect any sort of achievement of meaning at all. Such an accomplishment clearly is not automatic. It requires a committed effort—often missing or only partially in place—on the part of the communicants. That effort is a mutual performance inside an implied social contract. In this section, we want to consider two aspects of the contract—intentional production and referenced reception—and two aspects of the performance—mutual participation in performance and the reciprocal supervision of meaning construction. We select these four concepts for development because they provide the points of greatest contrast between interpersonal communication and mediated communication. We will, therefore, use them in our discussion of mediated communication that follows this section.

INTENTIONAL PRODUCTION

Intentional production holds that a speaker is doing more than making noises—he or she intends to mean something appropriate to the receiver in context. Further, the intentional performance meets the standards of good workmanship. That is, the expression used is selected from all the speaker knows about language, culture, the listener, and the context of the utterance-to-be to produce a message that is open to the intended interpretation.

Certain care must be taken not to extend these concepts too far: First, intentional production is not meant to suggest that each utterance has a singular intention that is clearly identifiable. Many motives can be simultaneously operating and any given action has the potential for multiple satisfactions. Utterances, then, can be initiated for *whatever* return might eventuate. Second, the code of good workmanship does not mean that one cannot be sloppy in creating messages or that ambiguity (plasticity) of meaning might not be the end goal of the message. It does mean that when one does poorly in forming a message not open to an intended meaning, it is considered a fault—an error. And when one is ambiguous, it is understood as expressing something about the situation. These judgments get made because the rule of good workmanship has obviously been violated.

REFERENCED RECEPTION

Referenced reception posits that the listener is required to invest meaning in what is heard, taking into account all that he or she knows about language, culture, the speaker, and the context of the utterance as referenced to the intent of the speaker. Again, there is an assumption of an honest effort—that the receiver will make a valid attempt to interpret according to what the speaker means. That interpretation becomes part of the context of the intentional production of the listener-turned-speaker.

The practice of accounting for referenced reception in intentional production permits turns of talk to develop a coherent interdependence in which each turn is in a recognizable relationship with another. Such a set of relationships produces a conversation. Think of the irritation felt when a listener will not grant a speaker an obvious license or does not pay attention or mimics the speaker as children will do. These listeners are not playing fair, and we reckon them to be outside the conversational contract.

Again we must be careful not to overstate this principle. An individual can carry on a conversation without deep engagement or deliberately pursue an interpretation that enables a particular turn irrelevant or in opposition to the presumed intent. Nonetheless it is ordinarily axiomatic that conversationalists function inside the boundaries of one another's intentionality.

A SYSTEM OF MUTUAL PARTICIPATION

Unlike mediated communication events, the interactive process of interpersonal conversation gives us the opportunity to participate mutually in the creation of content that will account for one another. Figure 1.2 outlines some of the components of interpersonal conversation[8] by returning to our eminent conversationalists, Ben and Lynette. We can see that Ben and Lynette with their individual conditions of membership, past history, personality, and purposes, as interpreted in the specific context of the event, are the coproducers of the conversational content that develops through their mutual turn taking. Each utterance is produced with intentional meaning and received in an interpretive process. Messages are constructed at each receiver end, according to the consequences perceived by the listener, not of whole cloth, but as constrained by the context and the sign/symbol content. These messages are not the words spoken, but the significance of the words for the individual listener implicated in the social process of sense making.

Looking again at our graphic in Figure 1.2, content and understanding develop through the interplay of turn taking. Ben and Lynette are coproducers of the conversation. Both are required. If one walks away, the content is irrevocably altered. What the content will be cannot be precisely predicted. Even when one knows exactly what she will say, she does not know what the other will or will not say in return. The presentation is rule-governed, however. Again the code of good workmanship requires a progression of turns that makes sense.

In accomplishing that task, both members participate in what the other will say and the messages that will be constructed. The last turn of a member sets the conditions for the next turn of the other. It contains the subject matter, the context, and perhaps some indication of the interpretations being developed. The next well-produced turn will have to deal with all of those elements. The message that one constructs from the utterance of the other typically attempts to account for what was meant by the speaker. And when the speaker notes the listener constructing an unwanted interpretation, he will often change the content of the conversation to address that interpretation. Consequently in our Figure 1.2, Lynette participates in what Ben intends to say by his understanding of her probable outcomes and Ben participates in Lynette's interpretation by selecting the content of his turn. And so this mutual system of participation begins.

That they mutually participate in a communication process does not imply that the communicant will achieve the same meaning from that process. Sense making is an improvisational performance—not a

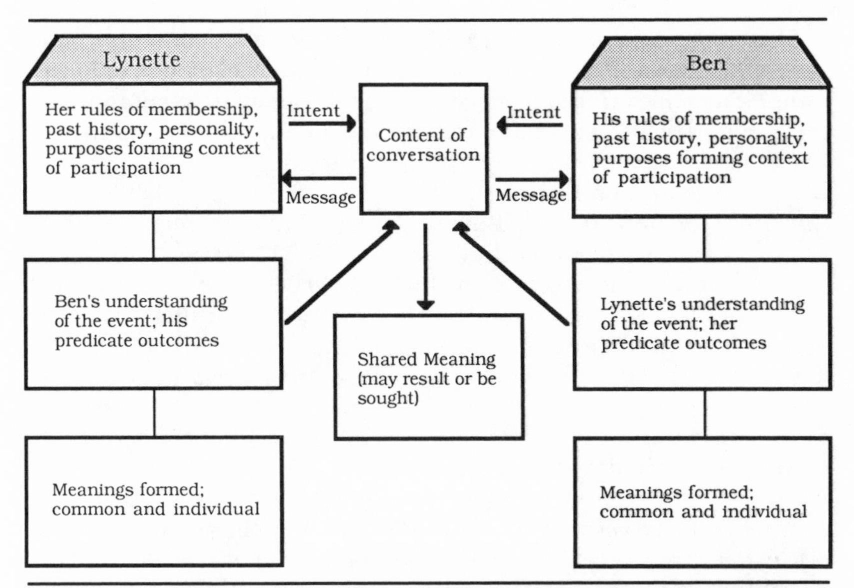

Figure 1.2 Some elements in dyadic conversation. Individuals are represented three-dimensionally as systems that govern the production and interpretation of conversational turns. Intent refers to the intentional production of meaningful expressions. Message refers to the interpretive assignment of meaning to the conversation as it develops. Predicate outcomes are the consequences interpreted by the individual for the individual. Meanings may be individually held, common through coincidental correspondence or shared by confirming correspondence in the conversational content. Content is the sum of the "objective" verbal and nonverbal text.

determined response. Consequently, the correspondence of meaning is a difficult issue that can be viewed from several standpoints. One complexity is offered by the nature of sense making, which itself is multilayered, ongoing, and purposeful. Meaning, therefore, is not objective, but produced in time and circumstance in relation to some end.

Nevertheless, as a conversation continues, a continually emerging understanding of what is going on appears to develop for each of the participants. Each individual's understanding undoubtedly includes some notion about what the other intends to mean, is attempting to accomplish, and understands about the ongoing event. These understandings can be called the predicate outcomes of the conversation. To the extent that the predicate outcomes held separately by each participant correspond in some way, there is a move toward a *common* interpretive stance. This common interpretive stance is common only in the sense that it happens to agree at some level. It is not recognized as an **achievement** by the conversing partners.

Shared meanings, on the other hand, are the product of a common interpretive stance that *is* recognized as an achievement of the communicants. Shared meanings reference the condition in which that common stance is part of the intent and effort of the communication performance. For example, a transactional technique is to use an explicit signal to indicate a correspondence test: "I hear you telling me that you are unhappy with my cooking." But most conversations test interpretations indirectly as our father and child did.

It is through the turns, then, that we shape the interpretive performance of one another to achieve our shared meanings. We may accomplish this shaping with subtlety and grace or in textbook fashion. The point is that *if we intend to achieve shared meanings, it is work that must be provided for in the communication situation and accomplished by the communicants.* It is, in short, an achievement of their practice.

Many times in day-to-day conversations, we choose to operate at a level of shared meaning that represents only a very superficial level of engagement. We actively choose *not* to supervise the actual meanings others have constructed, or we seek purposely to avoid the discovery of what many of those we interact with actually mean. We do these things because we simply do not want to know, because we do not want to spend the time dealing with the consequences that further supervision brings, or because we do not care to expend the effort to accomplish a mutual understanding.

A psychiatrist recently lamented the excessive frequency of superficial levels of "communication." He observed that many of the conversations he had with people outside of his work amounted to nothing more than the exchange of words that appeared to be communication but actually involved little or no work toward shared meaning. As an example, he cited the usual circumstance of being introduced to someone. Upon being presented, the person replied "I'm so glad to meet you." Instead of his usual conventional response, he asked: "Why are you so glad to meet me? You don't even know what kind of a person I am or who I am." Following an awkward pause, the person made a feeble, stumbling attempt to try and salvage the situation and quickly excused herself to move on to a more comfortable conversation.

The psychiatrist (who appears to be something of a creep) was making his point that much of what passes for communication in ordinary conversations at work, school, home, or out and about operates at a level of engagement that is characterized by few, if any, attempts to manage or supervise precisely what meanings are actually shared. (He, of course, erred in assuming that every discursive performance is an act of communication. The woman was clearly performing a conversation—taking her turn in a conventional way.) To supervise actively our interpretations and those of others can be a difficult, time consuming, and uncomfortable process. (One way in which we manage this effort is through the routinization of social action—a subject of Chapter 4.)

There are indeed, risks involved in shared meanings because the understandings accomplished are mutually owned. Convenient fictions that may have permitted a relationship (like "I'm happy to meet you") are lost. The mutual accomplishment of some meanings is not necessarily good.

RECIPROCAL SUPERVISION OF INTERPRETATION

Communication, therefore, does not imply full disclosure. Communication involves the management of meanings to permit (or empower) the social action in place—a premise the psychiatrist violated. One of the strategies that communicants invoke in order to heighten the likelihood of inducing the appropriate meaning construction is the supervision of interpretation. Again, it is the interactive nature of conversation that permits the reciprocal supervision of the construction of meaning by the communicants. While we usually may not go much beyond the surface in supervising interpretations, it is the capacity to do so that gives interactive conversations an enormous advantage over other forms of communication. In the Fuzzy Bear conversation, the daughter appears to perform a supervisory act when she directs her father's understanding of her intent with the turn, "I know I can't have it." We would argue that the little girl does not intend to confirm the rule of ownership when she indicates that she knows she can't have it. She does indeed want to have Fuzzy Bear, but doesn't want her father to anticipate the request. We can presume that in listening to her father's responses she had anticipated or detected an inappropriate (or perhaps inopportune) move on his part. Her turn can be analyzed, therefore, as a move to eliminate that route of interpretation for her father.

Supervision attempts to create a referential frame of interpretation from which we can manage the coproduction of the social action. For example, supervision is a common conversational move in the classroom. The teacher will ask the student to use a concept in a statement and then correct that performance until the student uses the concept "properly." That proper performance is taken as an indication that the right meaning has been achieved. And it probably has for that time, place, and circumstance, but it doesn't preclude a different performance in a different context.

The capacity to participate and to supervise are singular advantages that interactive conversation has over forms of mediated communication. It is *not* by happenstance that we do not turn over the bulk of the education of our youth to textbooks or audio-visual instructional forms. Such communication forms do not provide adequate control over the interpretation process.

SUMMARY

To review this look at interpersonal communication prior to our full entry into mediated communication, let us summarize our discussion of the nature of meaning and the performance of conversations.

First, we have found meaning to be fluid, taking different forms given different times and circumstances. The signification of content may be fixed, material, and indisputable—competent members of the same semiotic community all see the same words and pictures. Meaning, however, is volatile, plastic, and interactive—dependent on an interpretation in a particular context. Content has many valid meanings; the one the author intended is one of them, but it is not *the* meaning. Notions about *the* meaning of any content are mistaken.

We found that the process of interpersonal conversations is not easily defined in time. Although we can point to where turn-taking begins and ends in a particular episode, those turns are dependent on an extensive history and will have implications in the future. A conversation is an ordinary thing, perhaps trivial, but each is an index of our history and leaves its mark, however small, on our future.

Finally, we found that the performance of conversations can be seen as a system of mutual participation in both the intentional production and referenced reception of content. Such mutual participation is fundamental to the nature of the well-formed conversation. Its very existence is dependent on the interaction of its members. Its content is formed in the interaction of turn taking. Each turn of talk while produced by one member is influenced by all members. As that content is formed it is interpreted by the members interacting with those signs and symbols in context. Those interpreted meanings flow back into the conversation to interact with the ongoing content production.

Through this system of mutual participation, common and shared meaning develop. One move in this mutual participation is the supervision of interpretation in which the supervisor attempts to constrain the possible avenues of interpretation available.

SOME CHARACTERISTICS OF MEDIATED COMMUNICATION

We have not forgotten that the primary interest of this text is in *mediated communication*—a term we prefer to *mass communication* in today's rapidly changing technology.[9] Consequently, as a way of making the move to mediated communication, let's see how the notions we developed for interpersonal communication stand up when we turn Ben and Lynette away from each other and toward an event of mediated communication.

SEPARATE SYSTEMS OF PRODUCTION AND RECEPTION

Figure 1.3 gives a graphic metaphor of the elements of the process of mediated communication. The first notable aspect of this model is that both the media and the individuals are drawn in separate three-dimensional representations. This depiction is used because it is, perhaps, most useful to think of the process of mediated communication as composed of two quasi-independent systems. The first is the content production system that involves a set of interlinked media industries

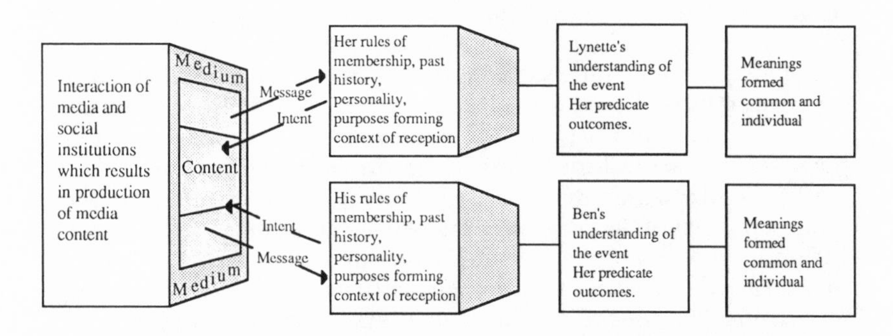

Figure 1.3 Some elements in mass communication from the perspective of individual attendance. Mass media content is represented as the product of a system of interrelated institutions. Content occurs within a medium that itself is part of the content. Individuals are represented as systems that govern their own attendance to and interpretation of mediated content. Intent refers to the process of intentional attendance; message to the interpretive reception of content. Predicate outcomes are the interpreted consequences for the individual of the messages constructed by the individual. Meanings formed may be idiosyncratic or coincidentally common.

that, in the United States, produce, package, and distribute a **commodity content** primarily for commercial purposes. The second is the system that describes the reception of that content by an individual locatable in some social system. Reception is also a system because it involves the integration of media use with other action performances and the accommodation of content within quotidian routines.

The fact of two mostly independent systems underlines an important difference between mediated communication and interpersonal conversations: Unlike a conversation in which content is created by what is said and not said by all the members, neither Ben nor Lynette participate in the production of mediated content. Nothing Ben, Lynette, or any other audience member does will change the content of an ongoing program.[10] Here we have individuals dealing with a commodity content developed within media institutions subject to the influences of other institutions. Similarly, the media institutions cannot participate in Ben's or Lynette's ongoing interpretation of messages through supervision strategies or content modification during Ben's or Lynette's attendance. Mediated communication, then, loses the system of mutual participation in the construction of content and meaning that characterizes interpersonal communication. Both the media and the audience operate at a distance from each other and within separate systems of action. As a result, they exhibit a degree of independence from one another. Media can and do produce content that is successful only within the purposes of the community of media practitioners—for example, content that is created solely to provide an inventory of advertising time or space.

For its part, the audience no longer shares a responsibility for the orderly production of content elements and is, therefore, not necessarily bound by any contract that directs its interpretations toward the purposes or intended meanings of the producer. Further, there is no mechanism by which Ben and Lynette as individuals can share their understandings of the program content with the creators of that content within the process of the mediated communication event. The loss of this interaction makes the interpersonal notion of shared meanings impossible. Because individuals as receivers of mediated content do not have the ability to confirm meanings extracted from the content by testing those meanings in the mediated communication process, there is no mechanism by which an audience member can accomplish a shared understanding with the production community. As a result, the receiver's responsibility for determining the meaning intended by the content's creator is no longer a given expectation as in conversations. Further, the media have little ability to supervise the interpretation of their product.[11] There is no longer the interaction between the producer and the receiver of content at any individual level, rather, that interaction occurs on an institutional level. Media receive feedback primarily on attendance by an audience institutionalized in a system of measurement. (This measured audience is the **commodity audience** sold to advertisers.) No matter what meanings Ben and Lynette construct, as long as they attend, the content will go forward as planned.

THE CONTENT PRODUCTION SYSTEM

Each geopolitical social system has its own structure of interlinked media industries. In most First-World instances, however, these interlinked industries develop an archived (fixed content) commodity of different contents that enter into a variety of distribution networks (shown by the content "windows" on the media-structure figure). As we shall see in some detail in the next chapter, that content has a standing independent of any individual's response to it because of its perceived intrinsic value (e.g., congressional hearings) or as a by-product in the production of an inventory of advertising opportunities and/or the commodity audiences to be sold.

The production of content is the responsibility of the **community of practitioners** that functions inside the media industry structure. Individuals such as Ben and Lynette have little access to this community. Given that individual audience members cannot directly participate in content production, their reflection disappears from the notion of intentional production to be replaced by an idealized image of the audience—called a **canonical audience.** Tim and Jim are writing to an idealized audience of colleagues and students within a very real community of reviewers, editors, and publishers.

THE RECEPTION SYSTEM

With the delivery of content, we shift our focus to the system of reception that begins with the attendance by an audience member.[12] Both Ben's and Lynette's attendance to their media is knowledgeable, intended in the broad sense that it isn't happenstance. Even the very young know what their media provide and seek them out for it. That is not to say that every content reception event is governed by well-articulated purposes. As with the reasons for initiating a conversation, the intentions that direct our attendance to the media can be specific or most general, simple or complex. But in the broad sense of the term, attendance is intentional, requiring a set of practices for its performance. In the model, intentional attendance is the substitute notion that corresponds to the action of intentional production in conversations. As that previous notion suggested, intentional attendance implies that meaning-making processes are to be invoked. That is why we are there.

These meaning-making processes are themselves embedded in the methods and practices we use to accommodate the media. Whether we view alone, in a family setting, or in public, media use is part of the flow of everyday life. We negotiate its place based on individual invention and multiple levels of social convention. When Ben and Lynette attend to this content, they bring to it their own interpretive skills, tactics, and strategies managed within the social action of reception that will interact with the content in sense making and other social action performances. Ben's and Lynette's interaction with the content is affected by the intentions they bring to that content, the characteristics of that content relative to those intentions, the conditions that surround the circumstances of reception, and the social action in which the meanings of that content will emerge.

In short, the media deliver a commodity content but not its meaning. Meaning is constructed by the receiver, within the culturally embedded social action context of reception and for the purposes that arise within that action. While we will spend all of Chapter 4 explicating that sentence, we can begin to break it down as follows: In order to understand the meanings that may arise from the content of the media, one must examine the methods and practices by which that content is interpreted. Those methods and practices are part of the set by which we constitute our everyday life. It is in the practices of being a couch potato, an avid basketball fan, a cynical consumer, a child of 4, a concerned parent that media content comes to have meaning. Such is the central interaction in mediated communication—the interaction between content and the interpretive social action in which we participate.

ACCOMMODATING EFFECTS

In the traditional analysis of media effects, content is used as the causal agent for the behavior to be explained. Viewing violent content leads to aggressive behavior; watching commercials leads to certain consumer behavior; and so on. We reject that traditional view because it ignores the complex patterns of social action within which we perform our lives. Media content, nonetheless, is a presence in our lives for which we need to account. Our manner of accounting for content is to consider its interaction potential.

The interactive potential of content is its capacity to be accommodated into the ongoing performances of every-day life. For the receiver, content has value for its utility in the production and maintenance of the routines of social action. Such value as any content might have, then, is added in the applications found for it in the concourse of our daily lives. Television news programs, as an example, therefore, have value not because of the intrinsic worth of the information they present, but because of what can be done with them by the individual audience members. For someone involved in the news business—that particular social action structure—a news program has considerable value across a broad spectrum of what he or she does. For another individual, in a different structure, the program may serve only to fill time, to preclude discussion at the dinner table, to permit the image of being informed, or similar limited application.

We'd like to underline what this value-added perspective does to the analysis of content. It shifts the focus away from the traditional concerns for the meaning conventions of content and the intended purposes of the content *producers.* Value-added analysis is only marginally concerned with content characteristics and intended meanings and then only to the extent that such elements have impact on the meanings that can be constructed within the multiple contexts of reception.

While we will shift the focus off of content and direct it to the strategies of interactive interpretation, we do not disregard the constraints that content imposes on these strategies. Content participates in the limits of its interactive potential. Arriving at an idea of how that potential is actualized, however, is not revealed to us in the meanings intended by the producer or in the meanings developed in conventionalized analysis of the content. An analyst cannot assume a single, reconstructed meaning for content or that the receiver must take any responsibility for the creator's intentions or the conventions of the content. How many folks watch a "Miami Vice" or a "Magnum P.I." for the plot?

For us, then, the value of content is not in what it is intended to do or in the manner in which it is produced, but is in the meaningful applications that appear. Where we will learn about meaning is in the everyday methods and practices that surround the use of media. *These methods and practices are the ongoing accommodation of media content in our lives.* And here we have sounded the major theme of this book. *The effects of media occur when their content is entered into the interpretive strategies that we use and the social action in which we participate.* These effects are, therefore, embedded in and not separable from the scenes of life in which we play. These scenes are not themselves the consequences of media but are the ecological expression of human individuals socially embedded in their cultural environment. We certainly hope to marshal the evidence for these concepts in the essays that follow. For now, we need to draw some specific implications of this perspective concerning the processes of mediated communication and the meanings that are constructed from it. To do that we will return to the four characteristics of meaning that we introduced in our discussion of conversations—the claim that meaning is embedded, emergent, promiscuous, and prolific.

EMBEDDED MEANINGS

It seems quite easy to see that the meanings that are derived from a conversation are dependent upon the social action of the conversation itself. It is perhaps a little more difficult to see that the meanings derived from mediated content are also dependent on the social action by which we admit such content into our lives. Usually our ordinary and academic discourse treats the content as the carrier of meaning—that the whole of it can be seen in the content. This analytical perspective is particularly common when the content of communication has been institutionalized. That is, when the content has no personal creator—the policy statements of an organization, memos representing an office, the content of our media. Suddenly, the meaning of the content becomes "there for all to see" as if the process of interpretation was entirely determined by the content. In this text, we take a contrary position. We hold that such institutionalized content may be "there for all to see" but the meaning of that content arises within social action and as a result of social action. To use ourselves as an example, both Tim and Jim can read the University of Utah policy concerning travel funds but only Jim can naturally know what it means in the practices of the university. On the other hand, of these two, only Tim can naturally know what it means in the eyes of an outsider.

When a critic such as Aimee Dorr (1986) says that "in the final analysis we all see the same content," what she is actually saying is that same content is delivered (p. 27). But content and meaning are not the same thing. Within the academic community, we can certainly bring conventionalized strategies of interpretation to bear and thereby achieve agreement as to what some content means. We have spent many hours of schooling to achieve the skills of those conventionalized strategies. Our agreement, nevertheless, is dependent upon those interpretive strategies as practiced within the social action of that community. Those are not the only interpretive strategies available, nor is the public interpretation of content by an academic community the only social action. Any meaning we can point to is only one of several that potentially can arise.

A somewhat facetious example can be drawn from the Meese Commission. If the Meese commission on pornography is correct (pornography leads to social decay), why haven't the commissioners run amuck? (Perhaps they have.) If they haven't it is because the manner in which they accommodate such pornographic content does not include that consequence. If content was the sole source of meaning, they should be doomed to their own conclusions.

EMERGENT MEANINGS

Meanings are constructed both at the time of reception and extended in time to other situations. Again the notion of latent interpretations emerging in given contexts is useful. Mediated content can be profitably viewed as raw material available to the receiver that subsequently will be shaped into meaningful constructions according to the demands of the situation at hand. As those situations differ the meanings constructed differ also.

The process of mediated communication is an extended one. To contend that a reception event begins when the television set is turned on or the newspaper opened is to ignore the level of integration typically required for these events to occur. That integration is an important part of the context of reception in which the content will be used and interpreted. In order to understand mediated communication processes adequately we need a much larger view than that ordinarily taken. We need to fit the particular act of reception into the larger constructs of the meanings held for the medium, the purposes for which it gets used, the context in which the content gets received, and the circumstances in which meanings emerge. Only by taking in the whole process are we going to make much sense out of the welter of fragmentary and sometimes conflicting research on the media.

PROMISCUITY OF MEANINGS

This principle describes the fact that content is open to sense making by all of us. We will make sense of it in ways appropriate to the social action at hand. It is not necessary for us to stop what we are doing to adopt a "proper" interpretive frame. We can view the news for entertainment or to pass the time or to appear informed. We need not adopt any of the interpretive frames advanced by those outside the significant social action. We are not suggesting an unbridled individual freedom here. We are suggesting that the interpretive strategies contained within the social action in place need not be constrained by the intentions of the content. The accommodation may require considerable invention, as we suspect the Meese Commission required in order to justify the release of a final report full of pornographic content to the general public. That move was fully justified within the social action of the Commission itself. That others cannot understand the move simply indicates that they are outside the significant social action.

PROLIFICACY OF MEANING

Vital content engages us again and again. It has a potential inside our methods and practices. As we have argued, the meaning of that potential is realized within those methods and practices. Each performance of these practices, however, is an improvisation on a theme. The realization of meaning is not textual button pushing. X does not mean Y. Content X enables meaning Y in many variations. Meaning is prolific in its offspring.

CENTRAL IDEAS OF SECTION III: SOME CHARACTERISTICS OF MEDIATED COMMUNICATION

1. Interpersonal conversations are conducted through the mutual participation in the production of content and the reciprocal supervision of its interpretation within an implied social contract in which one produces content intended to be meaningful to the other whose own interpretation is reference to that intent.
2. Mediated communication proceeds in two quasi-independent systems of production and reception. In the production system of interlinked media industries, a community of practitioners produces a commodity content for its own end, or as a byproduct in the manufacture of advertising opportunities or commodity audiences. In the reception system, attendance is an intentional performance in its own right, and content is interpreted through its accommodation in the methods and practices of everyday life.
3. The shared meaning of interpersonal communication is the achievement of the joint performance of production and interpretation. Shared meanings do not develop between producer and receiver in mediated communication. Shared meanings involving media content will arise among participants in the social action performances of reception and subsequent accommodation.

A SUMMARY

In this chapter we have laid out an interpretive theory dealing with communication and meaning. In broad strokes, we have argued that communication is an interactive process, the study of which requires an understanding of the unique character of all the elements involved. The producer of content, the content itself, and the receiver are all parts of that process, but only parts. One cannot use the characteristics of one to predict to another.

An act of communication begins with the intent to mean something, it continues in the creation of the content, that content is interpreted by those that receive it, and the act reaches a conclusion in a meaning emerging within a context.

Meaning is not delivered in the communication process, rather it is constructed within it. We have seen that each communication act generates at least three separate and potentially different sites of this construction. Meanings arise in the intentions of the producer, in the conventions of the content, and in the interpretations of the receiver.

Content is not limited to a single meaning. Content is the raw material for immediate and emergent meanings. Emergent meanings may find their expression in interpretive processes arising in other contexts at other times.

Mediated communication is an extended process involving elaborate structures of production and reception. To understand the process we must understand these structures and not focus merely on the presentation of content at a given moment.

The interactive processes of mediated communication involve the accommodation of its activities (viewing, reading, listening) and its content in the practices of everyday life. The meaning of media and its content is embedded within those practices and emerges in their performance.

The promiscuity of meaning suggests that though content may be attended to by millions, its meaning can be realized in radically different ways as meaning is open to all. The prolificacy of meaning suggests that the social action of sense making is not rigidly performed but is improvisational in nature. We work the themes not the rote of our methods.

We then examined the sense-making practices of interpersonal communication, focusing on conversations. We found conversations to develop within a system of mutual participation in which communicants coordinated the intentional production and reference reception of conversational turns and reciprocally supervised their interpretation.

In the last section, we considered the characteristics of mediated communication. We found that system to be composed of two relatively independent systems—that of production and that of reception. The production system was found in a structure of interlinked media industries in which a community of practitioners developed content commodities in the image of the canonical audience and for the sale of commodity audiences.

The reception system was analyzed at the simplest sociological level—the individual. Here we found that individual located in an ongoing flow of social action that accommodated mediated content. It was in that accommodation that media effects arise.

A TRANSITION

For most of the history of research in mass communication, content has been seen as a silver bullet shot from a media gun to penetrate a hapless audience. As research became more sophisticated, scholars developed the position that content had differential effects on individuals. It was thought that some segments of the audience were resistant and others susceptible to the effects of certain content. Being in one group or the other was the result of genetics, age, personality, development, training, and/or enculturated traits. Like exposure to a virus, there was little the susceptible person could do at the moment of reception to control for the effects of exposure to the content. Modern theory holds that individuals interact with mediated content within the social action routines of their everyday life. In this theory, it is the social action performances that provide for and explain media effects. This is the position we intend to explore and develop throughout this text.

We have noted in this chapter that mediated communication functions in two mostly separate systems—one that accounts for the content itself and the other for its interpretation. The next three chapters do the work of demonstrating this claim. Chapter 2 examines the structure, conduct, and performance of the media industry; Chapter 3, the conventional characteristics of the content that is produced by that industry; and Chapter 4, the social action process in which that content is accommodated.

NOTES

1. We make extensive use of lists such as this one. Our intent is not to claim that the list defines the nature of the subject—there are any number of ways of considering the fundamentals of communication. Rather, we are presenting a way of looking at that subject—those dynamic, ongoing, seamless processes.

2. One of the despairing concerns of present-day social critics is that modern social forces are moving to create a society in which the individual is isolated from extensive, direct human contact and the actual doing of things. They are concerned that our shared experiences will no longer be in the face-to-face performances of parent and child, teacher and student, master and novice. Rather our common experiences will be only the media texts—we will see our sunsets on the tube—with all the attendant distortion and manipulation possible. For these critics, if our experience is primarily mediated, the meanings that we can have will be only those of the media. There is a bit of irony here, since the urban, elitist academic who spends a professional lifetime reading and writing is the most likely person to express these concerns.

3. You may be aware of the arguments that present language as both empowering and enslaving. That is, through language we are able to understand the world around us, but only within the structures and terms provided by language. Though the authors accept the central theme of this argument, they would not limit human knowledge to language alone.

4. Not all languages are equal. Languages have different capacities for the expression of the ongoing. Multilingual communities use different languages for different transactions (e.g., English is often the language of choice for the economic realm). Language systems can be brought into competition. To remain viable, a system has to be protected from other systems and made responsive to the external demands of change. Language systems die when they no longer have the capacity to constitute an adequate understanding of the world in which the users live.

5. It is difficult to think of nonsymbolic meaning, but it is one's response to experience as experience. Not all that can be known can be or must be spoken.

6. To show how much we have embedded that conversation, consider it as a drug deal on a New York street corner.

7. The vitality of content is our capacity to use it in sense making. As a metaphor turns to a cliché, content "dies" when it loses its utility to attract the sense-making act.

8. This and the other model in this chapter are presented for their explanatory utility not as full-fledged representations of the communication process.

9. Our interest does not extend equally to all forms of mediated communication. We are primarily interested in mediated communication that is the product of our media industries. We are less interested in the letters written to Aunt Nell.

10. The obvious exception to this statement is a call-in show, such as talk radio.

11. Press releases, social commentators, critics, and other agents work to influence that interpretive process, but the media will not break off delivery because we view the news for entertainment and not information.

12. The reception system at its least aggregated sociological level is composed of the particular methods used by each individual in the reception of the media. As one goes up the sociological ladder, the perspective changes to social viewing, such as family viewing, and on to the aggregation of individuals into audiences. For now, we are operating on the simplest sociological level—the socially embedded individual.

RELATED READINGS

Belsey, C. (1980). *Critical practice.* London: Methuen.

An intelligent review of modern criticism. The final chapter is particularly provocative as the author advances the thesis that "meanings circulate between text, ideology, and reader, and the work of criticism is to release possible meanings" (p. 144).

Dallmayr, F. R., & McCarthy, T. A. (Eds.). (1977). *Understanding and social inquiry.* Notre Dame, IN: University of Notre Dame Press.

A reader of some grace that deals with the issues of interpretive understanding as applied to the study of the human condition. Part 4 on phenomenology and Part 5 on hermeneutics and critical theory are most useful for our purposes.

Guiraud, P. (1975). *Semiology.* London: Routledge & Kegan Paul.

Barely 100 pages long, this book provides a quick introduction into the field of semiotics, focusing on the nonlinguistic signs of fashions, customs, rites, and the like.

Innis, R. E. (1985). *Semiotics: An introductory anthology.* Bloomington: University of Indiana Press.

This book provides a sample of the writings of most of the main actors in the field. The introductions to these writers are helpful summaries of their positions.

Keat, R., & Urry, J. (1982). *Social theory as science* (2nd. Ed.). London: Routledge & Kegan Paul.

Chapter 7 is especially useful for its discussion of social action as a structure in theory.

Meltzer, B. N., Petras, J. W., & Reynolds, L. T. (1975). *Symbolic interactionism: Genesis, varieties and criticism.* London: Routledge & Kegan Paul.

A serviceable analysis of symbolic interactionism that itself is part of the social action formulation.

Sigman, S. (1987). *A perspective on social communication.* Lexington, MA: Lexington Books.

The author takes a social action perspective on the process of interpersonal communication. He does a good bit of the basic work of connecting social action theory with previous positions. This is a useful companion to the present volume.

2

Thoughts on the Mediated Communication Industry

SYNOPSIS

In the previous chapter we considered how symbols come to have meaning. In this chapter, we will consider those institutions that direct the appearance of symbolic content in our media. Members of the media are organizations that produce content for distribution to audiences. Although a rapidly changing technology makes any list of media somewhat suspect, at this writing, we would want to include audio recordings, books, broadcast radio, broadcast television, cable television, magazines, newspapers, theatrical films, and video recordings. There are also theatrical performances and computer communication services, among others, which you might want to consider. Each medium has a population of organizations that include the media outlets themselves and the supporting and even parasitical firms that function with them. (Newspapers, for example, are totally dependent on the firms that make newsprint, whereas insulation companies make money from the discarded product.) This population of interrelated organizations is generally called an industry.

While we certainly talk about the television industry, the newspaper industry, and so on, the interdependency among media also points to a more global concept of the media industry. News organizations produce content for magazines, newspapers, radio, and television. Radio could not survive in its present configuration without the recording industry. Theatrical films are the primary source of video recordings. The examples are numerous. In our analysis in this chapter, we will often adopt this global notion of a media industry. (The points that we develop, nevertheless, can be applied to any of the media individually.)

Because the creation of mass media content occurs inside this structural framework of interlocking organizations, mediated content is not the creation of an individual artist in the process of exchange with other individuals; it is the product of organizations and is developed to serve organizational goals. As you know, it is our claim that individuals and media institutions function in relative independence. Media institutions have little interest in the personal motives, uses, gratifications, and effects attributed to the individual viewer as long as certain institutional requirements are met. The individual viewer, on the other hand, is indifferent to the ledger-sheet requirements of media business as long as personal requirements for content are being met. The two do interface, of course. For the media institutions, the primary point of interaction occurs when individuals are **aggregated** into audiences. For the individual, the interface is in the methods and practices of use—those everyday performances of reading, listening, and viewing—a subject we consider in Chapter 4.

The implications of this separation are substantial. The primary of these addressed by this chapter is that the characteristics of mediated content are not the result of the meanings people make of that content but are the consequence of the marketplace in which this industry functions. In this chapter, then, we will look at the structure, conduct, and performance of the media industry in relation to content, and consider their effects on content.

THE MARKETPLACE OF MEDIA

Economists examine the "marketplace" of an industry—that is, the realm of activity for that industry—on the basis of three characteristics: (a) structure, (b) conduct, and (c) performance. As you might suspect, so will we.

The market structure of an industry concerns the conditions under which all players must participate—the nature of competition, the sources of revenue, the **rationality of the market place** (transaction uncertainty), the number of buyers and sellers (transaction demand and competition), barriers to entry (restrictions on membership), and **product differentiation.** The structure of an established industry is relatively stable, although it can be manipulated both from within and from without. In computer software, for example, we are now watching the larger companies buying out the small, reducing the number of sellers. This inside action will continue until it begins to raise antitrust questions that will ultimately halt these structural changes through outside governmental intervention. Such structural changes certainly affect all players.

Conduct refers to industry behavior—the practices that characterize that industry. For example, pricing the final product is an activity common to most industries, but the practice in given industries varies widely. It may be very competitive, as in the first days following deregulation for the airlines, or mutually beneficial, as in the most successful days of OPEC. Conduct is both internally and externally governed. The larger society always makes demands on the conduct of industry through customs, laws, regulatory agencies, and the like. There is a relationship between conduct and structure. Structure is usually used to explain why something was done, and conduct to explain how it was done. In short, all players must respond to structure, but not all players must follow the same practices. Different members can conduct themselves in different ways. Nevertheless, in general, the range of conduct of all players can be predicted from market structure.

Performance is the consequences of conduct within a given structure. Performance is always evaluated against some set of criteria held by the industry itself. Performance may also be evaluated by criteria different from those of the practitioners by other **stakeholders** (any group with an interest) in the industry (e.g., child action groups in television). An industry may have many different stakeholder groups with radically different performance criteria.

SECTION I: STRUCTURAL CHARACTERISTICS AND CONTENT

Remembering the focus of this chapter, we will examine the structural characteristics of the media to the extent that this analysis helps us understand the institutional and corporate influences on content. We will comment on (1) the institutional status of the media industry and its members; (2) the interlocking relationships between members of the media that both segregates and standardizes the content product; and (3) the limited creative community that is the result of high market uncertainty and stout barriers to entry, which produces formulaic content.

MEDIA AS INSTITUTION

The notion of an institution is an important one. It is not an organization, a company, or a physical plant, rather it is an element in society—a definable pattern in our social fabric. An institution has identity, position, status and power, and rights and responsibilities within the larger structure of society. The institution gains this identity, position, status, and power in a set of negotiated and practiced social contracts that establish the constraints and freedoms of conduct for its members—in this case the organizations of our media. Organizations become "institutionalized" as the number of direct, reciprocal relationships with other parts of society increase.

Media in the United States have achieved a high level of institutionalization as shown by their formal and practical relationships with government at all levels, other industries, and social organizations. Our system of governance, our system of competitive enterprise, our leisure practices are all interlinked with media organizations. The consequences of this institutionalization are threefold.

First, the reciprocal relationships that create the institution involve the exchange of autonomy for privilege. The media have a number of privileges—privileged access to government, privileged control of information, a privileged voice in society. But these privileges are bought by giving up the right of self-governance. In exchange for its privileges, the media must be responsive to the demands of government, the capitalist system, and other powerful social organizations. It is a tenet of relationships that each member of the relationship is a stakeholder in the other. (A stakeholder is one who has an interest in the other's welfare—good or bad—and works to protect that interest.) The content of our media, taken as a whole, is therefore the grand compromise between the competing and complementary demands of its stakeholders.

Let us work just one example: We have a long history of complaint against violent media content. Social scientists have developed an extensive literature that critics claim demonstrates the harm of such content. In spite of efforts to develop one, no policy has ever emerged to control the appearance of violent content except those policies of the industry itself (movie ratings, television standards, and practices). We presume that the reason for this lack of outside policy is that if one stakeholder (say, government) were to develop a policy to control harmful violence, another stakeholder (say, sports) might be denied its good violence. The industry, however, must be responsive to all such stakeholders. The violence that we see on the media, its forms, modes of distribution, and target audiences is the natural (as opposed to principled) compromise. The relative success of the compromise can be read by who is complaining.

The second consequence of institutionalization follows from the first—that the media are relatively protected from attack from any one quarter and at the same time must frame their own behavior vis-à-vis stakeholders according to their power. An attempt to control the media by any one stakeholder has implications of risk for all other stakeholders. Demands for time and space by government reduces that available to critics; nonetheless, government will get more space and time because it is inherently more powerful than is the opposition (media call it newsworthiness). As the power of stakeholders declines, they become an increasing target of exploitation by the media. The make-you/break-you cycles of political candidates, televangelists, and entertainment figures are good examples.

Finally, institutions are inherently conservative of their ongoing practices. As the number of relationships increase, the costs of innovation in the consequences for these relationships increase. Innovation places the balance of relationships, whether cleverly or clumsily crafted, at risk. An examination of the corporate culture of most media organizations makes this inherent conservatism apparent. The larger media organizations are typically hierarchical bureaucracies heavily encumbered with standard operating procedures that result in highly specialized work activities. This is a textbook portrait of a very conservative organization. This conservatism is reflected in the content of our media in the practices of imitation, regeneration of older forms, and repetition of format. You may or may not like what you get, but you know you are going to get it again and again.

INTERLOCKING RELATIONSHIPS

Mass media in the United States have responded to content demands, the forces of regulation, and economic competition by forming an interrelated system of ostensibly independent organizations that are actually dependent on one another. We can analyze this system by using the economic concept of **niche.** Niche is a metaphorical reference to the **ecology** of living organisms and is used to describe how organizations survive in their economic environment. A niche is a specific enclave within the larger environment that has particular conditions that can be exploited by the organizations within it and at the same time are detrimental to organizations outside of it.

An economic niche is formed when an industry or an organization within an industry is able uniquely to exploit elements of the environment as resources for its own viability. Resources for media organizations are generally considered to be types of content, types of audiences, and types of capital (venture, income, growth). An organization can be successful in the media ecology by having access to or controlling one or any combination of these resources.

The ecology of the economic niches of media develops in the interaction between the resource elements (content, audiences, capital) in the market environment and the operational scope of the medium. The operational scope of a medium is its performance characteristics and is a combination of capacity and competence. Capacity refers to the potential of what can be done and competence to the craft of what can be done well. Environmental elements become *exploitable* resources for a medium when they fall within the operational scope of that medium. (They, obviously, cannot be exploitable resources if they are outside that scope.) When those elements are exploitable resources to some and not to others, niches begin to form.

As a quick example of how niches are formed, consider "R-" and "X-" rated movies as a type of content. Because of the restrictions on broadcast television, this content cannot be readily exploited by that medium. Cable television and video recordings, however, can readily exploit this content and its audience. In this example, R- and X-rated movies are a type of content that can be bought by any of the three video media; the environment—other media organizations—makes it available. This content type becomes a resource for cable and VCRs and not broadcasting, because the operational scope of broadcast television prevents it (in this case, because of regulation and custom) from accessing that content. Both cable and VCRs, then, are protected from competition from broadcast television on this content resource. In this manner, one boundary of their "protective" niche is formed.

Media survive in the presence of one another by creating their niche in the market environment. To understand better our media and their content, we need to understand the ecology of their relationship. In the sections that follow, we will consider four elements of the interrelated media niche structure: Systems of content, sources of income, barriers to entry, and the functions of operational scope.

SYSTEMS OF CONTENT IN MEDIA

Media can be separated and identified by virtue of the type of content that predominates within them. This claim is not trivial because there is much more differentiation than can be expected from the "natural" characteristics of the media. (Though it is certainly true that we can't hear music in newspapers, it is not true that newspapers must carry news.) Much of what we do and do not see, hear, and read in our media is best explained by the structure of the industry. There are three loosely organized, certainly overlapping, content subsystems that are appropriated in different ways by different media, and provide for one aspect of the interrelationship among media. They are, as follows:

(1) *The creative system* that generates fictive content—content that needs no claim to empirical validity. This content system is composed of narrative (any content that tells a story) and music. Narrative is the primary content of broadcast, cable, and VCR television programming, theatrical films, books, and even music lyrics. Music is the mainstay of radio and sound recordings. Music and narrative mix in the now moribund musical movie genre, and are uniquely combined in the very vital music video.

(2) *The information system* that generates content dependent on a claim to empirical validity (did happen, will happen, might happen, should happen). The information system is composed of news, exposition, and explanation. Information content dominates the serial print industry (newspapers and magazines) with a definite presence in books (you're reading an example) and lesser presence in television.

(3) *The canonical system* that provides content valued for its adherence to the forms and conventions maintained by an intellectual elite distinction similar to that of the popular and fine arts. The literary magazines, a specialized book industry, some movies, and, at least currently, much of public broadcasting are identified by canonical content.

SPECIALIZATION OF CONTENT

Media position themselves between and within these content systems by generating a reliable set of characteristic content specialties that segregates that medium and identifies it to an audience. In this segregating and identifying process, the content of one medium has to be responsive to the content of the others.

Consider the entertainment system in which the appearance of television has irrevocably changed the character and content of radio and motion pictures. Upon the arrival of television, a true technological revolution, radio lost nearly all of its story-telling function. (What remains is nostalgia.) Radio shifted its content base from narrative to music (which in turn revolutionized the music industry). With that move, radio became a personalized, local medium—a one-to-one relationship between sound and listener.

As a further consequence of television, the "G-" rated movie is no longer the mainstay of the film industry. Films have chosen stronger themes in violence, sex, and horror than the formula of broadcast television will allow.

The relationship between film, broadcast, and cable television allows us a third example. If broadcast television were not constrained by its network/affiliate relationships, government regulation, and its advertising base of income, cable television would not have had the content niche of uncut, uninterrupted films to fill. The film industry responded to cable's demand by, at first reluctantly and then gladly, providing cable's content (but, at the same time, protected itself by reserving first run, theater rights). As cable continues to grow, its need for product grows. The semiannual cycle of the film industry (movie product peaks in summer and at Christmas) was not providing the continuous product flow that cable demanded. Consequently, cable has made a **vertical integration** move by creating the made-for-cable-television movie that is a product of neither broadcast television nor theatrical film. And, the film industry has altered the semiannual cycle by releasing movies throughout the entire calendar year and by shortening the length of time in between theatrical release and release to pay-cable channels and for videocassette sales and rentals. Such a strategy, at least in part, resulted in 1987 setting all-time records for box office revenue and for cassette sales and rentals, despite the absence of any dominating runaway hits.

News shows the same kind of segregation. Broadcast news makes no attempt to compete head-to-head with newspapers by using the same content product. News magazines establish their niches by synthesizing the disjointed events of an unfolding story into a more meaningful report. A news consumer, consequently, finds a different product in each of these media even when covering the same story.

STANDARDIZATION OF CONTENT

Media not only differentiate their primary content, they also take single product concepts that show success in one medium and spin them off into separate products for other media. These spin-offs produce a standardization or homogenization across media (what computer technologists call a "common interface") as the same characters, characterizations, plots, and so on appear. Their success across media, however, is aided by the fact that the final product and our experience of it are different as that product appears in the specialized form of each medium.

This product interrelationship among media can be shown in the current marketing practices for theatrical films. American film is no longer solely dependent on the line at the box office. Box office receipts are only one revenue source of many. Other sources are export and domestic broadcast television rights, various pay-per-view and subscriber pay channel television options, video recordings, and music and consumer goods spin-offs.

We see a similar relationship in print. Books are serialized in literary magazines and newspapers, and magazine serials are made into books—which are often then adapted for film or television.

SUMMARY—CONTENT SYSTEMS

The fact that American media operate with an interactive system, then, places the content of our media in a dynamic relationship. They are unavoidably responsive to one another. This dynamic helps define the service offered by each medium, positioning that medium with certain content characteristics. This positioning, in turn, reduces the competition among media as they tend to serve different purposes for the audience. This positioning also constrains one medium from moving into content areas held by another. On the other hand, the system relationship permits the development of content in one medium for its subsequent flow into another. Perhaps, the system notion can best be demonstrated simply by considering what would happen to the recording industry if we were to remove radio; or to the film industry in the absence of broadcast and cable television.

It is, of course, not all peaceful symbiosis out there. Media do compete for the finite time available to the audience. We are watching, for example, the decline of the X-rated movie theatre as the primary distribution mechanism of these films. Consumers of such material are showing greater likelihood to watch sex films on their VCRs. Further, for the first time in the history of television, network viewing is in decline. Network TV is still far and away the dominant force in television, but it has been in a slight but steady decline since the late 1970s, slowly being eroded by the pressure of cable and video movies.

STRUCTURAL SOURCES OF INCOME Media content is a commodity that is bought, sold and traded like any other. The buying and selling of content, however, has little to do with an *individual* viewer, listener, or reader, and is, in many exchanges, only indirectly connected with an audience.

In the United States, there are four very different market conditions that may govern the trade of content. These different conditions all have different impact on the content itself. The four conditions follow.

(1) The direct sale of content by the production agent (or distributor) to the audience. This transaction provides the sole or principal income source. Direct sale is the primary source of income for most audio and video recordings and pay-per-view cable, and subscriber pay channels. It accounts for one method of marketing theatrical films although most theaters break even on ticket sales and earn a profit only on concessions.

A modified form of direct sale is subscription. Subscription involves the direct sale of a content service (rather than a unit of content) by a production and/or distribution agent. Subscription sales as the principle source of income (no advertising) is rare, accounting for a very few magazines and newspapers and some small segments of cable. Subscription sales in combination with advertising (access sales) is, of course, quite common. Advertising has also moved into movie theaters and video cassettes.

(2) Access sales.[1] This income source often starts with the direct sale of content distribution rights by production agents to distribution agents. These distribution agents, such as broadcast stations, add advertising space to the presentation. The content is then "given away" to the audience, but advertisers pay for access to that audience. That is, the distribution agents receive no income from the audience but from the sale of audience access to advertisers and other "users" of the audience. In this system, the audience is the commodity being sold. Most commercial broadcasting is handled in this fashion.

(3) A combination of direct and access sales that involves subscription and access fees. The audience pays for the content product and advertisers pay for access to that audience. This system accounts for most magazine and newspaper economies and for a growing proportion of cable. In the print media, subscription fees generally account for less than half of the total income.

(4) Patron grants. This is the subsidizing of content producers (not content) through government or foundation grants (patrons). This condition is one of several funding techniques used in public broadcasting.

These four conditions have very different consequences for the character of content. *Direct sales systems* are clearly more responsive to the content consumer than to any other. The more the system is directly dependent on sales to an individual consumer, the more the content will specialize in the particular interests of a dependable audience. The force of the specialization is to fractionalize the audience through multiple outlets, as has been the case in records and videocassettes. As one moves away from the direct sales model, considerations other than the consumer demand for content become significant factors in shaping content.

The access sales system of broadcasting, for example, must produce content that will be appropriate vehicles for the insertion of commercial messages. This necessity affects both the shape and substance of content within advertiser-supported systems. A half-hour television program is 26 minutes long; content material tends to avoid central social conflicts and to be nonpoliticizing so as to not disturb the commercial material. These characteristics tend to maintain some program content at a level that audiences would not directly pay for, and to limit the testing of boundaries of audience interest.

The combination of *direct and access sales systems* shows a similar conservatism in those cases in which advertising dollars are the major source of income. When subscribers bear more of the costs of the content, specialization develops, as we see, in the broad array of magazines available in the marketplace.

Patron systems tend to be canonical in their approach to content. Canonical content demonstrates its worth by exhibiting certain characteristics. It becomes "fine" art, if you will. The worth of the content is considered intrinsic, centered on the characteristics of the content, rather than extrinsic, centered on consumer response. Canonical programming or publishing requires a subsidy because it cannot be responsive to changing consumer demands. It has shown itself to be concerned with maintaining past forms (fifteenth-century English drama, sixteenth-century music) that pushes it toward the esoteric. Full enjoyment requires some training in this esoterica that restricts its plasticity or potential for sharing of this content.

In general, the more limited the economic structure of the market, the more clearly drawn are the economic influences on content. Films for teenaged audiences, for example, have a dulling similarity. When sources of income are diverse, content producers are freer to manipulate content. This notion does not suggest that content will, therefore, become "better" by some standard. Witness the current situation in theatrical films, for which the box office, as we have noted, is no longer the sole economic tyrant. The consequence has not been more finely wrought films but a resurgence of the "B" movies, the potboilers of the 1930s updated in teen, space, and horror form. We need not seek any deep cultural meaning for the appearance of this content; it is cheap to make and, at the moment, sufficient for the demands of the marketplace.

BARRIERS TO ENTRY The number of sellers in an industry is a significant structural aspect. Once an industry is established, the number of sellers is controlled by the conditions of entry. Barriers to entry are erected through entry requirements of capital investment, skills and competencies and other resources, government regulation and licensing, restrictive practices within the industry, and so on.

In the United States, broadcast television, theatrical films, and newspapers have traditionally maintained high barriers to entry. The result in these industries has been an **oligopolist** ownership structure (few owners controlling many outlets) most noticeable in television networks. Each member in an oligopolist structure generally attempts to service the maximum revenue source, which means that they compete head-to-head rather than by dividing into specialties. Again, to use television networks as the clearest example, because networks sell audiences, the same type of mass-appeal programming content is selected by all three networks to attract the maximum audience. In short, all three networks mine the central audience vein with the same programming tools. Public television, on the other hand, with a different income structure works the lesser runs to provide an alternative.

By contrast, magazines and radio (particularly AM radio) have relatively low barriers to entry. They have developed an **egalitarian structure** (many owners for many outlets). In this structure, a few of the more dominant players stake the center but most seek specialty positions with well-defined boundaries. In periodicals, we have a huge proliferation of specialty sheets and radio offers the listener the multiple classifications of music and talk.

Economic theories of structure predict the content product outcomes of the oligopolist and egalitarian ownership characteristics well. When a particular market structure of ownership characterizes a media industry, it clearly defines the type of content product that will result. That is, content is not free to vary within ownership conditions. Despite some social critics' claims, the content of network television, for example, cannot be radically different from what it is. If changes in network television programming were to be effected, then the barriers to entry that support the ownership structure that motivates current programming would have to be lowered.

TECHNOLOGICAL INVENTION AND BARRIERS TO ENTRY Mediated communication shows an interesting disjuncture that should continue to widen. On the one side, the microchip has placed very high production capacities in the hands of the ordinary householder. Desktop publishing, near-broadcast-quality video cameras, and audio recording equipment are a yuppie commonplace. Incredibly sophisticated Christmas letters in print and video are being produced (countered by a resurgence of the handwritten letter). This widespread distribution of technology advances the possibility of substantial change in the clublike ownership structure of most media.

As we type and edit on our word processors, we cannot predict the outcome of the socializing of technology on the life of this club. For, on the other side, although the means of production may be rapidly coming into the hands of the people, the means of distribution are still beyond their reach. At the present, the club controls the means of distribution. Even if both production and distribution become more available to those with discretionary income, we may have learned our forms and convention lessons too well to expect high invention. It is true that MTV has shown that radically different visual narratives—the home movies of the rock-and-roll rich now have an outlet—but the lavish praise that Janet Jackson received for producing Gene Kelly routines suggests a revival of the musical, albeit in miniature and in modern dress, as this video art form "matures." Having worked with children for many years, we know that even very young children create the image of a news program, a commercial, or narrative when given the assignment to "do something on TV." Should the old ownership structure crumble with the loss of exclusive access barrier, new content products will have to await the rise of new artistic communities.

STRUCTURAL ASPECTS OF OPERATIONAL SCOPE We noted at the start of this discussion on the structural components of niches that the operational scope—the range of action—within an organization is a combination of capacity and competence. Capacity defines what can be done; competence what can be done well. Capacity and competence define the operational scope by establishing the organizationally accepted view of what is appropriate activity for the organization. While hard-edged realities of technical limitations and market conditions impinge, both capacity and competence are also defined within the organization itself. It is, then, the organization's view of its capacity and competence that provides the answers for the organizationally equivalent questions of who we are and what we can do. Operational scope is a str than imposed from without. The value of this concept, however, is the component centered in the organization rathersame as for all other structural concepts: It helps us to understand the forces independent of the audience that shape content before a single newspaper is delivered, a set is turned on, or a ticket is bought. We will stay with capacity and competence just long enough to set these concepts in a single example.

CAPACITY The characteristics that an organization uses to describe itself can be seen as its functional capacity. Television, for example, offers a description of itself as bounded by a small screen, poor sound (although some improvement has been made here), an audience at large, an access sales system of income, and so on, that limit TV's ability to create an extended content product dependent on detailed images and fidelity in sound. Television content emphasizes small scale action in close encounters (hence, why personal violence is so prevalent), within short self-contained segments. This type of content best fits this medium's capacities.

Theatrical film, on the other hand, has a large screen, excellent sound, a captive audience, a direct sales system of income and so on, that creates a demand for a different sort of content. The recent history of theatrical films shows the interface between content and capacity. As the energy and maintenance costs of the physical plant of the theater rose spectacularly in the 1960s and 1970s, theater owners divided their houses or moved to smaller plants. With the resultant smaller audience, the owners had to rely on audience turnover for adequate ticket and concession sales. Consequently, they demanded a product of consistent and shorter length that could turn an audience more frequently. Films greatly in excess of the 90-minute standard cannot return enough income because the number of showing cycles in the prime attendance periods is reduced, yet the theater size remains the same. The average size of the movie house, then, as it defines the limits of distribution, is a characteristic of capacity that in turn significantly affects content.

COMPETENCE The idea of competence as a structural characteristic may not be readily apparent. Competence develops out of practiced efforts and may seem more appropriately a matter of conduct. Competence as a structural component, however, is not the performance itself, but the limiting and empowering beliefs about what can be done well and the reservoir of technique that supports those beliefs. Local television news, for example, believes that what it does well is to bring the immediacy of the moment into the home. The time span of presented stories centers about the day of broadcast. Local television's news competence, therefore, is in the presentation of 12-14 stories, each of which can be completed in less that two minutes. The reservoir of technique is found in the people and tools necessary to do that job. (A news director remarked to one of the authors that "what we do is shallow and superficial, but we do that well.") Stories are rejected for being too long, too complex, too old—in short, not competent.

Could television news be different—say, four or five stories, five to six minutes long? Of course, but the change would require a new set of beliefs about the nature of news and the development of technical resources—in skills and tools—to accomplish the new design. Such a change would require the organization to be incompetent for the period of transition, which may be predicted to be several years long as the practitioners develop viable presentational techniques. This incompetence is uncomfortable ("Charley, what the hell are you people doing over there?") and places substantial pressure on the supporting rationale ("John, this has gone on long enough; you're fired!"). If the change fails, which it often does, that failure reinforces the beliefs about the traditional competence.

MEDIA STRUCTURE: A SUMMARY

In this section, we have first focused on the interlocking relationships among media. Media are inescapably intertwined because on the face of it they compete for the attention of the same audience (mostly to sell to the same set of advertisers). The structural response has been the formation of niches in which the media can be positioned vis-à-vis one another. By working even slightly different sections of the audience ecology by segregating content, media receive their share of the audience cycle and reduce head-to-head competition with one another.

The niche structure also permits product flow—a homogenizing process. Just as the automotive industry uses the same undercarriages and engines in many different products, the media can transport central themes, characters, narrative, and the like from one presentational niche to another and offer them in specialized forms.

Product flow is enhanced by the fact that the media community is relatively small and well protected. The modern history of media has been one of interlocking directorates and consolidations. Though antitrust regulations and the **Federal Communication Commission** (FCC) have forced some diversity, the industry economics have pressed consistently in the other direction. The result is a community protected by strong barriers to entry in the form of capital investment requirements, government regulation and licensing, and contractual relationships among present members.

A particularly instructive example of the limited community in media is the recent history of low-powered television. This new service, in which several new television stations with limited (25-mile) broadcast range were to be introduced into existing markets, did not bring in substantial numbers of new players. Instead, most of the licenses were acquired by existing media conglomerates. Perhaps as a result, LPTV is still a hazy dream of possibility.

The structural components of our media can also be seen in their sources of income. We identified three separate systems that alone or in combination generate the revenue structures of media: direct sales, access sales to advertisers, and patrons. Content maintains its greatest intrinsic worth in the patron form of revenue. It is least likely to have intrinsic value in the access sales form, in which it is essentially given away in order to generate circulation, the real source of money.

Finally, we examined the structures of operational scope—the living framework of organizational activity. We saw operational scope as a combination of the described capacity and the competence beliefs and resources that are internal to the organization. The answers to the questions of who we are and what we can do have far-ranging consequences on the shape of media content.

Structure is significant to us because it does shape content, and it shapes it prior to contact with an audience. Our media have been described by their practitioners as democratic because their audiences decide what appears. This statement is best seen as self-serving rhetoric with little explanatory power. The powerful forces of market structure determine the general form of content long before any of us gets to cast a vote. To show this power, we'll begin the next section on conduct by considering how these structural components form the operational contexts for the conduct of media organizations.

CENTRAL IDEAS OF SECTION I: STRUCTURAL CHARACTERISTICS AND CONTENT

1. The media industry is an institution of our society that participates in the

construction and maintenance of that society. It is not an outside or oppositional force.
2. The institution of media is composed of interlinked media industries that position themselves in relation to one another along the resource dimensions of content, audiences, and capital.
3. The structural characteristics of income, ownership, and operational scope have explicit consequences for the content of the media, much more so than does creativity or individual leadership.

SECTION II: INDUSTRY CONDUCT AND CONTENT

Within the member organizations of an industry, we are concerned with two separate processes—the process of organizing and the process of producing. It is within these processes that we finally meet the people who actually do the work of our media. The process of organizing is an endogenous or inward-looking process that governs the relationships among the members. It results in the structures of leadership, characteristics of communication, institutional values, corporate norms—in short, all of the activities that identify a particular organization. The process of producing while nested inside these organizing activities is an exogenous or outward-looking activity by which the organization maintains its principal contact with its clients and larger society. This process involves the codes of workmanship, resident technology, and the methods and practices by which these codes and technology are performed. When economists speak of industry conduct, they are speaking of the patterns within the process of producing—the public behavior of organizations, if you will. (Organization scholars, on the other hand, are more concerned with the private—member-only—behavior of the organizing process.)

The media products that we see, hear, and read are the result of people performing work within an organization that is a member of societal institutions called the media. Although aberrations and mutants do occur, the ordinary article, program, record, or film is not some dream child of creation freely wrought by an individual or even an individual organization. It is a precision product delivered to specifications arising both within the organization and within the industry. It is well beyond the scope of this text to consider the particular strictures that an organization would apply—suffice it to say, for instance, that the particular newspaper one works for will have its own rules for producing an edition that will be recognizable everywhere as a newspaper. We can, however, spend some time considering a few of the industrywide influences—those patterns of the production process that appear in content. In the next several sections, we will examine some of the behavioral characteristics of the conduct of production. Specifically, we will take a quick overview of the operational contexts, decision-making conduct in an irrational market, and the trading and competitive practices that may have an impact on content.

OPERATIONAL CONTEXTS OF MEDIA INSTITUTIONS

Institutions, as well as individuals, operate within contextual arenas that define the permissible choices of behavior or, in this case, the permissible goods of symbolic content. The media's choices are clearly circumscribed by contexts of law, regulation, sources of income, operation of the marketplace, **technology, codes of workmanship,** expectations concerning the responses of other institutions, and the institution's own inertia, given its history and characteristic modes of operation.

Analysis of these contexts of activity demonstrates that it is simply not possible to print, film, air, or distribute certain content and still remain viable within the operating economic, legal, and/or social systems. Some content is expressly prohibited by law. Other content is prohibited by custom or cultural mores (such as a situation comedy based on incest). Still other content cannot meet economic criteria imposed by the media institution.

While these contexts do restrict activity, they cannot be seen as constraints alone because in the act of constraining they also empower performance. That is, they make it very easy to do things in a given way. For the professional reporter, it is easy to write a story in the inverted pyramid style; so easy that it becomes difficult to perform outside that style. In the same vein, but in a larger scope, the very federal regulatory agencies designed to control certain media industries also protect those industries within their regulated performance. Broadcasting was protected for decades from cable, and now cable is being protected from local-area, low-powered broadcasting. It has been said that if we had a Federal Computation Commission we would still be counting on our fingers.

Another example of protectionism can be seen in the Failing Newspaper Act, which permits newspapers in the same market to combine production facilities in order that both might survive, even though the market would not naturally support both. Critics have argued that this "artificial" support simply continues an outmoded presentational form and blocks innovation.

The argument that we are creating here is that industry conduct is deeply embedded in structures and contexts. Conduct is not the independent actions of capricious men and women. If one wished to change conduct in order, perhaps, to achieve different products, the system that produces that conduct would have to be changed. Such change is possible, of course, but approaches that seek to change just one industry representative or some subset of behavior would clearly appear to be futile.

THE CONDUCT OF DECISION MAKING IN AN IRRATIONAL MARKET

Economists measure the rationality of a market by the extent to which performance can be predicted. In general, the media market is very uncertain. The failure rate for content product is very high. The extent of the understanding of the relationship between content and audiences is such that even when everything is done right—all the rules followed—the content is about equally likely to fail as to succeed. This high rate of failure is not for the want of testing; the industry is heavily into research. It is probably true that if a distributor followed only research results, a profit would be turned, suggesting a rational marketplace. Research offices, however, also produce spectacular embarrassments in predicting the hits and misses of content. The result of the unpredicted smash and the highly touted failure is that the market appears irrational to content producers, who then substitute inside knowledge (indeed, gut feelings) for, perhaps, the more objective arguments of the testing house. We have seen publishers, for example, decide on a book over lunch and then work up a treatment to sell it to the research and editorial board. It is also mildly amusing to watch television praise its latest content seer (remember Freddie Silverman?), knowing the inevitable fall will come. Grant Tinker timed his exit well.

An irrational market obscures the relationship between decisions made and the consequences of those decisions in performance. That is, one can make all the "right" decisions and still fail, or all the "wrong" decisions and still succeed. It produces a gambler's mentality, full of hunches, high risks, and safe bets. This conduct, of course, simply confirms the market irrationality. Regardless of the insufficiencies of research and the actions of the audience, the content marketplace is irrational, in part, for no further reason than the conduct of decision making by media producers.

Decision making in an irrational market becomes increasingly insular. The result is a community driven by its own stories of how things happen, some of which are shrewdly insightful, others face-savingly political. In this set of stories, any decision can be justified, any audience fact explained. This decision making is protected from nonmember influences, such as social action groups or media critics. The consequence of this isolationism is that the artistic and technical communities become increasingly inbred. There are fewer innovations and more imitation in this type of community. The rules of conduct are more tightly drawn. One reduces risks by working with the tried and true whether that be people or programs. It is not surprising, then, that media content has been criticized for being conventionalized—highly predictable in style and technique. Practitioners circle the wagons in uncertain markets.

Popular arguments to the contrary, the media are responsive to their own interpretation of performance, not to unmistakable audience demand. Audiences have media needs that transcend the content (an issue we more fully develop in Chapters 3 and 4). That is, content is only a partial predictor of why the audience is there. Estimates suggest that half of the audience is there for reasons other than content (e.g., to pass time, be with family, avoid work). Even though half of the audience is not predictable by content, the success or failure of content turns on a few percentage points rather than clear audience demand. As a result, as Dick Cavett has been credited with observing, "The people get what they get."

THE CONDUCT OF TECHNOLOGY

Technology, whether changing or not, has a profound effect on the content of the media. Technology is the sum of the tools and knowledge that generate an accepted way of doing things. Most news stories are now written on CRT devices, not typewriters. Nearly all video editing is done by computer, not razor blade. Whatever the task, the effort must conform to the technology currently in place. One often thinks of changes in technology as liberating—giving new capacity. But at the same time, those capacities impose a new set of demands for their use whether wanted or needed.

Technology, therefore, establishes general rules of workmanship, which govern the character of the content produced under them. These rules define the difference between "home movies" and theatrical films, or between a mimeographed newsletter and a magazine. In broadcasting, some of these rules of workmanship have been institutionalized in the FCC's technical regulations. In all commercial ventures, an understood and often explicitly stated premise of the contract is that the effort shall meet generally accepted standards of workmanship. Technology, then, regulates a way of doing things, which involves both method and means: A commercial in black and white (except for special effect) simply isn't done. Broadcasting a program from a home VCR isn't even legal.

Technology as a way of doing things is not limited to the engineering departments of the media. The transformation of ideas to finished media product resides within its own technology. The creative effort is sifted through layers of judgment by editors, directors, producers, publishers, programmers. Technical forms, conventions, and formulas develop. From the simple requirement of the inverted pyramid (all pertinent information in the first sentence of a story; details follow) to the AP stylebook (which decrees grammar, structure, usage, and so on) in print, the standard characters and settings of television, and the engineered endings of rock and roll music, media practitioners create a formula to accommodate a form. It is because of this institutionalization of the creative act that ordinary media content is just that—ordinary. Bound by team consensus, content production does not attempt to explore new territory but walks the well-known paths. For example, "Mork and Mindy" was introduced as a "fresh, new show" and enjoyed some critical and much popular success. One premise of the program, a visitor from outer space with special powers, had been worked years earlier in "My Favorite Martian" and the other premise of a culturally inept but winning character had been well developed by Grannie and the rest of the Clampett gang in the "Beverly Hillbillies." Even the remarkable contribution of the Norman Lear group in "Mary Hartmann, Mary Hartmann" and in "All in the Family," in introducing adult themes and dialogue into American television, was well established in Britain and other European countries.

In ordinary, everyday living, how things are done is well-defined. The media have their ordinary, everyday procedure also. Some of it may be written down in policy, but most of it is simply understood by individuals who have been socialized as competent members of the institution. One creates the form by the formulas existing at the time.

THE CONDUCT OF TRADE

Trade demands a price, and price establishes value. Our interest in the conduct of trade, then, is the value that it places on the content commodity. What is the value of a Marlon Brando cameo in Superman? How is it determined? By his performance? By the beliefs that the producers have for his box office power? To give the obvious answer, producers clearly felt that Brando's million-dollar-plus fee was justified in the box office return they would receive. Could the film have done as well without Brando? Of course, perhaps better, but we'll never know—the market is fundamentally uncertain.

Pricing is the contract between the seller and the buyer. If price is to reflect a valid performance value, the contract has to be negotiated between knowledgeable buyers and sellers. The terms *performance value* and *knowledgeable* are technical ones that simplify the transaction analysis. Performance value refers to the transaction's return in the units of the performance criteria—minutes or lines of competent content in subscription and patron models; number of impressions in advertiser-supported models. Knowledgeable buyers are those who pay no more, and knowledgeable sellers those who set prices at no less than the worth of the performance value of the commodity. Many of the players in the media market are not knowledgeable. Public television patrons (friends) donate far more than what they receive in content value. They do so for charitable, community, and other altruistic reasons. Advertisers on local television news buy time for reasons other than circulation (number of impressions). They do so for prestige, personal vanity, tradition. Movie producers buy stars on ephemeral hopes.

When the buyer is not knowledgeable, products with the same performance value can be differentiated and price manipulated. Advertising time on local television news, for example, can be priced higher than its performance value because buyers are willing to pay more for a product that has been differentiated on prestige. Similarly, an advertiser can use the controversial nature of a program to force the seller to lower the price of access below its performance value because those time slots can be differentiated on conflict. In strict economic terms, both of these exemplar transactions reveal players who are not knowledgeable even though they all may be very satisfied with the deal.

That the media product can be differentiated on criteria other than performance means that forms of content not justified by their performance value can be "artificially" supported in the market, and that content that is justified in performance can be denied presentation. Both of these consequences are important to us. That the media market allows product differentiation on criteria other than performance means that content can exhibit at least some independence of its logical audience worth. Analytical models that explain media content essentially on the basis of audience demand are, therefore, flawed. The primary conclusions of such models (now shown as flawed) is that our media are a mirror (albeit distorted) of the social action of our culture. The conduct of transactions in the media market demonstrate that this "mirror" is not only distorted but fundamentally unreliable. You cannot read our culture in our media! There is too much content presented that is not directly supported by audience and too much that would be supported, but which never appears. Now that is an iconoclastic claim; yet, it is well-evidenced in the empirical and theoretical studies of transaction conduct.

THE FORCE OF COMPETITION

The economic structure of the marketplace establishes the rules of the game, but it is the competition that sets the level of play. The forward pass was a creative solution for the problem of moving the football down the field. Introduced by a competitor, it forever changed the game. Media content in the United States (but not everywhere) exists in a competitive market—who the players are makes a difference, at least in understanding content at any given point in time.

The skill of a competitor may lead to a higher competence in the marketplace, but competition itself appears to breed more imitation of success than fertility of innovation. That is, imitation is the simplest form of competition. It is certainly safer to imitate success than to risk failure. Media industries have been charged with competition by imitation. To a certain extent this charge of imitation is unfair. Innovative content can seek the level of demand in the marketplace only through repetition or imitation. In broadcast television, for example, one production house cannot provide more than a single episode of a series per week because of production time constraints. Consequently, if market demand exists for content involving one blonde female lead and one brunette female character living in close proximity with a barely competent male, then imitation will be assured until it is filled.

Whether to limit risk or to respond to demand, competition seems to force a cycling and recycling of content formats and genres. A successful content format enjoys so much exposure that it soon fails because of its own success. The demise, of course, is temporary since it will reappear, phoenixlike, in its next incarnation.

CONDUCT: AN ANALYTICAL SUMMARY

The questions of conduct are praxeological questions—how things get done. For most economists, it is structure that generates the causes of performance. Conduct is the means of getting to those inevitable consequences and is, therefore, primarily a concern of the curious. Our media structure is oligopolist (few owners over many outlets), its products differentiated, and its markets characterized by high uncertainty. These structural components result in conduct embedded within these operational contexts in which decision-making is technically irrational, innovation is technological, transactions can be shrewd but unknowledgeable, and competition motivates imitation. It is our contention that *structure* and *conduct* are the primary terms in the definition of the content product. Content producers are responsive to performance criteria only within the terms of structure and conduct. Practitioners are analogous to players of a game: They are given the conditions of play—the court, ball, racquet, rules, and so on—and told to develop the best performance within those conditions. To look at that performance and to claim that it is the "natural expression" of a society is to ignore completely the fact that this "natural expression" would be forced into a different mold with a change of structure and rules of conduct. At the same time, it is egregious elitism to hold that, true or not, the audience believes that the media are a clear expression of society. Our ethnographic studies demonstrate that individuals can quite easily distinguish their own value positions from those expressed in the media. But with that comment, to be explored in the next chapter, we have slipped ahead of ourselves. We turn now to consider the measures of performance of our media.

CENTRAL IDEAS OF SECTION II: INDUSTRY CONDUCT AND CONTENT

1. Conduct is the set of practices that characterize an industry. The conduct of individuals in an organization is governed by the premises of action of the organization.
2. The premises of action arise in the context of the marketplace, the resident technology, the terms of trade, and quality of competition.
3. Simple claims of audience demand cannot explain the presence and success of content.

SECTION III: MEASURES OF PERFORMANCE

Performance, we remember, is the consequence of conduct within a structure on some set of criteria. In our primarily commercial system of media, it is tempting to consider only the bottom line of a ledger sheet as the criterion. It is not quite that simple. Certainly, income is primary, but significant criteria are contained in law and regulation, consumer demands (subscribers and time buyers in this case), industry practice, and individual and organizational style. We will visit with each of these.

INCOME AND AUDIENCES

In the United States, media performance on the criterion of income is more or less directly tied to an audience. We say, more or less, because in each of the income systems there are other variables that intervene in the relationship. In the direct sales systems, income increases only with paid ticket holders or subscribers, so audiences are routinely padded with freebies. Therefore, audiences can be much larger than the bottom line would show. With access sales systems, increases in audience have a minimal effect on income at the very low end and at the very high end of circulation. Audiences must be of a minimal size to attract advertisers, but audiences that are too large can become priced out of the market. And in patron systems, only a very small percentage of the audience actually contributes. We have little experience with the effect of very large audiences on funding.

Nevertheless, audience size—circulation—is an extremely important performance measure. We do wish, however, to draw a very careful distinction: Circulation is not the same as readers, viewers, and/or listeners. Circulation is a measured value. That is, it is an index developed within a set of counting procedures; it is not a measure of reading, watching, or listening. A reader, viewer, or listener is an individual attending to content who *may* or *may not* be included in the circulation count. Magazines and newspapers regularly claim a readership beyond their circulation. (Three people in the Anderson household read the one newspaper subscription, and think of all the *Sports Illustrated* readers in medical waiting rooms.) Broadcast television, on the other hand, routinely claims a circulation beyond its viewership (so we will see) as an **artifact** of its data-collection system. (Many public television stations and most public radio stations have only the haziest notion of either their circulation or their actual viewers and listeners because they do not meet the minimum standards required by the measurement companies.) Audiences count, therefore, but only in the way that they are counted.

One of the arguments that we have advanced is that institutions respond to institutions and not to individuals. We want to extend this argument into the distinction between readers, viewers, and listeners, on the one hand, and audiences on the other. It is our claim that individual satisfactions or dissatisfactions have little meaning for the media institution. What is meaningful is feedback from an *audience*. An audience is the institutionalization of the individual through some system of circulation measurement. The method of measurement defines the audience. In magazines and newspapers, circulation is defined by rates of subscriptions in given demographic areas. In film and recordings it is by the number of unit sales. In broadcasting, audiences are defined by responses to one or more of a variety of survey methods.

Audiences are significant to the commercial institutions of media because they generate cash in hand, or they are the commodity that these institutions sell to the institutions of advertising in the form of circulation. It is in the latter circumstance—in the access sales system—that the distinction between audiences and users becomes most clear. We'll spend a few paragraphs on this issue.

In the access sales system, circulation represents the number of people of given kinds who will be available for the advertising message. Circulation has value to the advertiser in two ways—sheer quantity and the mix of quality. Sheer quantity is the raw power of the number of exposures that can be anticipated by the size of the audience. The mix of quality is the percentage of potential buyers within that audience. Commercial media sell both size and quality.

In television, size is measured by the percentage of households with television (TV households or TVHH) or by the number of viewers tuned to a particular program. In the simplest form of measurement, there is no guarantee that anyone is watching or, if watching, that they are doing so in a manner receptive to the advertiser's message. Nevertheless, this form of measurement is the most common. This circulation figure is called a **rating**—a familiar term to many.

Ratings are calculated by taking a sample of households (usually around 1,700 for a national sample) or people (approaching 4,000 by 1989) selected from telephone or housing directories. If the household members agree, one of three data-collection procedures is set in place. The simplest is a viewing diary in which each member keeps a record of any program viewed for 10 minutes or more. Less prone to error is the "Auditron," a simple recording device that records when the set is turned on and the channel to which it is tuned; it must be used with a diary to get "people information." The newest procedure is the "people meter," which is a push-button device connected to a computer link. When a household member (or a timer) turns on the set and logs in on the people meter, an impulse is sent to a central computer and is recorded—one more household and viewer for program X. As the sample is presumed to be representative of the whole audience, the percentage of households tuned to the program in the sample is simply multiplied by the total number of TV households in the audience (in the United States, better than 95% of all households).

The measurement of audience quality and, therefore, of the people in the circulation requires the audience member to volunteer information about him- or herself. This information is collected by people meters or through the use of diaries. The information collected classifies people into selected categories. These classifications form the audience types that can be sold. In this system of measurement, there are actually very few audiences. For the television network, there is no white, middle-class, Christian, woman audience because the rating companies do not use these categories. There is an 18- to 49-year-old, working-woman audience because such measurement classifications do exist. The choice of measurement classifications is dictated by the economic system in which commercial television functions. Television sells the audiences that are wanted by advertisers. The system of commercial television measures only those audiences that are economically worthwhile. If the white, middle-class, Christian, woman audience were to become an economically desirable audience, it would be measured into existence.

Networks select programs to generate the audiences they measure. Consequently, they certainly do program for the 18- to 49-year-old, working-woman audience, but not by seeking out the individual reasons that the persons who would meet these classifications tests might have for viewing. Imagine the wide variety of women who are both working and 18 to 49 years of age. To assume that this aggregate of individuals is likely to present single-minded reasons for viewing a particular program is ludicrous. A woman may be there because she is tired from her working day, the car broke down, dinner is late, the kids are on her nerves, it's her favorite program, she enjoys the leading man, the scripts are witty. The list is potentially as large as the number of women involved.

As noted, it is estimated that about half of the reasons for attending any particular program have nothing to do with the content of the program itself. Rather, attendance is the consequence of the availability of the opportunity to view television, one's evaluation of the alternative activities, reaction to the programming on the other channels, and so on. Further, viewing is often part of another activity, or is used to accomplish some other task (such as avoiding another activity or maintaining power status and the like). Networks select content that is responsive to common issues of this audience, issues such as relationships with fellow workers, boredom, family problems, status, success, sex, and so on. They do not program for the reasons of the individuals.

As the audience exists only in measurement, the methods of measurement have substantial implications for the character of feedback and its impact on content. If these measurement methods misrepresent or poorly represent the intended audience, the content actually misses its mark, but the media institution is never privy to that failure. Well, do they? The answer depends on whom you ask. There is substantial evidence from studies conducted by the television industry itself that circulation is substantially overestimated and that the categorical estimates of audience types may be unreliable. Analysis of the procedures used to collect the data show that over half of the households selected for inclusion in the sample fail to appear in the final analysis. It is an incredible act of faith to presume that the greater portion is exactly the same as the lesser one.

Audiences can likewise be underestimated as an artifact of how they are measured. Ratings companies typically have not included a number of different settings in which TV is viewed as meeting their definition of "household"; places like college dorms and bars have been excluded. For most programs, such an exclusion probably matters little, but for programs like "Late Night With David Letterman" and "Saturday Night Live," the difference in audience estimates can be substantial. A privately commissioned study showed that Letterman's audience was underestimated by nearly 25%—2.92 million, as opposed to Nielsen's estimate of 2.19 million. A 25% increase in ad revenues would make for an even more profitable show than it is now. With a smaller than expected audience, however, the program might have been long since canceled. Therefore, if you ask us, the answer is yes, measurement procedures do distort our understanding of the viewers of television (and is true of other media as well).

The point of this very brief description of television audience measurement methods is that what we know about people using the media is, in fact, very little. And it is known only because of commercial necessity. Commercial media must have circulation information to sell time and space to advertisers. But, naturally, only that information that prompts the advertising sale is collected. Furthermore, the quality of the research is the result of an ongoing, negotiated compromise between the demands of the advertising institutions for information and the willingness of the media institutions to pay for that information. Larger samples, better measurement methods, and more complex analysis are all available but at a cost the industry is unwilling to pay—a quite understandable unwillingness as their practices have developed in response to the present system of measurement. Changing the system would only cast the market into higher uncertainty.[2]

Most of what we read about what TV audiences feel or what newspaper readers want are either presumptions or projections from the limited information of commercial research. We do not know how many people watched the Superbowl, although it certainly was a lot.[3] Nor do we know how many commercials a child will watch, although that, too, will be many. The claims in these areas are presumptive claims. Rhetorically effective presumptive claims are often used to promote social policy action, but they are not factual.

There is one final twist to this discussion: Pragmatically, it is of no concern to the industry whether circulation figures represent the audience. What matters is an acceptable set of measurement procedures that returns usable information about the relative audience strength of different content. Whether the numbers represent only the number of TV sets turned on in 1,700 sample households, or the viewing habits of America, is irrelevant. The industry doesn't sell the viewing habits of America; it sells a **commodity audience** as measured in rating points. What the industry needs is measurement with predictable characteristics by which they can evaluate their programming decisions in order to have a consistent product to sell.

REGULATORY AND LEGAL CRITERIA

Laws and regulatory agencies also establish significant performance criteria. Newspapers, in order to be classified as newspapers for a variety of postal privileges, cannot average more than 40% of their space in paid advertising. Broadcasting and cable industries have had a long history of regulatory controls on content either directly or by the hint of action. In the late 1970s, after a study of television content, the FCC proposed to establish a rule requiring seven and a half hours of programming a week aimed at children that would "inform and educate, not merely entertain." The networks responded to this threatened rule in a number of ways. They attacked it directly through legal briefs, but they also modified their content to weaken the case against them.

Legal actions affect content: The seizure of materials under the "community standards" interpretation of the First Amendment has led to the modification of magazine content and to distribution restrictions on X-rated films.

The definitions of paid advertising, educational content, obscene material, and the like are the obvious criteria of performance in law and regulation. The courts and agencies supply these definitions; the media manipulate them. What, for example, is a paid advertisement? The relationship between news copy and advertisement becomes blurred in the standard practices of using press releases without attribution or the sale of advertising around a feature story. And what gets left out of the newspaper is of even greater significance.

CONSUMER CRITERIA (OTHER THAN PRICE)

In all but film and books of the major media, the primary consumer is not the audience but the time or space buyer who represents the advertiser. The advertiser buys access to an audience of a certain size and quality to increase sales of his or her product (or other advertising purpose). For media, the delivery of an audience of the given size and quality at a good price is not enough. That audience must also be responsive to performance criteria set by the advertiser. A knowledgeable merchant who does not see increased traffic from a magazine spread doesn't buy the space again (granting all the possible exceptions to that statement). The harshest answer to a sales rep is "you didn't deliver." The rep's reply that the audience was there is no answer to an empty store.

The effects of the advertiser's criteria on content are many, both obvious and subtle. We will consider three examples, format, controversial content, and product differentiation.

FORMAT Format, here, describes the manner in which advertising copy is intermixed with the story and other content. Commercial media attempt to use format to lead the audience to the commercial message. Television narratives are broken at enticing moments to hold the viewer for the ads. In fact, it is a requirement of the narrative form to provide those breaks. Print outlets split stories, lay out columns, and arrange pages to bring the reader to the advertisement. Again, writing style that will provide for that manipulation is encouraged.

Format also concerns the content matrix. It affects the relationship between the number of ads within the space and time inventory. Both print and broadcasting have a fixed inventory; one set by law and the other by industry practice (and the threat of regulation). How one uses that inventory—in a few large messages or many smaller ones—affects the overall matrix. Television, for example, has recently set the 15-second commercial as the standard, with 10-second messages common, and the 5-second ad on the horizon. Television has done this because it lowers the total price to the advertiser while it increases the per-second revenue to the medium. The viewer sees no more advertising minutes, but many more ads.

CONTROVERSIAL CONTENT Content vehicles not conducive to advertising messages cannot be the mainstay of an industry whose income is derived from advertising. Advertisers hold a number of stories about proper content to be true. These explanations generally reject content that is intense, depressing, or highly charged politically. Advertisers are not in the business of taking risks by supporting content that may negatively affect sales. One of the most effective weapons of the social activist groups trying to constrain media content may be the threat of a product boycott.

A very good example was the recent decision of the Southland Corporation, a convenience store chain, to discontinue the sales of *Penthouse, Playboy,* and similar magazines. They were responding to boycott threats and picket action on their neighborhood outlets. This decision implicated a large revenue potential for these two magazines. The Southland Corporation is not an advertiser in Penthouse or Playboy, but as a retailer it represents an important link in the connection between content and reader. The Southland Corporation apparently felt that its business was in danger because of the controversial nature of these entertainment magazines. It was safer to drop the magazines—a very small part of its business—than to risk revenues.

Controversial content can also extend to other advertisers. Male birth control products are still expressly denied access to network television and many print outlets because of the fear of organized response. Feminine hygiene products are often rejected in local markets for the same reason. In these cases and with other similar products, the message about a legal and useful product is denied presentation because of its potential effect on revenue.

PRODUCT DIFFERENTIATION We return, just for a line or two, to the subject of product differentiation and knowledgeable buyers. Economists consider products *of the same type* to be differentiated when price can be manipulated because of differences in characteristics other than the primary purpose of the product. Soaps are a good example. All can be shown to clean effectively, but their price varies on qualities such as scent, color, minor ingredients, and the like. Soap, then, is a differentiated product whose differentiation is supported by unknowledgeable consumers. (Oh, yeah?!) We have noted that content, especially in local markets, is also a differentiated product. That is, advertisers will pay more for certain content even though the circulation delivered is the same, record buyers pay a premium for getting an early copy instead of waiting for the recording to migrate to the discount bin, and so on. The media industry makes money on this differentiation, and this revenue supports types of content products at a level not justified by its circulation. (News and cartoon shows are two good examples.) This effect, of course, is the opposite of the controversial content effect.

INDUSTRY PRACTICES

Owners, stockholders, and creditors establish the conditions for the conduct of business for all commercial institutions. Financial stakeholders profoundly affect the content of our media by the performance demands they establish for their investment. In the early months of 1986, CBS was forced to release a significant portion of its news staff. The move had little to do with the performance of this staff or with policy decisions about news content. One analyst saw the move as the result of a depleted cash reserve brought on by a relatively weak, but still threatening, takeover attempt. CBS stockholders and creditors, according to this analysis, demanded a more secure financial condition that forced management to reduce costs. News, a high cost/low profit item, was an obvious target. As a result, the CBS morning news program, a fixture for many years, was lost.

For over two decades, the National Association of Broadcasters' Code of Good Practice set the limits for the number of commercial messages members could present during various portions of the broadcast day. These limits effectively established the inventory of commercial-access minutes that member stations had to sell. Given a fixed inventory of access minutes and a relatively stable audience over all programs, broadcast revenues would soon go flat. Efforts to increase revenues from this large but finite inventory led to the decision of reducing the standard time sale from 1-minute slots to 30-second slots, and, as noted, most recently to 15-second ones. The Code of Good Practice has subsequently been struck down as a violation of antitrust provisions of free competition. Nevertheless, though the official code is dead, the practice continues.

A similar example of formalized industry practice is the Motion Picture Code. The Code, as you know, is the rating system by which films get their alphabetical insignia. Industry analysts believe that an "X" rating significantly lowers the box office potential of a film, whereas an "R" rating can increase its potential among certain audiences. Films are, therefore, edited to achieve the rating deemed appropriate for the intended audience. The Motion Picture Code may one day be challenged as a collusive practice. It certainly can be argued that the ratings do constrain trade by limiting the competitive effectiveness of the content product. The courts might also find the Code providing a greater public good in disseminating information about the rated films, which is, of course, the argument the Code board presents.

It takes intensive insider knowledge to identify industry practices. It is rare when such practices are formalized as the broadcasters' or film codes. Nevertheless, everyday business requires a large number of accommodations in order to conduct an orderly industry. Such accommodations include the tacit agreements between news sources and reporters as to who will get information first; between program producers and networks as to who has first refusal rights, under what conditions news outlets will share information, how contracted artists can work for someone else, and the like. Outsiders rarely learn of these agreements except when complaints surface about their violation.

A most recent dispute to surface was Ted Turner's decision to "colorize" black and white films from the 1930s and 1940s. The Screen Directors Guild expressed outrage, claiming that such action violated the traditional artistic ownership of the work. There is, of course, no apparent legal ownership involved in the dispute, although the courts have upheld claims based on practices. At some level, Turner will have to deal with the Guild, either economically or politically, because if an organization is to survive, and money is to be made over the long haul, how it is done is significant. Organizations need to be good citizens of their industry.

SOCIETAL STAKEHOLDERS

There is probably no more interesting potpourri of performance criteria than those held by the variety of societal stakeholders in the media. The greater number of these are directed toward content characteristics. A few examples: Dramatic content should "realistically" portray women and minorities. Dramatic content should not realistically portray violence or explicit sex (although affection between married couples is generally acceptable). Content that children watch or read should be educating and encourage imaginative play. News should emphasize government actions (hard news), rather than life-styles or happy talk. In short, there are a number of criteria that are generally outside those supported by the resources of the market environment in which media perform.

The activity of these stakeholders has had some effect particularly during periods of activist regimes in the FCC and **Federal Trade Commission** (FTC) agencies, and on the Motion Picture Code. Most members, however, would express frustration at the small effect achieved. One reason for this frustration is in the tactical naivetè exhibited by these groups. In the past, their attempts have been directed at getting a protectionist government to change ordinary practice or to get nonexistent audiences roused to action. Recently, more sophisticated approaches have been developed in product boycotts (or threats thereof) and attacks on distribution outlets (Southland). For these stakeholders to achieve significant results, however, they must gain status within the structure of the industry. As of now they are Cassandra voices outside the fortress.

INDIVIDUAL AND ORGANIZATIONAL STYLE

We want to end this long discussion on what might seem to be the invisible, inevitable, and involuntary forces on the shape of content with a section on the difference that people make. And people do make a difference, but those who do are people who have been successful within the system and have achieved position within the industry structure; then they make a difference, but mostly for the time that they are present.

USA Today is a good example. The Gannett organization has established content criteria for that newspaper that differ significantly from ordinary industry practice, although they themselves follow those ordinary practices in their other newspaper outlets. Their *USA Today* product has had some effect on what others can and will do. So far, however, their capsules, graphics, and color have not resulted in high revenues, although *USA Today* has turned a small profit. The organizational choices that resulted in *USA Today* may have created a player briefly on the stage.

Bill Cosby is perhaps another example in which the force of the individual is clear. Cosby and his organization have made distinctive choices in creating their very successful program, the form of which is a traditional situation comedy. It has been described as the creation of a white, upper-middle-class family with black faces, in order to destroy color as the basis for distinction. Ethnic behavior and white actors are both almost entirely missing.

While these two examples are powerful in presenting the force of style, it is important to point out that *USA Today* is still a newspaper and Cosby is clearly a situation comedy. Every piece of content is the result of individuals improvising within the requirements of structure and the rules of conduct, according to their own standards of performance. The final character of what we see is first the result of those structures and then the innovations of individual improvisations.

PERFORMANCE MEASURES: A SUMMARY

We understand the performance of our media according to the criteria we hold for them. It is the criteria that organize the action into something visible in analysis. The media have an extensive presence in our society. As a result there are many criteria by which we understand their performance. We have examined the following: revenue and the effect the different sources of revenue have on content choices, the nonprice requirements of the consumer in both direct and access sales systems, the values contained in industry practice that provide for orderly transactions, and last, the values expressed in individual and organizational style.

CENTRAL IDEAS OF SECTION III: MEASURES OF PERFORMANCE

1. The audience of the media industry is not the collection of viewers, listeners, and/or readers that we individually compose. The industry audience or commodity audience is the measured circulation that appears only in the methods used to survey it.
2. As a societal institution, media are integrated with other institutions and stakeholders through a system of laws, regulations, and agreements. This integration establishes constraints on content.
3. The consumers of the commodity audience place demands on content appropriate to their use of it as an access to that audience.
4. The industry itself is a community of practitioners that has a degree of autonomy in establishing its own measures of performance. These criteria are the codes of workmanship in the industry to which the content product ordinarily attends.

STRUCTURE, CONDUCT AND PERFORMANCE: FINAL COMMENTS

When we examine the media we are looking at a set of interrelated institutions whose operational scope includes the initiation and distribution of symbolic content. As in interpersonal communication, this content is initiated and distributed according to its consequences for the initiator, the corporate organizations within these media institutions. That is, the content is chosen to result in a successful transaction for the organization involved. The parameters of that choice reach far from the desk of the individual editor, program manager, or producer who ostensibly makes it. The system by which content comes into our media is complex. It involves communities of practitioners with enculturated rules of behavior, market forces, relationships with other segments of society and economic utilities. The industry-measured audience is a part of this system, but only a part. The individual media consumer is nearly invisible.

We have spent this length of effort on the institutional nature of media—a group of organizations embedded in the system of American business to moderate the prevailing view of conspiring media moguls feeding nutritionless cake to mindless masses. The sort of view that Robert Reno of *Newsday* mirrors in writing:

> The worst that can be said of the networks in their prime is that they rotted the minds of a generation for profit. The best that can be said of them is that they were an exquisitely democratic institution. If the Nielsen ratings showed that more people would watch reruns of "The Newlywed Game" than an extra half-hour of news, the public always got what it wanted. (Reno, 1986)

It is our claim that the networks have neither rotted minds nor given the public what it wants. The first is simply elitist drivel and the second, as we have seen, ignores the realities of the business. Those realities are that there are a limited number of content alternatives that fall within the networks' operating scope and are, therefore, available for production by the networks; these alternatives are further modified by the demands of the primary revenue source for the networks—the advertiser—plus the demands of any other stakeholder of power; then and only then do you and I get to choose; and if our choices are not those of the measured audience, they are never known.

What we know of media behavior in general is pretty simple: People have the time and inclination to use the media. Their reasons for doing so are many and varied and extend beyond the characteristics and ostensible value of the content. In advertiser-supported systems, media exploit that time and inclination by giving content away to sell the resulting circulation. One cannot read the face of our culture or the condition of our minds in this relationship.

SECTION IV: CONTENT—CHARACTERISTICS OF THE INDUSTRY PRODUCT

In our preceding analysis, we have directed attention to the points in which the industry system affects the content that appears in the media. In the next chapter, we will work the particulars of the codes, conventions, formats, and logics that characterize the content of various media. In this last section of this chapter, we want to consider three global consequences of the industry system that constitute a significant part of the fundamental character of media content. The first two concern the nature of content that becomes available for use; these are the characteristics of disposability and plasticity. The third determines what will not appear; this is the question of access. The next sections examine these consequences.

DISPOSABLE CONTENT

The character of disposability of media content is best exemplified by what happens to the morning newspaper come evening time. Once the coupons have been clipped and all the members of the family have had their shot at the comics, it gets thrown away. The newspaper editor does not expect that his or her audience will continue with a given edition for an extended period of time. In fact, economically, the editor depends on the value of the edition to expire rapidly.

The newspaper, like television, is essentially an advertiser supported medium. It must place a fresh product on the table before the same audience in order to sell space to advertisers. If its content fails to produce the daily turnover of product, the business dies. Therefore, the emphasis is equally, at least, on what is to come next.

Disposability also permits production on a large scale by keeping the standards of production appropriate to the projected length of use. No one is expected to write *the* situation comedy or *the* article on yet another traffic accident. The impact of the notion of disposability is that previous content offers little constraint for current content. Large amounts of media content are directly repeated as a technique of comic strips, soaps, reruns, sequels, and syndication. News practitioners update stories with small additions or by rewriting them in subsequent presentations. What was printed yesterday is generally considered dead and gone.

Disposability is also shown in the interchangeability of common kinds of media content. One situation comedy is much like another; whether one reads *Time* or *Newsweek* is more a matter of personal taste than substance.

The disposable character of media content affects the investment we place in it. Most homes we visit in our ethnographic studies do not have large collections of current media content. There are, of course, the newspaper clippings on the refrigerator and the VCR collection of a half-dozen movies, but the scrapbooks and libraries are notably missing. Undoubtedly, the issues of space and indexing play a part in this absence. The major part, we would claim, however, is in the fact that this content is always there. Its fundamental value is in its continued presence; not its particular representation.

One source of evidence for this claim is seen in one interesting side effect of disposability. Given time, the disposables of one generation become the collectibles of another. Dime novels and early comic books are now held in the special collections of libraries. Public broadcasting has elevated the radio drama of the thirties. Word has it that *Spiderman* comics will be a hot item—but only if enough readers throw their originals away.

PLASTICITY

The second characteristic of media content that we wish to consider is its plasticity. Attempts to define the notion of "*mass* media" generally focus on the distribution system (simultaneous delivery of the same message to large numbers of people). However, the capacity to engage large numbers of people resides not in the distribution system but in the content's utility as an arena for social interaction. What used to be

Educational Television has given us numerous examples of content distributed through a potent mass medium that garnered little or no attendance. Any number of arguments had been constructed to explain this failure: People didn't understand Educational Television; they didn't know where it was on their dial; they didn't have UHF converters; and the like. Most of these arguments can be construed as avoidance of the fact that people *chose* not to watch. The content did not have the capacity to be shared in large measure; it did not resonate through the culture. The texts of Educational Television were closed texts whose distribution was funded by the patron (foundation grants in those days) system of support.

In circulation-driven systems of content, the texts of the media have to be open—texts in which many different kinds of people can find their problems, their ideals, in short, themselves. For media texts to disseminate, not simply be distributed—across large numbers of people, they have to be *open* to their colonization—their exploitation—by the minds of individuals for common purposes. Cultural scholars describe such texts as **polysemic** because they can be approached from radically different interpretive stances. Our term for this characteristic of media content is **plasticity.** It is the plasticity of the symbols—their capacity to be shaped by individuals as useful tools for responding to the requirements of common social memberships—that created the phenomenon we call mass media.

ACCESS

What the institutionalized system keeps out of the media pipeline is an exceedingly important effect that has received little play in analysis. Modern theory of effects is turning more and more to the notion that the prime effect of media is not change but the maintenance of social values and relationships in society. In Marxist terms, the media are a major part of the method by which the operating order is seen as right and proper—the method by which the class hegemony is maintained. One means of maintaining this hegemonic order is to deny access to content that would validate iconoclastic values; that is, that which would show antiorder values as right and proper. That is not to say that such values do not appear; but that when they appear, we know them to be wrong and improper (cute, naive, impossible, dangerous) by manner of their presentation.

But there is also content that is simply absent. The complaint about gender in writing (the continued use of the male pronoun and references) is a good example. The female person is invisible in such writing. This invisibility, of course, confirms the hegemonic position of lesser status by denying the expectation of a feminine presence. Justifications for gender in writing usually claim that the English language requires it. The practice of the language, however, is owned by the language community. Therefore, it was (is) our use of the language in the male form that was considered right and proper.

Our media are the product of larger geopolitical systems that govern the accessibility of ideas. The presence of contrary ideas is managed by the media as a native response to those larger systems. The genuine presentation of contrary ideas is effectively prohibited in our media either by out-and-out rejection or by demonstrating the inviability of the ideas at the onset through some presentational device (e.g., use of a lower status spokesperson, manner of introduction, and so on). This naturalized management is the noncollusive result of the perceptions of "what will sell." A scenario that demonstrates the process might look like the following: "If we have the main character espouse these notions, we're sure to have a backlash. Advertisers will pull out. Have the *kid* say it or don't say it at all."

With notable exceptions, the view of the press as the "watchdog of society" is more mythical than reflective of practice. In the first place, the media are firmly entrenched as an institution in the system they are supposed to be watching. No media news organization can survive without the special privileges granted by government and industry. What often appears as a media coup is usually discovered, under closer scrutiny, to be the work of one power elite against another.

Further, most local news outlets simply do not have the resources to cast an equally jaundiced eye on their advertisers and nonadvertisers, political friends and outsiders, perpetrators, both large and small.

News media participate in the order of things both by what they don't report and by those to whom they grant daily access. Wonderful examples of the effects of access can be seen in almost any story produced by "60 Minutes"—the award-winning investigative reporting program of CBS. A typical story might show a succession of complainants directed against some corporation. "In fairness," Mike Wallace might intone, "we tried to reach a corporate spokesperson. . . ," dramatic pause while the camera scans a building up to a corner office window, "but they refused to be interviewed on camera." Boom! Guilty! The corporation may indeed be guilty, but the corporate spokesperson knows that whatever could be said in an interview will be edited according to the purposes of "60 Minutes," and surrounded by material that makes the program's point. "60 Minutes" owns all the terms of access.

In spite of all these examples of the power of access, the question of access remains a suspect one in the eyes of the establishment. The people who claim problems with access are clearly those not in power. It is the outsider who argues that the media are closed. The response by the powerful is that the outsider has all the access deserved. We analysts sometimes exacerbate the problem by acting as if open access were possible. That is, we argue for principles of action as if a media system could be system-free. It seems much more useful for us to consider carefully what constraints are in place and to expose them in the analysis. Access is a part of every media system. Each system grants some and prohibits others.

CENTRAL IDEAS OF SECTION IV: CONTENT—CHARACTERISTICS OF THE INDUSTRY PRODUCT

1. The structure, conduct, and performance characteristics of the media industry have consequences for media content that transcend the particular medium of presentation. They are: disposability, plasticity, and access.
2. The primary value of media content is not in any particular example but that it is always there.
3. The "mass" of mass media is not defined by the system of distribution but by the open, plastic, and polysemic nature of its content.
4. All systems of media must establish priorities of access. Each system will deny some ideas and valorize others.

CHAPTER SUMMARY

This chapter began with an examination of the media as a societal institution. In this examination we found that the media are not an addendum to society but an inseparable part of its performance.

We then turned to focus on the structure, conduct, and performance of the media industry. In structure we considered the interlocking relationships among media: the fictive, informational, and canonical content systems; barriers to entry; structural sources of income; and the capacity and competence of the media's operational scope.

Conduct was defined as the behavior of an industry within a particular structure. The structural components were shown to form the operational contexts in which conduct was embedded. The particular aspects of conduct of decision making, technology, trade, and competition were studied.

Performance was seen as the consequences of conduct within a structure on some set of criteria. The criteria of income and circulation, law and regulation, consumers, industry practices, societal stakeholders, and the individual and organizational choices of style were discussed.

Three global effects on content were presented: disposability, plasticity, and access. Disposability considered the time value of media content showing that such content is designed for current use, not longevity. Plasticity argued that media content must work broad general themes that resonate through the culture. And finally, access demonstrated that every media system valorizes some to speak and denies others.

This chapter has been concerned with the processes of intentional production of content by media organizations. It has been charged with demonstrating that media manufacture a content product to a set of specifications established within the institutionalized system in which these organizations operate, but that such content is developed in relative independence of the individual viewer, reader, and listener. The media's responsibility to the individual user is simply to create a useful product. As a matter of practice they (and their analysts) develop conceptualizations about this usefulness, but audiences need not correspond. Unlike the typical conversational contract, media do not participate in the sense making of their receivers and do not supervise the meaning constructed with their product. In fact, an important specification of media content is its plasticity—its relative freedom from constraints such that redneck and reformer alike can find pleasure in Archie Bunker.

In the next chapter, we begin the analysis of the construction of meaning by examining the conventions that surround the different media products and the contexts in which individuals might interpret them.

NOTES

1. We will generally use the term *access sales* to stand for time sales and space sales to advertisers in order to underline the fact that the audience is the commodity being sold.

2. As of this writing, all three networks have held up their contracts with A. C. Nielsen Co. because of proposed changes in methodology by the ratings company. The new measures will require individuals to register their viewing electronically. The networks' apparent concern is that many will not comply.

3. In 1986, there were 22 people who watched the Superbowl at a party in Anderson's home. At least the set was on. The game was so dull few watched past the first quarter. All of us, however, would have been counted as part of the audience for each and every commercial in diary measurements.

RELATED READINGS

Blum, R., Lindheim, R. (1987). *Primetime: Network television programming.* Boston: Focal.

This book provides an excellent, detailed description of how television programs come into being within the context of the operations of the commercial television networks. The role of personnel in various roles and the institutional constraints are well documented and explained. The authors also pinpoint the lack of sorely needed information on audiences that would account for the high rate of failure for new programs.

Caves, R. (1977). *American industry: Structure, conduct, performance* (4th ed.). Englewood Cliffs, NJ: Prentice-Hall.

The classic development of this line of thought on the structure, conduct, and performance of markets, presented in a readable style. The last chapter on competition and monopoly has special application to the broadcast industry.

Gitlin, T. (1985). *Inside prime time.* New York: Pantheon.

An "inside" view of network decision making, full of the voices of the decision makers.

Meehan, E. R. (1986). Conceptualizing culture as commodity: The problem of television. *Critical Studies in Mass Communication, 3,* 448-457.

Meehan examines the television program as a commodity subject to market forces rather than as an artifact of creative endeavor and considers how ideology is embedded in that product. She continues this line of argument in her article in *Communication Yearbook 11* (1988).

Wimmer, R., Meyer, T. (1988). Audience research in broadcast and cable programming. In S. Eastman et al. (Eds.), *Broadcast and cable programming* (2nd ed.). Belmont, CA: Wadsworth.

This chapter examines the industry's use of audience research for programming decisions. Problems and limitations are stressed in the analysis including the move to people meters by the major rating services. What current methods do and do not measure are also discussed. How audiences are "counted" via various measuring instruments and how those data influence programming decisions is presented.

3

The Contexts of Reception

IN THE LAST CHAPTER we examined the forces that control the manufacture of the content product of the media industry. We found that the audience was only one of many such influences and the individual viewer, reader, or listener was more a shadowy conceptualization than a real presence in this process. In this chapter we want to examine the completed product as it appears in the contexts of use. As we have presented it, our argument is that meaning emerges in the interaction among content, context, and communicants. An understanding of meaning (a prime determinant of effect), then, requires the examination of all three of these elements.

The last chapter had our feet firmly planted in the media industry and described the contexts in which content gets produced. This chapter will find us on the audience side of the exchange and will explore the contexts of reception. This chapter will first examine the access the audience member has to the context of content itself, which is composed of the identifying forms and conventions that describe that nature and character of the content, and finally, direct our focus to the contexts in which the content is received and is accommodated in the ongoing lives of individuals. In this effort, we are still one step removed from the individual musing over the morning newspaper, but we are considering the interpretive conventions that surround the content and the social action contexts in which sense making gets done.

Context is easy to define—it is the set of relevant, interpreted influences on some act in place at the time of the act. Context is, however, difficult to analyze because such influences are, of course, part and parcel of the act itself. We will muddy the waters a bit more in our discussion of three separate contexts of reception: the context of content, the context of content attendance, and the context of emergent meanings.

Conventions are the socially negotiated signs of these contexts. They inform us of the interpretive grounds from which meaning is to emerge. For example, as members of the audience of mediated communication we do not participate in the context of production. Nonetheless, that context—the intent of the producer, the intended or assumed contract between author and reader, producer and viewer, artist and listener, the criteria of workmanship, the signification of imagery, and the like—is a necessary part of our understanding of the authority of content (nature, character, intent).

Media logics develop out of the orderly patterns in content, which are the achievements of the community of practitioners. A logic is a set of rules governing the nature and relationships among content elements. Each medium and content type has an overlay of logic that permits us to recognize its good continuance and execution.

Conventions and logics also appear in the context of attendance. In that context, conventions are the signs of the rules that govern the behavior of audience members as they receive, interpret, and use the content delivered. They are, for example, the signs of the credence and affective value invested; the uses one would have for the content; and the gratifications received. The logics that develop are those that appear in the orderly patterns of social action, which are the achievements of the members of that action. The logic of that social action, then, contains the rules of that order. These logics will be taken up in Chapter 4.

We have noted that there are three separate contexts for which the communication analyst is responsible, the context of content, the context of attendance, and the context in which an emergent meaning appears. The analysis of contexts of content, attendance, and emergent meanings leads to concerns for (1) the conventional rules that were governing the production of the content; (2) the medium of presentation and its meaningful properties; (3) what the communicants, both producers and receivers, intended to accomplish by communicating; (4) the conventional rules that were governing the reception of the content; (5) the social conditions, whether private, familial, public, work, or play; (6) the setting of reception, which includes the physical characteristics of light, temperature, noise levels, proxemics, and so on; (7) the subsequent actions the individual may see as relevant to the communication; and (8) the value of the communication both as act and as content.

The list appears complex, yet it is undoubtedly incomplete. Nonetheless, each of us as competent communicators routinely take these concerns into account when we listen to another, read a magazine, watch a television program. That is, we make adequate estimates of the particular and conventional influences on where the communication is "coming from," which is where we, as the receivers, are, and then make knowledgeable applications of that communication in the current and in subsequent circumstances. Our discussion of conventions and contexts of each of those processes follows.

SECTION I: THE CONTEXT OF CONTENT

We have adopted this heading to allow us to talk about certain understandings we have about the qualities of content that are not immediately apparent in the content itself. These qualities concern the nature, character, and intent of the content: What is it supposed to be? How true is it to its class? What is it supposed to accomplish? For example, the sentence, "The Martians are coming!" is surrounded by different understandings when it appears in a national newscast, a science fiction novel, a television commercial, or a textbook on mediated communication. One can claim that the content is the same in all four of those presentations but the contexts composed here of the **genre** and the medium are different and materially affect what the sentence can signify. No, the medium is not the message, but then, neither is the content nor the genre the message. The message is the total complex of interpretation. This section begins to disassemble that complex by considering the master identities that relay the nature, character, and intent of content and the media logics that provide a structure for understanding.

MASTER IDENTITIES OF NATURE, CHARACTER, AND INTENT

Any fully recognizable piece of content carries with it a set of **master identities** that inform us of what the content (claims it) is (truth, insight, representation, reflection, vision, fantasy, deflection, deception), how true to its nature it is or can be (the idea of character), and what it can intend to accomplish communicatively. Master identities appear in the intersections of institution, genre, medium, codes of workmanship, and the like. For example, this textbook carries its master identities, in part, in its location in the institution of education, the genre of a text, the medium of print, and the codes of workmanship appropriate to an advanced level of content. Similarly, a local television newscast carries its master identities, in part, in its location within the institutions of societal surveillance, the genre of news, the medium of television, and the codes of workmanship appropriate to the market. When one of us sits down to read this book or to watch that newscast, those master identities are also in place.

CONVENTIONS AS SIGNS OF MASTER IDENTITIES

At this level of abstract analysis, the concepts of master identities can be very tidy. In practice, any particular piece of content more or less represents its class, can never be fully true to its nature, and is often ambiguous and conflicted in intent. Content, as the product of human performance, is as improvisational as any other performance. Part of the management of this improvisation is the set of **conventions** that arise within the production process. Many of these conventions involve the practitioners talking to themselves, confirming the truths of their community, in codes of workmanship and the like. But some of them are directly relevant to the audience member's right interpretation.[1] For example, newspapers have separate sections for the presentation of hard news, soft news, and editorials. Different rules apply to the content that appears in those sections. A televised drama about police work has a different license from a televised documentary. The different genre hold to different content standards.

The force of these standards has been institutionalized as part of the contract between producer and audience. Proof of the binding nature of this contract on the party of the first part is shown in the regulating and supervising actions taken by the production community and by society at large to enforce them. Three examples are that CBS was censured for allegedly faking a news story, producers of wildlife programs have a code governing permissible editing, and weather reporters now have a certifying association.

Conventions, then, first of all, are standard ways of doing things that gain their stature through longtime usage. Conventions are also the signs of these practices that appear in the ways the content is presented or formatted and that signal to the **auditor** (audience member) the presence of certain master identities of the content. Conventions as signs of conventionalized practice gain their stature by their consistent referencing of their associated practices and by their authorized interpretation by academics, critics, other media forums, interpersonal networks, and the like. The receiver is expected to be knowledgeable of these conventions and, in turn, content that shows them is expected to meet those standards.

In media, content carries these conventionalized signs of master identities in ways that vary according to the particular content involved. For example, a newspaper article, by virtue of it being a newspaper article, carries with it the convention of being an objective presentation of the facts surrounding some event. It is expected that the reporter will be attempting to inform rather than persuade, with no ax to grind or ox to gore. (Now, of course, journalism analysts point out that this convention is often violated in blatant and subtle ways, but the violation is notable because it is a violation, which means that the norm exists.)

Given this conventional guide, the reader can interpret what is read as a straightforward account to be accepted at face value. Such is not the case, however, with a newspaper editorial or commentator's column. Here the intent is to express and promote opinion or to play with humor or to comment upon. It is inappropriate to the intent to accept this writing as an objective account. The newspaper signals the change of context by location (front page versus editorial page) and by layout.

When a newspaper deliberately blurs these distinctions, as some grocery store, sensationalist rags do, it is considered outside the community of legitimate journalism and *caveat lector* (let the reader beware).

The notion of conventionalized news content shows itself in the continuing criticism of local television news programs. The introduction of personality and banter in these programs, some claim, has turned that objective account into entertainment and trivialized the news that is reported by discounting its importance. Proponents claim, on the other hand, that conversational transitions and such are merely moments of relief from unrelenting seriousness. They add that the audience clearly recognizes it as separate from the news just as readers recognize the comics and the opinion columns in a newspaper.

Whatever the resolution of this argument, we do recognize that a news program is different from an entertainment program in what it intends to accomplish. But there are a number of programs whose master identities are unclear. What is a program like "60 Minutes"? Is it news, comment, editorial, or entertainment? Perhaps all of that. What are professional sports? Always a fair contest, or often manipulated entertainment? What is a historical novel? Truth or fiction? The context of presentation is ambiguous in these cases. It is, therefore, difficult to understand fully the meaning of the content presented. Is it fact, fiction, assertion, opinion?

As a reader, viewer, or listener, one has to depend on the conventions of presentation to signal the nature of the content. One, obviously, cannot interrogate the producer as can be done in an interpersonal setting (You're kidding, right?). If the context is misinterpreted, substantial errors as to intent can result. Perhaps the classic example is that of the Orson Welles Mercury Theatre presentation of the *War of the Worlds*. Without commenting on the authenticity of the reports of mass hysteria, it is certain that many folks were confused by the presentation of entertainment content in a factual setting; a confusion that reportedly has since been repeated in the NBC television docudrama on D-day.

The following are some generally accepted conventions of media context: (1) Front page newspaper articles are objective accounts; columns are opinion; life-style reports may mix the two. (2) Films are fictional unless specifically billed as documentaries. (3) Television is also fictional with specific exceptions, but even in these, television shows a consistent bias toward entertainment. There is very little straight reporting in the total mix of television. The news story is held to the objective criterion, however. (4) Newsmagazines are rarely as factual as newspapers. They have claimed an interpretive function. As a result they mix fact and comment to report implications, predictions, and conclusions.

Understanding these conventions, the consumer is better able to discern the rules that monitor the production of content and may be relevant to the worth of the content, relative to some subsequent purpose. For example, the student who uses a citation from *Time* magazine in an academic term paper will generally discover that the conventions that govern the content of that newsmagazine do not meet the scholarly criterion. That student has failed in understanding either the conventions or the criteria (or both), and has wrongly applied content to this end. That content may be perfectly good for some other purpose, however.

The context of production establishes constraints on what intentions are permissible, what images and symbols may be used to accomplish them, and what interpreted meanings are appropriate to the intended meanings. These conventional rules are, of course, rules not laws. Individual media products can fail to observe them and, over time, they can be changed for all such products. They accomplish an important service, however, for producer and receiver alike: Producers accept the constraints in return for the increased likelihood that their intended meaning will be gained. Receivers benefit by the lowered uncertainty concerning the type and quality of content that will appear in given media outlets.

In our analysis of mediated communication in Chapter 1, we discovered that the relational contract so apparent in interpersonal communication was not a necessary feature of mediated communication. Nevertheless, mediate practitioners produce content with a contract, in fact different contracts for different content. It is a contract that exists between the producer and an idealized audience member, the "model reader," as it were. The conventions that signal the nature, character, and intent of content also signal the relational contracts that are expected. The terms of the contract tell us what the content is and what we are expected to do with it, thus defining our relationship to it. In three major headings that follow, we will consider the conventions that surround fantasy content, reportage, and advertising.

CONVENTIONS OF FANTASY CONTENT

Fantasy content is first of all released from a strict reality criterion. We are expected not to demand that this content represent our everyday life; rather it may heighten, illumine, comment upon, or even fly from the mundane. Participation in fantasy content requires the receiver to enter into a contract to permit the artifices of the drama. This active process has been called the "willing suspension of disbelief." In it, the receiver agrees to relax the requirements of reality in order that the author may tell the story. In essence, the receiver must agree to pretend the reality of the story. This process of pretending merits several observations.

First the willing suspension of disbelief needs to be learned. While such learning is apparently not difficult, it does require members of the audience to put themselves actively into the manipulative hands of those who exercise the creative content controls. We do not see this as an abandonment of reality on the part of the audience but an active participation in the creation of fantasy.

This participation enhances or perhaps is even essential for a certain type of enjoyment to be derived from the narrative structure. Allowing oneself to be exploited (not necessarily in a negative sense) has its rewards. Emotional or intellectual involvement would appear to be dependent on suspending disbelief. Such vicarious experiences can evoke a rich variety of emotional responses, often with enormous intensity. Children learn that involvement often produces satisfying and pleasurable experiences. A father once observed that his 6-year-old son was an avid viewer of horror movies on the pay movie channels, saying that his son "just loves to get the crap scared out of him" by these movies because he knows he is really safe. Viewers can control their participation;[2] some may enter a little at a time, preferring not to stray too far from their own environmental "anchors," which offer security and, as in the little boy's case, safety. The individual may not wish the consequences of an intensely involving experience. Higher levels of involvement require a higher level of participation.

An individual's suspension of disbelief can be prevented or interrupted by content factors and environmental factors. Narratives that are poorly structured or constructed erratically or illogically often have the effect of jarring any state of involvement out of existence. If the story has events that don't follow or seem to fit the conventional requirements of narrative or are poorly executed in the craft of the medium, the audience can no longer pretend that the events are actually happening. A toy ship that explodes but still looks like a toy ship exploding may devastate the viewing experience because it fails to look like the disaster it purports to be.

In television, commercials are a built-in form of interruption of the narrative. As a consequence, commercial television does not ordinarily achieve, or is not likely to aspire to, very deep levels of viewer involvement. The medium's time format is also not conducive to high levels of involvement. Programs ordinarily are much shorter than feature films. Building complex plots and narratives with sophisticated nuances is, in effect, negated by severe time restrictions. These restrictions, however, may very well promote the child's use of television. The literacy required is rather easily learned. External factors also play a crucial role in affecting the suspension of disbelief. Domestic use of media appears among the normal household interruptions. Another's questioning of a narrative (How can they do that!) may ruin it for all. The whispering or coughing audience member may distract participation.

In sum, the willing suspension of disbelief is a learned process in which the receiver actively participates in the formation of fantasy. This participation enhances or even determines the individual's enjoyment from and involvement with fantasy content as fantasy.

CONCERNS ABOUT FANTASY CONTENT

The terms of the contract for fantasy material have raised a number of perplexing issues in the study of mass communication effects. For example, one may ask if all the members of the audience realize that fantasy content is not reality or that, in the terms of the contract, fantasy content has no responsibility to be true to reality even when mimicking it. Concerns are raised that children might mistake entertainment fare for real events or that the less experienced might see media-presented images and characteristics as true. Further concerns are raised that even with those who recognize their suspension of disbelief, this relaxed state of vigilance might increase their susceptibility to subtle influences on values or attitudes.[3]

There are also demands that fantasy content must represent reality in certain politically charged areas, such as the presentation of women or minorities. While this position clearly confuses the role of fantasy content, a more active position calls for fantasy content to present such issues in a positive light for the betterment of society. This position is clearly appropriate to the fantasy content contract, but it is interesting to speculate about what the effect of the suspension of disbelief might have.

THE REALITY CONTRACT

The contract that comes with reality content, such as documentaries, news articles, broadcast news reports, and the like, is quite different from the fantasy contract. Here it is assumed that members of the audience will be comparing the reports that they read, see, and hear with their actual experience. If these do not compare, it is legitimate for the model reader to cast the validity of the content into doubt. It is expected, therefore, that this content will represent reality. This expectation has institutional standing. Individuals and institutions can be sued for misrepresenting reality in reportage. (A very well-publicized case was *Westmoreland v. CBS.*)

The other major convention of reality content is that it is important. What is reported is considered a necessary part of the potential audience. It is presented as a service to the community of the audience. The model audience for news, however, is less likely to be the person in the street. Most news, except perhaps the most egregious forms of entertainment journalism, is directed toward an elite of academic, social, political, and business leaders.

For most individuals most reality programming has little to do with the realms of their actual experience. News is something out of the ordinary, in distant places. One has little opportunity to compare with the reports from Lebanon or wherever the latest trouble spot is identified. For the nonelite audience, reality programming may show little difference from fantasy programming, becoming "the soap opera of life."

Nevertheless, there are some members of the audience who have both the availability of experience and the vested interest to provide a critical review of the content. This vulnerability to criticism and attack over how well the content achieves its representative purpose provides the major constraints on the production of reality content.

The decision as to what is important has often been described as the editor's gatekeeping function. As a matter of practice there are definitive conventions as to what shall and shall not appear. Individual practitioners are socialized into those conventions. One newspaper looks much like another; the local evening news broadcast in Indianapolis has different content but the same decisions as that broadcast in Detroit. There is some latitude within these conventions, of course, which gives the editor considerable power.

CONCERNS OVER REALITY CONTENT

Concerns over reality content fall generally into two classes, those relating to the quality of the reportage and those relating to the commitment of the audience to the importance of the content. Those of the first class are concerned with how well the content meets its intended purpose. These criticisms involve accuracy, fairness, breadth of coverage, and the like. Those of the second class relate to how well the audience is discharging its side of the contract—the time spent, the amount of effort expended, the content remembered, the knowledge gained. These criticisms make a notable assumption that the agenda of the reality practitioners is the agenda of the audience. When the audience fails to show an adequate response in any of the foregoing, it is the audience that has failed to complete its side of the bargain. That the reality content itself may be irrelevant and therefore not worth the effort, is not one of the arguments advanced. Most research has assumed that the conventional intentions of reality content validate the use of that content by the audience. That assumption is questionable. Most of one's functional knowledge about the particular world in which the individual lives still comes from interpersonal, not media, sources. (Our discussion of this issue is presented in Chapter 7.)

THE ADVERTISING CONTRACT

The methods by which goods and services are marketed in the United States (and in most Western economies) and the commercial nature of our domestic media have given the domain of product information a particular character. The amount and type of product information available is considered a competitive factor by most industries. There is, therefore, the standard practice of attempting to control what is said about one's own product and to object to any advantage given to a competitor. As a result most of our product information comes from those who benefit from our purchase of that product. Commercial media, of course, make money by selling access to audiences to the enterprises attempting to control the information in the marketplace. The media, then, are reluctant to provide "free advertising" in news reports. Further, as these media are dependent on the advertising dollar, many of the most widely circulated commercial media are constrained, or act as if they were constrained, from giving named product evaluations, comparisons, or criticisms.

The result of all of these forces is that our primary source of mediated product information comes to us under the advertising contract. That contract is clearly to persuade.[4] The expectation of that contract is that content will be created to present the product or service in a favorable light. There is little responsibility for advertising product deficiencies and the truth may be expanded in legalized puffery.

The advertising message comes to us as an advocate bound by, at least, some rules both of practice and law. It is further constrained by the conventions of presentation that are directed toward ensuring that an advertisement is recognized as such, although, as we shall discuss, this distinction is sometimes blurred even in reputable presentations.

The reader, listener, or viewer of the advertising message is assumed to be forewarned with the knowledge of this advocacy, this intent to persuade. The standard of the forewarned consumer is, in fact, used to justify the deceptions practiced under the puffery rubric.

CONCERNS ABOUT ADVERTISING CONTENT

The concerns expressed about advertising content fall into three categories: (a) Foremost is the concern that the receiver of the message is not competent to "read through" the advocacy to interpret properly the omissions and commissions of persuasive intent; (b) second are the claims that this class or that class of advertisements have overstepped the bounds of deception; and (c) third are the concerns that the conventions of separation have not been met.

The first concern we have seen before; it is an extension of the incompetent audience position expressed under both fantasy and information content. With advertising, the concern is directed toward right decision making as knowledgeable buyers in getting true performance value for one's consumer dollars and toward good nutrition. Fancies, fads, and fast foods are generally held up as examples of incompetence, along with sweets and sugared cereals.

These same products are often the target of complaints of improper deceptive practices. Product advertisements are generally careful not to make deceptive claims concerning facts. Claims concerning judgment and opinion (Improved! New! Best! and so on), those made by association (people having a good time with the product), or by imaging (famous spokesperson), however, are on a much looser standard. The advertisement for a sugared, artificially flavored, and colored cereal that shows children having fun with a cheerful cartoon character sets the nutrition activist's teeth on edge. The argument is made that this commercial, and others like it, practice deception in claiming positive consequences from a product full of nutritional defects. The argument gets expanded into the protection of children who are the target of these ads, and when presented on Saturday morning cartoons, into the issue of separation of program and advertising content.

The enforcement of the conventions of the separation of program and advertising content is a well-established issue in presentations aimed at children. The "rules" of television now require an explicit separation ("Monster heroes will be right back after these messages."). At present, there is a continuing controversy over product-theme programs (Rainbow Brite, heroes of various ilk and hulk). These programs feature characters that are also products for sale and are characterized by some as program-length commercials. But the issue of the conventions of separation go beyond children. When a newspaper publishes a press release (usually unedited according to critics) announcing a new product, it also blurs the distinction. Political coverage of the incumbent as news ("The president campaigns for the Senate") raises the question of news versus advertising value. Is the president speaking as a president or as a politician? A campaign speech, so the argument goes, should not be news. The reply states that, by definition, anything a government official does is news.

The arguments over the execution of the advertising contract have value in and of themselves. Advocacy can be quickly corrupted. The continual review of such content by critics provides a different voice, another perspective on the claims advanced, even though the critics are also advocates.

MEDIA LOGICS

Beyond the coded conventions that transmit the master identities of content, the capacity and practices of each medium constitute separate logics governing the relationships within that content and, by extension, of the reality it represents and helps construct. A logic is a set of rules as formulated, or in practice, that governs the relationship among things. Media logics are the rules that govern the relationships among content elements in the media. For example, there is a logic (set of rules) for the layout of newspapers and magazines, a logic for scheduling programs on television, a logic for the way a news story or even a situation comedy is structured.

As with conventions, media logics begin in the practices of the media professionals and serve primarily their purposes. The argument for the significance of media logics to the audience begins with the notion that our knowledge of the world is shaped by the methods we use to accomplish that knowledge. The importance of media logics—in fact any logic—is not in the content that they carry, but that they provide a cognitive tool for understanding. We are not concerned here about the images of the world in media. We are concerned with the fact that the rules that govern the relationships within that content can be used to model the relationships in reality. For example, a rule in formal logic is "if/then" as in "if A, then B." This rule states that given an A, a B will follow, and that no B shall appear without an A. This rule can be used to model relationships in the mundane as in "if sex, then babies," which also implies that given a baby we can presume sex. (Of course this rule is not accurately stated, which doesn't prevent it from being expressed.)

Similarly, The B-grade westerns of the 1930s and 1940s had a rule that evildoers be punished—a sort of "if crime, then pay." This was a logic of the story told and was expected by the audience. The rule may have transferred to their understanding of the consequences of everyday crime. It certainly would have been congruent with the concrete stage of moral development of many of the audience members.

The examination of media logics is an extensive study. In our space we can do little more than touch upon the three major forms: the logic of narrative, the logic of media space and time, and the logic of media formats.

THE LOGIC OF NARRATIVE

Media transmit their information in stories. Stories reconstruct our moment-by-moment experience into events, punctuated by the concepts of motive, intent, purpose, and cause; goals, outcomes, consequences and rewards; attitudes, values, morals, and judgments; agents and receivers; perpetrators and victims—in short, all of the notions that create events and connect them over time. In its broadest sense, a story narrative is any discourse that pilots a set of connections among claims (elements, facts, assertions, and so on). The writing of a news story, for example, involves the determination of which individuals are party to the story, what facts are involved, how the facts and individuals are related, and so on. The logic of the narrative essentially accomplishes two things: It carves the continuous action of experience into discrete units and posits the relationships between them. An interesting narrative is contained in the sentence "She deliberately dropped her pencil on the floor." Framing that experience into the dropping of a pencil now permits the narrator to tell you what happened before and what will happen after and, equally important, why. The word *deliberately* infuses the action with motive; we anticipate a consequence. Note that another interesting narrative that frames exactly the same experience is "As she gestured, the pencil fell from her hand." The logic of the narrative tells us that the world is composed of connected events "things happen because." The narrative permits us to see experience as "events," to consider the nature of these events, determine the connections among events, and to evaluate the connected sequence.

The narrative also encourages the dramatic convention. Drama is based on conflict, its character, resolution, explanation, and consequence. Most of our news is presented within this convention. That is, the news story reflects the agents of the story as antagonist and protagonist meet in conflict, however brutal or civil, out of which we expect a winner and a loser. If there is no conflict, it isn't news. One of the purposes of news, then, is to create the conditions under which we can see the conflict. Whether that conflict is objectively there or symbolically created is a matter of great debate. Whether represented or created, however, the conflict *cannot be seen except through the device of the dramatic narrative.*

The narrative is more important than is its mediated form. We all tell stories. We all tell different stories about the same experience. (A good reason why there are so many theories about media.) The narrative is at the center of human knowledge. We discover what we know and don't know by how well we can tell the story. The separate media logics develop because the media tell their stories in ways that accommodate the technology of the medium and the practices of the community of practitioners (hence their master identities). The television soap opera, for example, is different from the romance novel, even though both approach the same themes, because of the technology and practices of their production. What we can come to know of the basic themes of relationships and responsibilities that characterize both soaps and romances varies, and we understand that variation by virtue of the medium in which they appear. Note that neither precludes the other or denies the stories we tell ourselves. We are, therefore, regularly exposed to multiple logics about the relationships in life.

SPACE, TIME, AND PROPORTION

The manipulation of space, time, and proportion represent powerful techniques within narrative. In narrative, we can move at will, bilocate, achieve a divine perspective. We can contract or extend time, we can fix it to see simultaneity, we can move forward to the future and back to the past or back to the future or forward into the past. We can see objects or body parts in nearly microscopic detail, magnified to fill the entire screen or examined in intricate detail; objects are made to appear larger or smaller than they are when viewed with the human eye. In no sensory experience can I see simultaneous images without regard to place, retrieve images of the past, move from a present image to that of the future. In no physical experience can I change place without regard to time. This manipulation of time and space can be accomplished only through signification. We are signifiers in our cognition, imagination, memory, communication. The media are signifiers in their creation of content. They—in signifying—can shape our understanding by violating the temporal and spatial laws that bind our experience in the here and now. In such violations, we come to know our present by reviewing its past and forecasting its future, a knowledge in which the media participate by giving us the techniques of these manipulations.

FORMATS

A media format describes the component elements and their relationships of a media product. The "who, what, when, why, and how," expressed in the inverted pyramid style of the typical news story is a format. It also becomes a way of understanding things. Full knowledge of an event requires an explanation for each of the four Ws and the how.

Media products are formatted in a number of ways. One of the simplest is duration. We are familiar with the 90-minute feature film and the 30-minute television sitcom. A quick glance at our watch can predict the next twist of the plot.

Content genre carry conventional meanings. The form of the detective story is well-set and provides the knowledgeable reader additional sources of interpretation not available to the neophyte. Formulas develop within genre: The horror flick works best when it uses the anticipation of the audience both in confirmation and violation.

Scenes within content are also formatted. For example, the confrontation scene in a horror flick usually proceeds through the recognition of vulnerability to a moment of misdirection, which leads to a heightened anticipation, which is followed by the sudden contact whose violent action is rapidly resolved into escape or destruction. Given escape, the same scene may start again.

Another type of formatted information is contained in the concept of a series. We know that a series will continue beyond the particular program we are watching. Darth Vader escapes so that another movie may be made.

Content in series also permits the development of meaning over time. Narratology shows us that successful character development involves the steady generation of a larger and larger context in which to interpret the actions of the character at any particular moment. As regular viewers of *Hill Street Blues,* the authors could understand Detective Belker's need to bite as a situational response, while a first-time viewer might be repelled by the act. Seeing a rerun of an earlier, more harshly portrayed Belker, we can understand what the love of a good woman has done for that character.

The current rash of sequels and even prequels in film also makes use of this serial development. The successful character is known and attractive. There is less risk for the audience member in selecting that content. On the other hand, the content must not be too predictable.

Elemental content analysis or studies based on a single content unit cannot be responsive to the **indexical** nature of characterization development and genre conventions. It can respond only to what is currently presented and cannot reference the larger context that can be held by the individual. Further, what is held by the individual can vary widely across individuals. If one is not practiced within a genre, the conventions have little value. If one has no history with the character, that development is lost. Studies that aggregate the knowledge and history of individuals create an artificial understanding of the content's interpretation.

Formats obviously establish expectations about the content. We know the series hero (and often the villain) will escape; the denouement will come 26 minutes after the introduction; the attack will come the moment we release our vigilance. Formats may also induce expectations about the everyday. Relationships between a woman and a man are clearly well-formatted in the media. Do we use these formats to describe what should happen in an actual relationship? Even as simple a thing as the proper length of a conversation may be expressed in mediated formats. In whatever way each of us may choose to use them, media formats are available as models for the nature and course of events in which we regularly participate. It should be noted that such formats vary from medium to medium and that the process of social action itself generates alternative formats of great power. We may find an adaptive way to relate through a particular media format, but such success does not imply that we cannot move on from it or use other relational tools in other circumstances.

SUMMARY: THE CONTEXT OF CONTENT

Content gains additional signifiers as it is contextualized inside master identities and finds its place in the logics of production. Both master identities and media logics develop within the consistent practices—the conventional solutions—of the media professional. These conventions appear as signs to the audience, denoting the nature, character, and intent of the content. Such conventions are necessary if we are to understand the terms of the contract under which the content is delivered.

In the preceding sections we have found that the contracts for fantasy, informational, and advertising content are quite different. In fantasy, the fundamental assumption is that reality concerns are secondary to the demands of the narrative. It is the telling of a good story that counts, not the representation of life. To accomplish the narrative the author asks the audience for its willing suspension of disbelief.

News, on the other hand, is expected to be "true to the facts" and that the facts shown will be those developed from a perspective without guile or special interest. That news often fails this test does not deny, but confirms the expectation.

Finally, advertising is presented in the advocacy contract—a sort of enlightened opportunism in which the content producer is expected to present the argument in its best light, but at the same time minimizing the risk of retaliation should it become too exploitative. The audience is expected to understand that the "facts" in advertising are of a different kind from the facts of the news.

Some of the criticism that mediated communication reaps appears to be directed toward changing the terms of these contracts. In fantasy content, for example, complaints are often voiced about the unrealistic images presented of women, ethnic groups, jobs, and so on. The assumption appears to be that the narrative should be told in a manner that promotes the "right view." Similarly, advertising is criticized for being opportunistic and for attempting to exploit, particularly, those considered less able to judge.

It is relatively easy to dismiss such complaints as elitist power moves. ("Who privileges your voice?" is often effective.) But the concerns are more likely to have arisen from a media influence model of the audience and the reply from a receiver control model. The media influence model holds the audience as passive and manipulated by content; the receiver control model has the audience active, molding content to its own ends. We will see these opposing views again in the sections on the contexts of reception that follow.

In the section on media logics, we found that the ordered patterns of content, which are the achievements of the community of media practitioners, can also provide techniques for defining and ordering our understanding and performances. Media logics are tools by which practitioners develop "rightly made" content. They are the devices of narrative, drama, space, time, and formats. These tools are developed in the process by which media signify the world. As methods of signification, they become available to us to signify our own experience.

Media logics are, of course, no more coherent or focused than are others. Further, other logics abound; particularly, as we shall see in Chapter 4, in the social action of everyday life.

Having completed our investigation of the conventions and logics of the context of production, we turn to those of the context of attendance.

CENTRAL IDEAS IN SECTION I: THE CONTEXT OF CONTENT

1. The "same" content cannot appear in different media as content gains signifiers when it is contextualized within the understandings we have for the locating institution, genre of content, medium of presentation and the instantiated codes of workmanship.
2. Two elements of the context of content are master identities and logics.
3. Both master identities and media logics begin as the standard practices of the media practitioner. These product conventions become signs to the audience of the nature, character, and intent of the content.
4. Media logics are sets of rules that govern content element relationships.
5. The logics of the media can become or participate in the logics by which we organized the elements of our experience.
6. Important logics of the media are those of the narrative, space, time and proportion, and format.

SECTION II: CONTEXTS OF ATTENDANCE

In this section, we take one step closer to, say, a couch potato munching through another evening with the box and one step further away from the industry itself. We are now at the point at which the product has been created and delivered, not yet into a real home with actual people accommodating media and their texts in their lives, but still into an idealized home where we can consider the common contextual elements that typically surround the ordinary act of attendance to the media. (There are always exceptions to the typicalities noted, but they are not of interest here.) Our emphasis on the commonalities will help us to understand how the media experience itself is a common experience and one of the bases by which we share in the lives of others (and therefore of at least equal import as the content itself).

We are, consequently, about to discuss the common contexts of attendance to the content of the media. We will do so under three headings: the technology of attendance, the textual matrix of media, and the social currency of the media experience.

COMMON CONTEXTS: TECHNOLOGY

Some restraints that mediated communication imposes on the receiver would appear to be nested in the technology itself. Technology is more than the devices of the moment; it also includes the knowledge that is imparted and the practices in which those devices are used.[5] Technology, therefore, imposes the capacity of the devices, a mind-set of what is valid, and a method of its application. We can see the jointery of these three in the history of the development of television. Television has been called the visual extension of prewar radio. Television adopted the forms and formulas of radio narratives as it became the dominant domestic entertainment medium. This adoption occurred, in part, as a result of the fact that the first sets had screens that were too small for public viewing (devices). This screen size was acceptable to developers of television because the research was conducted within the radio industry in which, of course, the domestic delivery of the broadcast signal was considered most appropriate (knowledge). Had the sets been large-screen projectors, too cumbersome for home use, it is likely that television would have at least started out as a theatrical rather than a home medium. Had television become theatrical, the typical television program would be quite different from what we presently see (practice). (See also our discussion of capacity in Chapter 2.) All of this work of the invisible hand of technology is imposed upon us when we turn the set on and sit down to view in our homes.[6]

Theatrical films, on the other hand, impose a public context of reception in a controlled ambiance (which can vary widely, namely, a

Saturday matinee at a $1-a-seat theater or an art film in a museum); radio appears in the background; and newspapers are individually read. But even these constraints are being lessened by the use of technology itself as home video becomes a film market, videotext presents the newspaper, and cable news reads it to us.

We can clearly sense the impact of the technological context when we experience ostensibly the same content in different technologies. *Raiders of the Lost Ark* has now been distributed as a theatrical film, videocassette, cable movie, and broadcast television program. It was immensely successful as a film, but not very successful as a television program. Not at the bottom of the reasons for this differential between its theatrical success and its televised failure is that broadcast television is a small screen, poor sound reproduction system, and it is ordinarily the last of these technologies to acquire the rights to a theatrical film (devices and practices).

Technology also establishes the direction of control in the presentation of content. The simplest, least interactive technologies establish a vertical column of control, with content being available from a few outlets at the time and in the order set by the producing/distributing agent. The clearest example of this form of control is broadcast television, as it was in the 1950s and 1960s, and theatrical films, as they are now. As more and more control is invested in the consumer, it becomes spread across a number of constituencies, groups, or individuals and is said to be more horizontal. A most recent introduction of **horizontal control** has been the compact disk changer. One model allows the consumer to select any cut from up to seven disks and to organize a presentation of 32 selections. Music can now be easily programmed, switching order, mixing genre, creating individual juxtapositions.

The more control is vertical, the more common the context of attendance is likely to be. As control becomes horizontal, this commonality is eroded. One's experience with an album of music rearranged and mixed with other presentations simply is not the same as when that album is heard alone as ordered by the producer. Generally, as technology moves from analogue to digitalized content, it provides the opportunity for greater and greater horizontal control. It is now possible with ordinary consumer electronics to capture visual images from television, frame by frame, and to alter those images, pixel by pixel (dot by dot). We don't expect a lot of this effort, but it is an example of how technology creates and modifies elements of the context of attendance.

COMMON CONTEXTS: THE TEXTUAL MATRIX OF MEDIA

One element of context of reception that is often ignored in media research is that whatever content the audience attends to is itself embedded in a larger **text.** Television programs are selected from an array of possibilities and are combined into the text of an evening's viewing. Newspaper articles are selected from the total paper, and form part of one's daily reading. Each of these media selections are part of the tapestry of one's media participation. There are two implications of this textual characteristic: (1) The attendance to mediated content ordinarily involves some act of choice. (2) Any particular content rarely stands alone but is in juxtaposition to some other content. We present a few comments about each of these:

THE TAPESTRY OF CHOICE The institutions of complex, multicultural societies have many voices. The individual who listens to all of them is presented with an incoherent babble. The individual, however, does not listen to all of them, not even to most of them. The individual assembles the influences of action and the mechanisms of maintenance through the process of choice within the freedoms available. Many postindustrial societies grant the individual substantial freedoms. In the United States, one may have a choice of religions, schools, political parties, geographic location, jobs, products, and media. (Without argument, all individuals do not share these freedoms equally.) With these freedoms one can attune oneself to a chorus of a single voice. A rock-ribbed conservative can join the American Party, attend a fundamentalist religion, send his or her children to a back-to-basics school, work in a nonunion shop, read William Buckley, watch the "PTL Club" and "Magnum P.I." These selections surround the individual with a cognitive environment whose value structure will reflexively maintain the norms of his or her conservative position.

Note that as this individual constructs that supportive, normative environment for him-or herself, and if a parent, also constructs an environment with which his or her children will have intimate contact. We might also note that as the children mature in their own selections of television content and music, they may expose the parent to different value-laden material.

It is clear that the cognitive environments that can be constructed in part from the content of the media vary widely in the amount and kind of normative content they admit. Individuals structure their cognitive environment in much the same manner as they structure their physical environments by the choices they make from the alternatives available. We find the cognitive environment being structured in the programs selected for an evening's viewing, in the print materials subscribed to, in the video technologies introduced in the home, and the like.

JUXTAPOSITION Though we can substantially structure the textual matrix to which we attend, media industries still exercise considerable **vertical control** over the delivery of the matrix. Our conservative may be settled in with Magnum, only to be faced with some liberalizing commercial. Technology continues to erode this vertical control; he or she may reach over and zap the commercial with the remote control. Nonetheless, part of the volatility of the meaning of content arises because the content itself is not static. Normal exposure to content is not partitioned off into neatly packaged units. There is a flow to mediated content. It is important to realize that any set of values, plots, settings, characters, and characterizations is ordinarily followed by another, different set. For example, how can one deeply understand the notion of the credibility of television news without seeing that it can be preceded by "Three's Company" and followed by "Hawaii Five-O"?

As noted in our introduction to this section, the commercial television program itself is a **matrix text.** We have recorded a program in which a particularly explicit scene of antisocial violence is immediately followed by a powerful drama of a boy succeeding in a remarkable feat that required the close cooperation of others. The conclusion shows the boy landing in the center of a highly supportive and congratulatory peer group. Together the members celebrated the feat with a soft drink.

A classic "Sesame Street" program has a Bert and Ernie segment in which Ernie steals a cookie from Bert, Big Bird gets rewarded for doing something nice, Oscar the Grouch gets his kicks from being mean, and a cook takes pratfalls with pies. This program alone is a kaleidoscope of ideas, norms, and concepts.

One may read in the newspaper of the front-page war scene, the tragedies of weather, the delights of the social whirl. This unending flow of content—this matrix text—means that content is not monolithic but equivocal, contradictory, and ambiguous. What is the montage of the soap opera heroine's infidelity with the toy commercial's happy family, or of rock and roll's Armageddon lyrics and the DJ's plea to tune in tomorrow? It is this ambiguity that produces a plasticity of content the audience can use to mold the meanings that are both indexical and reflexive of the social constructions in which they live. One has to make sense out of mediated content in an accommodation to the other elements of life.

COMMON CONTEXTS: THE SOCIAL CURRENCY OF COMMON EXPERIENCE

One of the significant characteristics of social institutions and organizations is that they provide a common reference for connecting our lives with others. The fact that others face the same daily commute under the conditions that we do, and are involved in the same office stresses and family confrontations provides a basis for mutual understanding. In the large societal view, the broadcast media are clearly preeminent in generating a common referential base. This referent is created in two ways—our participation in attendance and our exposure to common content texts.

Whether in Wisconsin, Utah, or even California, we all have a common experiential referent in attending to television, the radio, movies, and print. We might not automatically expect a new acquaintance to be able to play tennis or craft furniture, but we would expect him or her to be able to watch television or go to a movie and to do so in a number of variations. The activity itself is something that is broadly shared. If one characterizes the individual in action, then, media attendance is one way in which there is communality. The "so what" of this claim is that our knowledge of one another begins in our communalities, from which we can assess our differences.

The content texts of media also provide a widely available set of referents. Political cartoonists can caricature the president as a "Rambo," knowing that the referent will be widely understood—not because most of us have seen the films, but because the qualities of the character have been widely disseminated in both mediated and interpersonal networks. The clarity of the characterization has created a useful symbol in the exchange of meaning. Beyond symbols, the texts of media also provide logical forms, dramatic and informational conventions, scripts for and representations of ideology and social action, and similar tools of signifying our world. Note that we identify them as tools not consequences because all of these elements can be used in irony as well as reverence—their presence does not predict which.

LOGICAL FORMS As we have noted, "media logic" refers to the premises and the rules of relationship that govern the fictive and nonfictive narratives created in the media. The concept of media logic rests on the twin notions that (a) reality does not speak to us, rather we interpret reality and (b) the narratives of the media are achievements by a community of practitioners—achievements that result in a consistent representation of the world. Media logic, then, gives a way of seeing the world, of constituting an understandable view. There is much work to do before the concept of media logic is understood within the practice of our social reality. Three comments are probably useful here: (1) Media logics are enforced within the production community by explicit and implicit codes of workmanship. As these communities differ across media, there are clearly media logics rather than a singular set of rules. (2) The media are not the only source of such logics. Logics appear in all technologies and practices. (3) It is uncertain that any of these logics are complete (able to represent all elements), how the various extent logics relate, or how such logics are put into practice. What we do know is that some such logic or logics are necessary in constituting the environments in which we live.

CONVENTIONS We have already spoken extensively about media conventions as signs of the nature, character, and intent of content. For our purposes here, we would like to advance our thinking about conventions one step further. Conventions can be seen as the standard solutions to the indeterminacies (or freedoms) of a logical form. Conventions are both enabling and disabling in their presence and absence. For example, the lack of a common convention in computer technology makes it difficult to network computers of different manufacture. On the other hand, the absence of convention permits the development of computers better suited to different tasks. The presence of conventional positions can be seen as inhibiting significant progress in arms negotiation. At the same time, the presence of these conventional positions provides the opportunity for making a spectacular offer.

Media provide a number of conventional solutions to the indeterminacies posed by their narrative logics. The transparency of sports commentary gives us some obvious examples of these conventions: A football that is beyond the fingers of a receiver is "overthrown." This explanation assigns a causal agent (the passer), a consequence (uncatchable ball), and absolves the receiver from culpability. It is, of course, impossible for the commentator to know if the ball was overthrown, the pattern underrun, or that the ball was subject to unpredictable forces in flight. Nevertheless, the construction of the narrative of "what happened on this play" requires a solution for its completion, hence, the convention.

Conventional explanations become available for other narratives. To continue our example, the overthrown ball is very useful to a receiver in a pickup game (much better than being too old, too slow, or both) and potentially damaging to the quarterback's contract negotiation. As these lines are being written, for another example, we are watching an extended struggle by the executive branch of the U.S. government to avoid the convention of overall responsibility and to retire to the convention of absolving ignorance (what's becoming known as plausible deniability). The logic of the narrative of how government operates permits either convention. The convention that gets set in place, however, serves different purposes. Different factions, therefore, are promoting the different conventional solutions to responsibility. Presuming that the facts of it can be maintained, the absolving ignorance is likely to be accepted, at least, to the point of disabling the consequences of overall responsibility, which again conventionally (since Nixon) would call for the fall of the government.

The conventions of agency and consequence are powerful determinants of what happened, what is happening, and what will happen. When the media consistently use violence as the solution to injustice, the presence of injustice in a media narrative calls for violence. We can, of course, immediately see that this relationship exists in other narratives: The terrorist who argues that his or her disenfranchisement justifies the killing of children or the high school athlete who claims that poor officiating justifies taking out an opponent are examples. We analysts invoke other conventions when we argue that the media conventions justify the terrorist or vice versa. The conventional relationship of injustice and violence is demonstrably in place in the narratives of media, terrorist, and athlete; the direction of influence is, however, indeterminable. Nonetheless, a catalogue of media conventions is not without value in understanding the potential empowerment of action. Convention can clearly travel between narrative forms.

SCRIPTS Social action involves a set of ongoing performances within common and uncommon contexts. The problematics of what to do, what to say, and how to interpret the doings of others are always present. We can extend the notion of conventional elements to the metaphor of scripts. The roles and role performances, the characters and characterizations, the action and dialogue, and the props and settings of media scripts are available to these problems. Some of these applications involve a direct transfer. One of our most recent examples was a party director acting like a game show host. A more common use of scripts that we have observed in our family contacts has been the indexing of a script in a description of one's own or someone else's behavior. "Tim and Elaine are involved in the very same thing" and "They had a fight like that down at school today." (We also hear, "People don't act like that" and "That's stupid.")

The performances of media scripts (extended conventions) are undoubtedly used in the same way that observations of interpersonal performances are used. Methods and solutions deemed successful or needed are incorporated with appropriate modifications into one's own performances. Social action provides the stage for our own performances that demand content that we can draw from the media. Rarely, however, are we permitted simply to replay a character without drawing comment on that performance. Most often we have to improvise on the material provided to give a satisfactory performance.

Scripts also have ideological significance both in the models they give for performing our beliefs and in the justifications they provide for the beliefs we hold. A value can be defined as a set of rules for the governance of behavior. The meaning of any value, then, emerges in action. The meaning of the value of honesty, for example, is unclear until such time that one can choose between actions that can be deemed honest or dishonest. (Values are, in essence, conventionalized solutions to choice.) Well-drawn media characters represent these conventionalized solutions so that we know them to be driven by value motives. What honesty is, then, is represented in the choices made by a character known to be honest.

A performing member (as contrasted with one that simply has the traits) of the white, female middle-class has to constitute her behavior in such a way as to re-create continually the social constructs of whiteness, femaleness, and the stratum of the middle. Such behavior involves accepting the rights, duties, and consequences of these performances. The scripts played in our media justify such constructs by "turning out" in accordance with the rules. For example, a script about a member of the lower economic class who comes into a lot of money typically uses the conflict inherent in the circumstance of *one who should NOT have money* having large sums available. Comedic or tragic events occur because this person has unentitled money. That events occur for this reason justifies the ideology that creates the lower economic class. It is right and true that such things should happen.[7]

It is right and true to the members of all economic classes. Ideological hegemonies (power relationships) function because all members agree to the basic terms of the contract. Even those who would ostensibly reform it comment from a position inside the hegemony. Media scripts, then, that critique the relationship (such as *All in the Family*) confirm the rightness of the inequities by showing them to be objects of humor (or dramatic power or academic analysis) rather than rage. Media criticisms of the lives that we live, therefore, become part of the methods by which such lives are lived. These criticisms are part of the consequences for position. They enable certain acts that function to maintain the **hegemony,** such as charitable giving, to become legitimated solutions of the hegemony.

It is clear that as scripts perform the premises by which we live, they create an expression of our living logic as interpreted by media practitioners. In providing this expression, these scripts reaffirm the validity of the logic itself. In the creation of believable performances, media scripts demonstrate that the logic works, that its premises are true.

The notion of the social currency of media—that they are part of the method of human intercourse—provides an insight into the analytical tensions involved in understanding the place of media in modern life. On the one hand we can conceptualize the product of media—the logics, conventions, and scripts as tools by which we can *or may not* manage the freedoms or indeterminants of the material reality. On the other hand, we must realize that as part of our life constituting technology, media determine in some/in no small/in large part the solutions to those freedoms. The concept of tools suggests a liberty to use or not; the concept of an in-place technology suggests that we are embedded or located within it. Can we avoid using the media? As individuals, of course; as this society, absolutely not. The significance of the media is not so much their messages, but the common ground they provide in their logics, conventions, scripts, and symbols. In these, they provide a common currency of exchange.

COMMON CONTEXTS: CONCLUDING REMARKS

In this section we have sifted through the contextual layers of reception to find those elements of context common to us all as receivers of mediated communication. We have found three: Those contextual frames that are imposed by the technology of the media, those that result from the textual matrix of media, and those that arise from the fact that media use is itself an embedded activity in the larger realm of social action.

Technology was defined as the devices, texts, knowledge, and practices (and texts) that govern an industry. The force of technology has its greatest effect on the conditions of availability—when, where, and in what form will mediated content be present. Television is an intimate, small-screen medium and film a theatrical one because of the different constraints of the technology of each. These constraints are, of course, present in our reception of mediated content and must be accounted for by the receiver. (The ways of that accounting, however, are not fixed by the nature of the constraints.) Technology also establishes the direction of control of the presentation of content. In noninteractive technologies, control is vertical from producer to consumer. In highly interactive technologies, control is horizontal across various consumers. Noninteractive technologies provide a setting of greatest commonality for content.

The textual matrix of mediated content imposes the demand for choice from that matrix and introduces the ambiguity of the kaleidoscopic presentation of facts, opinions, values—stories in merry juxtaposition. The demand for choice finds the media user constructing cognitive environments by virtue of the selections made. At the same time, the inevitable juxtaposition of competing positions introduces a volatility in the meaning potential of any content. The implications of these two conditions led us to conclude that content cannot be understood independently of the matrix or the social processes that lead to the cognitive environment of attendance.

In the final section, we argued that the true nature of mass communication was that it provided a common experiential base that becomes part of our currency of exchange. The media are something that we know about together and their contents provide conventional solutions and even extended scripts of action that we can all recognize.

CENTRAL IDEAS OF SECTION II: CONTEXTS OF ATTENDANCE

1. Our attendance to the media involves common elements that we all experience.
2. The common elements under discussion here are technology, the matrix text of media, and our common attendance and use of the media.
3. Technology is significant when it imposes conditions of attendance and/or control of content. Not all technologies are, therefore, significant at the consumer level.
4. Digital technologies are moving control from the producer/distributor (vertical control) to the consumer (horizontal control).
5. Media present their text in a matrix of texts that both has a logic of organization and is internally inconsistent and contradictory. Each medium speaks in many voices. But the consumer need not listen to all of them. In choosing which voices to listen to, the consumer creates a cognitive environment.
6. The significance of the media is that we participate in them, creating a vast reservoir of common experience by which we can share in one another's lives.

SECTION III: THE CONTEXT OF EMERGENT MEANINGS

We have in this text made a very careful distinction between what content signifies and what content means. The processes of signification have been located at the sociological level of the linguistic and/or symbolic community. At that level they have a broad scope and transcend the particulars of any individual interpreter. We have found the process of meaning, however, at the local level of the situated individual—the individual operating in reference to his or her recognized others.

A person does not simply act, but acts as a person in a particular time and place—as this student in that classroom, as this single female talking to that single female, as this employee interacting with that co-worker, as this respondent to that survey, or this customer in that store. Every particular situation carries with it expectations for what are the acceptable and likely behaviors. The analysis of any communication act involves what *you* said to *me* under *what circumstances*. In face-to-face communication we share those circumstances. We are both at a party, in a classroom, in a department store. These circumstances have conventions associated with them that govern our behavior, including our communication behavior. We each have our own interpretation of those circumstances; therefore, though not everything is held in common, the external characteristics are the same. In mediated communication, there may be no contextual circumstances held in common. Ordinarily, there is a wide separation between the context of production and the context of reception. Conventions help to bridge that gap. As we write this paragraph we have no idea of the circumstances in which it will be read. Rather, we hold before us an idealized context, a convention, if you will, that this text will be read by inquiring students participating in a media effects class. It will not be read by individuals sitting down for an evening of entertainment. (No cheap shots on writing style, please.) Note that these are not different people referred to in those two sentences, but the same people in different contexts. This same book in the first context is an intellectually stimulating work; in the second it may be a waste of time. As you read this work, you have a similar problem in that you can have no guarantee of the context in which it was written. You have to assume the convention that as a textbook from a reputable publisher this work is being presented seriously and is worthy of your intellectual effort.

Perhaps we can illustrate the effect of context with this example from a classroom.

Discussing the effects of context within the conventional modes of the classroom, the instructor moved to the center of the blackboard and wrote, "Do not erase this blackboard." Turning back to the class, the dialogue was as follows:

Instructor: There isn't anyone competent in the English language who does not know what these five words mean individually and in this sentence. But what does this sentence mean to us now? Does it mean "Do not erase the blackboard?" [Various students answer.] Brian says, "No." You say, "It could." What do you mean that it could?

B-student: Well, I'd have to know what you meant. You might just be writing on the board or something.

Instructor: If I told you what I meant, would you then know what those five words mean?

B-student: Well, I'm not going to erase the blackboard no matter what it means.

A-student: What you have written is an example not a command. It does not mean that no one is supposed to erase the blackboard, but as an example it shows that words depend on the circumstances of their production for their conventional meaning.

Instructor: And from the words, how can I tell the difference?

A-student: You can't. You have to know the context in which they were produced.

Instructor: Marvelous, you are indeed an A-student. [The instructor turns to the whole class] When we leave this room those words on the board present a problem to those who follow because they do not know the context of production. Are the words an order? If so, by whose authority? What risk does one take in erasing the blackboard. Is it not the convention that all have the right to use this public blackboard? And so on. When the janitor comes in, she has a different problem. Part of her job is erasing the blackboard, but she is also bound by the convention of this workplace to honor the requests of the instructional staff. Is this one of those requests? Next Monday when we reconvene this class, perhaps you will walk into the room with one of our members who is missing today. Looking up you'll see those now famous words still on the board. With a laugh, you'll nudge your companion and say "Look, they still haven't erased that blackboard." Your companion might look at you strangely and reply, "Of course not, it clearly says, *Do not erase this blackboard.*"

EMERGENT MEANINGS AND "AUTHORIAL INTENT"

The point of this parable is that texts come to have meaning in what philosophers call the "here and now," the actual situations in which sense making is called for. Meanings emerge, therefore, in and as appropriate to the *context of their achievement.* Although mediated content often carries with it the producer preferred terms under which it would be received, it doesn't necessarily follow that the context of interpretation will meet those terms. Unlike interpersonal communication there are few constraints that can be imposed by the initiator on the manner by which an individual receives mediated content. One can be entertained by commercials and never buy the product; read the newspaper to pass the time while commuting to work and not be informed; use this textbook for bedtime reading and never worry about tests. In the consideration of the local meaning of mediated texts, one cannot assume that the conventional terms of content are the terms under which the content is received.

The circumstances of reception may also convene to enhance or inhibit certain modes of reception. Involving content may be inappropriate to an individual ready for sleep. Complex plot structures may be difficult to follow in an open atmosphere of a family viewing situation in which conversations and other interruptions are intermixed. On the other hand, comedic values may be enhanced by viewing with others and the social viewing of sports can add to the intensity of the game.

As a receiver, one is, therefore, free to move mediated content into a host of interpretive contexts that will instantly join with that content to cocreate its meaning potential. It is the receiver, however, taking an interpretive stance within that context, who will bring that potential into the fruition of meaning.

EMERGENT MEANINGS AND THE SOCIAL PROCESSES OF INTERPRETATION

The receiver, however, does not stand alone in this process. For us the attendance to and interpretation of mediated communication is essentially a social process—a social process that arises within the context of meaning production. This social process is not a question of whether one reads, views, or listens separately or with others. It is, first, the process of making sense of content in reference to others. It is the fact that all of one's identities and memberships are in play at the moment of reception even though a particular response may not reveal them. In short, an individual's interpretive capacity is many-layered. The **structuration**—to use Giddens's (1984) term—that is accomplished is equally complex, although not necessarily unified or coherent.

Second, it is the fact that we interpret content in the connections to others that it provides. The content of the media is often immaterial. Anderson writes:

> I don't read the newspaper because I need to find out the price of lettuce or because I have to carry on a conversation at lunch or because Miss Manners will tell me which fork to use. I may indeed accomplish those things, but they do not inform me of why I read the newspaper. I read the newspaper because you read the newspaper. Our reading of it together provides a method and sometimes the content by which we can constitute our social worlds.

Communication is wholly dependent upon a continuing base of common experience. As we have noted, our common attendance to the media is one of the methods that we use to provide for that base of experience. Our culture provides a number of such methods: Each member knows about driving a car, shopping in a department store, using a telephone, watching a movie. Each of those experiences is a part of those actions by which we constitute our everyday life. The full knowledge of those actions is itself an indicator of membership. We share those experiences and the sharing becomes part of our currency of exchange.

In the proper season, either Tim or Jim could walk into any downhome tavern in America and strike up a football conversation. Something like: "Did ya see that guy from Green Bay who put McMahon on his ear. That's stupid football—cost them the game."

Whatever conversation ensues will enlarge and confirm our understanding of our social world and of that game. We may discover an argument that claims that the risk of a deliberate foul gives courage to the team; the sacrifice of a member disqualified from the game focuses the efforts of the other team members and so on. How do we now know that game and the values that were expressed in the action?

It is clear from the football story that meaning emerges over time and in the social action process. Each individual enlarges the knowledge of his or her experience in social action. Attendance to the media is an experience that itself is experienced in the action of our lives. As the one of us who wrote the football story sits in his office and reflects on that game for the purpose of advancing this argument, the content becomes something other than experienced in the watching on Sunday. Even though alone, he participates in the social action of framing his thoughts for himself, his co-author, his colleagues and his readers. In doing so, that game transcends its content, and its effects cannot be discovered in a thousand replays of the tape.

"But wait there's more," as the pitchman says. The story that references the game has become a text that engenders comment within more social action. In weblike strands, meaning continues to emerge around this focal event. So what is the effect of viewing this game? The game itself is a trivial but convenient bit of common experience that has been used to accomplish a larger task. The event of viewing was equally trivial—a Sunday respite. It was the discovery, found in subsequent effort, that the content that marked that game for its significance of meaning could be useful. It became important and more meaningful because it was available to fill a need that arose independently of the reception process. The author did not view "to find examples for a book." The author viewed because viewing has long been a legitimized practice within his social action frame. One of the legitimizing factors is that viewing is successful in accommodating at least some demands of the social action process—it is, in fact, enough that others who are significant in that social action do it. That we do the things that others do provides us with the vital source of connections that permit us to be members of the society around us. When we do not do what others do, it becomes quite clear that society systematically excludes those who act in radically different ways.

EMERGENT MEANINGS AND INTERPRETIVE FRAMES

The axiom of this section is that the media speak only inside an interpretive frame of social action. Therefore, media have messages only when the content is interpreted by an intellect that is always embedded in social action. Let's begin to explicate the complexity of this claim.

The practices that form the social action of attendance and sense making are the interpretive strata through which media content passes in the process of becoming meaningful messages (plural intended). They are not content in the traditional sense, and are, indeed, lost to those who would attend to the archived record even a few years in the future. Nonetheless, they are crucial to an understanding of what the content means. These strata include the manner in which media are constituted; the functions that are allocated, attributed, contributed, and/or performed by each medium for communities of record and membership and for the individual;[8] the rights, privileges, identities, standing, status, and power claimed by and/or granted to each medium by accountable entities; the ideological practices that are both legitimate and legitimated by the constitution, functions, rights, privileges, identities, standing, status and power of the media; the indexicality of the content (the material and constituted world that is referenced and sustained); and the circumstances of the performances of attendance and sense making by the interpreting intellect.

Looking at this rather imposing list, we see that all but the last item develop at the societal level. What this means is that many of the terms by which we know the media are simply givens. They are what is natural and ordinary. Being natural and ordinary, they are not remarkable or problematic. It takes effort to see these terms and the manner in which they shape our understanding. For example, terms associated with news usually concern objective and factual reporting. Consequently, when we read or hear "Lebanese terrorists, today, kidnapped . . . ," we generally fail to question the political characterizations in the words *Lebanese, terrorists,* and *kidnapped.* The same event could be reported as "Freedom fighters of the Brotherhood, today, arrested . . ." News, of course, is never objective as it must be written from some perspective, usually that of the power elite. In essence, news has the same responsibility as advertising copy to "sell" a point of view, in this case, of a particular political and social system. That we have institutionalized a separation allows us to question the claims of advertising (thereby allowing an economic system of competitive enterprise) while ordinarily accepting the claims of the news (thereby maintaining the system in which we live).

The point of this excursion is not to raise the blood pressure of journalists, but to demonstrate the "naturalness" of our understanding of the media and their content. As noted before, we are born into the system as it is. Understanding the terms of the system permits us to use it within our own sphere of activity. That understanding is typically integrated into performance involving an acting "as if" the terms were in place and true, rather than as establishing a decision point to determine the validity and utility of the terms. It is that integration that constitutes its naturalness.

The terms of the system empower the system—create the conditions under which the system can successfully function as that system. These terms develop at the points of interaction or transaction, both internal and external, to the media organization. That the terms develop at the points of interaction means that anyone's knowledge of those terms is always localized and partial. One's accounting of the media involves that local and partial knowledge rather than some encyclopedic view. Again, we are brought into that tension between the sociological and psychological, there is far more that needs to be true for the media to function within society than what needs to be true for the media to appear within the social action of individuals. It may be true that *we* must have the news to continue as a society; it is not therefore true, however, that I must be informed.

We can call on our work up to this point to reflect on the systemic terms of the media for they arise out of the processes of signification, constitution of the media, and the resultant mediated forms and conventions. What remains is to consider what appears to be the least part of the list—the circumstances of performances of attendance and sense making. In this effort we are finally at that point at which one of us picks up the newspaper or flips on the television set. Such acts seem trivial and disconnected—something any of us could do at any time. What we will argue (primarily in the next chapter) is quite different. What we will argue is that media use is an invested routine that is meaningful in and of itself—regardless of content delivered. Our media use, therefore, has meaningful standing in our lives—it is an accomplishment not a happenstance. As a meaningful accomplishment, it is parts of the interpretive frame into which content is delivered and within which sense making begins. The accomplishment of media use is a richly varied and powerful activity. It is a significant part of the social action by which we together constitute our societal world. For the moment, these few comments will suffice, but a fuller analysis is the business of Chapter 4.

CENTRAL IDEAS OF SECTION III: THE CONTEXT OF EMERGENT MEANINGS

1. In any act, including any act of interpretation, the individual performs as situated in a social matrix. The act of sense making is, therefore, a social action.
2. Sense making as a social action is performed in, and as appropriate to, some context of the social matrix.
3. The intent of the producer may or may not be relevant to the act of sense making. Unlike interpersonal communication, the producer is not necessarily "present" in the interpretive process.
4. Participation in the media is a communal activity, one that gives us a common ground of interaction. What is signified in the content is of less import than its availability as a site of interaction.

5. The content of media has to be understood according to its location in the strata of social practices penetrating from the overburden of societal constructs to the local performances of interpretation.

CHAPTER CONCLUSIONS

This chapter continued our move from the grandest sociological scale of cultural institutions to the unique realm of the individual that we began in Chapter 2 and that we will finish in Chapter 4. In this chapter we examined the elements of the contexts of reception that are common to most acts of media use.

Our first concern was with the concept of the contexts of content and the conventions that display those contexts for us. Conventions, we found, were metacommunications that directed us to the nature, character, and intent of the content of their master identities by identifying the rules governing the production of content. We examined the contracts of fantasy, reality, and advertising content and showed that those rules changed markedly from type to type.

The logics of mediated content were our next stop. Logic was defined as a set of rules governing the relationships among content elements. Any patterned content implies a logic of order that, in turn, imposes upon the interpretation of that content. We examined the logics of narrative, space, time, and proportion, and formats.

Finally, in the section we just left, we made the transition from the realm of the media institution to the realm of the individual engaged in the social action process of media use. We found that content is never context free. Any act of reception is embedded in some social action in which content and context join instantly to form the message to be interpreted by the receiver. Because context is always present, it can never be ignored, and because the individual is an active element within that context, its aggregation across individuals raises serious questions.

We are now prepared to explore the logics of social action in which media use is embedded. That is the stuff of Chapter 4.

NOTES

1. "Right interpretation" means the interpretation of the content according to its culturally held master identity and the intended meaning of the producer. It involves a legitimized (though not necessarily pragmatic) standard of literacy. While the "normal contract" of interpersonal communication implies a responsibility for both what is being done and the producer's intent, this contract is weakly held in mediated communication. The relationship in place is of a different sort. The audience member certainly has no responsibility for the conduct of production or for the intended goals of the content source and is "free" to do whatever with the content received. Nevertheless, if the audience is to be responsive to authorial intent, that intent must be accessible in some conventional manner.

2. We have observed any number of practices, including hiding under a blanket, starting a conversation, walking out of the room, bossing the kids around, and putting the book down for a while.

3. These concerns and the ones we shall report under our analysis of the other contracts motivate programs in media literacy instruction. These programs of instruction are concerned with both the "right reading" of content and its forms and conventions and "right action" in monitoring one's thoughts, values, and behaviors (see Anderson, 1980).

4. Even the more objective consumer-oriented magazines intend to persuade the reader to accept the terms of their comparative evaluations. Regardless of how objective the analysis, the performance value of a product is determined by a particular set of criteria for a specific application. It is often easier to accept someone else's evaluation, but, in the final analysis, it is the end user who must determine the worth of a product.

5. A fourth element, texts, which references the treaties, laws, regulations, and policies governing the relationship between technology and the larger society, is also in this list but not central here.

6. Not all technological differences are significant, however. Broadcast television does not change its nature when delivered by wire (cable) rather than by the "airwaves." Cable television, nevertheless, as a whole, is a significantly different technology from broadcast television.

7. One can see and hear this script played out in the news stories and conversations that surround the latest lottery millionaire. Both the claims of the winner that "I'm still going to go to work at my old job as a trucking company foreman," and the subsequent stories—when they appear—of loss of family and funds are part of this script.

8. Communities of record transmit a codified position (in this case on media) to nonmembers. Communities of membership maintain master identities. The individual in forming an interpretation has to account for all such positions and identities, plus his or her own experience (the empirical requirement). The sum of these are the "accountable entities of interpretation."

RELATED READINGS

Altheide, D. L., Snow, R. P. (1988). Toward a theory of mediation. In J. A. Anderson (Ed.), *Communication yearbook 11* (pp. 194-223). Newbury Park, CA: Sage.

In this article, Altheide and Snow continue their work started in *Media Logic* (1979). The premise of both works is that media provide schemata by which we can come to know the world around us. The foundation of their mediation theory is in contrast to the social action theory worked here, but their notions of logics and formats correspond. The commentary of this *Yearbook* piece provides some useful analysis of the authors' concepts.

Deming, J. (1988). For television-centered television criticism: Lessons from feminism. In J. A. Anderson (Ed.), *Communication yearbook 11* (pp. 148-176). Newbury Park, CA: Sage.

Deming's work is essentially a cry for the legitimation of television criticism. Her most useful work for our purposes is her examination of television drama as melodrama and her analysis of the serial nature of most television drama. As with all chapters in this volume, the commentary that accompanies each piece is equally important.

Fiske, J. (1987). *Television culture*. London: Methuen.

A very useful application of the methods of cultural inquiry to the study of television. A complex but coherent analysis of the nature and character of television's texts including an analysis of intertextuality, polysemy, and narrative.

Gumpert, G., Cathcart, R. (1986). *Inter/media* (3rd ed.). New York: Oxford University Press.

An interesting collection of something for nearly everyone, it explores the mediated/interpersonal communication interface primarily in the direction from media to interpersonal. Interpersonal relations are seen as corseted by the media; their languages, conventions, and formats by most of these articles. This perspective is not one the present authors prefer, but this reader offers a wealth of valuable comment.

Jamieson, K. H., Campbell, K. K. (1988). *The interplay of influence* (2nd ed.). Belmont, CA: Wadsworth.

These authors provide an engaging discussion of the conventions and contracts of news and advertising. They also provide chapters on the commodity audience and methods of influencing the media.

Lindlof, T. (1981). The television fantasy construct. *Communication Research, 8,* 135.

The author explores the nature of the unwritten contract between the media and the individual audience member, focusing on the particular case of television viewing. He speculates on how viewers interact with television content and how their environment, individual interpretive structures, and histories interrelate to make sense of television as a medium and of the content it presents. Also included is a description of how the variety of viewing contexts and viewer interpretations account for the apparently universal popularity of television and film narratives.

Newcomb, H. (Ed.). (1987). *Television: The critical view* (4th ed.). New York: Oxford University Press.

Another reader of excellent quality, it works the critical analysis of text and media. Probably the most useful section for our purposes in this chapter is titled "Thinking about Television." Of the eight articles here, the ones by Booth, Karp, Newcomb, and Hirsh, and by Kellner resonate well. But also take a look at Anderson, Barker, Himmelstein, and Corcoran's contribution.

4

The Social Action of Mediated Communication

IN THE *CLAN OF THE CAVE BEAR*, a particularly inept film about prehistoric life, one of the characters is sentenced to death for violating a taboo. The method of execution is to drive the person from the security of the cave and to deny her the social interaction of the clan. The narrator rather patiently explains that though one might find another cave, there could be no true life outside the company of the clan.

Like the persons in this film, our lives are spent in the company of others. More to the point, our lives are jointly produced. The manner in which we confront reality is in language and behavior passed on to us from others. Human knowledge and understanding are rooted in the process of communication and appear within extended acts of communication. To accomplish the work of this chapter, we need to turn away from the prevailing metaphor of the individual as the element unit of human life and turn toward an understanding of the individual as incomplete. The elemental unit of human life is the one joined with the other. This turn is not an easy one to make. Western cultures have idealized the individual acting in free agency with an independent intellect, grasping an obstreperous but ultimately yielding reality. As Frank Sinatra would have it, the highest order of praise is that each of us is out there fully autonomous—doing it his or her own way.

Much of the theorizing about human life has taken the notion of the complete individual as the center. Theories of maturation, for example, are concerned about the development of such an entity. Theories of the mind create cognitive structures like knowledge schemata or value systems so that each of us is a self-contained microcosm of society. While undoubtedly valuable for understanding some things, these theories, unfortunately, leave uncharted the vast terrain of social action on which the majority of human life is performed. They do not speak to the coordinated, mutually supervised life world of human accomplishment.

It is to this life world and the manner of its accomplishment of mediated communication that this chapter is addressed. In this effort, we will not find the traditional notion of the individual to be very useful. In considering communication, that notion draws a picture of a complete, intact, and reacting intellect marked by capacities and predispositions that will respond with predictable outcomes given the right perception of content. Our view is of an incomplete, interacting, and interpreting intellect, functioning within and enabled by strategic social action using the tactics of sense making to improvise the good continuation of that action. While we will spend the next several paragraphs laying out the implications of these two views, we can alert you here to two key differences: (a) We come into being as humans in a social, communicating relationship. As isolates we are incomplete. (b) What is being done and who we reference in the doing is more important than are the tools—here the content of the media—of the performance. Let's see how these ideas develop.

The essence of our life is the performance of social action. Even the answer to as basic a question as who we are appears inside the social action in which we participate. The creation of our own identity clearly requires us to distinguish ourselves from others. Granting that, then who we are is a performance governed by the others in whose presence we are to appear. For example, if you are a student, the kind of student you are depends on the school you attend, the classes you take, the teachers assigned, and classmates you get as much or more than your native ability. You may be able to modify but you cannot resist these social forces and, in fact, cannot be a student without them. In short, you could be an "A" student at Harvard and barely survive at Green Bay or Utah.

Despite the obvious social nature of education, the traditional view focuses on the individual's traits, skills, motivations, and the like in relation to the content mastery task, as if both the traits and task were "out there" somehow independent of the social action. A similar model has traditionally been in place to describe the process of mediated communication: Individuals are classified according to characteristics of age, socioeconomic class, race, gender, education, and so on; content is classified according to another set of characteristics; and the measurements taken after exposure are explained as outcomes of the relationship. The social action nature of meaning and effect is lost.

In the study of media, the locus of control is typically given either to content or to the individual, reacting intellect; we, on the other hand, posit control in the system called "us." In that system of relationships, the intellectual "I"(the independent, intact intellect) is a fiction of the material individual (the fallacy that separate bodies mean separate minds). The "I" is a particular, partial representation of "us." That "us" is created in a series of relational expansions from the intimate to the societal. It is inside these relationships that the media themselves are created and our understanding of their contents arise.

SECTION I: THE ROUTINES OF SOCIAL ACTION

There are two ways to work toward an understanding of the complex performances of human behavior. The traditional method is to "build up" an understanding by beginning with some very small part of behavior and tracing the consequences of that small part through to the whole. For example, one way of looking at the meaning of content is to investigate the effects of visual vectors, light intensities, color, scene change, and similar content elements and devices on, say, attention and/or retention. Once the elemental effects are known, the larger effects of messages are inferred from content that contains the known elements. The reasoning here involves the linking of a causal chain initiated at the elemental level, the consequences of which influence the next level, which influences the next, and so on until the whole of some larger social action is known. In this reasoning, the parts direct the action of the whole.

A contrary approach sees human behavior as sets of culturally influenced routines, with a routine being a discursive performance of connected acts governed by a syntax and grammar. Routines produce recognizable actions. There are large and small routines, a large routine might be "working" or "being a student," a smaller routine would be "going to a movie" or "laying out." A routine is essentially a governing understanding about what is being done. It contains the premises by which acts are chosen and connected to other acts to create the social action of the routine. What creates the social action nature of routines is not that the performances occur in the presence of others, but that the premises are developed in the interaction with, or in some way accounting for, others.[1] It is not necessary that every human behavior be considered routine. In essence, however, any action with a name is a routine. A routine, therefore, contains the answer to the question, "What is being done?"

Routines do not specify the nature and sequence of acts. Rather, they provide the meaning by which a set of sequenced acts is understood. The performance of a routine is an improvisation on the premises or themes of the routine. A colleague recently told us of the difficulties he had in making sense out of his sabbatical leave:

> This was my first leave after 20 years in the office. I really didn't know what I was supposed to do. But, I knew I wasn't supposed to do what I had been doing. I had gotten my leave to write a book. But then, how do you write a

> book when that's all you have to do—I mean what's a day's work? It was disturbing enough that I talked it over with some more experienced leave-takers. After we got through the mutual boasting and with some trial and error to make it all fit with what I could do, I hit upon four finished pages as a day's work. Then I had something to report: "Boy, I did two days' work today" or "What a godawful day, worked all day for just two pages." I had some way to share my successes and disappointments. And, by the end of the leave, I had my book.

This recounting shows most of the elements of a routine. Here was an individual with enough savvy to get a leave, but not enough experience to know what to do with it once received. He is faced with the question of how does he fill the time. Note that the premises of the leave mean not doing what he had been doing. He is denied the classroom, and showing up for committee work would garner criticism from others wanting to protect their own leaves. Liberated from his routine, he discovers that he has a diminished sense of what he is about. He does not know the performative meaning of his leave. With the help of others, he finds that the premise of four pages a day and all that it implies in time and supporting activities is within his abilities. Further, it was acceptable and understandable as a day's work. He checked around to get a reading on the worth of four pages as a day's work. His quoted sentences near the end suggest that he didn't consider it a heroic effort. Nonetheless, his final sentence shows him fully justified.

The colleague of our story is a well-socialized member of his profession. He wouldn't consider violating the premises of "work." His confusion and desperation arises because in the changed circumstances of his status, he cannot fulfill those premises. His solution is to negotiate and adopt a routine approved by his colleagues and appropriate to his abilities.

The routine establishes the conditions of satisfactions and stresses—good days and bad days at work can be recognized. The routine also contains the terms of its supervision. He knows when he has done a day's work. He can report to his colleagues that he has done his work. Others can participate in that supervision—"Did you get your work done today, dear?" Both the performance and the supervision of the performance maintain the premises of the routine.

Finally the routine has standing among the other routines in this person's life. A "day" must account for this routine in its presence or absence. Decisions can be justified on the basis of the routine—"I have to work in the morning."

This sabbatical example is useful because of the relative simplicity of its development. There are routines, however, that develop in complex negotiations, are unstable in their organization, have conflicting premises or terms of supervision. Routines are not always clearly integrated within a "day." Many of our routines can be more or less available; an individual can readily shift among them. Larger routines contain smaller routines and elements of other larger routines (e.g., "taking a break" or "going for a run" during "work"). The answer to the question, "What is being done?" can be very complicated.

The concept of a routine is a device for recognizing the influence of the whole on the action of the parts. It directs us to understand that an act under the routine of "work" does not have the same meaning as that act in a different routine. The relational terms of a given act—its antecedent and consequential qualities—are determined, not by the elemental nature of the act but by the semantic frame of the routine. There is, consequently, no simple quality of, say, attention or retention. There is, rather, attention and retention as practiced within some routine (including experimental protocols).

Social action, then, is the performance of a semiotic and semantic frame—which we have called a routine—that invests the elemental acts of behavior with a potential for meaning as expressions of the action and provides for the interpretation of their meaning within that action. Let's disassemble that complex thought. As a semiotic, social action creates the signs—routines—by which the performance is understood. That is, it is in the performative routines that one knows that one thing is being done and not another.

As signs, these performative routines are liberated from a particular set of performance requirements, such as time, location, or props. Routines can "speak" inside other routines. As a sign, for example, one can do "watching television" inside "serious discussion" as a point of argument—She: "John, our relationship is falling apart." He: (turning on the television set) "So?"

As a semantic frame, social action creates the rules for its own internal consistency. That is, the meaning of this act is known in reference to that act inside the frame of action. The meaning of this moment of action is interpreted by the moment preceding and the moment to follow, all of which are understood as moments of the social action in progress. John is not about to watch television in any ordinary sense. Watching television is not the meaning of his act of turning on the set. His move is to use the sign value of the act as a meaningful statement within the argument.

Because they are a semiotic, routines are accountable within the sociological rather than the psychological dimension. Routines are not the habits of individuals.[2] Routines are the invested actions of a community: Driving, going on a date, listening to the radio, eating dinner, taking a leak, getting drunk, vandalizing, murdering, falling in love, and dying are all signifying and meaningful social actions. All of them are performed in reference to others and represent a sign to others as to what is being done. Because these actions belong to the community, a given performance is subject to supervision, comment, and criticism. (Garrison Keillor gave an extended dissertation over public radio on the proper performance of male urination in a public restroom—where one looks *is* significant, especially to a shy person.)

The argument within what has been called the "social construction of reality" is fairly straightforward. It begins with the assumption of a relatively indeterminate, interpreting intellect that is delivered by birth into an ecology of conjoint action. Our place in this ecology is always in relation to another. The axioms of human understanding arise in that relationship. It is from these axioms that we act and understand our actions. Together, therefore, in the performance of social action, we reproduce the axioms of human understanding. This, in very condensed form, is the concept of the social construction of reality—not that we cocreate material reality but that we cocreate and maintain our understandings of it.

SOCIAL ACTION AND INDIVIDUAL PERFORMANCES

In this ranging discussion of social action, we have emphasized the cultural thematic of routines. Such routines, as we have noted, are the product of the community, but they are not fixed specifications to which we respond in lock-step fashion. The performance of a routine is an improvisation on that cultural theme. A performance is an expression of the understandings we hold together, created in and maintained through the actual interactions we have with one another. These understandings do not exist "out there" in the social mists; they are under our local control and are partially held by each of us. The principle of local control means that, as the "actors," we negotiate or improvise any performance within those understandings. The improvisational nature of any performance implies that it is a construction using practiced and unpracticed acts, interpersonal and mediated texts, local materials and settings, appropriate technology and technique, and so on, all of which are referenced to what is being done. Any individual has only a partial grasp of the improvisational range within a routine because any individual's understanding is cocreated within a finite and particular set of others.

The concept of social action, then, refers to that broad spectrum of coordinated, indexical, and reflexive human endeavor by which, together, we cocreate the cognitive and behavioral worlds in which we live and through which we interpret material reality. The concept of routines refers to the culturally embedded sense-making understanding that defines what is being done and provides the interpretive context for the meaning of any act performed within a given routine. Performances of routines are improvisational expressions in varying dialects that are interpreted from the province of the routine. Understanding that the routine provides the contextualized meaning of one's social action of the moment, performances, then, are the creative improvisations on the themes set by the routine. These improvisations are granted by the indeterminacy present within the boundaries of the routines. These improvisations are the material expressions that reinvent the routines they express, a process that provides for both the stability and adaptiveness of the routines. Performances answer the question (undoubtedly, never asked), "In the face of the elements made significant by the context of possible routines, how shall I constitute an expression that is true to that context?" The individual seeks an expression that is true to a participative understanding of the world. That seeking is not done alone. There is a repertoire of performances with well-practiced expressions. Any expression is anticipated, supervised, and retrospectively evaluated by all the participants. The strokes of the performance, however—the manner of its doing—are given to the moment-by-moment reinterpretation of "what's happening."

Finally, in this extended comment, there is a useful parallel to be drawn between social action and discourse (while understanding that they are inseparable). Social action is analogous to discourse in that they both use signs in context to potentiate meaning. Social action frames discourse and discourse reflects on the course of social action. Both improvise their outcomes in ongoing performances that can be intentional, are retrospectively interpreted, and from which meaning emerges. In both cases, then, the answer to "what's happening" is a process of interpretation that accounts for the configuration of the past, may look to the future, and directs the adaptation of the next act. To relieve the excessive burden of proactive sense making, much of this interpretation is well-practiced in supervised socialization. In social action as well as discourse, it is our constraints that set us free.

SOCIAL VERSUS INDIVIDUAL EXPLANATIONS IN UNDERSTANDING MEDIA EFFECTS

The point of this theoretical stance is not to arrive at some finite number of culturally determined routines that "explain" all of behavior. Our social action stance is taken to provide a viewpoint on the multiple, emergent, and coconstructed nature of meaning. The meaning of a television commercial, for example, might begin as a simple act of interpretation inside a performance of "watching television," in which it might be intermixed with the opportunity to grab a snack or engage some conversation; emerge with different significance as it is reinterpreted in an episode of "going shopping," in which it may provide a moment of recognition or a justifying text; and yet again, as a topic of conversation in the process of doing "lunch."

At any point when the question of meaning is explicitly or implicitly addressed, the answer is generated within the social action of the moment of interpretation. Message "effectiveness" arises within the terms of the social action that enables the interpretation of that message. Message effectiveness, then, is not transportable across the terms of message interpretation. Without a doubt, we do not have to lose the memory of a previous interpretation. Interpretations interact and one's history with content is available to an interpretive act, but other interpretations and the history are both reinterpreted in the action of the moment. *No content resides as a primitive force evoking the same interpretive spasm each time it is invoked.*

The stance permits us to recognize that we live in constructed environments that we fill with recurring performances that are coordinated with others who participate in and comment upon and often directly supervise. Information, then, is interpreted from the historical and ideological perspective of the routine—I am led to understand who I am and what something means to me by what I do. What "I do," however, is a permitted, improvised, social construction, not the independent creation of free agency or the mechanical reproduction of attitudes, schema, or similarly loaded black boxes or the response demand of content. The problem with the latter three in the preceding sentence is not that acts of creation, attitudinal responses, and unthinking replies to content do not occur. The problem with all three of those is that they misdirect us by either denying or ignoring the social character of human action. They begin and end their analysis with the individual and do not account for the performances of sense making and the social action constitution of effect.

For example, we have a long history of trying to explain violence in society by examining the "effects" of exposure to violent content. The method of investigation for these studies is essentially the same: Selected volunteers are in some way angered; they are then divided into two groups: one group views violent content, the other views nonviolent content; both groups respond on a measure of aggression. The consistent empirical evidence is that the violent content group scores significantly higher rates of aggression than does the nonviolent group. The conclusion: Watching violent content leads to violent behavior. Unfortunately the conclusion fails when one returns to the purpose of the study—to explain violence in society—because most of us are exposed to violent media content and yet almost all of us (over 90%) never participate in an incident of socially violent conduct.

How can we reconcile these conflicting sets of evidence. One way is to take a much more careful look at what is going on in the experimental protocol. (A more detailed discussion is provided in Chapter 6.) These studies all begin when the individual is taken out of his or her normally functional routines by accepting the invitation to participate in a socially constructed episode of "science experiment" that itself produces a semantic frame for social action. That experimental protocol will enable action that, in the process of its performance, is defined as some socially acceptable act (evaluation, usually) but, in subsequent scientific argument, is defined as an act of socially unacceptable violence. The researcher will argue that the meaning of the experimental protocol is kept hidden from all respondents. This claim allows the researcher to argue that the criterion performance of aggression is sequentially determined by the events of the research design: being angered, having one's aggressive state heightened or maintained by violent content, and then being given the opportunity and appropriate target for aggression. The aggressive act of the respondent, then, is a consequence of exposure—as mediated by the other conditions—without any interpretation or understanding on the part of the respondent.

There is an alternate argument, of course, that the meaning of the **protocol** slowly unfolds. For the violent-content group it unfolds in an eminently sensible way; for the control group, it offers little consistency. The argument that one continually makes sense of the whole scene—reinterpreting what has preceded in accord with what is happening now—seems considerably more plausible than one in which respondents wait numbly for what happens next. It is clear that the experiment itself is a socially constructed environment in which the viewing of televised violence and the performance of subsequent violence is encouraged for some members and discouraged for others.

The researcher is able to conduct his or her experiment because of a set of agreements, both implicit (social practices) and explicit (recruitment statements, release forms, disclosure statements) that are entered into by researcher and respondent. The respondent is typically a student drawn from the introductory psychology or communication pool who accepts the authority of the experimenter as the representative of the authorizing institution and who has been called on in various classes to support texts that purport to explain, but actually mystify and valorize, social science experiments. These agreements and contexts create a functioning environment for the respondent's performance. It is from within this environment that the respondent makes sense of being yelled at, being shown a movie of a fight scene, and then being asked to grade someone's work by giving electrical shocks.

These studies, whether on violence or pornography or even on the informing effects of news, are more than a bit like studying the effect of a brick. A brick can be used to build a house or break a window. The presence of the brick contributes to either action but is neither necessary nor sufficient. What evokes the brick as a method of building or breaking is the meaning we attach to it. In the day-in day-out performances of our lives, meaning is found in the routines of social action for both the builder and the breaker. The continuing buzz of social violence is not the aggregation of the sporting acts or those suddenly deep-ended by a rock-and-roll lyric. Violence is a practiced achievement supported in the social networks of the perpetrators.

Television as a cause of violence? Nonsense! Television as part of the method by which we sustain violence? No objection. But the differences are substantial. In the first case, a reformer works to remove certain content from the media. In the second, the reformer works to redistribute wealth, develop opportunity, provide education, or in some way to change the social action conditions in which violence arises. Violence is a product of and, in fact, is defined by the society in which we live, so that it is considered an act of violence for the thief to steal from the millionaire, but not to permit a homeless one to die of exposure beneath a viaduct. One interpretation that can clearly be made is that the belief in the scientific hypothesis of effects on individual action that aggregate to rates in society can be used to support the existing order of things. The belief that media violence is the cause or a major cause of violence in society effectively eliminates the need to redistribute wealth, power, and status to effect its control. The practice of science arises in the society in which it operates.

THE METAPHOR OF ACCOMMODATION

As children we do not have to "invent" a system of mediated communication. We are given one and gradually taught how to use it. As we move from instructional site to instructional site—family, friends, school, commerce, work—we increase the range and space of our improvisations. It is a process of accommodation—of making sense of action inside other performances. One understands the routines of media use in reference to the other routines of life.

The metaphor of accommodation characterizes this formulation of social action. *Accommodation is the practiced method by which we manage the multiple understandings that constitute our view of reality.* These understandings arise from our relationships, technologies, and texts of every sort. In no way do these understandings "naturally fit together." They are, rather, melded into action by continually reinventing (or reinterpreting) them in the context of the moment. One's concept of the media and their messages is not fixed in rigid cognitive formats that determine consequent action. One's conception is part of the improvisational response to the perceived demands of action. In short, we make sense of the media inside the framework of action. What is important is not so much what we believe, but what we believe we are doing.

SUMMARY

Social action is that set of supervised, improvisational performances of embedded, culturally accountable routines that constitute and maintain our understandings of the world. Social action is central to an understanding of the human condition. Without social action, there is no science, no theories, no beliefs, no language by which to construct them all. An individual performs his or her life in the routines of social action not in senseless, moment-by-moment adaptations to a material universe. From the initial exercise of our genetic potential to an understanding of the moment of our death, we depend on others and they depend on us.

CENTRAL IDEAS OF SECTION I: THE ROUTINES OF SOCIAL ACTION

1. The notion of an independent, intact, reacting intellect as the source of interpretation deflects analysis from the dependent, coordinated, cocreated lives we live.

2. An understanding of human behavior is not built up through the analysis of elemental acts. Rather, we understand the elemental acts by their location in some meaningful action.
3. One device that helps us recognize the influence of the whole on the parts is the concept of the routine. A routine is a semiotic and semantic frame that constitutes a sign of what is being done and provides the context for recognizing the performance.
4. Routines appear in improvisational performances that are under local control and are partial representations of the cultural thematic of the routine.
5. Interpretation of the texts of media is itself a performance that can be located in several routines. As the location changes, the progress and consequence of interpretation also changes.
6. Media and their texts, therefore, are accommodated within the routines of everyday life. That accommodation is the practiced method by which we manage the understandings of our socially constituted reality.

SECTION II: SOCIAL ACTION AND MEDIA USE

The words *social action of media use,*[3] perhaps irresistibly, conjure a picture of folks gathered around the television set or sharing tidbits from the newspaper. Such scenes are certainly part of the concept. But social action does not disappear just because an individual happens to be viewing or reading alone. Mediated communication is not restricted to the moment of exposure. The process of mediated communication is an extended one. It is a process that we are born into and die out of—a process that we maintain and modify in the course of our lives.

MEDIA USE AS COMMON EXPERIENCE

Mediated communication is an institutionalized system of communication with the same institutional character as our systems of transportation, education, religion, government. Each of us is a participant in all of those systems whether or *not* we drive a car, go to class, attend church, or cast a ballot.[4] The systems account for our action or inaction within them by providing a "place" (good, bad, or indifferent) for each of us. It is this provision of place that identifies them as societal institutions in that they are a common resource for all of us to sustain the world in which we live.

At the end of Chapter 3 we introduced the view of the media as a common resource in the broadest view of social action. Here we would like to extend that view as the background for the study of the characteristics of media use performances. The media permeate our society just as our monetary system does. An individual can certainly live without either (bartering in close interpersonal networks); it's simply a great deal more work; it is not the "natural" thing to do. It is not remarkable for us to watch television, listen to the radio, or read a newspaper. It is as remarkable to avoid these activities deliberately (No, I won't have television in my house) as it would be to never carry cash in any of its forms ("John, would you pick up the tab; I'll trade you some work later.").

The point is not that we *have* to participate in the media. The point is that it is *expected* that we will have participated in the media. The media are there for us as a currency of social exchange. They provide a broad base of common experience—the sine qua non of communication. The resource metaphor is a useful one. It suggests all the problems attendant to resource management and uses—production costs, use characteristics, unwanted effects. But note that the resource is not the content but the common experience of use. At this societal level of analysis, it is that most of us watch television, not that some of us watch a particular program, that is important. Note also that every societal institution is a resource of common experience. We don't create our worlds out of the stuff of media alone. All of society's institutions provide the building blocks of our world.

Content becomes more important in more restrictive memberships. Individuals can build particular and peculiar communities around types of music, political tracts, and even 30-year-old reruns. Once again, however, media institutions are among many available to us. The work place, the family, schools, churches, clubs, and the host of shared activities with common practices (sports, parties, dating) are rich in their own texts. One does not need the texts of the media to understand the problems of getting from one place to another or how to form a relationship or the exercise of power. Many institutions provide the terms by which such experiences can be understood.

With the caveat firmly in mind that the media are an influence among many, the next several sections *examine the accommodation of the experience of media and their texts within social action.* In this examination, we hope to demonstrate a symbiotic relationship between the action that accounts for media and the media as a method of the action. The accommodation of any social institution in the social action of our lives not only uses that institution in performance but creates the meaning of the institution within that performance. The living social institution is the product of human effort to create the realities of life's work. Social institutions die when they can no longer provide the terms of our activity.

The media, therefore, are not some noxious addendum to twentieth-century life. They are a significant and necessary element in the constitution of lives that we live. On the other hand, this is not the only life-set that can be lived, and the media are not the only (or even the paramount) constituting element within it.

THE EMBEDDED NATURE OF MEDIA USE

Earlier in this chapter we wrote of the social process of media reception in which we claimed that individuals made sense of media content in reference to others. In this section, we will add to that claim by arguing that the ordinary attendance to or participation with any medium as a recognizable routine ("I'm reading a book," "I'm watching television," "I'm going to a movie") is not an unstructured pastime. It is the normal case that every such incidence of media use has a coherence. The source of this coherence is the routine that stands as a sign of what is being done. This coherence connects the particular incident with what has happened in the immediate past and with what will happen in the immediate future. Media use happens within connected skeins of behavior, the routines of social action, the accomplished practices, if you will, which constitute and maintain our social realities. Family viewing of television, for example, is no more casual and spontaneous than is the family dinner. Such viewing involves all of the relational elements of the family—status, power, rights, responsibilities, and the like. Family viewing, then, is accomplished by competent actors with great improvisational skill. Every family that the authors have visited in their ethnographic studies has a set of practices of media use. Every individual—from the youngest to the oldest—shows a practiced accomplishment of media use. All of us, therefore, have a common context of media use in that such use is embedded in and defined by a set of practices. It is in these practices that media content comes to be interpreted.

Each day of our lives can be seen as an achievement—something that *is* because of the contributions we make to it. This notion is neither maudlin nor egocentric. It is a recognition that there are choices to be made even within the most severe of constraints—choices that make differences. These choices are managed within the scope of our understanding of the alternatives. The management of these alternatives leads us to two kinds of work—provisioning and rendering. Provisioning generates alternatives by providing for their requirements. One provides for media-use alternatives by subscribing to newspapers, magazines, and cable services, purchasing video equipment, buying and maintaining record collections, and the like. Provisioning does not imply that a choice will be exercised, simply that it is available.

Rendering is an interpretive act that, within the premises of the ongoing social action, creates alternatives by determining the permissible, given the constraints in place. One cannot make choices without alternatives and those alternatives arise within our social action. To return to our discussion of television and violence, television does not create violence as an acceptable alternative—a possible choice. It is the terms of cocreated social action that permit violence. Television may provide method or even means, but not the possibility.

Provisioning and rendering are both ongoing work, which means that they maintain the sense of our lives. The "sense of our lives" is a phrase that we are using to reference the order (even the order of disorder) that prevails. That order is an accomplishment in which we and others participate. We may hate it or love it, but, in fact, we do it. Media use is part of that accomplishment and is not independent of it.

It is our argument, then, that media use has a created place wherever it appears as a routine in our lives that is also cocreated in the lives of others. This created/cocreated place is an inevitable reference and context for any media use. In this argument we have developed the requirements for an important distinction: the difference between media use as a routine in its own right and media use as an element in some other routine. As a routine, the act of, say, watching television is a sign of what's happening; as an element in some other routine, that same act has to be understood in accordance with whatever central, organizing action is being performed. The point of this comment is that sitting down to "watch television" is a different activity from watching television as part of an "evening with friends" or a "classroom exercise" or a "communication experiment" because the sense-making premises of the action are different. To understand what is being done and the character of the performance, we have to understand the semantic frame that enables the actor to make sense of the performance.

We should exercise some care with this argument by noting that we are not claiming that we all have the same set of practices or that an individual uses the same practiced method for, as an example, reading the newspaper. We are claiming that a person knows what she is doing when reading a newspaper. Her rules for the performance of that reading, the significance she attaches to the content, her expectations concerning both content and act, her history with content and act, her understanding of how this activity is distinguished from and related to others, and her knowledge of how her reading of the newspaper is provided for and interpreted by the communities to which she belongs are firmly in place. It is, therefore, of great interpretive significance that when asked, she responds, "I'm reading the newspaper."

This concept of the sense-making routine needs further explication. To do so, let us retrieve the partial listing of the components by which the analyst would recognize that a routine is in place: the rules, significance, expectations, history, and so on that we listed previously, and develop examples for each.

RULES

Performance rules are ways of doing that define the ordinary appearance of a particular action. Our patterned achievements of performance establish what it means to do the activity (such as read the newspaper) and the preferences we will show in action. They are the proper order of things. Our exemplar newspaper reader takes a morning rather than evening daily because she makes time for reading during the first part of the day. She starts with the front page (while her husband reads the local section), then to the comics, and ultimately, through each section, systematically sampling each article, reading thoroughly those of interest. She then returns to go through the newspaper for coupons and ads. A person with a different set of rules—patterns of performance—will have a different experience in the reading. Whatever pattern of media use one achieves, it will become an expectation of the others that share in that pattern. The others will supervise the performance of the patterned use by accommodating it in their own practices, by remarking on its deviations, and so on.

SIGNIFICANCE

The importance one attaches to an activity is certainly part of its significance. Our reader could value that activity highly, organizing her day to ensure its performance, expressing irritation when delivery interruptions prevent it, and the like. On the other hand, she could approach it as an activity available when and if she has the time in the morning. Significance, of course, is more than importance. It is the variety of meaning the activity has within this person's life. The method of accommodation implies that wherever a routine appears, it is in a sensible place. This implication, in turn, suggests that the wider the sensibility of a routine the greater accommodation one should find.

In any case, by talking about meaning variety, we are deliberately avoiding the concept of *the* meaning of an activity. We believe that meaning is situational rather than fundamental. Further, the meaning of media use changes as the situations in which we participate change. For example, we see the greatest frequency of television use in those between 6 and 12 years and in those 60 and older. It's not hard to find an explanation in time availability, potential of competing activities, and other circumstances. Similarly, television viewing declines in the summer months and rises in the winter. An individual who may have no interest in watching TV on a bright summer's night may be delighted at the opportunity in mid-February. Postmodern cultures provide a number of different solutions to most human intentions. Which resolution moves to the fore depends on the decision-making situation.

EXPECTATIONS

An important element in that decision-making process is the expectations we have for content and action of media use. Our expectations exist because, for each of us, media and their contents reside in a dynamic, ever-evolving semiotic field into which we are first born, then are trained to accomplish—a training that we embellish with our own learning. Our media use is well-practiced and both supported and supervised in the relationships that define our social life. Those practiced efforts, support, and supervision ensure that, on the whole, media and their content will be what we expect. Please note that we are not arguing for a rigid set of a priori, deterministic motives but for an understanding of the range of possible methods and outcomes for the accomplishment of media use within the improvisations of our daily life.

PERSONAL HISTORY

Most media content that one engages involves some personal history with that content. This personal history develops a larger context that can be indexed by any particular example of that content. No analysis of content, of course, can tap into the individual's history of participation. The 11-year-old child who has fought for and won the right to stay up to watch a favorite syndicated program brings a particular point of view to that attendance. The history of success and failure with a medium and its content can motivate choices made from that medium. One's personal history is, therefore, part of the context of media use that forms the core of interpretation of media content.

NESTED ROUTINES

Lynn Johnson, who draws the comic strip *For Better or for Worse,* captured the notion of one routine providing the arena for the work of another routine in a strip that showed the younger sister standing in front of the TV set interminably changing the channel. Finally, the older brother yells in exasperation, "What are ya doing!" "Looking for something you don't like," comes the reply. In this drawing, a performance of watching television becomes the setting for the **enactment** of the power relationship among siblings. Spouses can read the newspaper to avoid interaction. Children can appeal to emotional entanglement in a TV program to extend a bedtime. Those who are quickly ready can read a magazine to manage the frustration of waiting for those who are more deliberate. A movie house is as much an arena for passion in the seats as on the screen.

Any meaningful activity can become a tool for the accomplishment of some other routine. A respondent in the Utah studies has a small library of pornographic videos that he uses as part of his conjugal sex play. "Let's put on the videos" is a clear invitation that establishes the conditions under which the content and the viewer's responses to that content are to be interpreted. This meaningful theme, however, can be used to reflect on the relationship. Played in opposition to the relationship, the videos can be read as a challenge, an expression of discontent, a normative violation, and so on. The content becomes embodied with this symbolism as the action is constituted by the players.

The utility of nested routines is the improvisational space provided by the "primary" activity. The signs and symbols of that activity can provide the devices to enact the themes of the nested activity. The "actors" can use them in exaggeration, irony, metaphor, deliberateness—all of the expressive measures available. They work because of the corecognition of the semiotic frame in which they are presented.

THE SIGNIFICANCE OF OTHERS

The last element in this partial list of the components of the embedded context of media use is one's knowledge of the other's understanding, supervision, participation, accommodation, and so on, of that use. We have referenced the concept of "the other" on a number of occasions. Setting *no* exceptions aside, the ordinary concourse of human behavior is in reference to (but not necessarily in the presence of) someone else. The typical human is born into a family (however defined) and lives enmeshed in social networks. The rugged individual is a western fiction that unfortunately has badly damaged the progress of social science. One *does not* respond to the world, including its media, as a freestanding intellect independent of his or her understanding of the others' responses to the world and its media. Both the production and the reception of content are referenced activities. In essence, in the act of being a member of the audience of some mediated presentation, we reference our performance of reception to our own audience of others.

On the other hand, my "others" are not necessarily your "others." We are not talking about some nameless, faceless cultural mass. We are talking about the 200, 300, or whatever hundred individuals with whom we actually connect and reference as individuals and as representatives of the roles and institutions of our society. The presentation of those others is not coherent, not unified into some forceful, determining influence. It is, rather, ambiguous, conflicting, situational. As a result, we improvise under the gaze of others, and gaze, in turn, upon their improvisations.

Each of us reproduces our society in the connections we make. Society does not exist "out there" as some invisible force. It resides in the conduct of our relationships. Each of us lives, then, in a locally produced, partially representative society. These societies have much in common: systems of governance, laws, technology, communication media, and so on. Nonetheless, these communalities can be made sense of in radically different ways. As teachers, the authors daily discuss societal themes. It is interesting that our own positions seem to be at the center for some, and beyond the pale for others.

SUMMARY

The consequence of this discussion, we hope, is that the concept of media use is now enlarged well beyond the moment the set is turned on or the newspaper opened. Media use is not a new adventure but an embedded routine that both contains the elements of a common experience—we all see the same programs—and provides for a wide range of improvisation—the meaning of that experience will emerge in the social action in which it arises.

The center of the argument that invokes this view of media use deals with the dominant character of human life. Human life is not characterized by freestanding intellects whose common features are the result of early socialization. Human life is jointly produced. As a species on this earth, we are continually in the company of one another—not as independent units merely aggregated together but as interactants linked in a common effort of understanding.

It is the fact that we are incomplete as individuals that leads this theory to the grounds of social action as the site for the investigation of the processes and effects of mediated communication. We have described the character of social action as organized into meaningful wholes, which we have called routines. Routines are social action structures that contain the premises of what is being done. As such they are a semiotic constituting the signs of the action and a semantic providing for their interpretation. Social action is what you and I know we are doing together.

Social action, then, is the jointly produced set of premises by which we know what it is that we are doing, which constitute the signs of its action, and provides the frame for interpreting the events within it. The performances of social action are the improvisational efforts of actors to accommodate the situate premises in ongoing behavior that is under local control at the site of its production and partially representative of what could be done. It is in the next section that we consider the implications of these characteristics of performances.

CENTRAL IDEAS OF SECTION II: SOCIAL ACTION AND MEDIA USE

1. Media are naturalized within our society and are an expected part of our lives.
2. As naturalized elements in our lives, media use is embedded in and as a routine of social action.
3. The course of each day is achievement within the choices among alternatives some of which are created through provisioning and rendering.
4. Routines are characterized by rules of performance, holding significance, expectations, a personal history, the ability to stand as a sign within other routines, and to be recognized by and referenced to others.

SECTION III: PERFORMANCES

The next several pages document three performances that involve mediated communication. The three performances have been drawn from our ethnographic field work or, in the case of the first example, from personal experience. The narratives that we present are, of course, pedagogical not anthropological. They have been written to instruct rather than represent. In the writing of these performances, we are trying to demonstrate the fundamental principles of the performance of social action: Any performance is an improvisation on the premises of the routines of social action, locally produced under local control; it is a partial representation of what can be understood under those premises.

DOING WRITING

As the one who writes these words, I sit alone in front of my CRT pushing the keys of the word processor in a referenced performance of the social action routine of professorial writing. As I do so, I invoke all the rules of what this performance should be—the time, place, and conditions of its accomplishment: how difficult, how engaging, and so on. My performance this morning has been granted—and supervised—by a number of others. Long before I was admitted to the practice, this industry had accomplished the fact of writing to be a central definition of the profession. Not all organizations "walk the talk" of course, but here the performance of writing has been legitimated by the meritocracy practiced in this department.

Nonetheless, it took over a year before writing at the office—as opposed to at home, where it is usually practiced—was accepted. One of the major problems was the word processor I'm working on. I own one myself—no writer should be without one—but with a two-career marriage and children in college, there was no way I was going to move it out of the house. My chairperson told me to "just stay home," which I would have been delighted to do except that the department wanted me to do other work that required calling all over the country. There was a period when I was in "Catch 22" in having to be at the office phone and at home at the same time. I understand that I should have been able to return to a typewriter or even a yellow pad. I also understand that academics don't want to make writing too easy at either the organizational or industry level, lest it lose its power to distinguish success from failure, but this seemed so unjust, even though it was wholly unintentional. It was very frustrating.

We also had to work out some enabling practices that were reached by mostly tacit agreements to provide the uninterrupted time I claim to need. Though I have been called "the mole," both students and colleagues respect my closed door before 10:30 a.m. My secretary slips notes under the door. (It's all a bit weird when fixed in writing, but quite natural in its performance.) I have participated in those agreements by moving my schedule two hours ahead to get into the office before 7:00 a.m.

That decision had repercussions at home. My wife is a night person. I had to learn to lay out my clothes the night before and to dress by flashlight. She had to learn to come to bed with something less than an avalanche of noise. It is still a topic of comment and negotiation. Nevertheless, I have overheard telephone conversations that indicate a certain pride in carrying the burden of someone who is up at work so early in the morning. Those old agrarian values are still strong around here.

My family participated in the coproduction and supervision of this morning's performance by making sure that I was up and out the door in a timely fashion. Two hours later, my next office neighbor gave his recognizable knock as he arrived both to connect and to know that I was doing what I ought. An ordinary lunch-time comment will inquire about my progress.

When this chapter is finished, the product of this performance will be audited by my coauthor (and the "I" in these sentences will lose its personal reference) who will appropriate it into our common effort. That coauthored work will then be audited by our and the publisher's reviewers to ensure that content and style are appropriate to the routine. There is a risk in doing this episode of writing. It is different and might not be understood. (It will probably be set in italics.) Their comments will be very practical—paragraphs will be excised, lines crossed out, insertions made, pithy comments written ("awkward," "dumb," "nice," "argh!"), lengthy recommendations given. If published, the chapter will be audited by our professional colleagues who in letters and convention comments and, of course, adoptions will tell us of the success of the work. With readers and impact on theory yet to come, the trail of supervision stretches far into the future.

In this writing, I have improvised a performance that in its particulars has not been given before (to my knowledge) but that is an ordinary accomplishment. The choice of words has been under my control as I reference the premises that govern that choice. There may be an infinite set of choices available; I have performed only one. I will learn from others of my success.[5]

EXEGESIS OF "DOING WRITING"

The writing episode just presented emphasizes the embedded character of one person's performance. It was included here because it focuses on what is ostensibly a single person writing behind closed doors—the lonely author in the solitary act of creation. As we examine this performance, however, we discover that his solitary circumstances are an achievement with many contributors. His position behind closed doors has been granted and accomplished by a very large number of individuals. That achievement took time and effort to initiate and takes time and effort to maintain. Colleagues avoid interrupting, students counsel one another about the peculiarities of faculty, secretaries type out notes, administrators assign resources and take the heat for the decision, family members adjust.

Having accomplished the conditions that enable the performance, the writing gets done in layers of effort. A draft is constructed in reference to what it is to be—a textbook that deals with established content by innovating in theory—a known form. The product of the episode of writing has to be referenced to that form. Referencing does not imply imitation or even conformity. It means that should there be nonconforming or oppositional writing, it has to be recognized as such. For example, in the episode, the author comments on the risk of what is being done. It's a preemptive move. By noting the risk, the attempt is to reduce the risk. The space for criticism has been narrowed. (This exegesis narrows it even more.) But as it is written, the author does not know whether it will survive.

All writing, but particularly nonconforming writing, is vulnerable to the collegial and corporate practices of publishing. Even a well-practiced author does not know if it is possible for others to achieve some representation of the meaning intended by a particular choice of words. Further, the writing has to evidence an appropriate level of craft in format, style, and convention. (In some writing, that craft alone is sufficient.) Such uncertainties open the work to review. One dictum of the business is that it's not the writing but the rewriting that counts. The writer, then, works to penetrate that phalanx of reviewers, to get through to publication.

The result is that the ownership of the text is muddled. The words and ideas of reviewers as well as authors are represented in any text. Some words and ideas of the authors will not be permitted to be presented. There are much larger problems with ownership, however. We have, for example, taught from typescript drafts of this text for a number of years. Students in their classroom arguments, for and against, have shaped the ideas. Graduate researchers working their studies from the perspective have colonized the area thoroughly. Both invention and its ownership are the decision of the social membership not the act of creation.

Any writer produces within an enabling milieu. Textbook writing particularly has to connect with current thought. The writing has to proceed from a field of agreements. Those agreements have to be in place before a book like this one can be produced. Some 20 years ago, the mainstream agreements as to what was proper for mass communication theory would not have been open to the arguments presented here. Our writing, then, though still different, comes from what is now a recognizable perspective in the field. The fact that we (Tim and Jim) can look into our own performances as actors in a mediated communication process (as we are here) and can find explanations for the success and frustrations personally experienced is another confirmation of the value of the social action perspective.

PICKING UP A FEW THINGS

In the episode that follows, we have constructed a narrative from field notes of our family studies. In presenting this episode, we have also worked the layers of meaning that were present during the performance. As participant observers, the ethnographers were part of the "us" that provided for the contextual meaning of the expressions recorded. The tale told has been thoroughly disguised according to common practice.

Ralph, 52, is deputy assistant director of Social Services for Morgan County, husband to Alexis, 48, treasurer of Data Inc. and father to Heli, a 14-year-old high school sophomore. Alexis, like many Indiana women, took on the responsibility of running the household at marriage. She has always worked outside the home, on a part-time basis in the past, but now full time in a career with a fast-growing computer application firm. As her responsibilities outside the home grew, she has repeatedly attempted to enlist her husband in the household tasks. He shows a passive resistive tendency in responding, agreeing to the assignments but often forgetting or delaying their execution. Alexis, for her part, while needing help, is also reluctant to give up her long-time power base. Ralph's practiced incompetence supports her primacy in household matters.

Today, Alexis has asked Ralph to pick up some things at the grocery store on the way home from work. Ralph examines the list and quizzes Alexis on the actual kind of lettuce (ruby leaf), ground beef (lean, not regular or extra lean), bread (wheat), and shampoo (see the coupon). In doing so, Alexis and Ralph reinvent her role as head housekeeper and his role as a visiting employee. Ralph could, of course, make all those decisions, but the move would be inappropriate to their well-practiced relationship.

Driving home in the 6 o'clock traffic, Ralph has to double back to the store remembering too late to make the turn. It was almost enough excuse to bag the whole expedition. Lettuce, meat, and bread are accomplished with reasonable efficiency. Turning down the "personal care" aisle, Ralph pulls the coupon his wife had given him and checks the brand—Revlon, 32-ounce size. He immediately recognizes the hole in the wall of products as the spot where that bottle ought to be. "Damn, she always wants something that isn't here," he thinks. The absence of the requested product forces Ralph into "action that will have to be explained." That fact opens up the space for a variety of performances. What may emerge from Ralph's decision is another passive aggressive episode ("I couldn't make a choice like that" or an attempt at "competent shopper"; "This brand is actually a better buy than the coupon one") or some other performance. The decision that Ralph has to make will be located in and interpreted from a number of places. On the face of it, the decision is part of the well-rehearsed practice of shopping. The rights and responsibilities of the shopper are in place and ready as criteria for the performance. The decision is also likely to involve his wife in their relationship vis-à-vis household responsibilities and easily moving across other areas. It may become embedded in his relationship with his daughter ("I thought you were going to buy some shampoo, Dad"). The decision requires a performance of self from Ralph as another materialization of who he is. That performance may also be a point of interpretation. Even in this rather limited analysis the potential dimensions of interpretation are many.

Some of this potential may have already been invoked prior to the actual entrance into the store. Alexis, in deciding to ask, may have reflected on Ralph's likely resistance. In the store, Ralph's attribution of blame "She always asks for something that isn't here" has the sound of empowering a particular interpretation that may influence later action. Whatever his decision, Ralph may be ready for a confrontation as he walks through his door, only to find a very sympathetic and appreciative

Alexis: "Thanks so much for doing this. It really is irritating when they run out like that." "Glad to," he may respond, "we've got to pull together." The potential of interpretive place is realized as the decision is presented to self and others. Ralph may recognize no alternative for representing himself in the decision, or he may debate the possibilities. Alexis may say nothing at all upon Ralph's arrival thereby denying one stance and allowing others. The uncertainty of outcome means that any effect of the decision will be improvised.

But for the moment, Ralph is still standing in front of the shampoo shelf. What do we need to know in order to make a reasonable prediction as to how he will decide? Basically we need to know whether the absence of the product is reason enough for Ralph to take action. The absence imposes the requirement of action but may not provide the basis for action. If Ralph and Alexis have a rule, "Never substitute on a coupon," absence is sufficient to accommodate the decision when the decision is interpreted within this rule. But there may be another clause in the relationship: "Ralph gets to buy whatever he wants when the requested item is missing." Alexis may supervise the first rule; Ralph, however, can invoke the second. The question of need may be made relevant— "How can I wash my hair with no shampoo?" (Lots of ways, of course, but none of them the "right way.")

In the final analysis it is Ralph himself who is the best predictor of the outcome according to the manner in which he reduces the indeterminacy of the alternatives. What set of conditions will he empower as he interprets the circumstances of the choice? The answer depends on what is available to him to make the move. Something useful may be available to him from his stock of information from the media. A commercial message or a news report may be the basis for identifying a product as an acceptable substitute. On the other hand, an article laying out tips for shopping may justify the no-substitution rule. Whatever decision Ralph makes will have to be made sensible from some interpretive stance, and most likely, from several stances. Whatever information is used, it will be used within that interpretation.

No media attendance by Ralph is best explained by the reason of Alexis's request. He doesn't watch TV, because a store may run out of shampoo. But one consequence of that attendance is about to be created as Ralph reaches his decision. Further, it is not the content attended that explains Ralph's action. It is Ralph's interpretation—his re-creation— of that content as sensible within the decision process that makes it work. Let's pick up Ralph again as he says, "Damn, she always asks for something that isn't here. Now I get to try this." Grabbing a bottle that advertises "A man's formula," he pushes on to the check-out line. Unpacking his purchases at home, Ralph is questioned about the substitution by Alexis, "How come you got this stuff?"

"Ah, they were out of what you wanted and that was the only one of the bunch that looked good."

"Good? Since when do you need a special formula? Does this stuff wash it or grow it?"

"Hey, watch it."

Sensing the potential argument, we'll leave Ralph and family. The point of the example is that a commercial viewed o such intent becomes justification for a decision when the circumstances are such that that decision has to be made. The claims made in the commercial are accepted at the decision point not because they are now seen as true but because the circumstances make it useful to accept them. It is those circumstances that permit that meaning to emerge.

We are continually faced with decisions that must be made. We must eat, clothe ourselves, provide ourselves with transportation, distinguish ourselves from others, fill our available time. We can use information from many sources to provide for those decisions. In doing so, we reinterpret the information within the very routines by which we accomplish these mundane responsibilities. Ralph's shopping is not independent but is referenced—to his sense of self, to his relationship with Alexis, and, perhaps, to his co-workers' commentary on his receding hair line. Given his performance of the routines that fill our lives, he would never walk into a store just to buy a bottle of "man's formula." It becomes a "permitted act," however, within the routine of his "shopping for Alexis," given the request, the rules, the absent product, the action at work, his persona within it, and his interpretation of the substitution.

Did the media play a part in Ralph's decision? Clearly. Could he have made the decision not having seen the commercial? Of course. Would Ralph have bought the product simply because he saw the commercial? Certainly not. Ralph, as a matter of practice, does not buy personal care products. Could that change? Yes. Ralph, however, could not simply walk in the door with a bag full of grooming goodies. Ralph understands the risk that Alexis and Heli would most certainly comment. He would need an explanation. He might find it in his daughter's *GQ*.[6]

There would be some beauty in such a move in that a good deal of his work would be done. First of all, it is both a common text between Ralph and Heli, and it supports the claims that Ralph would have to make. Ralph would not have to "educate" Heli about the acceptability of men's grooming aids, at least within some social quarters. Ralph can also use the fact that Heli commits herself to the reading of the magazine as a legitimation of those claims. Ralph can, further, use that text to introduce the legitimacy of his claims to Alexis.

There are some difficulties about that text too. Ralph may be considered by both Alexis and Heli as a person outside *GQ*'s purview—too old, too married, and so on. By appealing to *GQ*, Ralph might be seen as a midlifer deep in identity crisis. His actions could be read as a serious threat to the relationships involved. With a gesture to the pictures on her wall, Heli might exclaim, "I don't want my *dad* looking like this." Alexis might respond to the threat by appealing to the Yuppie caricatures that appear in the media, "Next thing you'll be wearing a gold chain and carrying one of those men's purses." Ralph might answer with claims of "dressing for power."

Note how readily we can find the content for this scenario from the media. The meaning of that content, however, finds its expression inside its appearance in this social action. Media content is one of many resources in the performance of our lives. Media use is another. Each finds its accommodation within and among the meaningful routines that fill our days.

TALKING POLITICAL SENSE

During the 1984 U.S. presidential campaign, a group of researchers conducted extended conversations with a selection of individuals from different parts of the country (Anderson, Avery, Burnett Pettus, Dipaolo Congalton, & Eastman, 1985). One point of the study was to discover how people made sense of the great outpouring of comment that fills the media during presidential campaigns. Conversations were held with each individual at the start of the campaign, in the middle, and at the end. The conversations were almost entirely unstructured, only the general topic was specified. Each conversation lasted at least 30 minutes. In this set of conversations, we listen in on how four people make sense of the vice presidential candidacies of Geraldine Ferraro and George Bush.

MARIANNE THOMSEN[7]

Interviewer: So, I guess we could start out by my asking you if you do have one of the candidates in mind that you are going to vote for?

Marianne: I would probably vote for Reagan. I've had a great soul-searching and I detest people who use personality to make a decision, but I do not personally like Fritz Mondale. I was crazy about his mentor, Hubert Humphrey. I feel all along that this man [Mondale] is just a politician's politician. Everyone is discouraged with the political. Now Ferraro—and not because of the women's movement or anything like that—but when I first read in *Time* magazine and I had seen a couple of shots on the TV news, I said to my husband, there's a woman I would vote for. I'm not out waving a flag for women, but I liked her. And he [her husband] said, how could you like her if you don't know anything about her. And I said, well I read in *Time* . . . [later in the conversation] I liked Ferraro when I saw her on TV very much. I have read glowing reports on her. Even though I knew she was a Tip O'Neill protege and I'm not an O'Neill fan. But I liked the way she addressed the issues. I liked her delivery. I liked everything about her. But not with Fritz. I do not like their program. Now if it were just between Ferraro and Bush, I would have a very difficult time, because, you see, I . . . [pause] maybe I hang on to lost dreams. But I think Bush is purposely staying undercover. He has refused from what—and everybody thinks they have inside information. I have relatives in Washington that are around the political scene. They aren't part of it, though. And I keep asking: In the Washington papers, is there anything with Bush? No, they say and he has refused to grant interviews. And I think maybe he's still the man I thought he was going to be. I just [pause] I just don't know.

MICHAEL RUSSELL

Interviewer: What about the vice presidential candidates? Does experience also mean anything to you there or do you really care?

Michael: I'm not really too concerned about the vice presidential candidates. I don't know why. I guess I'm just not. I could care less really if the vice-president's male or female when it comes right down to it. You know if they were a very, very outstanding individual or a very, very bad individual then I might look at them, but so far I haven't seen anything that's really made me stand up and look carefully at the vice president candidates. However, the financial disclosure stuff with Ferraro, I was a little concerned about that.

Interviewer: Did you have the same concern when there was a lot of talk about Bush's finances too?

Michael: No, for some reason I had them more against Ferraro. And I think that was probably because, you know maybe, I don't know why but for some reason I was more interested in her. She's Italian?

Interviewer: Yeah.

Michael: I think that's probably why. You always connect money, Italian and Mafia. [laughs] You know.

JOHN TAYLOR

John: Like I already warned you I'm not really into . . . I'm still uncommitted on the presidential election. The vice president, I've already chosen, though.

Interviewer: [laughs] Who do you like for vice?

John: Ferraro.

Interviewer: Do you?

John: Yeah. She's just more honest. I think she's sincere. She talks from her heart, and I think Bush has everything memorized and he's just trying to. . . . He just tries to please everybody in the public.

Interviewer: Yeah?

John: And I don't think he's being sincere. He's just doing what he just says, what everybody wants to hear.

Interviewer: You mean he's kind of a "yes" man?

John: Yeah. He just looks and sees what everybody favors, and then he'll go along with it. He doesn't say what he thinks would be better, things like that.

Interviewer: Did you see the debate?

John: Yeah.

Interviewer: Did that come across in the debate?

John: Yeah, I mean, I figure he won the debate, but I didn't like the way he approached the debate. She made a lot of mistakes, but she didn't have the knowledge. She doesn't have the, you know, he's got the experience because he's already been a vice president for four years. So, of course, he can answer a couple of questions better. But she wasn't going to make these real big decisions on a split second like in a debate, you know. She was going to take more time to think about it, and she just wasn't familiar with the topics. And him being in the White House already, he has the experience.

Interviewer: Yeah. You said you didn't like the way he handled himself?

John: No. I mean he just handles himself too coolly. It's like he doesn't . . . Everything's memorized. Everything's, you know, I just don't like his attitude [laughs].

JEAN GOODWIN

Jean: There's no reason why a woman could not be president. I've always said women are more diversified than men. I see this in our family. Women can take care of the baby, cook dinner, clean the house, answer the telephone, do 15 things at once, and get them all done on time as they should be done. My husband cannot clean the garage and barbecue chickens without burning the chickens. Men can do well what they do, but they do them one thing at a time. I see this so often and by so many men. By working with men in two or three of the jobs I've been in, men do one thing, and if you ask them something else, they're totally wiped out. They cannot continue. So, I'm not too sure that a woman wouldn't be great in the White House, to take care of the warfares and do all these things at once which is, I'm sure, necessary for a president now.

Interviewer: That's an interesting view [laughs]. Think Geraldine could do that?

Jean: I don't know, she may. Right now she seems to be a fighter. I don't know, she seems to be very defensive. She's a nitpicking lady, I think. She finds little things and she digs at them. I don't think this is necessary. She's got a lot more talent. She's beneath herself doing this. I think she's a very, very brilliant woman. She shouldn't be going this low with herself. She should hold her head up and give her qualifications.

Interviewer: I think her qualifications have been questioned. . . .

Jean: Oh I think she got a terribly dumb deal over what her husband made. It's nobody's cotton-picking business what her husband made. What she makes is all that's at stake. They don't ask what Nancy Reagan made or what Mrs. Mondale made in a year. I'm sure Nancy Reagan made a hefty salary going out speaking for all those events she did. She doesn't do that for free, I'm sure, and yet, they didn't ask for her financial statement. She could have come from a wealthy family. So, I think that was a terribly dumb deal. I think it was only setting precedent since she was the first lady for this position.

Interviewer: Yeah.

Jean: And I just really feel she got ripped over good on that. It's nobody's business. And that did not sway me in either direction on how I felt.

AN EXEGESIS

We can clearly see Jean and Michael making sense of the same mediated information (the financial disclosures about Ferraro's husband) in radically different ways. Both Jean and Michael are Reagan supporters, but for Michael the disclosures confirm an old prejudice and are one more reason to vote against the Mondale/Ferraro team. Michael has no apparent difficulty in simply dismissing the negative information about Bush. For Jean, Ferraro is the victim of a muckraking press. Perhaps, more confident in her Reagan decision, she does not use the financial information as part of her decision. At the same time, however, she is not pro-Ferraro. She finds her flawed—"nitpicking . . . beneath herself." She upholds the principle of a woman in the White House, but not this woman.

John takes Bush's smooth, cool approach and Ferraro's inexperience and lack of knowledge and makes them a liability for Bush and a positive factor for Ferraro. His argument makes the most of Ferraro's "soul" and "heart" and devalues the slick performance he sees with Bush.

Marianne has won an argument with her husband by appealing to a source he apparently respects—*Time* magazine. In an earlier part of the conversation not presented here, she carefully tempered her remarks about that source saying that she knew of its Republican bias, most likely anticipating a response from her college-aged interviewer. Marianne's comments are a good example of the shifting value of information as one moves from one situation to another.

The analysis of political campaigns is particularly vulnerable to post hoc reasoning. In every election, there is a winner. The claim that this event or that event was significant is verified in the fact that this individual won and that individual lost. It is the outcome that creates the significance of events within the campaign. Unfortunately for the validity of the claim made, the outcome of any election is simply the aggregate of thousands of decisions, each ecologically located in some social action. In all but the fewest of cases, each of these voting decisions is bounded by a history of such decisions and an ideology that directs it. In a series of presidential campaign studies we have conducted since 1976 (Anderson & Avery, 1978; Anderson, Avery, Burnett Pettie, Dipaolo Congalton, & Eastman, 1986; Anderson & Avery, 1988), over 80% of voters living in family settings had determined their candidate of choice following the presidential conventions but prior to the "official start" of the campaign. It is clear that the cultural significance of these national campaigns is something other than the persuasion of a large undecided electorate. One cannot have it both ways: An analyst cannot boast about the power of the media to effect voting without noting that in most elections, it is the majority that does not vote at all, and the majority of voters make their choices independent of the campaign efforts.

In all of the conversations audited here, we see the obvious presence of the media. What these respondents know about the candidates is what is presented in the media. That presentation, nevertheless, is not capable of evoking a consistent response. To begin with, that presentation is conflicted and incoherent. But more importantly, from our perspective, substantial work of interpretation is conducted by these participants to accommodate the workings of their own social environment. Individuals bound in their own networks of interaction come to different conclusions working from the same information.

SUMMARY

The thrust of this section on performances has been to locate seemingly independent and isolated acts that involve media use inside the ongoing social action in which they arise. The effects of mediated content cannot be determined from the characteristics of that content alone. Significant to the analysis of effects are the interpretations of content accomplished by recipients and the potential outcomes empowered by the premises of action. It is of no significance that a piece of content be judged violent by an analyst when recipients interpret that content as fantasy, childish, or in other ways incapable of directing behavior, or if the premises of action do not enable aggressive acts.

Any consequence of mediated content is an improvisational performance under local control that partially represents the variety of performances incorporated within the boundaries of the premises of action.

CENTRAL IDEAS OF SECTION III: PERFORMANCES

1. Any media product, even those attributed to a single author, arises within an enabling community and has contributions from various sources. The content of the media is, therefore, a joint effort, even if ostensibly produced by a single person, and ownership is a social practice.
2. Communal codes of workmanship are referenced even in nonconforming production.
3. Media texts are reinterpreted within the social action context of their application. "Others" will always participate in this context. The particular interpretation accomplished will be improvised in an accommodation with local conditions.
4. Attendance to the media is a routine in its own right, provides a common currency of exchange, and can be seen as an act of provisioning of enabling and rhetorical texts.
5. Content of the media is accepted or rejected within the social action frame of the interpreter. The so-called same content can, therefore, receive opposing interpretations.
6. Certain mediated content, such as news, public events, and campaigns, are better understood as ritualistically reaffirming certain truths rather than serving informational or persuasive ends.

CHAPTER SUMMARY

This chapter began with the claim that our lives are jointly produced. It rejected the traditional Western notion of the autonomous individual operating as a self-contained microcosm of society. It posited, rather, the "I" as an incomplete and partial representation of "Us," the site of the coordinated, mutually supervised life world of human accomplishment.

In order to understand social action, we reversed the common order of analysis, which starts with some independent, elemental act and moves through a linear chain of causality to action, and began our analysis with a view from the top down, where elemental acts have meaning according to the premises of action. These premises of action are organized within a semiotic we call a routine. A routine is the understanding that we have about what is being done.

The understanding of the causes and consequences of any act arises within the routine of its practice. An act of interpretation of some mediated content, then, is understandable according to the premises of its performance.

A performance within a routine is an improvisation accountable to the premises of the routine. As an improvisation it is under local control—negotiated by the actors—and a partial representation of possible performances within that routine.

It is in performances that we find social action. Social action is that set of jointly produced, mutually supervised, improvisational performances of the culturally accountable routines that constitute and reproduce our understandings of the world.

Media use appears within that set of performances as an embedded component of social action. Media use, therefore, varies according to performance rules, the meanings or significance one holds for that performance, the personal and communal history of performance, the local conditions of performance, the ecology of routines, and the relevant communal networks, to give only a partial list. How media become an often integral part of our daily lives both helps and hurts our attempts neatly and clearly to classify mediated effects. The theoretical perspective one uses, the assumptions one makes, and the methods selected to study media effects combine to determine how effects are defined and interpreted. The often confusing and elusive search for such media "effects" is the theme of the next chapter.

NOTES

1. An accounting can be made by anticipating or extrapolating a response from another, by working from "texts" of the performance of others or those of the media (e.g., this is how something is done). Even when we hike into the mountains to be alone, we follow the trails made by others.

2. Habits are methods by which we reduce the burden of choice. If one always gets up at 6 o'clock, the uncertainty of each day is reduced by that much. Habits can be tied in with routine performances, but can also move across routines. Getting up at 6 on a Sunday morning permits a different statement about oneself from getting ready for work on Monday morning. Routines do not determine performances, but performances account for the routine in which they are performed and are judged according to the criteria of the routine of which they are presumed to be an expression.

3. The term *media use* refers to any interpretive act involving the content or technology (knowledge, texts, devices, and practices) of our public media (television, radio, recordings, film, books, newspapers, magazines, in some circles, computers, and so on). It does not depend on intention or purpose or outcome, although such may be present.

4. Not acting is as important as acting in these systems. For example, our system of government works well or poorly depending on the criteria in place, but it does work. Historically, however, for it to work the way it does the majority of enfranchised citizens *must not vote.*

5. This episode is based on a series of notes taken over a two-week period. No particular morning is described, however.

6. Many will recognize *GQ* as a men's fashion magazine that has also found great favor among high school—and older—women.

7. Names and places have been disguised but gender is preserved. The conversations have been slightly edited to bring the spoken grammar more in line with the written form.

RELATED READINGS

Bryce, J. (1987). Family time and television use. In T. Lindlof (Ed.), *Natural audiences: Qualitative research of media uses and effects* (pp. 121-138). Norwood, NJ: Ablex.

The author presents a discussion of how three different families studied over an extended period of time come to different patterns of use and meanings for television as medium and for its content. Her research provides a clear demonstration of how the meanings arrived at for television's content cannot be determined by an examination of the content independent of the context in which that content is interpreted or of those engaged in the interpretation. A small part of the chapter seeks to compare some of the findings from the three families with interview results from another sample. This comparison is less successful.

Gunter, B. (1988). The perceptive audience. In J. A. Anderson (Ed.), *Communication yearbook 11* (pp. 22-50). Newbury Park, CA: Sage.

Biocca, F. A. (1988). Opposing conceptions of the audience: The active and passive hemispheres of mass communication theory. In J. A. Anderson (Ed.), *Communication yearbook 11* (pp. 51-80). Newbury Park, CA: Sage.

Lindlof, T. (1988). Media audiences as interpretive communities. In J. A. Anderson (Ed.), *Communication yearbook 11* (pp. 81-107). Newbury Park, CA: Sage.

These three authors provide a symposium on approaches to understanding audiences and their relationship to mediated content. Gunter takes an enlightened social science view that grants the audience some control over the effects of exposure to content. Biocca is more traditional, seeing the audience member as being in the vortex of influences beyond control. Lindlof takes an interpretive stance (more to our liking) that holds that the effects of the media are in the interaction between the content, the semiotic community of membership, and the individual audience member. See also the sections that follow (pp. 108-146, same volume) in which each author comments on the positions held by the others.

Traudt, P., Lont, C. (1987). Media-logic-in-use: The family as locus of study. In T. Lindlof (Ed.), *Natural audiences: Qualitative research of media uses and effects* (pp. 121-138). Norwood, NJ: Ablex.

While stretching to impose a preexisting framework onto their analysis of how a family uses media, the authors, nonetheless, provide a useful description of how the social context and related interpretations of family members are used to maintain this construction of social reality. Also of interest are the ways in which parental uses and interpretations of media are used in the socialization of their children. The material on what was learned about the particular family studied can be read separately from the theoretical framework introduced in the first part of the chapter.

Part II

The Search for Effects

5

In Search of Effects

BRAD SAMSON'S WIFE had dragged him out to the PTA meeting last night. They had a speaker from Chicago who had traced most of society's ills to too much television. Brad had found a new crusade that night to carry him through his middle years and was trying to recruit his neighbor, Milt, while they pulled their adjoining dandelions.

"Milt, you just don't understand, there's children all over this country, right now glued to the TV set. Their minds soaking up that swill that the networks pump out day after day."

"Well, my kids watch a lot of TV and though they're not the best in the world, I like 'em. They don't seem to have had their little psyches hurt."

"Oh, sure, but you're a responsible parent. I mean you take care of your kids."

"Aren't most parents responsible?"

"Now, listen, we're talking about the ghetto kids. The ones who smash windows, steal cars, smoke dope. Do you know that research shows that those lower income groups are among the heaviest users of TV?"

"Does TV make 'em poor?"

"It makes 'em poor in the head!"

"Come on Brad, you know as well as I do, that Barbi next door is a TV zombie, to use your words, yet she does OK in school and I've never seen her steal a hubcap much less a car."

"Damn it Milt, you just won't understand, will you?"

Media effects are real and imaginary, impressive and elusive. The media are unmistakably a part of everyday life in our culture. Some estimates suggest that about one-third of the U.S. population is watching television during any prime time minute, about one-half wake up to radio, some 50 million households receive newspapers and magazines, and each week, movie theater box offices ring up millions of dollars in ticket sales. All that participation is itself a "media effect" and is the prime move behind a great deal of social concern and scientific interest. It is also what makes the analysis of media effects so very difficult. Consider the following:

(1) Almost every item in a supermarket is advertised in one way or another. Yet, we all have to eat. If one buys an advertised product, is that a media effect? Further, if advertising shifts food choices from one brand to another, though important for the manufacturer, is that effect socially trivial or important?

(2) The newspaper reports of the early 1900s of the authors' western states are replete with killings, robberies, rustling, and barroom fights. Were the newspaper depictions the cause?

(3) Teenage pregnancy rates per thousand population have been estimated to have risen and fallen at various times during the past five decades. Why is television (or rock and roll lyrics) now the cause for its present direction?

(4) College aptitude test scores have shown a steady decline for the past 20 years, yet a steadily increasing percentage of the population is attending college. Could the media be responsible for both?

(5) Media effects research has shown that viewing media violence increases the likelihood of subjects in the laboratory responding with greater aggression, but most prime-time viewers watch TV without starting a brawl in the living room. Do media have different effects in different conditions?

If there is anything consistent about media effects, it is in their inconsistency, contrariness, and contradictions. This inconsistency of effect and impact emanates from the interplay of the media and other institutions as elements in a cultural soup. The metaphor is apt, for just as in a well-prepared soup, one can identify the individual contributions; nevertheless, they cannot be separated from the effect of the whole. That is our problem, that media effects are cultural effects as well. And that any media effect on individuals can also occur in individuals independent of the media. Consider, for example, the purchase of a breakfast cereal. One can easily analyze the popularity of generic cold cereals without reference to the media: They are satisfying, good tasting, quick, efficient, can be served by a child, can be stored for long periods without special care, are readily available, and offer many choices of selection. They provide, in short, a response to obvious consumer needs and demand.

On the other hand, no major cereal manufacturer would introduce a new brand into the market without a well-orchestrated media campaign including television, newspapers, cents-off coupons, and point-of-purchase displays. The success of cold cereals is clearly not media generated or media dependent, but the successful introduction of a new entry into the field may be.

This chapter begins a "search for effects" that will not end until the final section of Chapter 8. The reason it is a search for effects rather than a catalogue of effects is that the effects one sees depend on where one stands on media theory, analytic methods, and the purposes of research. This chapter explores the concept of effect as it is constituted in the various theories and perspectives taken in the study of media. Chapters 6 and 7 will examine the analytic methods of social science for the manner in which they establish the character of evidence. And finally, Chapter 8 will analyze the nature and purpose of how theory, claim, and method come together in a study to produce useful statements about the effects of mediated communication.

In this search for effects, our work of the first four chapters establishes the standards we will use to evaluate the theory, method, and claim that we find along the way. The reader, therefore, can anticipate our difficulties in this chapter with theories that do not account for the interactive nature of communication, ignore the realities of production in mediated communication, or do not provide for the interpretive accomplishments of an audience. The chapter is divided into three sections: The first examines how effects are defined within different perspectives and provides an analysis of the major perspectives that populate the study of mediated communication. The second considers the confusion that often arises in considering the power of the media to create an effect and the **scale** of its operation. Scale, as we shall see, is often mistaken for **power.** The last section looks at the affinities of the different theories of media effects for different analytic methods and considers their consequences.

SECTION I: THEORIES OF EFFECTS

DEFINING EFFECTS

An effect is some circumstance that would not have occurred without the presence of some other circumstance. An effect, then, requires an agent and a reactant in a relationship. Theories of effects vary over what they define as the agent (it can be content, intent, interpretation, and so on), what they specify as the reaction (behavior, beliefs, social structures), and the characteristics they ascribe to the relationship (indirect, direct, culturally or socially mediated, and so on). In the sections that follow, we provide an overview of the different kinds of effect definitions that appear in the research literature.

INDIRECT EFFECTS

In the study of activity, the simplest effect is probably the trade-off. Assuming some degree of exclusivity and alternatives, going to a movie means not doing something else. Currently, claims are being made that television is a leading cause of obesity in children. The reasoning used follows the trade-off effect pattern. Children watching television are not exercising and are, therefore, gaining weight. If they were out slopping the hogs, kicking a soccer ball, or running from the police, they would be in a more healthy condition in obesity terms. Obviously television viewing does not directly cause obesity, but, in this argument, contributes to weight gain by not providing for exercise. Trade-off effects have been implicated in school performance, church attendance, participation in politics, marital discord, and other social activities.

DIRECT EFFECTS

A trade-off is considered an indirect effect in that the consequence cannot be explained by the choice alone. A more direct effect would be shown if the content of television induced viewers to overeat (a claim also part of the obesity argument). To see the difference, consider that in the first case, turning off the television set would not necessarily lead to more healthy activities, but in the second case, turning off the television set would eliminate the influence of the commercials for snack and fast foods that are claimed to induce overeating.

The concept of a direct effect varies widely in definition according to how direct and how immediate the effect is. Directness is determined by the number of other conditions that must be accounted for in the relationship between content and behavior. Less direct effects require the presence of other conditions such as prior states of mind, enabling response conditions, and/or type of respondent before the relationship is exercised. Immediacy has two components: The first concerns the number of exposures before an effect occurs; the second is how long the effect will stay in place once established. The first component distinguishes between "single dose" and cumulative effects. Cumulative effects are the consequences of repeated exposures. For example, the presentation of particular images of women and men over and over again is said to establish the expected values of these images. Women and men are supposed to be as they appear in the media. These effects are still direct effects in that exposure is the governing condition.

The second component gives rise to classifications of short-term and long-term effects. Short-term effects have to be executed quickly or they dissipate; long-term effects remain in place, exciting a demand for resolution for a lengthier period. (The analogy to the effect of a drug is apparent.)

Direct effects then are understood according to a three dimensional classification scheme: The first dimension is the contingency requirements of the relationship between exposure to content and resultant behavior (noncontingent versus contingent); the second is the number of exposures needed before the effect occurs (single dose versus cumulative) and the third is the length of time the demand for the effect remains in place (short-term versus long-term).

The power of an effect is usually evaluated in terms of directness and immediacy. The most powerful effect would be one in which the presence of A (exposure to content) leads inevitably to the condition of B (resultant behavior) with the need of few if any concurrent states and the demand for B remains in place over a long time. For example, if you settle down with a newspaper, see an advertised product, and with no prior interest in or knowledge of the product, make a purchase decision that you maintain over a period of time on the basis of that single reading, that is a powerful direct effect. On the other hand, if you are in the market for a product that has wide acceptance in the culture, have studied the choices, determined prices, and so on, and make the decision to buy at a dealer who advertises a special sales price, that is a much less powerful effect. We have little evidence of direct media effects of the first kind and much evidence of the second. Both of these effects are called direct effects, but clearly we would be much more concerned with the more powerful of the two.

Nevertheless, we are also concerned about the subtlety of cumulative effects, particularly with those who make frequent use of the media. Though it may take multiples of exposures before consequences appear, the effect on the frequent user is just a matter of time. (We often read a note of insidiousness in the analyses of such effects as if the media were "sneaking up" on us.)

FUNCTIONS AS EFFECTS

In most of the research and social activist literature, effects both indirect and direct are considered outside the control of the media user. When the consequences of media use are sought after, a third category of effects is created. These effects are called **functions.** Generally, functions are the purposes served by behavioral, institutional, or cultural structures. The functions of media can be invoked at the societal level (as in, "The function of a newspaper is to create informed citizens") and at the individual level (as in, "I watch television to forget my troubles").

INTERINSTITUTIONAL EFFECTS

When the institutions of society are considered in relation to one another, it is clear that the practices of one institution have effects on the action of others. The effects of these interrelationships establish the institutional ecology of a society. For example, technological changes in the telecommunication industry have greatly affected the practice of political campaigns, the operation of businesses, and the conduct of government.

CULTURAL EFFECTS

A fifth category of effects has developed in the research of the past decade. These effects are called cultural effects. Culture in this formulation is the set of reality constructions that are actively maintained by a collectivity into which we are born. As we become enculturated, we learn these constructions as the set of naturalized, unquestioned assumptions about how things are (e.g., we are the people, and they are our enemy). The cultural effects claimed for the media are of two kinds: (1) the long-term creation or modification of cultural premises sometimes called ideology; (2) participation in the maintenance process usually called hegemony.

The study of cultural effects is currently divided into rival camps (see S. Becker, 1984; Hardt, in press; or Hall, 1985) each making an exclusive claim on these terms that makes any attempt to sort them out inadequate. Nonetheless, there is some useful central tendency around each of these terms. Ideology is the more widely dispersed of the two. When not coupled with hegemony, it refers simply to the underlying set of beliefs that enable a society. In this reasoning, it is a static force.

Hegemony is a larger term that describes a dynamic process by which a particular social structure (usually based on class, race, or gender in these writings) is maintained. Hegemony is larger because it assumes the management of multiple ideologies with the dominant one.

In the formulations that treat ideology as a static force, creation (or maintenance) effects depend on the consistent presence of particular texts or textual genres within the media. In a manner similar to cumulative effects, the presence of these texts and their premises of narrative action provide for the premises of social action as well. (We have encountered this idea in our study of logics of media in Chapter 3.) Modification effects depend on the persistent presence of oppositional texts. The civil rights movement and the Vietnam conflict have often been cited as examples of the modification of cultural premises that grounded civil action through the media presentation of oppositional content. While such claims are often self-serving and usually ignore the extended interpersonal networking efforts that existed long before media attention, they do suggest media participation in an effect.

Hegemony effects involve cultural processes that maintain the power of the dominant structural element. Culture is an enactment, a performance by one and another in all the interactions of the collectivity. The continual reenactment of its premises is the process by which a culture is maintained. A culture contains a set of fundamental power relationships that govern the status and conduct of individuals. These power relationships inscribe the hegemony or the "proper order" of a culture. When the media resolve narratives, describe events, or project images in accord with this proper order then they are said to participate in the hegemony of the culture. Therefore, when women are presented as supporting members of a patriarchy or the aged as members of lesser capacity, the proper order of gender and life span is maintained.

On the other hand, the presence of oppositional text is also said to provide for the good continuation of this order. Oppositional text permits the expression and release of the tensions within the structure, thereby abrogating the power of that tension to institute change. In this view, while both the civil rights movement and the Vietnam movement instituted new directions, the fundamental structure remained in place, resistant to change.

The creation, maintenance, modification, and extinction of cultural premises are in the purview of every social institution no less or more than the media. Obviously, however, not every institution is equally powerful or powerful in every circumstance. We have had few comparative analyses of the cultural effects of institutions, whether ideological or hegemonic. Analysts have generally selected a single institution and sought to show the influence of that institution on some subset of notions. It is most likely that any premise is widely connected within the institutions of society; that is, after all, the underlying concept of culture.

ACCOMMODATION EFFECTS

There is one final set of effects that we tentatively advance here and spend considerable time with in the final chapter. We call these effects accommodations. They involve the appearance of media and mediated texts in the social action routines of everyday life. Because they are the product of accommodation theory, we will hold their discussion for that chapter.

AN ANALYTIC SUMMARY

These categories of effects can themselves be grouped into three types: those that aim at explaining consequences for the individual; those that explain institutional consequences; and those with a cultural focus. Indirect, direct, and **microfunctional** effects are explanations for the individual; **macrofunctional** effects concern institutions as do the accommodations that other social institutions make of the media; and cultural effects, obviously, cultural.

Within each of the individual, institutional, and cultural levels, we can further direct our study according to the three major divisions of understanding: **ontology, praxiology,** and **epistemology.** These divisions, in their turn, approach the questions of "What is it (ontology)?" "How does it get done (praxiology)?" and "Why does it happen (epistemology)?" Full understanding requires answers to all three questions, that is, we must understand the nature of an action and how it gets done in order to comprehend fully why it happens.

Most of the study of media effects (indeed the very word *effects* implies the approach) has been from an epistemological framework. Effects are seen as consequences, the "why" of which is explained by the media. In only very recent times have scientists begun to approach the major questions of "what" and "how." As a result, we have very little scientific understanding of what it means to watch television, read a newspaper, listen to the radio (except "what everybody knows"). We cannot describe with any richness of detail the wide variety of how attendance to the media gets done, though we know from individual experience the many different conditions in which media play a part. Readers, then, will have to be sophisticated in supplying the essence and conduct of the variables scientists are attempting to explain as cause or consequence. Effects studies have admitted little variety in the nature and context of performance in their analysis of human behavior. These studies must be understood from their limited perspective. With this caveat in mind, we begin the analysis of individual effects.

INDIVIDUAL EFFECTS

Effects on the individual are at once the most enticing to study and the least likely to provide one's study with success. Each of us operates within a complex communication matrix. To isolate a single communication event or even the content of a single medium as the primary source of some significant behavior is for all intents and purposes, impossible. Scientific study of individual effects, then, ends up as a catalogue of "might be's," "could be's," and "may be's." In short, no scientist can explain why you voted for the candidate of your choice as opposed to all the others in the campaign; why you purchase some advertised products and not others; why you select to watch some programs and not others. Scientists can construct plausible scenarios for those decisions, but cannot show evidence for **causal relationships** or even adequate probabilistic models. We cannot know, therefore, the effect of the media on violence, sex, change, what have you in our society because we have nothing to compare it to. There is no way to show the functioning of our society without media.

In the process of constructing these plausible scenarios in the arena of individual effects, scientists have typically made use of different models of the agent (content), the reactant (the audience) and the relationship (manner in which content affects the audience). Before discussing these differences, let us offer a word about models: Models are scientific metaphors. They serve to organize one's thinking; determine the variables of interest and their relationships, and they direct the course of analysis. Most often they are used to accomplish those things without any overt expression. Reading scientific articles, you will not find a description of a model. Rather the model is where the scientist is "coming from." It is his or her view of reality. It need not be spoken because it is obvious, taken for granted. Models, then, are the creation and the tools of those who study scientists. They are aids to classification; they specify the unspoken postulates that are the foundation of a particular avenue of study. In doing so, models identify the conceptual and pragmatic limits of the approach, and every approach has these limits. Finally, scientists generally do not like to be classified, to be identified with a particular model. They would rather consider themselves to be doing "their damnedest" to generate new knowledge unfettered by ways of thinking. Such is not, nor can it be the case.

Knowledge must be shared, and to be shared it must be understood within a context of acceptable axioms.

To return to the models of agent, reactant, and relationships within the study of individual effects, there is a dominant model of content, two descriptions of the audience and three relationship models that organize most of the literature in the area. A description of each follows.

CONTENT MODEL(S) IN INDIVIDUAL EFFECTS

The primary model of content used in most individual effects studies is that of a meaning delivery system. Content is a "closed text" whose right interpretation can be practiced by any competent auditor. The interpretation practiced by the researcher becomes the fixed reference for the analysis of all other interpretations. Different interpretations are seen as "distortions" or "biases" or "errors" or the result of "insufficiencies" of development, experience, or training. (To paraphrase Professor Higgins: "Why can't a child be more like an adult; why can't they all . . . be like me!")

Recent developments in theory but not research practice have offered, as we have seen, the concept of the open text that motivates multiple interpretations, all of equal standing. The closest approximation we have seen in research applications have been studies that explain different interpretations by virtue of differences in training, motivation, or socialization practices. Even in these studies, however, the potential of meaning is fixed in the content because the clear implication of the analysis is that if we all had the same training, motivation, and socialization, we would all produce the same interpretation. Differences in motivation, and so on, actualize different meaning potentials of the text. Interpretation is not seen as an achievement of an interpreter but as a consequence of the text characteristics coming in contact with the external and internal characteristics of reception.

There are good reasons why we would expect this "delivery system" model to remain dominant in research while theory continues to explore the achievement metaphor. Most social science explanations require a single vision of content in order to make their claims; many theorists are dissatisfied with the restrictions that this requirement places on our understanding. But we are surely ahead of ourselves as these are points to be developed in the next several chapters. For now, we turn to models of the audience.

AUDIENCE MODELS IN INDIVIDUAL EFFECTS

We have two longstanding and opposing conceptions of the audience in mediated communication research and the recent development of a synthetic position somewhere distant from these two. The earliest tradition is that of the passive audience often called the media influence model. This model held that "rightly formed" messages were nearly irresistible by the common person. Only the specially educated could be inoculated against them. The passive audience was called up in horrifying visions of the masses being led by tyrants which, given the history of the 1930s and 1940s, may have appeared to be the case.

By the early 1960s, however, Bauer (1964) had introduced his notion of the "obstinate audience," and Klapper (1960) had determined that effects were contingent on a "nexus of **mediating factors.**" In this conceptualization, the audience became an active processor of messages: It could resist the seductions of media and could even deliberately use mediated messages for its own purposes. While these arguments were sufficient to lead to a viewer control model, they were not sufficient to extinguish the media influence model. These two conceptions of the audience—the media influence model or the viewer control model—continue to dominate research.

The third—as yet developing—concept of the audience is that of audience communities. Membership, whether explicit or implicit, in an audience community produces the ideological frame in which interpretation is practiced. The model of communities has had nearly no presence in the study of individual effects but is common in cultural studies, being particularly apparent in hegemony studies.

In practical terms, nearly all studies of individual effects can be located on the active/passive continuum. It is also not unusual for a study to jump its position from an initial passive position in hypotheses to more "active" explanations when the results are not clear. In the next section, we will see how models of relationships make use of these different conceptions of content and audience.

RELATIONAL MODELS IN INDIVIDUAL EFFECTS

Relational models explain how content and the audience are bound together in power relationships. There are three models: The exposure model grants most of the power to content and little to the audience; uses and gratifications, however, grants more power to the audience; the interactive model grants power to both. An explanation of each model follows:

EXPOSURE MODEL When scientists use content characteristics or attributes as the source for subsequent behavior they are operating from the exposure model. The major works in media effects have been conducted from this model: Media violence as the instigator of subsequent aggression, campaign effects, children's advertising, and the like are all content dependent. The model makes a number of assumptions that are instructive to inspect. First, in general, the model requires meaning to reside primarily in the content (content as delivery system). That is to say that meanings for words, images, persuasive techniques, plots, settings, and so on, are commonly understood by the viewers or, at least, functionally equivalent. We can essentially agree on what is violent, funny, persuasive, informative, educational, entertaining. If it is not true that meanings reside primarily in the structure of the message, then what is violence to the experimenter might be seen as simply foolish to the respondent, which would, of course, negate any conclusions the experimenter might wish to draw about the effect of violent content.

The second major assumption is that there is a causal or **conditional relationship** between the content presented and the subsequent behavior noted as an "effect." Causal and conditional relationships both posit a direct connection between some antecedent condition (as a television commercial) and some consequent condition (as the buying of a chewing gum). The difference between the two lies in the strength of the relationship. Causal relationships are one to one: If A, then B with no "buts." Conditional relationships are probabilistic. If A, then B is likely (but not surely) to follow. Both causal and conditional relationships imply that if one wishes to control the consequent condition, one controls the antecedent. Consequently, if purchasing behavior is desired to be controlled, one controls or manipulates advertising messages (power to content).

The third major assumption is that the individual who attends to media messages is essentially a passive recipient of the message (media influence model). That is, exposure is the sufficient condition; the message works its magic with little resistance offered by the audience member. In its egregiously elitist form, this assumption of audience passivity expresses itself as justification for protectionist moves primarily directed toward children and outgroups (the poor, the ethnically unassimilated, and so on).

Because the strong media influence model is rarely supported in research findings, researchers have been directed to analyze the internal and external conditions that mediate the effects of exposure. In the violence studies, for example, the greatest effect occurs with respondents who have been angered prior to exposure, and are given the opportunity to aggress against an appropriate target in a socially approved action. When those four conditions are present and exposure occurs, content effects are heightened. Note that no internal, cognitively mediating action by the respondent (such as interpretation) is used in the explanation.

The exposure model is, of course, an epistemological model. It casts the content and technology of the media as an explanation of "why" subsequent behaviors occur. While focusing on content, it does not provide insight into the nature of content (how it transmits meaning) or how content is created, or the nature of attendance in its variety of expression. On the other hand, it makes no claim for these insights. The readers' problem, then, is to determine whether such things make a difference.

USES AND GRATIFICATIONS The uses and gratifications model shifts primary attention away from the content of the message to the needs and purposes of the individual. The model is based on the notion that the individual selects media material for some purpose, to accomplish some end, to gain some satisfaction (viewer control model). Content does not do something to the individual; rather individuals do things with content. Content is no longer the reference point as different uses can be found by different individuals for the same content. Content, then, is not seen as a reliable predictor of use.

In the exposure model, individuals are seen as responsive to the content of the media. In the uses and gratifications model, the content of the media is seen as responsive to the needs of the individual audiences. Particular forms of content come to the fore in a circulation-driven system not because of manipulative decision making by media moguls, but because of consumer demand. Content is shaped by its utility. For the uses and gratifications theorist, a clear example of consumer demand on the content of the media has been the changes in newspaper content over the last decade. The growth and proliferation of "leisure living," "suburban life," "dining out," and "entertainment" sections have shifted the balance from hard news and advertising to soft news and advertising in many newspapers.

In the uses and gratifications model, media are a tool for the solution of some individual need. There may be some side effects along the way, but the control of individual effects does not reside in the control of content. Restrict some content needed by a given audience in a given medium, and that audience will simply seek it or its equivalent elsewhere. This maxim includes advertising content. Controlling gum purchases, to continue our example, does not begin with the control of advertising messages but with an understanding of the reasons why individuals chew gum! Gum commercials are simply a response to an audience's need for information about a product they want. Consider any of the many substances that are not advertised in the media. Demand creates a supply and builds an information structure about that supply. (One's imagination springs to clandestine gum runners bombing remote Utah deserts with thousands of Chicklets.)

The most individualized version of the uses and gratifications model can be summarized as follows: Some purpose (demand, need, want, desire), conscious or not, initiates some behavior to serve that purpose. When the use serves the initial purpose, gratifications are gained that heighten the likelihood that should the need again arise, one's solution would be the same. In short, motives for action arise within the individual, direct the individual toward action, and provide the criteria for determining satisfaction. For example, if one is motivated by information-seeking, then the work of attending to the news will be in extracting and remembering information and the satisfactions of that work will be in the information gained. On the other hand, if one is attending for reasons of sodality then the parasocial components of the newscast—the interactions and reactions of the newscasters—become the focus, the work is the bond between auditor and anchor, and the satisfactions are affective.

More sociological versions of this model are seeing the demand for media use arising in different life-styles that can be led rather than the psychologistic explanations of individual purposes. If, for whatever reasons, one is lead to be, say, upwardly mobile in a particular social unit, then certain behaviors, including certain uses of the media, will be demanded by that life-style. (We provide an extended analysis of one such study in Chapter 8.)

Finally, one line of uses and gratifications studies has begun to study the problem of the relationship between the gratification sought (the notion of purpose) and gratifications obtained. Because these studies do not show a one-to-one relationship between **gratifications sought** and **gratifications obtained,** the purpose-use-gratification chain comes into question. The consequence of these results for the model are yet to be known. It is clear that when gratifications sought do not match gratifications obtained in a continuing practice of use, then the model will be forced to move from its traditional teleological formulation. That movement may be underway.

The uses and gratifications model is useful for explaining why institutions develop (to serve use demands), how they are shaped by consumer demands, and to describe patterns of human behavior. Its problems are those of any functional analysis: We must infer purpose or social demand from use, and for every use, there must be a purpose or some motive for that use. The model produces its greatest explanatory power when it can document a necessary, one-to-one relationship between use and purposes. When purpose does not match gratification and use does not change, the traditional explanation breaks down. And last, because the theory is epistemological, it gives us no insight into the nature of purposes and uses or how they arise or get fulfilled.

INTERACTIVE MODEL In general terms, the interactive model argues that the primary behavioral meaning for the individual is constructed by the individual from the symbolic content that has been presented. That is, meaning is in the interaction between content and its user. That meaning can change from individual to individual and within the same individual from time to time.

Let's give some examples. Suppose four students walked into a classroom and found this message written on the board: "The 9:00 Mass Communication Effects class has been canceled today. Go to Union 323 for the news conference at 11:00. Attendance will be taken." First of all, let's assume that all four individuals are competent members of this culture and native speakers of English. These two assumptions assure that the four will receive the same literal meaning from the message. They will know that the class will not meet today, but is expected to meet at its next regularly scheduled period, and that the instructor has issued a directive to attend a news conference at a specific time and place. They will also recognize the implied threat in the line "attendance will be taken."

"What a waste," the first might respond. "I drove all the way up here for this class. It's my only class of the day. Now I have to hang around here 'til 11:00 to go to that stupid news conference."

The second might decide: "That's it, pal. I'm gone. I can't go to that conference. I've gotta go to work."

And the third might exclaim: "Great, I can put two hours in at the library and get to go to the conference too."

While the fourth mutters: "Why does this always happen to me! Last week I would have pushed the instructor down the stairs to get the class canceled. Today I'm all prepared and zap, no class. I'm gonna skip that news conference. They can't take attendance there."

These four students have crafted very different messages from that same content concerning the class and the conference. The first is irritated, has to make a decision about how to spend the next two hours and will attend the conference under duress because of the threat implied. The second sees an opportunity and nullifies the threat. She leaves making a mental note to inform the instructor of her work assignment and to let him know how important work is. The third, or typical student, also sees an opportunity that is greeted with pleasure. He will attend the conference regardless of the threat. The fourth exemplifies how different meanings can be generated for the same content by an individual at different times and also how one can refuse to accept the expressed intent of the message.

The key to this example is that there is nothing in the content that would predict the pragmatic consequence for the four. Those consequences vary according to the interpretive stance of each recipient. Content becomes a message as it is interpreted by the recipient according to the perceived consequences for the individual. The interactive model emphasizes these interpretive processes as the source of explanation concerning the outcomes. Analysts working from this model focus on these processes rather than the characteristics of content as one would in the exposure model and presume that these processes provide the basis of gratification rather than some prior purpose as a uses and gratifications analyst normally would.

The interactive model has been the site of considerable conflict among its advocates as they struggle with the conceptualization of these processes. The majority of scientists, for example, are not prepared to posit interpretation as a freely occurring cognitive act. Interpretation is seen as governed or at least predictable according to conditions outside of it. Conditions that have been used as predictors are typical demographics and psychographics of analysis, age, sex, race, and so on; motivation, attitudes, values, and so on. The reason for this **reductionistic perspective** on interpretation is that if interpretation is wholly independent then no additional information can be learned about it other than an unending series of cases of its expression. This circumstance is generally not acceptable to scientists.

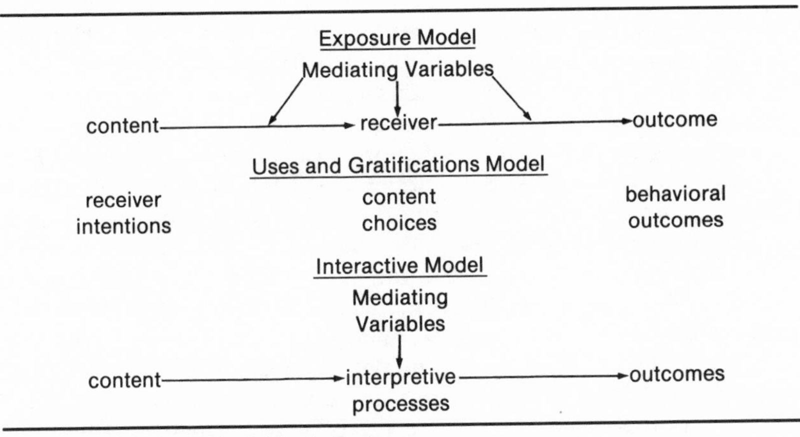

Figure 5.1 Models of individual effects.

Returning to our example then, scientists would likely create four categories of students (perhaps these: unmotivated, outward valued, inward valued, and alienated) and claim that all students in each category would respond in similar ways. And, in fact, we make much the same assumption when we use the scenario of the four students as an example.

A COMPARISON OF MODELS

The differences among the interactive model, uses and gratifications, and exposure model now become apparent. Content is the explanatory agent in the exposure model, although content is often used in conjunction with other conditions. Content is the explanatory agent because the researcher is directed by an interest in the effects of certain types of content. In the uses and gratifications model, it is the intentionality of the receiver that is the explanatory agent. Here the researcher wants to explain the functions of content for individuals. Why the receiver attends explains the outcomes of attendance. In the interactive model, interpretation with its governing conditions is the explanatory agent. The researcher is seeking to account for the differences in outcomes observed among different individuals.

Figure 5.1 gives a graphic representation of these different models. Figure 5.1 shows two important differences among the three models. First, the uses and gratifications model is the only one that attempts to explain content choices. Both the exposure and interactive models begin with the given of exposure to content. The explanation of why individuals are in the audience of particular content is not within their explanatory scope. It is also clear that exposure and interactive models are more alike than different: When the mediating conditions are held constant across interpretation or exposure, the effect of content is the same for all members within those conditions. The difference is that the exposure model would then discuss the characteristics of content and the interactive model the processes of interpretation.

Second, the exposure model attempts to explain the consequences of exposure in terms of a single-valued outcome. Exposure to violent content leads to aggression; exposure to pornography to the devaluation of women. The presence or absence of this single outcome is generally all that is measured in such studies. Both the uses and gratifications model and the interpretive model predict multiple outcomes across a group of individuals attending to the same content. These models are, therefore, called active audience models because, unlike the exposure model, these models assume that the audience member must participate in the outcome. The exposure model is considered to be a passive audience model because once exposed under the proper conditions, the effects of content cannot be effectively resisted (much as one cannot resist getting drunk after four martinis[1]). The notion of an active audience, however, does not necessarily translate into a celebration of the individual. Intentions are often seen as culturally derived and the processes of interpretation the consequence of socialization. Classes of intents and interpretations have homogeneous outcomes.

SUMMARY AND ANALYSIS

In the exposure model (often called "direct effects"), exposure to media content is considered an adequate basis for explaining subsequent conditions. The exposure model underlies most studies that look at particular types of content or make claims about the consequences of media logics, formats, or other characteristics. The well-known studies on violence, pornography, ethnic and gender images, value formation and attitude change are typically conducted from this framework. The general challenge to these types of studies concerns their external validity—their ability to model the real world. Few critics question the facts of the data—that higher rates of the criterion behavior are recorded. Most critics point out that many other conditions of the study could equally and as easily explain the outcomes as the content itself. They further claim that the effects predicted do not appear in society as the greatest proportion of its members use media content with no apparent ill effects.

The uses and gratifications model begins with the assumption that media attendance is in some way purposeful, has some conscious or unconscious intentionality. These expectations motivate attendance and provide the interpretive context for understanding the subsequent outcomes. The uses and gratifications model, therefore, provides insight into why the audience is there and what they expect to achieve as a consequence. In this model, content characteristics are important only in relation to use or gratification sought. Uses and gratifications studies have been used to explain audiences for various types of content; audience demand for content change; and the differential patterns of use across audiences differing on class, race, gender, life stage, and other demographic and psychographic variables.

Criticisms of the uses and gratifications model have been many, directed mostly at its undeveloped state as a theory and the naivéte of the of the methods used with it. Generally, uses and gratifications studies present respondents with a laundry list of reasons for media use (I read the newspaper to be informed; I watch rerun television to relive my past). Critics argue that the reasons are often trivial, self-justifying, and fail to distinguish levels of importance. They also claim that there is no evidence that the reasons selected truly motivate media use rather than being simple, post hoc explanations for that use. If what is considered to be the a priori intentions are only the post hoc explanations, then the fundamental purpose of explaining why the audience is there and what they seek is lost.

Development of the interactive model has been motivated by desires to correct the deficiencies of the exposure model. In its most traditional form, the exposure model makes no accounting of the audience member. The central premise of the interactive model is that what the audience member brings to the reception situation is as important as the content itself.

But critics do carp, here picking on the fact that the interactive model offers little advancement over the exposure model. Two principal points are made: that the interactive model doesn't explain attendance and that present studies simply posit interpretation with little description or apparent understanding of its processes. Consequently the interactive model is seen as a slightly more sophisticated form of the exposure model in which cognitive states are accountable within the mediating conditions of attendance.

INSTITUTIONAL EFFECTS

Institutional effects are a second level by which we might define the notion of effect. The institutional focus has been developed in three ways: public opinion research that considers the cycle of media influence on individuals whose private opinions become a public force in the influence of societal institutions, a cycle we call Lippmann effects; interinstitutional accommodations, the manner in which the interrelated practices of its institutions creates a society; and the analysis of institutional functions in the maintenance of that society. Our discussion follows this order.

LIPPMANN EFFECTS

Walter Lippmann (1922) in his pioneering work on public opinion called the reality constructs that direct our decisions and actions the "pictures of our mind." The idea that we develop mental views of reality has led to questions of media manipulation of those views, as we have seen. The question addressed in this section is how the private views of individuals aggregate to influence public policy and institutions. Public opinion research has been founded on the notion that a democratic society pursues a course of action founded on the "will of the people"—a sort of collective focus that permits political decision making. Early forms of public opinion research sought a direct link between a coherent public opinion and the progress of a democratic government in society. With totalitarian governments, it was only one more linear step for theorists to create the mass society in which media controlled public opinion, which justified governments, which, of course, controlled media.

A radical break with this formulation came in **agenda setting** research. The theoretical stance of agenda setting reflected the failure of researchers to find simple, direct effects of media influence on public decision making. Agenda setting claimed that media did not tell us *what* to think but what to think *about*. That is, the issues over which the public formed opinions that then had to be accounted for or could be exploited by government were presented to the public by the media.

Agenda setting held the concept of a more or less unitary public retiring to a more or less coherent agenda of discussion in common with earlier mass society theories. More recent theories have taken these concepts to task. Such theories generally see that there are multiple publics that hold to different opinion centers and are catered to by different media messengers. There are, therefore, both multiple publics and multiple agendas. Elements of government exercise some freedom to move among these publics seeking justification and empowerment for some chosen action.

A second set of research concerns has developed around the methods by which collective opinion arises. These concerns trace a history back to the two-step flow hypothesis that posited opinion leaders within interpersonal networks who interpreted media content for their followers. Current interests investigate the dynamics of a collective in which individuals read the opinion climate and are either privileged to speak by their identification with and commitment to the "winning" position or are constrained to silence because they are known to be or will reveal themselves as connected to the "losing" position. Winners and losers both work to maximize their gains from their respective positions. Studies within this set are just beginning to wrestle with the concepts of a collective, the communication methods that institute an opinion climate within them, and the perceptual processes by which individuals ascertain the opinion climate and their own position within it.

A third set of studies has developed around the idea that public opinion is a useful myth but does not actually exist except in the popular methods of measurement used to create (rather than reveal) it. In this cultural-based argument, the creation of public opinion occurs when the commercial polling organization asks a question with a restricted set of answers—"Do you approve of X? Yes. No. No Opinion." Only silence by all would stop the creation of a "public opinion" as the responses are tallied. The creation is accepted, so the argument goes, because the myth of public opinion is institutionalized in text books, government practices, and the like, and sanctioned by the media as valuable content. This is, however, no "will of the people," no concerted force for action being expressed. Each of us accepts the myth because it is a method by which we can locate ourselves in a larger society—"My ideals are quite different from most people's" or "More people agree with me than with you." Public opinion is created to form the ground of the generalized other against which the figure of the individual can appear.

Much of the movement of theory in public opinion reflects the perceived changes observed in First World societies and their Second and Third World relations. The traditional notion of public opinion (pre-World War II) can seem better suited to an age in which individuals within the purview of a government could gather in the square to discuss the issues and then retire to the town hall to vote their opinions. Whatever one's position, it is clear that western, democratic societies have refashioned themselves in the 65-year period since Lippmann wrote. Whether this reconstruction is superficial or fundamental is the debate. Postmodern critics often see societies as fractionated with individuals holding multiple memberships with commitments to all and, therefore, to none. Governments are equally fractionated, in this view, both horizontally within a level and vertically through them. Any action involves a momentary coalition. Seen through to the end, of course, this view predicts the end of the First World (brilliantly presented in the French-Canadian film, *The Decline and Fall of the American Empire*). Theories are instantly politicized on this issue. A belief in a true public opinion directing a responsive government preserves the power of the past just as a belief in a public opinion myth predicts a particular future.

There is another fracture readily visible in public opinion research that also underlies the differences that appear elsewhere in effect studies: This unsettled issue involves the location or site of the effect claimed. For most media theories, the effect occurs in the mind of the individual. An effect occurs when the cognitive structure of the individual is modified in some way—Lippmann's pictures get changed. Public opinion, in these theories, occurs when the attitudes held by individuals are congruent because all individuals within the public are subject to the same external influences. In these formulations, there is no collective action, no achievement of a membership needed. Each individual is motivated to a decision by a common set of forces. Such formulations constitute the individual as the smallest, complete unit of analysis from which certain societal effects can be observed as individuals independently act. From this position, a society's opinion can be measured by polling individuals because that opinion is simply the aggregate of opinions held by them.

A contrary position, gaining new presence over the past decade, holds that a true public opinion has to be the consequence of an achievement by a public. For a public opinion to appear there has to be a collective action by a membership with recognizable processes of member-to-member communication and commitment. Any opinion—if it is to be truly public—is present in and only in that collective action. In this perspective, the individual is incomplete and is realized only in the community of intellect that membership allows. This claim is a far cry from both LeBon's inferior group mind and the American ideal of free agency. Here, a public opinion could not be measured in polling individuals but would become known through participation within the ongoing action of a membership as it creates and processes an understanding of what it is doing. The common myth of public opinion is created in the conjunction of the press, the pollster, and the political elite.

When theorists use the individual as the location of effect, they enable certain methods of analysis—aggregated, quantified data subject to statistical analysis—and certain lines of argument—external influences on cognitive structures. When theorists use social action as the location of effect, they enable different methods of analysis—participant observation motivating analytical interpretation—and different lines of argument—opinion as ongoing achievement. The wave of theory has been away from the individual and toward social action, though the ocean of previous thought remains.

INTERINSTITUTIONAL ACCOMMODATIONS

We can think of political parties as societal institutions. And we can think of the media as societal institutions. The interaction of these two institutions, political parties and the media, generate political campaigns. The campaign is the symbiotic consequence of the effect these two institutions have on one another. We can claim, for example, that the media had a tremendous effect on the 1984 presidential campaign—over half of the potential voters didn't vote at all. What! How was that a media effect? It certainly isn't one that has been ascribed to the media. But, then, how would we know? Because media are part of an integrated social system, it is very difficult to sort out what is and what is not a media effect. When a researcher focuses in on the consequences of a campaign, he or she is looking at something larger than individual effects. The campaign operates in both the political and media context and must serve the conventions of each. American politics have been consistently shaped by the presence of the media and the media are what they are in part because of American politics. The effects of a campaign then, cannot be limited to media explanations but must be understood in the larger picture of the interaction among the social institutions involved.

Another example of institutional effects lies within the mercantile system of the United States. The concept of a private ownership of competitive enterprises was established in America before the arrival of mass media. The development of the mass media was, in fact, largely shaped by the presence of that mercantile system. The interplay between the two systems brought about the present structure of advertising as content for the media and the marketing notions of brands, mass distribution, and the like for private enterprise. Again, the effect of an advertisement has to be understood within the context of the entire marketing system, not just the media presentation. Advertising is an integral part of our merchandising and consumer practices. Every advertisement is embedded in those systems. Consider the following scenario.

Let's presume that Meyer and Anderson decide to get out of academics to bring out a line of designer jeans. They want to get into the big money. Investing their life savings in a back pocket signature, they hire the advertising firm of Derierre and Co. that develops a clever advertising campaign. The jeans sell 400,000 pairs in the first quarter. Certainly Meyer and Anderson would have to conclude that the media advertising played a significant role in the sale of those 400,000 units. The question that remains is how did it play that role. The following bits of conversation heard during that period might give us some insights:

"During the prime shopping hours about 3,000 people will pass through the doors of our four stores. With jeans of this quality, I can sell 50 units a day just by displaying them properly. Put me down for an order of 1,500 units to start."

"I can't give you an inch of rack space in juniors, but we'll sell almost as many in preteens."

"Oh, these are the Tim Meyer Jeans that everyone is wearing. I want a pair."

"These Tim Meyer jeans are just like the Vanderbilt ones you saw on TV. At 20% off, we'll go with them."

"John, you told me that 60 million people saw that campaign, yet we sold only 400,000 pairs. What happened to the other 59,600,000?"

When we attempt an analysis of the effects of the advertising campaign we suddenly find ourselves in the midst of a mercantile system that can sell on its own inertia, and a welter of individual decisions that lead to a purchase. You can see what is going to happen if we claim it was the content of the advertising campaign that caused the sale. We simply have no basis for explaining why it worked for some and not for most. Here's why: Each purchase decision is an independent decision. That is, a full understanding of one person's purchase gives us no basis for predicting another person's purchase. The next person's entire set of reasons will be unique, and so on for all 400,000. The communalities that we find in such reasoning sets are created when the researcher chooses to ignore the differences or uses a measurement device that does not reveal those differences.

In attempting to explain the impact of the advertising campaign on the sale of the 400,000 pairs of jeans, we are faced with determining the effectiveness of one element within an event involving interlocking systems—manufacturing, wholesaling, retailing, advertising, and each individual purchaser. What part did product design play, the quality of manufacture, the success of the wholesaler in getting retail outlets, the point of purchase displays in those retail outlets, the image the product has within the social circles of potential buyers, the inherent need (got to wear something) for the product by the buyers? Certainly if the factories in Hong Kong burned down or all the cargo ships got lost in the Bermuda Triangle or retail outlets were managed by khaki-crazed preppies, not a single sale would result from all the advertising. Again we have to keep the larger system before us when considering the effects of media.

All of the major media effects occur within some set of interlocking systems. The effects of media on politics cannot be considered as isolated from the network of lobbyists, political action committees, precinct organizations, party memberships, and the like. The effects for children cannot be considered independently of the school, the family, and peers.

Until most recently media theorists had done little in the study of interinstitutional effects (Howard Becker's, 1982, *Art Worlds* and Eileen Meehan's, 1986, political economy theory of content are two notable exceptions). Such studies were left to economists and market analysts. Studies coming out of these camps are generally driven by structural models. Structural models find the causes of institutional performance within the market structure of the industry rather than in, say, the creative genius of given practitioners. We, for example, advanced this kind of argument in our examination of the structural influences on content in Chapter 2. Conspiracy theories of the media that sometimes appear in fundamentalist writings or demands for unilateral change on moral bases are antithetical to these arguments. Media executives cannot conspire to do what the market demands nor change the market by themselves.

FUNCTIONS

Societal institutions are organizations and structures that serve the functions that make a society a society. It is the nature of this functional service that motivates the creation, maintenance, and evolution of the institution. When an institutional structure fails to show functional value it collapses. When a function is required by a society an institutional structure arises to serve that function. As has been noted elsewhere, humans have legs because they walk. These tenets form the characteristic axioms of structural functionalism, a theory that has a clear presence in sociological research for several decades. Because many of the first researchers in mass media came from sociology, functionalism made an early entry into media theory. It appeared in two forms: First, in theories about what the structure of the press (media) should be in different sociopolitical societies (democratic, totalitarian, and so on). Second, in theories about the functions of media for a society (surveillance, correlation, and so on). Although introductory texts routinely cite the four theories of the press and the functions of media in their reviews, the functionalist model has, at least temporarily, passed its moment on the stage replaced by its heir, uses and gratifications, and its rival, cultural studies.

SUMMARY AND ANALYSIS

The analysis of institutional effects from a functional perspective was an early direction of media theory. The analysis of effects across institutions has generally been outside the purview of media theorists, although the past five years have shown a growing number of examples. Functionalism held a dominant position for a relatively long time and was also the target of much criticism. The most telling of this criticism starts with the fact that in this model, functions are the explanatory agent but structures are of that which we have the most direct evidence. That is, one can see that the media exist, that they have various kinds of content, but one cannot demonstrate, with the same clarity, the functions served. There seems little additional value in making the claim, after observing the media to be filled with entertainment content, that the reason for that content is that society has an entertainment function that must be served.

Structural approaches to interinstitutional accommodations have been criticized because they dehumanize the process, deny the importance of the individual practitioners and, consequently, eliminate accountability. Structural theorists would generally agree with those criticisms but argue that those are the facts of the marketplace and that accountability must either be developed in the regulation of the market or be to the market as it freely functions. (We can see that contrast in the active regulation stance of the 1950s and 1960s and the deregulation forces of the 1980s.)

The public opinion studies that started this investigation of institutional effects are founded on a particular view of how democratic societies operate. Often this view appears to be a naive and unprincipled acceptance of a particular political framework and supporting views of the electoral process and the functions of the press. Certainly, the public opinion literature shows little careful study of the processes by which public opinion (as opposed to lobbyists, special interest groups, and other political elites) presumably influences political decision making. An exciting opportunity for study is clearly present in this arena.

CULTURAL EFFECTS

The study of the broad area of cultural effects can first be divided into two parts: the first encompassing the more traditional social science approaches to the study of the processes of socialization and encultura-tion, the second involving studies that arise from the critical perspective but that have an empirical, generally ethnographic, foundation also.

TRADITIONAL SCIENTIFIC APPROACHES

Most of the traditional work in cultural effects have used either models of cognitive structures or social learning theory as their base. A more recent theory—**rules theory**—has lineages in each. We'll look at them in this order.

Models of cognitive structures typically posit a hierarchy of statements (called knowledge claims, reality claims, attitudes, beliefs, values, and so on) from which action emanates and is explained. (He voted for Nixon—action—because he believed in an imperial presidency—mo-tivating belief.) These cognitive structures are known as cognitive maps, **schemata,** value systems, belief systems, structures of moral judgment, and so on. Socialization and enculturation studies both consider the processes by which these cognitive structures develop and are main-tained. The quality of these structures is considered to be the basis of social competence and cultural membership. The difference between socialization and enculturation is primarily one of perspective: Socializa-tion adopts the psychological perspective of the individual and encultur-ation, the sociological perspective of society. Media studies of socializa-tion or of enculturation consider how the content of the media enters or is reflected in these structures. Both perspectives have used exposure as the most common explanation for an effect, although the interactive explanation is now also appearing. Other media studies make use of the concept of cognitive structures by examining the mediating effects of attitudes, beliefs, prior knowledge, and the like on the consequences of exposure to content (e.g., how voters react to messages from their chosen and the opposing candidates).

While not informing us about our cognitive libraries, social learning theory is a broad spectrum attempt to understand how we come to function competently at various levels. The primary premise of social learning theory is that we learn through others mostly by participating with them but also through observation. It is with this latter tenet that media studies are brought in. Social learning theory predicts that we can learn value and behavior through exposure to media content that contains performances that can be transferred to our own situation. **Imitation** and/or **vicarious learning** are the mechanisms of transfer.

Social learning and cognitive structure ideas are teamed in the rules perspective. This perspective presents a somewhat different model describing the effects of media. It states that the premises of social engagement are set in a complement of **rules** that operate much like the rules of a game with prescribed and proscribed behaviors. Within the rules, however, there is considerable space for particularized performances—episodes of "playing the game." The rules themselves develop within sociological processes, vary in explicitness and completeness, are more open to interpretation than rigid, and are more or less "known" by each member of a culture. For example, every member of a high school class knows the rules for being a student and a peer in a classroom. Various roles and performances are taken and given, applauded and criticized, but all within the rules.

Media effects appear in two ways in this perspective: First, the media can provide content for the rules per se. This claim shows the most traditional lineal connection with social learning theory. Second, media effects can arise in the performances of episodes of social interaction governed by a complement of rules. Media content is understood within the ongoing interaction. This claim is more modern. It rejects exposure as an adequate condition of effect and grants power to the collective understanding of "what's going on."

One can see the parallels with the reasoning of cognitive structures. Here a complement of rules has taken the place of a set of cognitive structures. The two major sources of effects remain the same. Media content can be brought into the rule structure in which it will have long-term effects and extensive power as it will participate in the governance of subsequent behavior. Media content will also be interpreted within the performances governed by the rules. The effects there are located within the particular performance and likely to be short-term and limited.

The difference provided by the rules perspective is the sociological view. Cognitive structure theorists generally restrict themselves to the boundaries of *the* individual finding their explanations in the processes of development each of us goes through. Rules explanations are located in social interaction.

CRITICAL APPROACHES TO CULTURAL EFFECTS

We must accomplish a delicate transition here. The reader will have to grant us some space and much tolerance. What we want to talk about are the ideological theories of class, patriarchy, and hegemony. These theories are located in critical analysis, a different practice of inquiry from that of science. The most visible differences between the two are that criticism is (a) charged with evaluation and (b) conducts its inquiry from an explicit value stance. Criticism describes what is from a view of what ought to be. As a human endeavor, science, of course, cannot be value free. Its claims, however, are diminished when the complaint of value can be issued against a particular argument. Further, science has more methodical requirements for the development and presentation of empirical evidence in its arguments. Within the last decade, the practices of critical inquiry and of the human sciences have moved much closer together. Nonetheless, the turf between them is still well-contested.

At this point we have crossed volumes in a few sentences to deal with three types of theories that come from critical analysis: critical issue theories, hegemony, and **interpretive communities.**

CRITICAL ISSUE THEORIES **Marxism** and **feminism** are two examples of critical issue theories.[2] For Marxism, the *critical issue* is the class structure of society. The analysis of the media is taken from the perspective that the media participate in this class structure. The traditional Marxist claim is that the content of the media reflect and support the ideology of the ruling class. (An example of this kind of argument is presented in Chapter 8.)

For feminists, society is organized into a patriarchy in which the voices of women are missing or subordinated. Media analysis from the feminist perspective has concerned itself with the image and presence of women in content and the use of that content by men and women in support of or in opposition to patriarchy.

HEGEMONY Hegemony is a theoretical concept taken from Marxist writings (generally, the idea is attributed to Gramsci, 1927/1971). The concept refers, as we have noted, to the dynamic process that maintains any given hierarchical social structure. (The critical issue of the hierarchy might be class, gender, race, age, and in recent writings, combinations thereof.) Hegemony appears in the "proper social and moral order" that serves to maintain the ongoing hierarchy. In short, the hierarchy is seen as right and proper and is supported by members of all strata. The critic's responsibility in the analysis of hegemony is to break its taken-for-granted nature in order to consider its consequences and often to radicalize those exploited by it.

Because all social institutions are considered part of the in-place hierarchical structure, critical media analysis considers the manner of that institution's support. Two claims are generally made: First, that the dominant character of the media is the repeated presentation of the truths of the hierarchy in the reality and fantasy narratives of its content. Second, that the media provide harmless opportunities for opposition through the presentation of diminished texts, the use of comedy as an outlet for hostility, the sacrifice of individuals to save sociopolitical institutions (Nixon resigns, the presidency remains),[3] and other techniques.

COMMUNITY A most recent and rapidly developing model in critical theory is that of audience communities. An audience community is one in which members hold in common both certain media texts and the premises of interpretation of those texts. The decoding of community-connected texts (not all texts) is conducted according to those premises and serves to maintain the community. Understanding how a text is understood, therefore, requires the analyst to look for communities of interpretation and to determine whether a given text is community-related. An individual may belong to many communities and a given text may be related to more than one community. Interpretation depends on where the individual is presently situated and how the text is connected. For example, feminists within British Marxist cultural studies might use working-class women as the site for oppositional interpretations of news reports on labor unrest. The intent of the analysis would be to show how these interpretations are achieved, how they serve principles of solidarity, and yet at the same time diffuse authentic responses of resistance.

SUMMARY AND ANALYSIS

Culture has been variously defined. But most agree that it involves an understanding of the world around us and the knowledge of how things get done. Culture is not fixed but always in some motion as it spirals through noted cycles of repression and freedom, war and peace, boom and bust, pushed on by environmental change and innovation. We describe our current history in decades of startlingly different character. Culture is the ongoing creation of human interaction. Albeit stabilized in memory, practice, and institution, it is still a dynamic in which we continually negotiate the relationships among its various elements. These negotiations get done in the living rooms of our homes, in the halls of our clubs, schools, and churches, in the statehouses of government and in the content of our media. On any given day, the whole panoply of issues is on the bargaining table where we come together and within the programs, plots, stories, and reports that appear in the print, electronic, and cinematic media.

It is no wonder, then, that scientists and critics have become deeply involved in the role media texts play in the dynamic of culture. Their involvement varies along three axes: The first concerns a focus moving from the individual to some form of community. Explanations on the individual side would privilege cognitive states, their development, maintenance, and change; on the community side, the processes of interaction are primary. The second axis varies across the dimension of exposure and interpretation. At the exposure end, the formal properties of the text have great explanatory power. As one moves toward interpretation, that power is increasingly mediated by the decoding activities of the receiver. The third axis concerns the primacy of text or practice (experience) in the cultural worldview. In the most radical of the text positions, there is no experience other than text, a notion that raises media to high privilege. At the other end, text is in the service of practice and/or must be validated in experience.

We can set for you the typifying model for each of those sectors:

Cognitive structure theory is concerned with the individual, accepts exposure as an adequate condition of effect, and with its empirical lineage would hold to the primacy of experience, although the theory predates the issue.

Cultivation theories attempt to explain an individual's cognitive structures through exposure to media texts. Cultivation theories, therefore, would appear high in the exposure-individual-text sector along with theories of media logic and format.

Most of the critical studies of cultural effects would appear in the community-interpretation-text sector. High in the section would be the hegemony model.

The community-interpretation-practice sector is the least populated. We would find some audience community models here, although they tend to differ on the primacy of text. Accommodation Theory, the promised subject of Chapter 9, would also appear in this sector, but more toward the center.

CENTRAL IDEAS OF SECTION I: THEORIES OF EFFECTS

A. Defining Effects

1. The theories from which we view effects produce six different perspectives on them: indirect, direct, functions, interinstitutional, cultural, and accommodation effects.
2. Direct effects can be further classified according to their contingency, immediacy, and lifespan with these three describing the power of the effect relationship.
3. Functions as effects have been studied at the micro level with individuals, and at the macro level with institutions.
4. Cultural effects are of two classes, one that views ideology as a static force the other is based on hegemony as a dynamic process.

B. Individual Effects

1. Individual effects explore the relationship between mediated content and the behavior of the individual. They generally include indirect, direct, and functional effects.
2. The three components of individual effects—content, the reacting individual, and the relationship between the two—are described in different models, one dominates content, two describes the audience, and three the relationship.
3. In most studies, content is seen as a "meaning delivery system"; the audience is either passively under media influence or actively using content; the relationship between content and person is controlled by content exposure, motivated by the purposes of the auditor, or governed by the interpretation processes in use.

C. Institutional Effects

1. Lippmann effects concern the relationship among the agendas of the media, the public, and the political elite. The media agenda is said to determine the public agenda that is exploited by the political elite.
2. Conceptualizations of public opinion range from the aggregate of individually held attitudes that appears as a coherent expression only in measurement to the achievement of an interacting community. Many public opinion studies collect data as if the first were true, but give explanations according to the second.

3. Institutions interact to produce societal conditions: Examples are the interaction between media and political parties to produce campaigns; the interaction of production, distribution, and marketing in the mercantile system; and the production of content for the media.
4. The study of the media has included structural-functionalist theories about societal demand creating the media. While their contribution remains, these theories show limited activity.

D. Cultural Effects

1. In traditional science, cultural effects are the product of socialization or enculturation processes that create cognitive structures or leave behavior-determining traces in the individual. The individual, therefore, is a product of society/culture.
2. Critical approaches to the study of culture have fixed on the concepts of ideology, hegemony, and community.
3. Ideology is the center of critical issue theorists who see the world as determined by the power of class, race, gender, or some other organizing structure.
4. Hegemony is the process by which whatever structure is in place maintains position through elastic resistance, deflection, diffusion, or accommodation of the forces for change.
5. Community is a membership that becomes the site for the practice of interpretations that maintain the community and the larger hegemony.

SECTION II: POWER AND SCALE IN THE INTERPRETATION OF EFFECTS

An interesting problem that all studies of effects have to deal with is the question of power relative to the effect of scale. Power is the capacity to cause an outcome. Power would be seen in the claim that ads cause sales. An effect of scale is encountered when the size or quantity alone is the issue (e.g., one ant is not a problem; 10,000 ants are).

Estimates vary, but presume that at any prime-time minute, 40 million people are watching television. An advertiser presents a commercial for half of that minute that results in 40,000 sales. If we attribute all of those sales to the commercial alone (certainly an unrealistic claim, as we have seen), its rate of effectiveness is one-tenth of 1% of the audience, but at that scale, the absolute number of sales is huge. The scale of the media tends to confuse us into making claims about power. It is considered a massive media effect when a news report of a shortage can cause a sell-out of a product. But such sell-outs are equally a function of inventory. Typically, inventories are kept very close to selling performance. It takes very little change in buying to create problems. In markets like Salt Lake City or Green Bay, the action of 1,000 people can have significant effect. To draw the point of this example, consider that it is estimated that 800,000 in this market of 1.5 million watch one of the evening news programs. An effectiveness rate of a message that induces a purchase decision in 1 out of every 800 viewers will sell out the stocks in a given day.

What is shown in this example is that the scale of the media is much larger than the scale of product inventory. It is this difference in scale that is as much responsible for the so-called media effect as is the message presented.

Are the media powerful? Perhaps, but often where we see power is actually the intersections of scale, those points at which the scale of one action influences the scale of another. The combined action of media functions on such a large scale that it can easily overwhelm the scale of another. It is a misinterpretation to confuse effects of scale for power.

Do the media have significant effects? Of course! Try buying a product after a shortage scare. In short, the effectiveness of the media is not dependent on their power but can be created in the scale of their operation. When we consider media effects we must always balance the units sold, votes garnered, information gained, with the number of impressions made. This ratio keeps us cognizant of the consequences of scale.

SECTION III: MODELS AND METHODS

We have been talking about ways to model the concept of effects. Models, as metaphorical representations of reality, organize one's thinking about that reality. Our methods of investigation also direct our thinking. The combination of organizing models and directing procedures is a powerful predictor of the conclusions we are going to draw about the world. For example, if one holds to the interactive model, it simply is not possible to argue that all readers will react to the same content in fundamentally the same way. Further, the methods used would focus on the differences rather than the similarities among readers.

In any form of inquiry, method is used to support claim; there is a symbiotic relationship between one's theory and one's selection of method. Certain methods are dependent on certain theoretical approaches. The models that we have studied across individual, institutional, and cultural effects have all shown affinities for particular methodologies. The next two chapters take up a detailed analysis of reference studies conducted from these different approaches. What we want to do here is to consider the relationship between theory and method. Our discussion follows for each approach.

METHODS OF CAUSAL/CONDITIONAL MODELS

The causal/conditional models that we studied were those that predicated the appearance of some effect on the presence of some prior condition or conditions generally involving exposure to content. Those models included the exposure and interactive models of individual effects, the market structure models of institutions, and the cognitive structure socialization model of cultural effects. The market structure model dealt with relationships among institutions but each of the others was concerned with the consequence of exposure to mediated content. In the simple exposure model, characteristics of content were used to predict the appearance of certain kinds of behavior (media violence begets aggression). In the interactive model, content characteristics and cognitive states were used to predict behavioral outcomes. In cognitive structure, it is generally content and maturational state that are used to predict system outcomes.

In all of these models, it is necessary to relate at least two but usually three sets of measures: a measure of exposure to a kind of content, a measure of the mediating or interacting conditions, and a measure of the outcome. The relationship is presumed to work linearly through time beginning with exposure working through the mediating conditions to the outcome. If our exposure model predicted that newspaper ads (content) cause automobile purchases (outcome) when the individual is "primed to buy" (a mediating condition in which the individual has motive and means but is looking for opportunity),[4] then the strongest evidence for our claim would be given if qualified individuals exposed to ads and only those exposed to ads—bought cars.

How could we generate that evidence? The easiest but least convincing way would be to collect **self-reports** from registered new-car buyers. In this procedure, respondent would answer positively to statements such as: "I read automobile ads in the newspaper before buying a car." This is a simple application of survey methods. Survey methods provide evidence of a relationship by demonstrating the presence of the elements in the relationship, in this case reading ads and buying cars. The evidence is weak because the dependence of the outcome measure (buying) on the causal agent (reading ads) has to be inferred. (Individuals could easily be reading ads because they were buying a car and needed the glowing phrases to describe it to their neighbors.) To use another example, studies have shown that school children who watch substantially more television get lower grades. It seems reasonable to assume that if individuals spend a lot of time watching TV, they don't have the time to prepare well. However, it is also reasonable to assume that bad grades may lead to increased use of television—if you can't do it well, why do it at all? Actually, bad grades and watching a lot of television may both be symptoms of poor motivation or some form of alienation. Finally, the two variables of grades and TV use may not be related at all but simply both present at the time of measurement.

To provide more convincing evidence of the relationship, the resentrol the alternative explanations. Instead of simply measuring naturally to provide testing conditions that would cooccurring television use rates, the researcher would probably want to manipulate these rates across students of each success level. This is a simple form of experimental methods. To switch examples again, studies have manipulated exposure to pornographic films to see if higher rates of exposure (pardon the pun) affected attitudes toward women.

The key to understanding experimental methods is in the concepts of control and manipulation. The problems with experimental methods arise from the methods necessary to accomplish control and manipulation. Let's say that while attending an establishment with a dance floor you become intrigued with the ebb and flow of the number of dancers on the floor (dancing, of course). In your mind's eye, you see a relationship between the tempo of the music and the number of people dancing. You want to test your hypothesis. In a survey approach, you would simply ask the dancers to indicate if the tempo of the music affected their choice of whether to dance or not. Clearly there are problems here. The respondents might not report or might not even recognize the effects of tempo on their choices.

In an experiment, you control and manipulate the situation that, in turn, causes the individuals to respond to the situation according to the normal consequences of the event. That sounds simple enough, but consider what the experimenter would have to control: The music would have to be the same except for tempo (which we might define as the number of beats per minute—not measure, as that is relative). It could not vary in rhythm, lyrics, or instrumentation because these might be the source of the change in the number of dancers. The dancers would have to be the same for each musical presentation—they couldn't be tired, bored of the same partner, or of the same music being played over and over—and they must be in the same state of consciousness. "Come on, now," you might say, "That's not how things are in real life." True, and you have identified the primary criticism of the experimental paradigm—it's not realistic. In the laboratory, most people who watch violent television exhibit higher rates of ostensible aggression. In the living room, most people who watch violent television get up and go to bed.

Nevertheless, experiments are the first-choice source for evidence of causal relationships. Laboratory experiments establish effects that *can* occur. If we wished to produce aggression, we know the content and protocol that will accomplish that outcome. That knowledge does not necessarily explain violence in society, however. The net of all of this discussion is that it is very difficult to generate solid evidence of causal or conditional relationships that describes these relationships as they naturally occur. We have hundreds of studies that show a relationship between violent media content and subsequent aggression. Yet, we have no national policy on such content. There are, of course, powerful economic and political forces arrayed against such a policy. But one of the reasons these forces are successful is that the evidence is inherently contestable.

FUNCTIONAL MODELS

The functional models of uses and gratifications at the individual level and structural functionalism at the institutional level are a special form of a causal/conditional reasoning. Functionalism applied to individuals or institutions is predicated on a preexisting need: Society needs informed citizens; therefore, news media develop. I need to spend time with my buddies; therefore, we go to the movies. The preexisting need is the motivation for the institutional structures and the individual action (a use *for* some purpose).

Because the researcher is always faced with an existing system of need and resolution, the methods of functionalism are essentially descriptive. In structural functionalism, the researcher attempts carefully to describe the characteristics of the institution both in isolation and in relation to other institutions. These descriptions are drawn from survey data of many types, census data, economic indicators, policy statements, legal documents, and the like. This description, then, is explained or accounted for by virtue of the functions that have been postulated for the institution. If the preselected functions are not adequate as an explanation, they are modified. (The four functions of the mass media were originally three: surveillance, correlation, and transmission of culture; entertainment was added several years after the initial formulation because content was inadequately explained.)

In the study of individual uses and gratifications, most studies have used a battery of statements, such as "I relax with the newspaper," to determine the relative frequency of choices across media, types of content, and classifications of people. One of the purposes is to build an understanding of the typical uses that appear for given media, content, and people. These uses would explain why individuals are attending and potentially their states of mind in receiving content.

Functionalism has been the subject of much criticism (the present authors included—Anderson & Meyer, 1975). It has serious difficulties as a meaningful research perspective for the mass media, because of its inherent tautological explanation. If one agrees with the statement that "I relax with the newspaper," that individual, therefore, uses the newspaper to relax.[5] A use or a gratification, then, becomes any descriptive statement that can reasonably be applied. The ontology of either a use or gratification is not explored or explained. A similar problem exists in the macroperspective that develops functions on the basis of content characteristics assuming that all characteristics must have a corresponding functional explanation. On that assumption no new knowledge is gained as one simply substitutes a function name for a content characteristic.

ETHNOGRAPHIC MODELS

The past 15 years or so have seen the development of ethnographic approaches to the study of media effects. Ethnographic approaches have three characteristic assumptions which distinguish them from survey and experimental methods: First it is assumed that sense making is a socially based process that happens in reference to some membership.

(Meaning is in the situated individual not content.) Second, it is assumed that the proper place of study is in the social action of everyday life. (Surveys and experiments are particular social actions, but do not necessarily inform us about other social action.) Third, the proper method of study is some form of participant observation in which the researcher becomes a member of the respondent group. (The researcher has to join the action rather than be an outside manipulator.)

Both the rules model and the various cultural models make use of ethnographic methods. In the study of rules, the membership—a notion of reciprocal identity; you claim membership, I grant membership and vice versa—is the site for the development and maintenance of the complement of rules that mediate and interpret our behavior toward one another. Rules for media use, then, develop in most membership settings—in one's family, work site, with one's jogging partner, and so on. Effects are created within these settings as permissible action alternatives are defined within them.

Ethnography is making its entrance into cultural studies after a substantial body of such literature had already developed. The primary mode of inquiry was, and to no small extent still is, the careful examination of content. This examination is certainly necessary. If one is making a claim that the media are the repository of the ideology of the ruling class, expressions of the ideology need to dominate the content of the media. The other half of the critical issues perspective—that other classes accept that ideology—cannot be demonstrated through **content analysis,** however. It is in the analysis of that part of the claim that cultural scholars from the critical perspective have turned to some form of ethnographic methods.

This effort is in its very beginnings; the work is immature. The practice of ethnography in the study of mediated communication is not well-developed and the criteria of excellence—a committed, complete engagement with the membership dedicated to learning and describing the socially constructed meanings of that community—are rarely met. Media studies in general and critical venues in particular have not supported an exemplary class of ethnographic studies. Ethnography itself has been an oppositional method—a weapon to attack traditional power bases. The most damning criticism is that the studies have been self-fulfilling: Marxists have found economic subjugation; hierarchical theorists, their hegemony, as we all knew they would. On the other hand, a central principle of critical writing is that an interpretive stance must be taken. If a well-developed argument for hegemony can be crafted from detailed descriptions of everyday life, we are informed about both. At present, we have so very few authentic ethnographies that a legitimate critical review of the practice is not possible. We will have to see how this practice develops in this discipline's studies before being able to recognize systematic problems.

SUMMARY

In this section, we have considered the relationships between the theories of effects and the methods used to gather evidence in support of those theories. We found that most theories used causal or conditional reason in which media effects were dependent on exposure to content of given characteristics. So, aggression came from violent content; an informed citizenry from news content; purchase behavior from advertisements; and various values from their expression. Survey methods that demonstrated the presence of the elements in the theorized relationship and experimental methods that control for the dependent relationship through manipulation are the prime source of evidence for these theories.

The functionalist theories of uses and gratifications and structural functionalism were seen to be special forms of causal/conditional models. Uses and gratifications studies use survey methods that search for different structural relationships within a battery of statements, each describing a possible use or gratification. The traditional study of the societal functions of the media has been directed by content analysis with the content characteristics so discovered motivating a claim for a societal function.

Cultural studies have also been based on content analysis. This analysis is conducted from the presumption that the ideological texts of content are a force in the development of cognitive structures and in the community of intellect within society. Content analysis has been coupled with outcome surveys of users of this content on the science side of cultural studies and with ethnographic methods on the critical inquiry side of these studies.

CENTRAL IDEAS OF SECTION II: POWER AND SCALE IN THE INTERPRETATION OF EFFECTS
SECTION III: MODELS AND METHODS

A. Scale and Power

1. Power is the capacity of content to invoke an effect; scale is the size and scope of elements in a relationship. In media analyses, differences in scale are often confused with power.
2. The scale of the media is usually much larger than is the scale of elements affected, thus contributing to that confusion.

B. Models and Methods

1. Causal and conditional models make use of survey and experimental methods to demonstrate the dependent relationship between content and auditor. Survey methods, however, offer weak evidence of relationships and experimental methods often lack mundane realism.
2. Functional models of the individual and of social institutions are dependent on survey methods because manipulation of the initiating

state cannot be accomplished. The relationship between purpose, gratification sought, or societal demand and some action or structure is, therefore, always in doubt.

3. Models that are based on concepts of interpretive achievements or social constructions have used content analysis and ethnography as their analytical methods from science. Content analysis permits claims about effects but does not provide evidence of them. The practice of ethnography in mediated communication studies is in an immature state. Few studies have been completed and most suffer from an oppositional character or a limited effort attributable to this stage of development.

EPILOGUE

We began this chapter in search of effects. What we have found is that in the very notion of effects itself is an explanation—an understanding about the way our world works. As our worldview varies, our understanding about what an effect is, changes. Some events seem clear: Candidates get elected; there is crime in the streets; products are sold at the stores; people act differently today than they did 50 years ago. And, campaigns are constructed; there is violence on television; there are commercials, ads, and billboards; you can buy magazines at grocery stores that show naked men and women. What isn't clear is what the relationship is among these events. Do candidates get elected because of the campaigns, or are the campaigns a public reaffirmation that we live in a democracy but of little consequence as to the outcome of the vote? Is the violence in the streets an expression of television content, or is television content an expression of the violence in the streets? If one shows one relationship, does it hold in all cases, or does it change with time and place? The answer to these questions lies in the understanding we hold about the world.

One of the very real problems in understanding social dynamics is that society is an ongoing performance by people, not a set of discrete components. Further, people have the capacity to improvise solutions that may not be predicted by looking at different partitions of this ongoing performance. To postulate the effects of some part of that performance, say, the interstate highway system (or even our media) does not preclude the conclusion that we could have arrived at the same place through other means. If we were able to rip the media out of our social fabric, would we be different? It seems incredible to think not. But those differences might not be where we now hold the media's greatest effects: People would still buy products; spend leisure time on something; participate in their governance; develop values and notions of the world. They would simply do them in some other way. Society is a multicausal, multiconsequential system. Effects are where one sees them.

Myths, stories from the past, common sense, scientific theories, are all explanations about the way the world works. Particular explanations rise to the fore and hold center stage for as long as they are useful to the people who hold them. In media explanations, behaviorism and direct effects have held sway for the second half of this century, replacing the sociological mass-man notions of the 1920s and 1930s. It does not seem reasonable to expect a final answer. Alternate explanations will continue to appear even as the exposure model is now being aggressively challenged.

A TRANSITION

This chapter has presented an overview of the theories and methods within which we come to see the effects of media. It should be clear to you by now that what is or is not a media effect depends on how it is arbitrarily defined, including how it is theoretically conceptualized, how the terms are operationalized, how the presence of such effects are measured, and how evidence of results are interpreted. Chapters 6 and 7 consider in detail the quality of evidence that is generated by experimental, survey, and ethnographic methods. Chapter 8 then considers the claims about effects that have been made from this evidence and provides both a set of examples of research from different models and methods and an analysis of that set.

NOTES

1. That's a metaphor, not a challenge.
2. In the short space we have available, we can hardly do justice to the power and quality of writing within either of these perspectives.
3. In the democratic theory of the press, the press is the watchdog of society. In hegemony theory, although individual reporters may believe themselves watchdogs, the watchdog function is an institutionalized strategy that deflects criticism from the possibility of true change.
4. A more powerful effect would be demonstrated if respondents had means and opportunity but no motive—to be induced by the ad, of course.
5. One of the authors claims to relax by refereeing adult soccer games. These games generally involve opposing ethnic groups shouting at one another and at him in languages he doesn't understand. Is this the same use as relaxing with the newspaper?

RELATED READINGS

McQuail, D. (1987). *Mass communication theory: An introduction* (2nd ed.). Newbury Park, CA: Sage.

A second edition that is a genuine improvement of what was already a good book on theory. This text is an excellent starting place for an overview of the various perspectives taken on mediated communication. Its major failures are the lack of integration of the study of communication and the inconsistent application of evaluative criteria. This author's 1984 review of uses and gratifications research (With the benefit of hindsight: Reflections on uses and gratifications research. *Critical Studies in Mass Communication, 1*, 177-193.) is also worth reading. In it, he provides a brief description of the issues that have plagued this perspective and offers a thoughtful response in defense of it.

Fisher, B. A. (1978). *Perspectives on human communication.* New York: Macmillan.

A much larger view of theory in communication than is ordinarily taken, Fisher avoids the detailed particulars of separate writers to illuminate the central themes around which they congregate. The result is a principled analysis of theory. Though now more than a decade old, this book still stands as a refreshing and informative look at what theory can do and has accomplished.

Becker, S. L. (1984). Marxist approaches to media studies: The British experience. *Critical Studies in Mass Communication, 1,* 66-80.

The author provides an excellent review of how some scholars have developed an analytical framework for studying media process and effects on society. Using Marxist interpretations, the author, a somewhat "reformed" American positivist, describes the major perspectives for thinking about relationships among the media institutions, government, groups in society, and individuals. For additional reading in this area see Hall (1986) and Hardt (in press).

Lee, C. (1980). *Media imperialism reconsidered: The homogenizing of television.* Beverly Hills, CA: Sage.

This author examines Schiller's major ideas on cultural imperialism and U.S. influence internally and abroad. He provides a thorough analysis of the pitfalls of classifying subgroups or subcultures too conveniently and easily. He provides a view that modifies yet extends Schiller's work. Coupled with Becker's article (see foregoing), the reader should gain an elementary grasp of what issues are at stake in Marxist interpretations and perspectives (see also Jameson, 1981).

Lowery, S., & DeFleur, M. L. (1983). *Milestones in mass communication research: Media effects.* New York: Longman.

Probably a "must read" for any serious understanding of the genre of the effects study. This volume documents the high points of social concerns and the response of the research community to them. Their conclusion that "mass communication takes place in a constantly changing social and cultural milieu that can alter both the process and its consequences" sets well with us (p. 360).

Jeffres, L. (1986). *Mass media: Processes and effects.* Prospect Heights, IL: Waveland.

The first three chapters set up the bulk of this book by briefly describing the societal context of the mass media, some views of the process of mediated communication, and the organizations and people in them who form the media institutions. The remaining six chapters look at the audience, content, and the traditional typology of effects—social, political, economic, and cultural. The author provides a standard literature review format but leaves out a great many studies of media processes and effects. Such omissions are common in reviews, but in this case, there are no discernible criteria directing what was included and excluded. The book provides a selective summary of the media effects literature up to early 1986 without any enduring framework into which subsequent research can be assimilated. It functions, therefore, as a summary catalogue of some media effects research up to the mid-1980s. (See also Klapper, 1960; Surgeon General's Report, 1971; Atkin, Murray, & Nayman, 1971; Murray, 1980 for other effects bibliographies.)

Severin, W. J., with Tankard, J. W., Jr. (1988). *Communication theories* (2nd ed.). New York: Longman.

A new edition of a very traditional look at communication theory, useful because it attempts to treat communication as a unified discipline. Don't expect more that a mention of anything past the mid 1970s, however.

6

Experimental Methods in Mediated Communication Research

THIS CHAPTER BEGINS an excursion that continues through the following chapter, into the realms of research methodology. This journey is a necessary part of our search for an understanding of the processes and effects of mediated communication. Research methods are one of a triumvirate of means by which we constitute knowledge claims (the other two being theory and instrumentality). What we know is in part shaped by the methods we use to provide the evidence needed to advance a proposition into a body of knowledge. To determine what we "know" about processes and effects, then, requires us to make a judgment as to the character of that evidence. The two chapters consider the three major methodologies of empirical research: experimental, survey, and ethnographic. We are concerned here only with the **empirical** forms of evidence, both quantitative and qualitative. The term empirical is granted to systems of evidence that are grounded in the material aspects of our experience. Generally, these systems of evidence are contrasted with the creative (artistic) and the critical. Our concern is limited in this manner because the empirical is the ordinary arena in which analyses of these topics take place.

We start our journey with an examination of experimental methods. Experimental studies are regularly cited as evidence of the effects of violent television and film fare on the violent behavior of viewers and the effects of viewing pornographic or sexually explicit content. The experiment is, in fact, the analytical method of choice when the suspected agent of an effect can be in the control of the researcher and the relationship between the agent and the effect can be shown or presumed to be a direct, causal linkage. Because of its importance as a method of study, understanding the logic of experimentation, how it works, and what it enables us to conclude and *not* conclude about mediated communication effects is of critical interest and provides the focus for this chapter. The chapter is divided, as is our wont, into three sections. The first considers the elements that go into the design of an experiment; the second, the assumptions that warrant the acceptance of experimental evidence; and the third provides a critical analysis of a classic, often referenced study of media, children, and imitative behavior.

SECTION I: DESIGN OF EXPERIMENTS

Social science experiments have their roots in the natural and physical sciences. Experimentation is used to identify and verify relationships among specific, definable elements. The design of an experiment begins when the researcher can state a causal relationship between one event, condition, trait, or state—called a variable—and another event, condition, trait, or state. There are two important elements that need to be explained in that statement: One is the nature of a causal relationship; the other is that of the variable.

CAUSAL RELATIONSHIPS

A causal relationship is one in which the appearance of the effect is dependent on the prior appearance of the agent. Simple causal relationships have two characteristics: (a) necessity and (b) sufficiency. The characteristic of necessity requires that the effect *not* appear in the absence of the agent. Sufficiency requires that when the agent is present the effect will also follow. The most powerful explanations come from simple causal relationships because they give us good predictive control. If one wants the effect—initiate the agent. If one sees the agent—expect the effect. We have talked about this relationship being the desired and expected one in studies using the exposure model.

VARIABLES

A variable is a defining or punctuation of our experience. It is a boundary that distinguishes one experience from all others and merges all similar experiences into the same concept. Variables in media effects research have been the different types of content (violent, nonviolent, sexual and aggressive, sexual and nonaggressive, nonsexual), the states of mind of the respondents (frustrated, angered, aroused, not aroused), their traits (level of education, social class, age, development), events (viewing, not viewing), and conditions (viewing alone, working while viewing).

Experiments divide variables into two major classes—independent and dependent. The independent variable set is considered the agent for the dependent variable set. The independent variables are the ones the experimenter will manipulate, and the dependent variables are those that are observed as the outcome of the manipulation. That manipulation gets described in various ways but it always involves the presence or absence of some form of the independent variable (causal agent).

Variables in experiments are defined by the procedures or operations used to measure or elicit them. Such definitions are called *operational definitions.* Operational definitions enable an observer to recognize the behavior or conditions and to measure or reproduce them. Operational definitions of aggression, for example, have been the frequency of hitting an inflatable Bobo doll, the number of painful electrical shocks given to another participant, coded observations of aggressive play, and self-reports on questionnaires. The key requirement for all operational definitions is that they tap into some dimension of the concept they claim. In this case it is aggression—either as it characterizes the behavior of some television or film actors or as it describes the behavior of the respondents

HYPOTHESES

A hypothesis is a statement that puts two or more variables into a predicted relationship. Examples are as follows: "Viewing violent content leads to increased aggression." "Committed voters show more interest in campaign texts." "Individuals who make more frequent use of television score lower in reading abilities." In each case, the first variable is stated as an agent for the effect that follows. The first hypothesis places exposure to violent content as the agent for increased aggression, for example. Hypotheses are predictions derived from some theory about how such things work that will be tested in the experiment. The experiment will set up the optimal conditions for a **fair test.** The experimenter wants the hypothesis to succeed but must provide for the opportunity of its failure. Those two concerns set the requirements for the design of the experiment.

CONTROLS IN EXPERIMENTS

A simple media experiment might include one independent variable—violent versus nonviolent television content (i.e., the presence and absence of violence in content)—and one dependent variable—a measure of viewers' aggressive behavior. If the group seeing the violent segment is more aggressive on the average than is the other group seeing the nonviolent segment, then the relationship is assumed to indicate that viewing violent TV content can cause increases in the aggressive behavior of viewers. Thus it is the manipulation of the television content that is assumed to cause the difference in the aggressive behavior that was observed.

The cause and effect assumption, however, is only an assumption and a big one at that. If there is to be a convincing argument made for this assumption, the experimenter must successfully rule out any other events or variables that might account for (cause) the differences observed for the dependent variable. The experiment must, therefore, introduce at least some elements of control. In deciding what controls to effect, the experimenter must determine what are the most likely elements to interact with the relationship between violent content and aggression. The ones that we would choose include traits of the respondents, states of mind, conditions of viewing, and the circumstances permitting an aggressive response.

TRAITS Certainly the experimenter would want to have the same kinds of people in the two content groups. If they were to vary widely on age, education, socioeconomic class, intelligence, and the like, we would expect differences simply on that basis. This control could be effected by using a relatively homogeneous group such as college students (a typical solution) for the respondents. It could also be done by random assignment. Random assignment means that each participant, whether high, average, or low on any given trait, has an equal chance of being placed in the violent television group or the nonviolent television group. With random assignment, each group should have a roughly equal distribution of participants. But, like the assumption of cause and effect, the roughly equal distribution of participants across experimental groups is still an assumption. Random assignment makes the occurrence of an unequal distribution very unlikely, but still a possibility.

STATES OF MIND In similar vein to the distribution of respondent traits, should respondents in one group be confused, frustrated, angered, or aroused to a different degree than the other group prior to the presentation of the content, or for some reason other than the content, differences over the aggression measure are likely to occur. If the researcher is not aware of these prior state differences, he or she will incorrectly attribute the outcome to content. To control for that possible error, researchers expose respondents to social conditions designed to elicit a common frame of mind—relaxed, angered, frustrated, whatever is called for by the theory in place.

CONDITIONS OF VIEWING Differences in viewing conditions might cause differences in outcomes. One group views individually and the other communally or one has a distracting environment and the other peaceful: Both are obvious sources of error. The researcher will attempt to standardize the conditions for all respondents.

CIRCUMSTANCES OF RESPONSE Response from the treatment and control groups have to be comparable. In most cases, the control instituted for this requirement is to collect or measure responses on the same instrument. This instrument might be a self-report on feelings of aggression or a set of responses that are ostensibly aggressive or imitate aggression, such as delivering mild electrical shocks or hitting a Bobo doll. Again, the researcher attempts to standardize the conditions of response for all respondents.

CONTROLS AND DESIGN

Controls are crucial to the proper design of a fair test of the hypothesis. In the foregoing example, the lack of controls over traits, states, or conditions of viewing and/or responding could result in the experimenter observing a difference in aggression because of differences in traits, states, or conditions rather than the content being tested. The experimenter, of course, would have no way of knowing that the source of the difference in aggression was not the content and would conclude, therefore, that violent content was the cause.

REPRODUCIBILITY

When experimenters report their results, it is imperative that the conditions under which effects are observed be as accurately and as completely specified as possible. This requirement means, in essence, that something about the conditions may have produced the effects reported other than the variables manipulated and controlled by the experimenter. Moreover, science also demands that findings be capable of reproduction. When findings are tested over and over again under the exact conditions, the process is called replication. Replication is one of the necessary safeguards in the scientific process that prevents a result that happens by chance or coincidence from being attributed to the causal relationship that the experiment was supposed to be testing. (This is the scientific equivalent of the "On any given Sunday..." rule.) Successful replication depends upon careful and exacting specifications of conditions and variables. When accomplished, replication adds substantial credibility to the validity of the cause and effect relationship reported by the scientist. When replication does not take place or when results are not successfully reproduced, the relationships reported remain highly tentative, questionable, and/or unclear.

PROBABILITY

Probability plays a wide-ranging role in science. To begin with, science maintains a fundamental skepticism about its own claims. They are accepted provisionally. A given statement is received as probably more true than another until or unless a better one comes along.

More directly, probability rules the relationships predicted among variables. Formal causal relationships in logic require that each and every time the agent is present the effect will follow and if the agent is not present, the effect will not occur. Pragmatic causal relationships in science are expressed in terms of probability: Given the agent, the effect is more likely but not absolutely certain.

Finally, the results of experiments are expressed in probabilities because the experiment represents only one expression of the relationship within a potentially infinite range. The experimenter, then, can be more or less certain of the outcome but never positive.

VALIDITY

Validity is the attribute of most importance in evaluating an experiment. The behavior as represented in the laboratory must be *isomorphic* to the behavior as it occurs outside the laboratory (or field conditions for that matter). In other words, the two behaviors must be at least roughly equivalent to one another. If not, the results produced are known as **experimental artifacts,** products unique to the experimental setting but unlike the behavior as it happens in the real world. Much of the criticism of experiments, especially those done in laboratories (usually college classrooms), focuses on this lack of isomorphism. This argument about mundane realism or external validity is that when variables and conditions in the experiment do not effectively simulate or approximate the variables and conditions as they occur naturally outside the experimental environment, the experimental findings are largely irrelevant. You would be sadly misled if you acted upon the implications of such findings. Looking forward, Chapter 8 will provide an extended discussion of the three levels of validity that should be evaluated.

SUMMARY

Experimental designs are warranted when the analyst has reason to believe that a dependent relationship exists between two variables. The point of the experiment is to demonstrate that the appearance of the dependent variable is contingent on the presence of the independent variable. To produce this evidence, experimental designs institute controls that aim at ensuring that the presence or absence of the independent variable is the only difference in two conditions in which the dependent variable can occur. The experimental hypothesis of the relationship is confirmed when the dependent condition occurs in the presence of the casual agent and does not occur in its absence.

The intent of the elements of design are to institute adequate controls and to provide for the application of the findings to the actual problem at hand—in our case the effects of media in society. The success in meeting this intent determines the validity of the experiment and quality of its claims.

CENTRAL IDEAS OF SECTION I: DESIGN OF EXPERIMENTS

1. Experimental research is designed to provide evidence on causal or conditional relationships by examining in controlled conditions the effect of one variable on another.
2. Controls in media experiments usually involve ensuring that respondents are similar in nature and in their current states of mind, that conditions of

viewing are equivalent, and the conditions of response save for the presence or absence of the causal agent are the same.

3. Experiments meet the requirement of intersubjectivity when the results are reproducible. Replication is part of the evidence for the acceptance of a claim.
4. Experiments must meet validity requirements by representing the conditions they attempt to explain.

SECTION II: ASSUMPTIONS OF EXPERIMENTAL MEDIA EFFECTS RESEARCH

Given that we now have some idea of the elements that constitute the experimental approach, we can turn our attention to the assumptions that allow the use of experimental procedures to inform us about conditions in the world in which we live. These assumptions also represent the criteria by which we can evaluate any particular experiment. These assumptions can be applied to any experimental study, done in a laboratory or in the field, in evaluating its effectiveness, validity, and worth. It is clear that the assumptions must be met before the findings of the experiment can have relevance to our understanding of media effects.

(1) *The known characteristics of the experimental data are isomorphically related to the behavior in the natural environment.*

This assumption means that the conditions in the experimental setting under which the effects are measured and the instruments used to measure a given dimension of media effects are very similar to those conditions as they occur in the consumer's own natural environments. If the experimental conditions are dissimilar in a major way, results observed may well represent experimental artifacts.

This assumption is cause for concern when the researcher must use a **surrogate** or **simulated measure** for the natural behavior of interest. For example, it has been argued by experimenters studying violent content and aggression (e.g., Bandura, 1973, Milgram & Shotland, 1973) that surrogate measures are the only plausible options for the study of aggressive behaviors. They claim quite correctly that creating an experimental environment that actually measures the aggressive effects of violent media content on human beings would be morally and legally unjustifiable. This position, of course, assumes that **simulation** and approximation efforts will provide effective representations of the processes and interactions that take place outside of the experimental setting. But in nearly five decades of media effects experiments, the experimental conditions and procedures used appear to be rather poor simulations of their real-world counterparts.

Another area of difficulty is in the ordinary processes of content selection that we all practice in our attendance to the media. In both laboratory and field experiments, exposure to media content is usually fixed by the protocol for the participants. Participants watch the experimenter-selected and/or produced film, television segment/program, or other mediated content. Exposure is not at all voluntary or self-selected.

In many experiments, exposure takes place in an essentially noncompetitive environment, one that purposely has few if any chances for interruptions, distractions, or competing alternatives that might divert the viewer or reader from the experimental role he or she has agreed to play. When exposure is mandatory as part of a "scientific experiment" and takes place with participants viewing alone and/or in an artificially created group (created for the purposes of the experiment), the hopes of approximating anything even close to natural viewing conditions vanish before the experiment can even begin.

Contrast the artificiality of the typical experimental setting with the host of different environments that occur in natural states. One of the key differences is that in natural environments, exposure and attention are voluntary and selective, largely under the control of the individual (not mandated by an experimenter). Another crucial difference is the occurrence of viewer/environmental interactions that are carefully and purposely prevented in experimental procedures and environments. Such interactions are avoided because they "confound" the process by introducing intervening variables that in turn mediate (change, erase, alter) the effects of the content on viewers under study. Of course it is precisely those effects that regularly occur in natural environments, but yet they are suppressed by researchers because they do not manifest themselves uniformly across natural environments and the same interactions do not occur in the same way from household to household. In brief, because they cannot be easily or practically accounted for by experimenters, they are procedurally "controlled" out of existence.

A small-scale but most enlightening study by Bechtel, Achelpohl, & Akers (1971) offers a solid indication of natural environmental effects on the "viewing" of television. Having videotaped 20 families' television usage in their own households, Bechtel and his colleagues reported that television viewing was largely not a sole activity. Viewers engaged in a host of other activities while the set was on, reading a newspaper or magazine, talking, sleeping, staring out the window, and so on. Counting viewing time as only those periods when viewers' eyes were on the screen (a highly restrictive operational definition of television "viewing"), results indicated that such viewing was actually going on less than half of the time for household members that were in the room at least some of the time while a program was on. While this study did not measure the degree to which naturally occurring factors mediated content impact on viewers, it convincingly confirms what you probably realized applies to your own viewing habits—viewing television usually represents a less than full-time commitment.

The variable nature of attention is well-recognized by the industry. Even a cursory examination of how television shows are paced and structured (formatted) indicates that industry practitioners take this less than full commitment into account. Because exposure/attention to content is not generally consistent and is reflected in the structure and pace of actual television shows and films, the generalizability of experimental TV or film segments (as opposed to entire films or programs) also comes into serious question. In some experiments, a segment is produced by editing together several scenes that participants view in a 4-7 minute block (e.g., Liebert & Baron, 1972; or in a longer set of segments, Frost & Stauffer, 1987); in others, only a short sequence is taken from an entire film or program and is shown to participants devoid of its original context. In any event, the use of segments introduces another artificiality for viewers in that not only are they expected to watch as part of the study, but they also view a condensed bit of content free of its context and unlike any content they have seen before or will ever see again.

At least with edited segments taken from actual films or television programs, the viewer sees content that is professionally produced and reasonably "slick." Experimentally produced originals, however, can be done with inexpensive, poor, or low-grade quality equipment and end up looking amateurish. That viewers would have problems recognizing the segment as being much like the content they are used to seeing is no big surprise.

Exposure and attention are processes that are influenced by numerous other factors that operate in the individual's environment. The presence of other people presents a frequent source of mediation that alters content effects. Research on children's learning from television, for example, has shown that those who view with an adult learn more and different things than do those who view alone.

Consider other atypical mediating factors that determine the type and extent of media content effects. In the case of the parent keeping one eye on a playing toddler, the food cooking on the stove, in the oven or microwave, the ringing phone or doorbell, the front or back door opening and closing with people coming and going, it is clear that by necessity or attractiveness, other activities are present in some combination and to some degree. All that we know for sure is that these factors influence the effects of media content on consumers. Not carefully and comprehensively accounting for these significant reality variables is a serious limitation in the applicability of experimental findings.

(2) *The sample used in the experiment represents some identifiable population.*

Experiments always use a small number of respondents to represent the human in general or some set of types within humankind. The respondent group is called a sample of the larger population. Researchers have limited interest in the sample alone. Rather, they wish to apply their findings to the larger population. Generalizing from any sample of individuals to the larger population assumes that the sample is representative of the population involved. Representativeness can never be demonstrated (unless one already knows the characteristics of the population, but then—why do the study?); it has to be judged. To make this judgment, the sample used has to be described fully and the results qualified to reflect the limitations of the sample itself. Studies also need to be replicated with different samples using the same procedures, design, and instruments but with a new sample. Only when a large number of samples show convergence is there any justification for some still limited generalizations.

Researcher Harold Mendelsohn (1974) has criticized much of the media effects research because of its use of samples with questionable generalizability:

Experiments on the alleged effects of mediated communications conducted solely on subjects who are college students or the children of university professors are almost certain to manifest changes as a direct consequence of exposure. These population subsets are literally trained to react to abstractions and to be receptive to innovative ideas. But the population as a whole is made up of both sophisticateds and provincials, professors and functional illiterates, those with flexible receptivity to ideas and those whose positions are literally immutable (even under the most intense bombardments of symbols inviting them to change).

The provincials, the functionally illiterate, and the immutable traditionalists rarely show up in the laboratory. Yet their distribution in the population far outweighs that of the types on which mass communication experiments are typically conducted. Their resistance to change is monumental. Small wonder, then, that the effects noted in much of behavioristic mass communications experimental research manifest themselves "in nature" only on occasion, if at all.

(3) *The content used to generate a given response generalizes to some class of content.*

When an experimenter like Berkowitz (1962) reports the use of a short segment from the movie starring Kirk Douglas titled *Champion* that contains an explicitly violent boxing scene, he does so under the assumption that this content represents violent behavior. At first glance, there seems to be little question that a scene with two men pounding away at each other could be construed as anything but violence. To the extent that the actors represent the purposive acts of inflicting pain and/or injury on one another, the segment indeed is "violent," but there are other factors that cloud the possible representativeness of this particular scene.

First, the segment, even when shown out of context, is clearly perceived by viewers as being fictional; despite any willing suspension of disbelief (which seems hard to induce under the conditions of viewing of only a segment in an experimental setting), respondents are aware as the scene evolves of the fictional creation that is part of the movies. Kirk Douglas is obviously not Mike Tyson or Sugar Ray Leonard.

Second, the violence in this segment is unusually long, involves repeated acts, and focuses on consequences, three unique characteristics. Those who have seen any of the *Rocky* films (I to IX) will grasp the meaning of this limitation. Most televised violence is far different in its typical portrayal. For starters, the duration of the acts is much briefer, and the violent act itself either is entirely implied (not shown at all) or only some parts of the sequence appear on the screen. Most important of all, televised violence is usually devoid of consequences. The results of violence are usually and purposely omitted from television programs. If *Champion* and its violence seems representative of only one series of popular movies and not all, as television's presentation of violence, then its representativeness is in serious doubt. The generalizability may be thus limited to the possible effects of violent movie fight sequences on the aggressive behavior of some viewers under some conditions.

Finally, the segment involves a fight in a socially sanctioned (ergo, not antisocial) event—boxing. Competitors willingly engage in the sport, they train for it, enjoy it (or at least the financial rewards), and a few are even paid very well for it (the same holds true for other violent sports, such as football, hockey, and basketball). Contrast this type of event with the everyday violence that occurs: Aggressors are usually not evenly matched; there are no rules previously agreed upon by participants; there are no substitutes, injury timeouts, referees; there are victims, many virtually defenseless; the setting is a household, bar, alley, or street, none of which is a location designed for violence.

As with the previous assumption on the generalizability of samples, this assumption looks at the media content whose effects are the subject of investigation. It is clear that there can be considerable variations within any given class of media content (all media violence is not alike). The researcher, therefore, is obligated to present the rationale for the representativeness of the content selected for inclusion in the experiment. It seems preferable for studies to use a random sample of actual television programs if the generalization to television content is supportable. If only one program or segment is used, the study's findings should be considered limited.

(4) *The operating elements of the independent variables are fully known.*

When a given type of media content is manipulated by a researcher and a limited range of effects is measured, the assumption is that the differences in content claimed by the researcher have in fact produced or accounted for the differences in behavior on the chosen dependent measures. Mistakes of interpretation are likely when complex process variables are used by media researchers. Such mistakes are perhaps best understood by the old cause and effect line of reasoning that goes like this: "I've tried scotch and soda, bourbon and soda, and whiskey and soda, and I've gotten drunk on them all. It must be the soda!" Mediated content represents a class of variables that is complex and process-oriented. What the researcher assumes is producing the observed effects may be misleading.

For example, some researchers have found that older children (e.g., 11- to 12-year-olds) are more aware of the manipulative intent of advertising content than are younger children (e.g., those under 8 years old). The explanation offered for this difference is that the two different age groups represent different levels of cognitive development, and, accordingly, the older children are capable of discovering and understanding the selling motive, while the younger children have yet to produce these skills. In other words, the state of cognitive development produces reliable (statistically measurable) differences in awareness of advertising intent.

But, the differences in age and/or cognitive development apparently may have little to do with the differences in understanding. Other researchers have shown that these differences may simply be a function of verbal ability and vocabulary differences, both of which mean only that younger children are less capable of expressing their awareness in comparison to older children.

The contrasting claims generate confusion as to what is actually going on, but they do show that the course of acceptance of a claim over time is more important than any occasion of its report. Science works to correct its errors. Any claim made sets itself up for review and criticism. While we may accept the role of maturation in perceiving persuasive intent—or not, our position is open to change.

(5) *The circumstances that led to the behavior measured can be present in a noncontrolled environment with sufficient frequency.*

In Berkowitz's research on film aggression (which became a prototype for this kind of study), subjects (college males) were told they were participating in a number of tasks. After this simple introduction, their base-line blood pressure and pulse were measured. They then were asked to design a house floor plan that would be evaluated by another male student via electrical shocks; the more shocks given, the less evaluators liked the plan. Regardless of what type of floor plan was drawn, the participant received seven shocks from an unseen confederate who was working with the experimenter. The shocks were intended to serve as a hostility arouser. Given only five minutes for the task, the subject was supposed to be angered when he received so many shocks.

Subjects were then to evaluate their evaluator's floor plan through the shocking method. While the other student was supposedly designing his floor plan, each subject watched a scene from a film. Subjects then saw the violent segment mentioned earlier from *Champion* or a short, nonviolent film. It was then the subject's turn to "grade" the student's paper, again via electrical shocks, with the more shocks administered by the participant, the worse the evaluation expressed. After the participant gave the shocks (actually the confederate in the other room simply counted the number of shocks supposedly being given by each participant) and after each task, blood pressure and pulse readings were taken. The idea in all of this is to see if those males seeing the film violence returned more electrical shocks (operationally, if they were more aggressive) than were those who saw the nonviolent film. Results from Berkowitz and his replicators have consistently shown a difference between violence viewers and nonviolence viewers in that those seeing the violent segment returned more shocks than did the nonviolent segment viewers.

Given the unusual circumstances present in these experiments (Have you ever graded floor plans—with electrical shocks?), how do we evaluate whether the circumstances in the experiment will appear with any frequency to be of import? The sequencing and nature of the procedural steps in the experiment are significant elements in the decision to generalize to natural settings. Experiments on media violence effects on aggression have shown that when conditions prior to viewing change, so do subsequent effects on aggression. It is thus incumbent on the researchers to present a rationale for their particular sequence of conditions as to its likelihood of (a) being present in the natural environment and (b) how frequently the particular combination occurs, when all other conditions are the same as they were in the experiment, that will produce the results demonstrated in the research setting.

If we set aside the question of direct external validity—none of us will grade floor plans with electrical shocks—and consider the more abstract components of the action, we can see how to conduct this evaluation. In the Berkowitz-type experiment—and their are several replications and variations-in the span of about 30 minutes, a person is angered by another generally in a scenario of injustice, injured (slightly), receives a brief exposure to a violent, fantasy segment of film content, and is given the opportunity to respond with the same irritating but not harmful stimulus in a socially acceptable manner. The components, time span, and sequence of the action all enter into the explanation of effect. For this explanation to work for violence in society, the components in that time span and sequence must appear in the mundane performance of aggression. Unless researchers can reliably estimate the degree to which experimental conditions are present in natural settings, the results stand as artifacts, interesting and perhaps even provocative, but still artifacts.

(6) *The state of mind of the participants established during the manipulation can and does occur in the participant's own environment and is consistent from one participant to another.*

This assumption says that the interpretation of the experimental procedures by participants must be comparable to what they experience in their own individual media environments. As discussed in the preceding chapters on human communication behaviors, perception involves a selective labeling and interpretation process. How one perceives the environmental conditions at hand depends in part upon what motivations are most salient at that time. The consequence is that tasks and expectations will be interpreted according to each person's identification of the nature of the task and its perceived purpose and consequences.

In terms of an experiment, the tasks performed by participants are selectively perceived. In the Berkowitz research and other similar experiments, the evaluation task may be perceived as just that—no harmful or punitive motives may be part of a participant's frame of mind. Similarly, when participants get a chance to return shocks, the interpretation for some may be: "I'm simply grading his floor plan according to the scale they gave me." In essence, the task may be perceived as simply mutual evaluation with little or no thought of actually "aggressing" or purposely hurting the other person. The point is: Because each participant's interpretation of the tasks is not known, there is no way to determine whether these people perceived that the mutual task involved aggressive behavior at any level. And, even when predicted differences occur for those seeing violent content versus nonviolent content, all that may be demonstrated is that the content will influence their evaluations but not their aggressive behavior. For a task to involve aggression, it must be perceived as an act of aggression. And, for the aggression to be antisocial in nature, its antisocial context must also be perceived as such.

Berkowitz's research suggests the absence of a consistent participant interpretation. First, he notes that few if any participants were able to discern the actual purpose of the experiments. This situation may well mean that the sanctioned scientific procedures were just that for participants—unnatural tasks sequenced in unusual ways in an institutionalized setting. Second, Berkowitz reports data that have high variability. This occurrence means that some participants, particularly those in the violent film groups, returned many shocks, whereas others in the same group returned very few. That participants were not giving consistent responses despite being in the same experimental group suggests that participants were not interpreting the tasks in the same way. Although the average score was higher and differed significantly (statistically speaking), the inconsistency of scores indicates the distinct likelihood of different interpretations occurring for participants.

If experimental procedures are to be generalizable to natural media environments, the conditions used must produce a state of mind in participants that can and does occur with some frequency outside of the experimental setting. Moreover, the interpretations (and subsequent state of mind) of the experimental tasks and what is happening to participants must be consistent from one person to another. And these interpretations must correspond to the researcher's intentions and meanings. A task intended to measure aggression must be interpreted by participants as aggression. Once again, if this two-part assumption cannot be met by researchers individually or collectively (through a series of studies), then the results are of only minimal value for our understanding of media effects.

(7) *The experimental environment allows for the measurement of all major potential responses for a given type of media content.*

After viewing the film (either violent or nonviolent) in Berkowitz's studies, subjects had only one choice of behavior—how many electrical shocks they could give in evaluating their partner's work. What if subjects were given the choice of returning shocks or talking to the other person? We suspect that if participants were allowed a wide range of responses, their display of aggression might have been far different. With the restriction imposed that allowed for only one type of response, the research channeled possible responses in the direction desired and deviated from the known operating conditions present in the natural viewing environment. Although the number and types of choices available to people varies greatly, when individuals are in control, as they are typically in their own media environments, there are options available in most situations that arise. A single or limited experimenter-determined choice(s) is not at all isomorphic to natural settings.

Further, we have all experienced aggressive impulses in the concourse of our everyday activities. Nearly all of us have developed mechanisms by which we control, channel, or repress those impulses. Experimental conditions that release or disable those mechanisms create abnormal conditions of performance. In most of the aggression studies, aggressive behavior is a protocol demand—the most reasonable response for the participant to give.

SUMMARY OF ASSUMPTIONS

The careful examination of the assumptions that experimental research must meet before the findings reach the credibility needed to inform us about the effects of the media suggest that most experiments would have difficulties in meeting the test. It puts the analyst in a quandary as to what to do with the body of claim that is generated by such studies. The ends of the decision continuum—to dismiss it out of hand or to accept it without concern—both seem inappropriate. Our decision is to accept readily what experimental evidence shows only in the specific terms of the protocol. We will not easily grant the move to generalize beyond those protocols—floor plans and electrical shocks are not muggings in the streets. On the other hand, we must be open to the opportunity to learn what can happen in actual settings even if these settings occur in the laboratory. Before making any level of acceptance, however, the reader needs to engage the study itself in a careful, unforgiving analysis. An example of which follows in the next section.

CENTRAL IDEAS IN SECTION II:
ASSUMPTIONS OF EXPERIMENTAL MEDIA EFFECTS RESEARCH

1. For acceptance of experimental evidence in the claim for effect, the following tests must be met: (a) The characteristics of the experimental

data must represent behavior in the natural environment, (b) the sample of respondents must characterize the population it is intended to represent, (c) the content used as the causal agent must correspond to the content of the media, (d) the agency of cause must be properly identified, (e) the conditions of response in the experimental setting must be possible and significantly occurring in the everyday, (f) the respondent must perceive his or her response as in the class specified by the researcher, (g) the experimental procedures must not create a demand for the expected response.

2. Experimental studies typically fail the tests necessary for ready generalizability to media effects in natural settings. The reader, therefore, must exercise caution in making claims from them, and then only after a principled and systematic engagement with the study itself.

SECTION III: A CRITICAL ANALYSIS OF A MEDIA EFFECTS EXPERIMENT

To understand better the limitations of experimental methods as ways of assessing media effects, it is useful to analyze a prototype experiment, one often referred to as a classic in the field. The analysis of this experiment raises issues inherent to nearly all experiments studying media effects. The experiment selected for analysis is not only representative of experimental research but also an excellent example of well-conducted experimentation. The study is titled "Imitation of Film-Mediated Aggressive Models"; the authors are the social psychologists Albert Bandura, Dorthea Ross, and Sheila Ross. And, despite the fact that it was reported in 1963, it still presents procedures and analyses wholly comparable to experiments being reported in today's scholarly journals. The same type of analysis can be applied to any of the media effects experiments reported in various communication journals or journals from noncommunication fields. It is interesting to note that how media effects experiments are conceptualized, carried out, interpreted, and reported have not changed in any substantial way, despite the publication of many hundreds of such studies over more than 25 years.

In the analysis that follows, we carefully review the design decisions and actions taken by the researchers. In mature methodologies such as experimentation there is a great body of literature—scripture nearly—that sets the standards for the research procedures. These standards are high; in fact unattainable, given the normal financial support provided such studies. The result is that the researcher has to make compromises that invariably move the research farther and farther from the standard. These compromises would be less of a problem if the results of the research were accepted within their context. What normally happens, however, is that the results enter the field as if the standards had been met. This is a convenient fiction in which all researchers participate; a sort of graceful gloss that allows us to conduct business as usual.

Our analysis attempts to probe that gloss that to some extent sets us up in an oppositional stance inviting rejection out of hand. Two points are offered to mitigate that reaction: (a) The study analyzed here is not a "bad experiment" that we are taking advantage of; it is as good as most and better than many. (b) It is true that what follows is sharply critical, but it is not unkind. Both Tim and Jim conduct and direct experimental studies making the same sort of compromises identified next. Our move here is an appeal for a realistic appraisal by the reader and for a modesty of claim by the researcher. Our critical analysis considers the following topics: rationale for the study, hypotheses, selection of participants, experimental procedures, results, and limitations.

RATIONALE FOR THE STUDY

The authors point out that while the area of violent content effects on viewer aggression is one that had to date received some attention, no previous research had examined how viewers might copy or model acts of aggression as presented on film or television. They cite a newspaper account of some teenage boys who apparently reenacted a knife fight scene from a movie as an example of imitative media effects. Referencing their own previous studies, they point to the findings that young children (3 to 5 years old) were influenced by observing live models who acted aggressively. Building on these findings, the authors indicate that the purpose of their study was to determine whether the effects of live models could be extended to models shown on film or television. Moreover, since mediated models take different forms other than "real" people, the researchers wanted to compare the modeling effects of real-life film models to nonhuman cartoon characters. They viewed the likely influence of models on a three-place continuum with real-life, nonmediated models on one end, filmed or televised models in the middle, and nonhuman cartoon characters on the other end.

COMMENT That children (or adults for that matter) can copy or imitate film or television characters is a phenomenon of no startling or insightful proportion. Ask any mother if her child ever behaves like an actor on television, and she will tell you that it goes on all the time. Ask any kid (or anyone who was a kid) if he or she ever "play-acted" or pretended to be someone on television or in the movies, and he or she will also confirm the obvious. Any study that seeks to verify what is common awareness is destined to produce results that should be greeted with "So, what else is new?" (But see also our discussion on instrumentality—Chapter 8—for an explanation of the purposes of these claims.) Beyond this obvious condition, however, the researchers' concern was also how different types of models might have different types of effects on the imitative behavior of viewers. The authors also attempted to measure any transfer or generalization of specific modeled behaviors to other similar behaviors that were not specifically demonstrated by the film model. In addition, the authors were interested in how male versus female models would affect the behavior of male and female children who viewed them. Finally, the study manipulated conditions that were thought to affect the nature of modeled aggression. When young viewers were frustrated, it was anticipated that they would be more predisposed to model aggression than would frustrated children who were not exposed to aggressively behaving models.

The strength of this study is its assessment of the characteristics that seem to facilitate or inhibit children's modeling of filmed or televised characters' behaviors. Conceptually, beyond the general imitative modeling phenomenon known commonly to exist, this study was significant in its attempt to measure various aspects of the modeling process.

HYPOTHESES

Hypotheses are the educated guesses of researchers. Based on their abilities to assess a problem area, conceptualize it, and build on the findings of other researchers, social scientists formulate predictions. These predictions link up the independent and dependent variables as they operate ostensibly in cause and effect relationships.

Hypotheses should be grounded in theory. This grounding means that predicted relationships should be the outgrowth of a larger, overall explanation of how a given process is presumed to function. This study's hypotheses are distinctly tied to previously developed theories and to research that had tested some of the theory's relationships.

The authors predicted (1) imitation of real-life models would be the strongest effect, followed by human models on film, and finally, cartoon figures; (2) children who were less favorably predisposed to aggressive behavior would imitate modeled aggression less than would children more favorably predisposed; (3) male children would imitate more aggression than would females; (4) frustrated children exposed to aggressive models would display more aggressive behavior than would those frustrated children not exposed.

COMMENT Before describing the research procedures, it is perhaps useful for us to summarize the implications of the theory-based hypotheses tested by the authors in their experiment. They are, in effect, setting up a series of proposed restrictions or limitations that determine the likelihood of children imitating filmed aggressive models. Children most likely to imitate the film model's behaviors would be males favorably predisposed to aggressive behavior who observe male film or real-life models acting aggressively. Further, these same children are then frustrated (denied something they were promised and very much wanted) and then, finally, given an opportunity to behave in an environment that allows the behaviors demonstrated by the models to be carried out by the children. Conversely, a low level of imitation is expected for females negatively predisposed to aggression who observe female film, real-life, or cartoon characters acting aggressively and who are not frustrated prior to having the chance to act out the model's behaviors. Other levels of variables should also bring about intermediate amounts of imitative aggression. In essence, the authors are stating that some types of children (3- to 5-year-olds) will imitate some of the behaviors of film models under some very specific conditions, and that the sequence of events and the presence of the specified conditions directly affect the amounts and kinds of imitation that occur.

PROCEDURES

Given specific conditional hypotheses and a well-conceived rationale for this particular study, we can now turn to the procedures followed by the researchers in testing the hypotheses. This juncture is one of the most critical for most media effects research (both experimental and nonexperimental)—the point at which a good idea or set of potentially meaningful relationships begins to disintegrate, often to the point of having little to say regardless of the outcome of the experiment.

It should be made clear before proceeding further into this section that methodological limitations, flaws, or criticisms are not usually statistical in nature. One of the myths of social science research is that the methods cannot be grasped without a good working knowledge of statistical tests and probability theory. This myth is most unfortunate because the critical concern is with validity, not the application of a tool of analysis. Validity refers to whether the researcher is actually measuring what he or she claims to be measuring. Do the operationalized definitions of key terms (e.g., *aggression*) agree with your sense of what the behavior in the experiment is supposed to represent outside the laboratory in the real world in which the effects under study actually occur? Do the procedures that subjects go through represent an effective simulation of the real world conditions under which the subjects usually operate? To what larger population are the participants used in the study generalizable? How substantial were the actual effects—do the rates of behavior as measured show large differences or very small ones (this question is independent of statistically significant differences)? These are all validity questions that must be asked to appropriately evaluate the usefulness of any media effects study, and as you might be able to guess by now, none of them requires any knowledge of statistics on your part.

PARTICIPANTS The authors report that they used a total of 96 boys and girls who were attending the Stanford University Nursery School. The age range was substantial, 35 months to 69 months, with the average age being 52 months.

Several interpretive difficulties immediately arise with the selection of these participants. The most serious problem is posed by the age range. In terms of cognitive developmental level, the differences between a child not quite 3 years old and one who is almost 6 are substantial. In brief, how a 3-year-old looks at the world and makes sense of it would differ to a great degree from a 6-year-old. And, because cognitive development researchers have also observed large differences between children of the same age (i.e., not even all 3-year-olds are alike), the researchers should have controlled for age and cognitive developmental-level differences. They did not, and therefore, a major problem in interpreting results already presents itself. In essence, the researchers used a sample of children that was convenient, maintaining control of cost and effort. Convenience samples, even when they contain substantial flaws such as this one, are most common.

A second limitation stems from the location of the nursery school, Stanford University. The children at this particular school would be expected to be atypical in major ways associated with the outcomes of the experiment, given their parents' level of education, orientation toward their children's learning and, presumably, intelligence. To whom is this group of children comparable in trying to generalize the results? Why would anyone expect this sample of 3- to 6-year-olds to be like 3- to 6-year-olds who come from different, nonuniversity backgrounds? And, given the likelihood of these children's heightened intellectual development, their modeling behavior could be expected to be of a different quality and nature than would those of other, more average children.

A related limitation that renders the sample atypical is that the children at the nursery school were functioning in an age-integrated environment. Working, playing, and learning in a group of various aged children make for children who become favorably predisposed to learning from new behaviors, especially in the school setting and from teachers or teacherlike adult models. These children in essence were primed to learn new behaviors from adult models when presented in their own educational environment. In this way, imitative behavior from the children is an extremely safe bet. That there will be some imitative effects seems guaranteed before data are even collected.

A final problem with the participants arises in the question: Why preschoolers, as opposed to older children? The authors cite anecdotal evidence of teenagers imitating film models as one basis of their interest, yet they test preschoolers in an environment conducive to imitation. It can (and Bandura has), of course, be argued that 3- to 6-year-olds are in the process of acquiring lifelong behaviors, but the susceptibility of older children seems a greater cause for concern given their greater abilities to perform antisocial acts and the presence of more opportunities. The attachment of an introduction that references our concerns with teenage behavior with a study of preschoolers is an interesting rhetorical turn.

EXECUTION OF EXPERIMENT The 96 children were divided into four groups of 24 each. One group observed two real-life models acting aggressively; a second saw the same two models on film; a third saw a person in a clown costume acting aggressively in a "cartoon" setting; the fourth group was a control group that observed no models at all.

The particular behavioral sequences for both the real-life and film models involved some nonantisocial behavior in the beginning, but after one minute, the rest of the time was spent "aggressing" toward the Bobo doll, making several novel types of responses in addition to merely hitting it:

> The model sat on the Bobo doll and punched it repeatedly in the nose. The model than raised the Bobo doll and pummeled it on the head with a mallet. Following the mallet aggression, the model tossed the doll up in the air aggressively and kicked it about in the room. This sequence of physically aggressive acts was repeated approximately three times interspersed with verbally aggressive responses, such as: "Sock him in the nose"; "Hit him down"; "Throw him in the air"; "Kick him"; and "Pow." (p. 45)

For some children, the model was a male, for others it was a female. The cartoon character was evidently "asexual."

After viewing (or not, for the control group), each child, participating one at a time, was escorted by a female experimenter (the same one for all 96 children) to an adjacent room that contained several "very attractive toys." The children were first told they could play with the toys in the room. At the point at which they had just begun to play, the children were interrupted. Each child was then told that while he or she could not play with the "very best toys," it was possible to play with some other toys in another room. This procedure was intended to induce a state of frustration, priming an aggressive response.

This next room contained various "aggressive" and "nonaggressive" toys. The aggressive toys included a five-foot tall Bobo doll, a mallet and peg board, two dart guns, and a tether ball with a face painted on it. The nonaggressive toys included a tea set, crayons and coloring paper, a ball, two dolls, three bears, cars and trucks, and plastic farm animals. Toys were arranged in the same way before each child entered the room.

Children spent 20 minutes in the experimental play room. The adult experimenter remained in the room to prevent children from leaving the room early and to allow participation of those children who refused to be left alone. The experimenter busied herself with paperwork at a desk in the corner of the room and avoided interaction with the child.

Two observers scored each child's behavior at 5-second intervals, using a one-way mirror that prevented the children from seeing them but allowed the observers to record the type of behavior displayed by each child at each interval. The observers' ratings were in near unanimous agreement.

The observers noted the following behaviors: *imitative aggression*—those specific behaviors demonstrated by the model; *partially imitative responses* —hitting objects other than the Bobo doll with the mallet and sitting on the laid-down Bobo but not "aggressing" toward it; *nonimitative aggression*—acts of punching, slapping or pushing the doll, other aggressive acts toward objects other than the doll, and "hostile remarks," like "Shoot the Bobo"; "Cut him," and so on; *aggressive gun play*—shooting darts, aiming the gun and firing imaginary shots at objects in the room. The authors also included the *nonaggressive play* of children as part of the overall observations. These behaviors comprised the *dependent variables* in this experiment.

The *independent variables* in the experiment were: sex of the model, sex of the child viewer, context of portrayed aggressive behavior—real life versus film, versus cartoon models. Thus there were 12 independent groups of children, with the following numbers for each group:

	Real-Life (24)		Human Film (24)		Cartoon (24)	Control (24)
	Female Model	Male Model	Female Model	Male Model		
girls (48):	6	6	6	6	12	12
boys (48):	6	6	6	6	12	12

Figure 6.1 Design of Bandura, Ross, & Ross (1963) experiment.

COMMENTS ON PROCEDURES

This experiment appears to be most thorough in its planning and execution. Unfortunately, the limitations and flaws, some avoidable and others inherent, make the results generally difficult to interpret and apply to our understanding of how media have effects on us. As you read through this discussion, or maybe even before, you may develop your own separate set of problems. You should remember, though, that studies like this one are never usually read by students (or even by a great many researchers). All that you may have read about is the outcome of the research. The results are usually prefaced by impressive-sounding credentials referring to a prominent social scientist at an equally prominent university who has studied a significant problem. Then comes a brief, overly simplified summary of only some of the findings. Such reporting of research in textbooks or in the popular mass media is clearly not the fault of the researchers themselves, unless of course they have written press releases that misstate or oversimplify their findings. But, the situation is nonetheless upsetting because the findings become accepted devoid of limitations and are often repeated in countless other sources as if the research has proven over and over that certain effects of media on some viewers have been occurring on a regular basis. In this particular study, the limitations are indeed crucial as they are in all studies. Some of these limitations may appear at first glance to be trivial or "nitpicking," but when their implications are exposed, their considerable significance becomes clear.

The authors are concerned with children's learning of aggressive behavior from mediated models. They do not offer an acceptable definition of aggression, however, and this is a paradox for those who seek and rightfully expect an unambiguous interpretation of what the experiment demonstrates. The authors chose to operationalize aggression in a peculiar way. Aggression, as a construct of antisocial behavior, involves a socially unacceptable act of inflicting or attempting to inflict harm, pain, injury, or death on another person or persons. Certainly the knife fight among the teen-agers, cited by the researchers, meets this definition. But the researchers used generally accepted behaviors directed toward inanimate, nonhuman objects. The Bobo doll is, of course, a toy designed to be struck—hit, pushed, or both. Any child who used the doll for its intended purposes was behaving quite appropriately. Whether aggression, typically defined, is involved cannot be determined but may be in doubt.

Bandura (1973) has argued elsewhere that his and others' research using toys as objects of aggressive play provide legitimate measures of antisocial aggression. He points out that boxers, for example, learn to punch by using a variety of different inanimate objects. Pilots learn to fly planes under simulated conditions. He thinks it rather foolish to do research in which actual interpersonal aggression can occur. That argument has obvious merit, but the "simulations" here do not stand up under close scrutiny.

Boxers hit the heavy bag and the punching bag in preparation for aggressive behavior, which they clearly understand while engaged in such training. Pilots are also well aware of their objective while simulating flying. Training military recruits for hand-to-hand combat necessarily involves simulated conditions, but again, the objective of the aggression is clearly understood and the training procedures are perceived as being means to well-known ends. We have no reason to suspect, however, that the children had any other objective in mind than simply playing with toys, perhaps in the same manner as the models. Adult presence and sanctions through actions and the absence of comment undoubtedly communicated approval to the children for their actions. And the children had no sense of learning to hit Bobo as preparation for a longer-range goal. In this sense, the analogy to simulated training fails.

Bandura has also argued that children learn behaviors that can later be used when the appropriate conditions present themselves. In simple terms, children who learn to hit and push a Bobo doll have learned the generalizable behavior of hitting and pushing. It requires little effort to transfer those behaviors to other settings and human targets. On the face of it, this argument appears to be a potent indictment of modeling hitting and pushing or of toys that evoke hitting or pushing. Of course, Bandura is not concerned about schoolyard hitting and pushing. He is concerned about a qualitatively different form of behavior—violence.

What does it take to evoke violence? Knowing a behavior is neither necessary nor sufficient. Hundreds of thousands of us through our service in the armed forces know efficient methods of violence and have learned them in a far more effective way than by watching images. We do not perform those acts, although the spectacularly frightful exceptions demonstrate what could happen if we did. How is it that we can train men and women to be killers and release them back to society with few ill effects? We would argue that the normal social action frames in which we live do not support that violence and, therefore, it does not appear.

How can we understand the children's aggressive play in these terms? Consider the fact that these children were given every nonverbal indication of approval and positive reinforcement for paying attention to the behaviors of the model and were by virtue of the environment either actively provided with or encouraged to show evidence of imitative learning; they were certainly not discouraged in any way from such "aggressive" activity. While the experimenter may have avoided speaking with the children in the play room, her presence and the absence of expressed disapproval in effect meant that whatever the child was doing was acceptable. The nature of the experiment thus created a particular environment in which the prescribed behaviors could appear. One can imagine the child thinking to him- or herself something like: "This must be okay to do. I just saw an adult do it" or "She's not saying anything or even looking like she's upset" or "This toy looks like fun. The grownup just showed me how to play with it."

Aggressive behavior may be learned independently of consequences (good or bad), as Bandura has maintained, but it nonetheless requires particular contexts for its performance. Positive play responses are generally separated from negative, hostile, or aggressive ones. Contexts for behaviors are learned as well as the actual behaviors themselves. Acquired behaviors are labeled and recalled accordingly.

Evidence for this argument comes from the Bandura et al. study itself. The authors report that the experimenter and a nursery school teacher rated the children prior to the execution of the study on four 5-point scales. These scales rated each child's display of physical aggression, verbal aggression, aggression toward inanimate objects (angrily throwing a book or toy on the floor), and aggression inhibition of actions by the child in the face of provocation (in which an aggressive response was highly likely). These observational ratings of the children's aggression were based upon the interactions and behavior of the children in their nursery school environment. Both raters ostensibly knew the children quite well and had experience observing and working with them. When these aggression ratings were used to see if they correlated with the "aggression" displayed by each child in the course of the experiment, the authors report that there were *no* relationships between the ratings of aggressive behavior and the "aggressive behavior" observed in the experiment. This means, quite simply, that children rated as being very aggressive in their day-to-day nursery school behavior were equally likely to display very little imitative aggression during the experimental play period and that nonaggressive children were equally likely to be aggressive.

This critical absence of any relationship between teachers' ratings of aggressive behavior and the behaviors displayed by children during the experiment may be explained in several ways. The first explanation warranted is that the experimenters indeed were failing to measure aggression and probably were measuring, therefore, a type of behavior that was independent of aggression. In brief, if aggression involves a purposive act to harm or injure another person(s), and the researchers measured the imitation of models by children in a "play" environment with inanimate objects, then there is no relationship between aggressive behavior and play behavior of these children. The lack of isomorphism impaired the validity of the study, its ability to measure what it claimed to be measuring.

Another plausible explanation that accounts for the nonexistent relationship reported is that the teacher and the experimenters were evaluating or rating the children with a different sense of what constitutes aggression. Had the definition been clarified, the ratings might have correlated at least to some degree. But, if the raters were using a different definition of aggression than the experimenters, then the question can be resolved only by evaluating the validity of the two definitions. While neither may be defining aggression at all, it seems most likely that the ratings of the teachers were closer to aggression (in the most common way people think of it) than was the definition as operationalized by the experimenters.

The third possible explanation is that the protocol itself created the conditions in which certain children found the expression of the behaviors defined as aggressive to be sensible. How does a 3- to 6-year-old child make sense of the sequence of events that led him or her to be in a room with a Bobo doll? Experiments of this sort provide no explanatory space for the interpretive processes of the "subjects" who are considered "subject to" the forces manipulated by the experimenter. On the other hand, do the events unfold in such a way that the child, at the point of the critical observation, says, "This is the way I am supposed to behave"?

A final comment needs to be made on Bandura's contention that it is unnecessary and irresponsible to expect researchers to show that children can learn to imitate aggression toward humans rather than just toys. We agree, but this argument cannot be the substitute for validity. If inanimate objects are approximations of human beings, it needs to be demonstrated in a clear and convincing manner. If a model airplane is a successful simulation of a real-sized working plane, then the equivalence of the model to the plane can be demonstrated by showing that both are the same except that one is smaller than the other.

Boxers would not argue that hitting bags is just like hitting another boxer. This "striking" behavior is primarily intended to develop timing, stamina, and strength in punching. No sane manager would send his prize pupil into the ring against an opponent without having sparred with other fighters first. Real boxers hit back and/or hit first; punching bags do not (except for a few inept boxers who get decked by an errant bag).

If violence involves human beings as targets in a perceptibly antisocial act, then research simulations must account for the qualitative distinctions implied if the isomorphism argument is to be convincingly supported. Playful aggression is not violence. This experiment, by virtue of its procedures, environment, and operations has well-documented some conditions of aggressive play, but it does not seem to be dealing with violent aggression at all, not at least in terms of that set of behaviors that most people recognize as "violent aggression."

The nature of the film segment that supposedly influences the imitative modeling of child viewers presents another area of concern in the analysis of this experiment. With all of the antisocial behavior that was (and still is) displayed on television, why didn't the experimenters select an actual segment? Or, at least, why didn't they enact a script that was closer to the television content that children watch? The key question is whether children will imitate some of the undesirable behaviors they see performed on television or in films. The normal conditions of transfer do not provide the exact environment equipped as shown in the viewed segment. In essence, some degree of generalization must be possible before any transferable imitation can take place in the shift from the screen to the viewer's own behavior that occurs in his or her own environment. If the children are not capable of making the generalization from regular television or film content, then the transfer would not likely occur.

A large body of cognitive development research would suggest that 3- to 6-year-old children are not usually capable of abstracting the characteristics of attributes of a given set of displayed behaviors and generalizing these attributes to other behavioral sets that may have elements in common. Such capabilities in fact often pose difficulties for adults whose reasoning capabilities do not sufficiently develop to the stage at which inferences are valid. If the researchers had used some actual televised content, or even plausibly simulated it, the amount of imitative behavior would undoubtedly have been substantially less.

Given the usually strange and different environments shown in most television shows, especially those that regularly feature violence, and the appearance of characters quite unlike "real" people whom viewers encounter in their own lives, the capacity for imitative behavior seems clearly restricted to only exceptional circumstances—those incidents that are occasionally reported by the media. Such instances are exceptions by the definition of what constitutes "news" in that they are unusual. If they were ordinary, everyday occurrences, their news value would be lessened just as when any unusual occurrence is repeated often enough to become usual. The incident cited by Bandura and his associates as well as those reported from time to time (e.g., teen-age gang violence presumably triggered by the movie *Warriors*; two teenage boys lighting drunks on fire as in the move *Fuzz*; kids playing Russian roulette after watching *The Deerhunter*) are rare, rare events, given the fact that millions of viewers watch numerous displays of violence on television and in movie theaters each day and night, 365 days a year. Instances of direct imitation of actual film and TV violence are so minuscule in proportion to the number of such potential instances that the power of invoking violence through imitation has to be seriously questioned.

RESULTS

The authors generally conclude that their results confirmed or supported their hypotheses. The control group displayed significantly less total aggression and imitative aggression than did the three experimental modeling conditions of real-life, human film, and cartoon figures. Based on the continuum of real-life to film to cartoon figures, it was predicted that such progression would yield less imitative effects. This was not generally the case; those exposed to the human film models were the most aggressive in their subsequent play.

Regarding the sex-related hypotheses, the data indicated that males were, as expected, significantly more aggressive than were females. Male models were also more effective than were female models in eliciting aggression from boys. Male or female models had a fairly consistent effect on girls except for the condition of human film models; girls seeing the male film model act aggressively engaged in more gun play than did girls who saw the female film model.

COMMENTS ON THE RESULTS The findings are most supportive of the author's main hypotheses, except for the one that predicted the differences in aggressive behavior that would result from live versus film versus cartoon models. There are several aspects of the results, however, that put the findings in a markedly different perspective.

In the procedures section, we noted that the experimental observers who recorded the children's behaviors made note of nonaggressive as well as aggressive behaviors. Given the total of 240 five-second units of analysis for the 20-minute play period, it is interesting to compare nonaggressive play activities to aggressive ones—a comparison that the authors did provide.

Table 6.1 shows some of the results of the experiment in average (arithmetic means) aggression scores (the average score for each group based on a total possible score of 240). The percentages in parentheses represent that part of the 240 total accounted for by that particular group total. For example, in total aggression, girls who observed a real-life aggressive female model had an average score of 65.8, which is 27% of

TABLE 6.1

		Real-Life Aggression Female	Real-Life Aggression Male	Human-Film Aggression Female	Human-Film Aggression Male	Cartoon	Control	Difference
		(percentages in parentheses)						
Total Aggression	girls	65.8 (27)	57.3 (24)	87.0 (36)	79.5 (33)	80.9 (34)	36.4 (15)	(16)
	boys	76.8 (32)	131.8 (53)	114.5 (48)	85.0 (35)	117.2 (49)	72.2 (30)	(14)
Imitative Aggression	girls	19.2 (8)	9.2 (4)	10.0 (3)	18.0 (3)	7.8 (3)	1.8 (1)	(3)
	boys	18.4 (8)	38.4 (16)	34.3 (14)	13.3 (6)	16.2 (7)	3.9 (2)	(8)

NOTE: Both categories include imitative and nonimitative aggression, mallet aggression, and aggressive gun play.

240. In other words, 73% of the total play time, or 15 minutes, was spent in "nonaggressive" play, while 27%, or 4 minutes, was spent in "aggressive" play.

It is interesting to note that only boys observing a real-life male model acting aggressively spent more than half (55%) of the 20-minute play period engaged in aggressive behavior (imitative or nonimitative aggression) as operationally defined by the experimenters. In total aggression, boys in the experimental groups averaged 44% of their time, or about 9 minutes, behaving aggressively and 56% (11 minutes) nonaggressively. The control group averaged 30% (6 minutes) acting aggressively and 70% (14 minutes) nonaggressively. The experimental boys, therefore, spent 3 minutes more on the average than did the control group in aggressive activities.

Females in the experimental group averaged 31% (6 minutes) for total aggression, as compared to 69% (14 minutes) playing nonaggressively. Thus the average female experimental group spent 16% more time than did the control group in aggressive behavior, or a total of 6 minutes as opposed to a total of 3 minutes.

For imitative aggression—those specific behaviors distinctly reproduced by children—the results are less impressive. Of the total 20-minute play period, boys observing a real-life male model had the highest proportion of time spent on imitative aggressive behavior at 16% or a little more than 3 minutes of the 20 minutes possible.

Girls in the experimental groups averaged 4% of their time in imitative aggression, or less than 1 minute of the 20 minutes possible. Boys averaged 10%, or 2 minutes. The girls' average was 3% greater than the female control group's (4% versus 1%), or 48 seconds versus 12 seconds, whereas the boys' average was 8% greater than the male control's (10% versus 2%), or 2 minutes versus about 30 seconds.

Such results are of limited magnitude. Given all of the favorable conditions created by the experimenters to foster imitative and nonimitative "aggressive" behaviors, there was evidence of little impact on the play behaviors of the children who participated. Children were presented with a distinct set of behaviors clearly displayed and repeated several times by an adult model; they were primed to be aggressive by the frustration brought about in the process of participating; and they were given a chance to play with some of the same toys shown in the film or used by the real-life model in the same environment (room), all in the presence of a tacitly approving adult. Despite an impressive manipulation of favorable conditions, the impact on children's behavior can be seen as minor.

It is also important to note that both experimental and control groups displayed aggressive behavior and even imitative behavior. Aggressive behavior, as defined by these researchers, was apparently already known by the respondents and seemingly was supported by the social environment. This finding suggests a channeling of respondent behavior by the varying conditions of the experiment rather than an important pattern of learning.

SUMMARY OF THE EXPERIMENT

What started out as an interesting area of inquiry with some useful conceptualizations of how mediated models can affect viewers turns quickly into a methodological nightmare that in essence precludes the ability of the researchers to say a great deal about the impact of aggressive media models on children's imitative behaviors. The authors had an excellent idea of what some of these effects are and how and why they manifest themselves; they may also be entirely accurate. But the empirical evidence for these hypothesized relationships and processes are still only guesses, unsubstantiated by clearly interpretable data and methods. The pitfalls highlighted by this experiment bring up the need for us to articulate the exacting requirements that experiments must meet before they can provide valid information on how media affect audiences.

CENTRAL IDEAS OF SECTION III:
A CRITICAL ANALYSIS OF A MEDIA EFFECTS EXPERIMENT

1. Research references but must compromise its own standards. Results are most often reported as if arising from procedures that were in accord with

those standards. The reader must be aware of the difference in evaluating the claims of the study.

2. Research studies seek to establish their social importance.
3. The major difficulties in research do not appear in the technical procedures but in the attempts to create valid conditions of sampling, measurement, and analysis.
4. Research has societal purposes in social advocacy that are independent of the quality of claim.
5. Knowing about something is different from either believing in it or acting upon it.
6. Operational definitions do not always validly represent what they claim. Evidence must be provided and the inherent claim evaluated.
7. Human beings are sense makers even in experimental protocols.
8. The magnitude of results and their social implications are of more importance than is their statistical significance.

CONCLUSIONS

Writing in their classic reference work on research methods, Webb, Campbell, Schwartz, and Sechrest (1966) reached the following conclusions about experimental paradigms in the social sciences: "It is a sad truth that randomized experimental design is possible for only a portion of the settings in which social scientists make measurements and seek interpretable comparisons. The number of opportunities is not staggering" (pp. 7-8).

While these conclusions would hold true for social science generally, it is even more applicable to the study of media effects. In this chapter we have tried to make clear the limitations that impair the usefulness of experiments in describing or predicting the processes through which the media have an impact on people's beliefs, attitudes, and actions. At present, the utility of experimental findings seems to be the suggestion of possible cause and effect relationships that may or may not be generalizable to the natural environment in which media impact occurs.

While the limitations of experiments are generally well-known among researchers, they are seldom articulated in much, if any, depth. This lack of discussion occurs perhaps because the limitations, although very real and very "limiting," require a certain degree of knowledge and sophistication to understand their nature. The arguments raised are indeed complex and, frankly, we cannot expect social science researchers to engage in prolonged debates about the limitations of experimental methods, because there is no convenient forum for such discussions. Such discussions are damaging to the impact that experimental research findings can have on our understanding of how mediated communication works or on the deliberation of communication policy. Further, there is no known resolution to the arguments raised when these limitations are discussed.

For those who seek to clarify the precise nature of causes and effects, the experimental paradigm remains, nonetheless, the empirical procedure of choice to test mediated effects. Given the limitations of our present practice, it may well be that experiments are appearing prematurely in the extended effort of identifying the complex processes that seem to produce those effects. What we have seen, at least, is that when the seven requirements necessary for the validity of experimental evidence are applied to experimental practices, those practices come up short. We do not grant the experimenter the easy conveniences apparent in most measurement and research design. The issues in mediated communication are too important to accept practices that can be so readily questioned. Our position is not a popular one, however. The media have been consistently seen as a "social problem" by researchers and critical analysts. Evidence, even faulty evidence, of its "problem" nature is readily accepted though it may fail to make sense in the company of other accepted propositions.

Others in our society are not so easily swayed. Despite hundreds of studies showing a relationship between violent content and subsequent aggression (Murray, 1980), we have enacted no policy to prevent its appearance in our media. Why? Certainly because other forces in our society are more powerful than is the voice that these researchers can raise. But essentially the success of the opposition is secured because we as a society don't believe the claim to be true—certainly not for our children although maybe for theirs. The claims supported with experimental evidence—supposedly the most incontrovertible, but in practice, easily dismissed—have not been able to hold their position in the political processes of society. This failure does not necessarily make them false, just impotent.

There are considerable ramifications of this apparent lack of utility for this body of claim for science in society, some of which we consider in Chapter 8. In the next chapter, we move to a parallel discussion of survey and ethnographic research methods. There, we discuss how these methods are used in media research, the strengths they possess, and the weaknesses they present. We will focus on the characteristics of these methods and their assumptions. At the end of that chapter, we consider briefly the place of social science in society.

RELATED READINGS

Anderson, J. A. (1987). *Communication research: Issues and methods.* New York: McGraw-Hill.

A modern look at research practices that considers the presumptions that empower those practices to be more important than methodological recipes. Nonetheless, the author also provides plenty of instruction on how to do it. The first two sections are most relevant for this chapter.

Bandura, A. (1973). *Aggression: A social learning analysis.* Englewood Cliffs, NJ: Prentice-Hall.

Bandura provides a complete summary of his research on aggression that includes a long chapter on mediated aggression from a social learning perspective. He presents his arguments against the criticisms of his and others' research using experimental simulations and the social learning perspective. He also argues forcefully for policy changes based upon the social scientific research findings that allegedly link mediated aggression with antisocial behavior in society.

Campbell, D. T., & Stanley, J. C. (1963). *Experimental and quasi-experimental designs for research.* Chicago: Rand McNally.

The classic in design, this work is still one of the best for understanding how to institute controls for conditions that are considered static forces influencing human behavior. The authors emphasize acceptable and unacceptable tradeoffs that are made in conducting experimental research. They also provide a discussion and illustration of the threats to the validity of experiments. The reader can't avoid coming away with a better appreciation of the difficulties in crafting an experiment.

Comstock, G., Chaffee, S., Katzman, N., McCombs, M., Roberts, D. (1978). *Television and human behavior.* New York: Columbia University Press.

This book presents a traditional social science examination of the impact of television on human behavior. Chapters 8 and 9 present detailed material that is relevant to the use and interpretation of experimental data. The authors conclude by calling for more and more rigorous experimentation to continue the sorting out of cause and effect relationships. The authors also address the nature of causality as it operates within social science.

7

Survey and Ethnographic Methods in Mediated Communication Research

IN THE PREVIOUS CHAPTER, experimental methods of researching mediated communication effects were described and analyzed. In this chapter we examine survey and ethnographic methods. Survey procedures will be described, with an emphasis on strengths and limitations regarding their usefulness for assessing media impact. An example, with "classic standing" in the media effects literature, will be presented and analyzed, following the pattern of the previous chapter. We will also focus on another type of inquiry in this chapter—so-called naturalistic inquiry. Naturalistic inquiry uses ethnographic methods that involve researchers as participant-observers of people in everyday life. In mediated communication research, they generally investigate how effects appear to manifest themselves in particular cases. Such investigations are often called **case studies**. We will describe common naturalistic inquiry procedures, again with an eye to strengths and limitations.

Showing our flexibility, we have organized this chapter in four sections: The first takes up the nature and limitations of surveys, the second analyzes a Roper survey on sources of news, the third considers the nature and limitations of ethnography, and the fourth, the place of social science in society.

SECTION I: SURVEY METHODOLOGY

The notion of a survey in social science is much similar to the topographical analysis provided by land surveyors. The idea is to identify the salient features of a domain, get measurements on those features, and map the territory. Babbie (1979) categorizes these goals into three different types: exploratory (identifying the features), descriptive (measuring them), and explanatory (creating the map).

In simple terms, survey procedures start with some question about the characteristics or states of people, events, or texts, identify a source of information for an answer, and devise a method of collecting the information. In mediated communication effects research, survey procedures include public opinion polling, broadcast and cable ratings, **circulation/readership audits, content analyses,** and the survey questionnaire. The elements surveyed could be people, households, subscription lists, content texts, whatever will yield the information sought. The appropriate measurement might be a procedure for counting subscribers, a recording device attached to household television sets, a set of content categories, or a questionnaire given to respondents.

Surveys differ from experiments in that they try to determine the presence or absence of variables but do not manipulate that presence or absence as an experiment normally would. Thus a survey straightforwardly attempts to "read" a set of conditions without the manipulation of or the establishment of environmental controls for those conditions. Surveys are a technique for describing relationships while experiments test relationships.

SOME USES OF SURVEYS

The media industries make extensive use of surveys. A most familiar survey appears in television, cable, and radio ratings (see Chapter 2). As we have seen, ratings surveys test the circulation of broadcast and cable programming. Print circulations are also tested in surveys, and readership studies measure exposure to advertisements or articles within newspapers or magazines. Advertisers often survey potential consumers about their product and brand preferences.

Surveys are commonly used to describe people's opinions or attitudes on a variety of topics. The Roper survey of people's attitudes toward television and other mass media that has been ongoing since 1959 is an excellent example of the use of surveys in the area of assessing people's attitudes toward the mass media. Each year that they are done, these surveys select a random sample of the general public and generalize the results to the population at large. Other examples of public opinion research readily come to mind, mainly the work of pollsters like Gallup or Harris. Curiously, what people think about a rich variety of topics provides a regular and convenient source of content for the mass media. Most major media outlets now routinely use surveys of one kind or another, suggesting some audience interest in them.

Surveys also frequently ask respondents to report on their behaviors. In media surveys, the emphasis is on how often people watch, read or listen, what they attend to, their motives for attendance, who they like and what they like, and so on. How many people have bought or intend to buy specific items are also of interest in surveys, as are questions on voting behavior—whom people plan to vote for in an upcoming election. The information gathered from surveys has shown itself useful to researchers in describing current conditions, to political analysts and politicians in determining the nature of public opinion or the response to campaign messages, and to industry and advertisers interested in consumer patterns among others. As we shall see further along in this chapter, however, the usefulness and reliability of surveys must be judged in each individual case. The source of information, the characteristics measured, and how the measurement is done present three key areas for evaluation of survey research. These areas are discussed in the following section.

SURVEY STRENGTHS AND WEAKNESSES

Surveys attempt to measure **phenomena** as they are represented via some research instrument, either things as they "are" or things as they are perceived to be (events that are alleged as factual occurrences or events that are perceived as factual descriptions). For example, a questionnaire may ask respondents to report the number of working videocassette recorders (VCRs) in their households and to report approximately how often the VCRs are used each day. The number of VCRs is the report of a fact (though the report could be false), whereas the amount of daily use would represent the perception of a factual situation (again, the perception may or may not reflect actual use; it is the perception, however, that has the power of "fact").

Surveys function as a camera taking a still photograph. The resultant photograph fixes a moment in time within a given frame of reference. What is present in the finished picture we have in our hands will be a function of the capabilities and limitations of the equipment used to take the picture, the nature and qualities of the film used, and the development process and developer's skills and objectives. Further, what is included in and excluded from the frame, the position of the camera, the clarity of focus on objects in the frame relative to one another, and so on, all influence what will and will not be visible in the photograph. What occurred prior to and after the photo was taken or why objects were positioned as they were and what the positions mean will remain unknown, but open to a variety of interpretations.

Surveys, therefore, are useful in that they can reflect representations of events but are limited by (1) the fact that the procedures always distort the scene (the map is not the territory). In even something as plain as the frequency of television viewing, it is not just a simple matter of asking people what programs they watch and how often. Such information can be assessed in many different ways. Each different way could lead to different answers, just as a photographer taking a picture of an event could produce a different picture with a different angle, different lighting, a different camera or film or developing processes. The results will vary with the procedures used to measure the characteristics. (2) Surveys ordinarily tell us little about *why* things are the way they are, how they got that way, and how they will be found in the future. In short, survey procedures tell us little about how variables operate in a process. Cause and effect inferences and the mechanisms underlying conditions are best left to experimental procedures in which variables are manipulated as well as observed and measured. Surveys of television viewing habits, for example, can provide an indication of what people watch and how often, but what brings them to the television set in the first place, what keeps them there, what they think about while watching, how viewing one segment of content relates to or helps to determine subsequent viewing interpretations and choices, the consequences for viewing in the short and long runs, and so on, are the kinds of factors that typically elude the measurement process.

THE PROBLEMATICS IN SURVEY METHODS

In any consideration of survey methods, a number of points at which these methods may have difficulties can be identified. In the paragraphs that follow we will consider the problems in sampling methods, measurement, descriptive versus causal reasoning, **ecological validity,** and the analysis of social action.

POPULATIONS AND SAMPLES IN SURVEYS

The questions survey-takers ask often involve large populations of people, events, or texts. Because large populations are difficult to deal with, survey procedures ordinarily use samples of the populations of interest. Most of us are aware of the U.S. Government Census, that activity whereby the population of this country is questioned and counted. The census does not make use of a sample in that it purports to study the entire population in question, not just a sample of the population. Most surveys, however, take a sample that intends to be representative of its larger population, study the sample's characteristics, and generalize the results to the population. In this manner, survey procedures can be useful for describing a population that is too large to observe directly or in its entirety. The U.S. Census involves the expenditure of a tremendous sum of money merely to "count" the number of people in the U.S. When there are insufficient resources to study an entire population, it is still possible to provide a reasonably accurate description of that population if it is possible to survey a **representative sample** (a much smaller group) of that larger population.

The principle here, of course, is that the sample must be representative before it can be of any use in describing the population. If the characteristics of the sample vary considerably on the measures of the survey from the characteristics of the population, inferences about the population will be false. The difficulty in all of this reasoning is that there is no direct way of demonstrating the **representativeness** of a sample. Typically, evidence for the representativeness of a sample is offered in a comparison between selected characteristics of the sample with known characteristics (usually from census data) of the population. For example, the sample's male/female ratio might be compared with the population's, the relative percentage of different age groups could be compared, and so on. Our interest, of course, is not in these characteristics but in the characteristics under study, for example, exposure to campaign messages. Unfortunately there is no way of knowing whether the sample is representative of the population on this measure because we have no baseline information (if we did, there would be no need for the sample).

Our way out of this thicket has been found in the principle of **random sampling.** The principle of random sampling was discussed in the previous chapter; the key notion to be recalled is that if all members of the population have an equal chance (probability) of being selected for the sample to be studied, the odds are that the sample will provide an accurate representation of the population from which it was drawn.

In fact, statistical theorists tell us that random samples are the only samples with the opportunity to be representative. That's the good news. The bad news is that random samples are nearly nonexistent in research. Most samples used in experiments are convenience samples, drawn from college classes or clubs. (Randomization of treatments occurs after the sample is in the door.) Most survey samples make use of some random procedures—like drawing names from telephone books. Of course anyone without a listing is excluded, but, more importantly, nearly all surveys rely on the respondent volunteering to participate. A key "unknown" in all survey research involving volunteer respondents is the effect of the cooperation rate of those selected for inclusion in the sample on its representativeness.

Obviously, some people cooperate with researchers and others do not. The unanswerable question is: Do cooperators and noncooperators differ in important ways in their media attitudes and behaviors? You might well suspect that there are differences.

One way in which they might differ is in their predisposition toward the topic. You can look at this problem in at least two ways: Either cooperators are favorably predisposed toward the study's purpose or noncooperators have little or no use for the topic and thus won't allow themselves to be bothered as a participant. In short, either cooperators are eager participants because they are already involved in the issue in question or noncooperators have so little interest that participating is a waste of their time. While research organizations use a number of different appeals to elicit cooperation, the ultimate conclusion remains that many people choose not to participate and are not represented in the report based on the sample that is generalized to the entire population.

Those that do cooperate, therefore, are the only ones represented in the sample and, by generalization, in the description of the population.

Is cooperation a genuine problem in media surveys? Yes, although it does vary by method. Short telephone surveys tend to have cooperation rates between 70% and 80%; cold contact, mail surveys less than 40%. Nielsen and other media ratings firms have always had a great deal of difficulty in gaining the cooperation of households selected for participation in the ratings samples. When respondents had to keep a diary of media behavior, the cooperation averaged below 50% of those originally contacted and invited to participate. Cooperation remains a serious and persistent problem with the shift to the new peoplemeters.

The theory of random sampling is a good example of an empowering text. It permits us to have good reason to believe in the representativeness of samples. The practice of sampling does not—and cannot—meet the criteria of the theory. Samples are always biased in unknown ways. We continue the practice because we have no alternatives, by the assumption of minimum damage. In truth, we have no idea how biased our samples are on the criterion of interest. In general, we can assume, however, that unless special procedures are in force, the very rich, the poor, the ethnically separate, the homeless, the rural, and even those in shared living quarters will not be properly represented. And, of course, the noncooperator will never appear.

It is not useful to reject all studies because their samples are necessarily biased. It is necessary to question the quality of the sample—to wonder if the claims advanced by the study aren't marred by the sampling procedures. It is also necessary to keep in mind that most of what we "know" about media comes from college students and white middle-class America.

MEASUREMENT

The end of survey measurement is to provide accurate description. Seems simple enough, but when we consider what we are trying to describe—the states and conditions of life; complex attitudes, beliefs, values; one's future in voting, purchasing, decision-making; one's past in media use; the motives that direct us—the task is daunting. Measurement is a highly technical craft with too many issues to consider here. We will take up, however, the broad concern of the character of survey questions looking at how the nature of the question can structure answers and the decontextualizing effect of standardization.

STRUCTURING QUESTIONS Survey researchers have to make many choices in devising their questionnaires. One of these is whether to make answers **closed-ended** (forced choice) or **open-ended.** Either choice has substantial consequences. When you use a forced-choice procedure, you automatically limit the validity and usefulness of your research in two ways. First, you "put ideas into people's heads" that may or may not have occurred to them spontaneously. Not only have you put people in an unusual circumstance (being asked to describe some natural practice), you have given them a list by which they must do it.

The second problem with the forced-choice procedure is that the research instrument structures the context of the available responses. If people think of the issue in a completely different way or in different terms or if they wonder exactly what is being asked of them in this question, they must now redirect their thinking and responses to the choices provided.

Open-ended questions pose validity problems too. First, they can put a respondent and the researcher in an awkward position. In a normal conversational question, both communicants can coconstruct what is being asked and what is being answered. But in the research situation, typical procedures prevent most discussion about the question and the answer. Different "rules," then, are in place for asking a question and for giving an answer. And if the respondents have only a vague idea of how to answer the question, they will, nonetheless, come up with an answer that they hope, at least, sounds good, whether or not it is a true representation of their position.

Most of us are not used to being "on the spot" in an interview situation. Perhaps if we had a considerable amount of time to think about what the question was getting at or how we could most completely and honestly answer the question, our responses would be considerably different. Indeed, when researchers study a particular individual over an extended period of time and get to know the respondent and vice versa, the quality and quantity of responses change. Whether such responses are more accurate or truthful cannot, of course, be determined. But they are different, and such a difference is a good reason to have some doubt regarding answers given to questions in a quick and off-the-cuff fashion.

STANDARDIZATION Surveys involve standardization of the measurement instruments. This standardization has both advantages and disadvantages. One advantage is that when the same questions are asked of a sample of respondents, the answers can be readily compared, assuming that the meaning of the questions themselves is uniformly understood by all respondents. In this manner, for example, one can reliably compare the hours spent viewing television by upper socioeconomic class viewers to middle and lower socioeconomic class viewers to identify any important differences among these classes of viewers.

Another advantage of standardization is that if the questionnaire is administered in a panel design using the same group of respondents more than once or a cohort design using different samples from the same population at different times, any differences measured can be attributed to changes in the population rather than differences in questions. These designs enable survey researchers to track movement in attitudes or reported behaviors over varying periods of time. If the questions were to change in major ways, then any differences in responses might be a result of asking different questions rather than an indication of any real changes in people's responses.

Polls that evaluate the overall performance of the U.S. president ask the same questions worded in the same way at various time intervals throughout the president's term of office. Although which factors may account for higher or lower ratings is open to question and interpretation, differences that may have been caused by changes in question wording can at least be safely ruled out.

Standardization can also work to the researcher's disadvantage. Even though such a procedure is useful, even essential for reliable comparisons, the questions that result from standardizing techniques may well yield questions that are either inappropriate for what the survey is trying to get at or too general to yield meaningful information. Babbie (1979) has commented: "By designing questions that will be at least minimally appropriate to all respondents, you may miss what is most appropriate to many respondents. It is in this sense that surveys often appear superficial in their coverage of complex topics" (p. 346).

If the sample of respondents represents a cross-section of a diverse population, which is usually the case when mediated communication effects are studied, then the questions must be designed with the "lowest common denominator" in mind. Complexity may have to be avoided to increase the chances of respondents uniformly comprehending and interpreting what was asked of them in each of the questions. Thus questions that may not be commonly understood by many in the sample will have to be either greatly simplified or lengthened to include appropriate definitions. And, since long questions tend to confuse many respondents, simplification is the usual route selected and followed. The consequence is, as Babbie suggests, superficial treatment of complex topics.

DESCRIPTION AND CAUSATION Surveys are a descriptive method. Description as a form of explanation is sharply distinguished from causation. Description is concerned with visible characteristics; causation with the nature of the underlying, and generally invisible, relationships among phenomena. The reason that surveys are descriptive methods is that although they can recognize the presence and absence of phenomena, they cannot manipulate the relationship as required for evidence of a causal connection. Nonetheless, relationship claims are often made from this descriptive method.

National surveys over the past 10 years or so have reported some interesting relationships between media use and academic performance in schools. The one key relationship that always seems to present itself is the one between amount of television viewed and school grades and/or standardized test scores. The surveys typically find that the most frequent television viewers tend to have lower grades and/or standardized test scores. Researchers, or those who have a specific use for the research, are tempted to infer some level of cause and effect as in "high television usage leads to poorer performance in the classroom and on standardized tests," suggesting that one causes the other.

Is there a cause and effect relationship between television viewing and school/test performance? With only the presence of a relationship, all that can be done is to describe the relationship in terms of its strength (strong, modest, weak) and its direction: A positive **correlation** means that as one variable increases in value, the other variable also increases in the same direction; a negative correlation means that as one variable increases or decreases in value, the other variable goes in the opposite direction. In our television usage/classroom performance example, the relationship is negative but generally weak to modest (persistent and consistent, but never very strong) meaning that increasing amounts of television viewing are associated with lower school grades and/or standardized test scores.

Note that the reasons this relationship occurs—the "mechanism" through which one variable affects another—is unknown: Certainly, you can argue that watching a lot of television means that students probably aren't studying, so they don't do well in school or learn enough to score well on tests. On the other hand, it can also be argued that because someone is not doing well in school, he or she turns to television and finds the ever-present innocuous programming to be a pleasurable alternative to a school environment that represents boredom and failure. In this case, doing poorly in school causes students to watch more television. A good argument can also be made that poor academic performance and more frequent use of television (or more frequent use of computers, visitations to shopping malls, use of drugs/alcohol, cars/trucks, and so on) are both manifestations of a separate underlying process that produces them concurrently.

This last argument is actually supported by the fact that the reported *correlations* are generally low (statistically reliable but small in magnitude). The character of these correlations means that the two variables have more connections with other variables than they do with each other. When this circumstance exists, it suggests that other more important variables in varying combinations exist that would provide a better account of relationships.

The point to remember should be clear: The presence of an occurrence (variable) or the presence of a relationship between or among variables tells you little about what either one means or what causes them, which is the cause and which is the effect, and so on. Accounting for relationships and predicting their occurrence via the controlled manipulation of the presence of variables is the province of experimental methods. Surveys are most useful, therefore, as indicators of what relationships appear to exist and not exist, couched against the limitations that impinge upon the procedures or methods used to arrive at the relationships.

SURVEYS AND ECOLOGICAL VALIDITY In the previous chapter, the act of participating in an experiment was described as posing a serious threat to the ecological validity or real world applicability of what is observed. How an individual responds to a survey also poses problems of interpretation because the act of inquiry puts the respondent in an "unnatural" position and usually asks for "unnatural" responses. For example, the simple (at least on the surface) question that asks respondents how much television they watch in a typical day puts respondents in a situation with which they are unfamiliar. To be sure, most of us watch at least some television every day, but we do not ordinarily think, in an active, conscious sense at least, about just how much we watch or keep track of some "average amount." Thus what this question calls for and how I must frame an answer are both "unnatural," suggesting that the process of being asked and having to frame an answer are in and of themselves intrusions that produce research **artifacts** in a certain sense. These artifacts, of course, may or may not bear any correspondence to the actual set of actions or behaviors referenced in the survey questionnaire.

This quality of the research act had led some methodologists to describe the process of being asked and answering questions, orally or in writing, as a performance in its own right. While the performance is usually not rehearsed in the sense of a stage performance, questionnaires or interviews put us in a context that requires an interpretation of what is called for and judgments of how we are to respond and how we are able to respond, given the demands of the situation. If given a considerable length of time to think about the information called for in the question, respondents' answers might be different from those given "on the spot." Again, the "how much television do you watch?" question might produce different answers from the same respondent if the individual had some time either to think about it carefully or to monitor systematically the amounts of time spent watching television. The most frequent comment from people who do systematically monitor the amount of television viewing is that they "never realized how much television they actually watched." Such a response points to an inherent problem posed by survey procedures: Questions may produce answers that are nothing more than research artifacts.

Closely related to the performance situations into which surveys place participants is the creation of arbitrary and often meaningless response categories. When asked about the performance of the President, respondents may feel that there are some aspects of the president's actions that they agree with, some that they disagree with, others of which they are uncertain. And they may have some qualms about the president's character or candor or may admire the person for having only the best of intentions motivating his actions, and so on. In short, their evaluation of the President's performance will probably be multidimensional in nature. Yet, they are virtually forced to choose from among a list of four or five adjectives. This "global" choice (e.g., "very good") may apply to only some aspects of the president's performance and not others. (And who will know what qualities were evaluated and the criteria used?) What comes out of this little intrusion is an answer that neatly and conveniently fits into an arbitrarily predetermined category. The evaluative question for us, of course, is whether the categories validly represent the way people make decisions about the president.

SURVEYS AND SOCIAL ACTION Surveys provide a convenient way to measure certain behaviors or feelings that are overt manifestations of social life, maybe the so-called tips of the iceberg. But, like the iceberg, its true shape and size remain largely undiscovered despite the visible peaks. Social life for individuals always occurs in a given context. It is this all-important context that invariably escapes survey researchers who "can seldom develop the feel for the total life situation in which respondents are thinking and acting that, say, the participant observer can" (Babbie, 1979, p. 346).

The limited view of the survey is compounded by its static nature. Once the questionnaire or measuring instrument has been developed and pretested and is presumed ready for administration to the intended sample of respondents, it is fixed across its entire administration. Unlike the field observer who is supposed to adjust and adapt to the course of events that occurs among respondents, the survey researcher either misses unanticipated changes in events that may have a bearing on the topics being studied or may have no sense of how to interpret many of the findings that are forthcoming.

Most social actions are embedded in complex social rituals or processes. Surveys, at best, measure only some parts of an overall process, usually those proverbial "iceberg tips." The underlying thinking processes, the interpretations of one's own and others' behaviors go unmeasured and can only be speculated upon by researchers in making sense of their findings. Mediated communication seems to involve a complex routine of rituals and/or processes that do manifest themselves at various points, and it is, perhaps, at these points that surveys provide some enlightenment. Underlying processes and the nature of interrelationships, however, would be the province of other research procedures, or perchance remain yet-to-be-solved mysteries.

SUMMARY

In mediated communication research, survey methods have dominated. Surveys are valuable in that they provide responses, usually from samples of various populations, to standardized questions; these questions can be and are asked over time to establish trends and to measure shifts in response categories. These are the strengths. The weaknesses actually stem from the strengths. Surveys generally oversimplify, especially when a more diverse sample is required; they frame the respondents' reality in possibly unnatural responses; they are inadequate for dealing with contexts in which various social actions are accomplished; and they usually measure only visible manifestations that may or may not accurately reflect the underlying processes and interpretations.

How these various strengths and weaknesses actually present themselves is treated in the next section of this chapter. In that section, an often-referred-to survey of public attitudes and behaviors regarding television and the other mass media will be critically analyzed. As in the previous chapter, our intent is not to discredit this research, but only to examine it from the perspective of what such studies are inherently incapable of telling us about the impact of the mass media. Again, all research methods are inherently constrained—there are no socioscopes in existence to reveal the "the truth." Survey methods, like all forms of inquiry, provide working constructions of knowledge. Such a construction tries to present a plausible explanation, but remains only one of many potential explanations for whatever is being measured or studied. It is characterized as a "working" construction, because it can be revised, given additional evidence, replaced if a better explanation comes along, or scrapped entirely if it is demonstrated to be fatally flawed. Research findings and explanations are thus temporary, never definitive or permanent.

CENTRAL IDEAS OF SECTION I: SURVEY METHODOLOGY

1. Surveys are a descriptive technique that is directed toward exploring, describing, and explaining the characteristics of a domain.
2. Surveys differ from experiments in that they do not manipulate variables or institute environmental controls for them.
3. Surveys offer a given perspective upon a domain, framed by the sample, the measurement instruments, and the methods of analysis.
4. Surveys use a sample to represent the population of the domain. Representativeness of the sample is always in doubt as the characteristics of the **criterion measure** are essentially unknown and requirement of randomness is rarely met.
5. Measurement techniques establish what can be learned from a survey. All methods of measurement force certain outcomes and those restrictions bias our knowledge. On the other hand, measurement techniques reveal what cannot otherwise be seen.
6. Responding to a survey is itself a performance of social action. There is no reason to assume that the respondent interprets the issues and questions as the researcher would or that his or her answers will be properly interpreted by the researcher. The hermaneutic character of meaning doesn't change just because its in a research context.

SECTION II: A CRITICAL ANALYSIS OF A MEDIA USES AND IMPACT SURVEY

The study selected for analysis is the latest in a series of surveys begun in 1959 by the Roper Organization. The findings and research methods are summarized in a 1987 report from the Television Information Office, "America's Watching: Public Attitudes Toward Television." In this survey, respondents were asked about why they watch television, how they feel about television, how important television is to their daily lives, how the media are used as sources of information, people's feelings about television as a news medium, as a medium popular with children, and as a commercial medium. Several of the questions have been asked each time the survey has been conducted to identify trends over the years since television emerged as a major social and cultural presence in American life. Our examination of the study will include a critical evaluation of the methods and findings.

THE RESEARCH SAMPLE

The Roper Organization reports that a **multistaged, stratified, area probability sample** was used. Such a procedure is designed to provide a sample that is representative of a nationwide cross-section of the "non-institutionalized population 18 years and older living in the continental United States." The Roper Organization claims that the sample selected was representative of all persons 18 and over, all sizes of communities, geographic area, and socioeconomic levels. The total size of the sample was 2,000.

Comment: Drawing a **simple, random sample** from the entire U.S. population of those 18 years of age and older is only theoretically possible and not at all practical. While random procedures certainly come into play, survey researchers must make certain choices before randomization can occur. This process was used in the Roper survey and closely resembles the generally accepted procedures for studying national samples of the entire population. The sample that is ultimately selected for study is compared to known population characteristics drawn from U.S. Census data. The characteristics identified by the Roper Organization included: age, size of community, geographic area, and socioeconomic (income) level. Whether or not the sample matches other population characteristics and/or those topics being studied (media uses and attitudes) cannot be determined in any procedure. The evidence for representativeness is always in doubt, since only evidence for nonrepresentativeness can be shown.

Roper's design allowed for a random sample up to the point of data collection. At that point, it failed the test of randomization because a large number of potential respondents refused to participate. Cooperation in the Roper study was undoubtedly affected by the methods of data collection. The Roper study involved household interviews that took a considerable amount of time to complete. Many people are extremely reluctant to allow a stranger into their households to talk about individual feelings and behaviors. Those who do allow such an intrusion would likely have at least some above-average interest in the interview's topics and, therefore, would be different from those with less or typical levels of interest. The results of this and other similar surveys may thus be based on unrepresentative samples—unrepresentative in terms of their behaviors relative to the survey's topics, even if not in terms of selected population characteristics (e.g., community size, geographic area, and so on).

The Television Information Office (TIO) report of the Roper study (TIO also commissioned the study) tells us nothing about the cooperation rate, although the Roper organization probably would. The manner in which TIO presented this study to the public is instructive. Because the representativeness of the sample cannot be determined, the problem is sometimes acknowledged but ignored when the survey's findings are presented and discussed. TIO's rhetorical move here is, therefore, common—ignore the limitations of research that supports the position desired. In evaluating research, the reader must remember that it too intends to persuade.

MAJOR FINDINGS

SATISFACTION WITH TELEVISION The Roper Organization claims that people feel positively about television as an institution and what it is providing for its audience. These claims are based on the findings of their survey—how respondents answered the questions as posed to them. Despite the presence of a small minority, most Americans describe television as being entertaining, informative, and interesting. Moreover, more respondents (46%) described television as generally good, as compared to the 14% who described it as generally bad. How did the Roper Organization come up with these results and conclusions? Let's examine some of their procedures.

In the interview, each respondent was handed a card. The interviewer said: "Here is a list of words and phrases that have been used to describe television. Would you read down the list and call off each word or phrase you would use to describe television?" On the card were a roughly equal number of positive and negative words/phrases. As the respondent called out a phrase, the interviewer made note of that particular response. Note, too, that any number of response categories were allowed and recorded.

Comment: You might have answered the question with another question: "Television in terms of what—entertainment programs, as a source of news . . . ?" But, because the type of answer had already been predetermined for you, your judgments had to be recorded within the confines of the list.

TELEVISION NEWS The Roper surveys have been the basis for many so-called truisms about people's reliance on television over newspapers and other media as their major and/or only source of news and as the most believable or credible source of information. We use the word *truisms* because the results are so frequently cited in the absence of any limitations or questions of validity that they must be "true." As you might suspect, however, the interpretation of these important results is legitimately open to question.

The Roper survey interviewers pose the question on source of news to each respondent as follows: "I'd like to ask you where you usually get most of your news about what's going on in the world today—from newspapers or radio or television or magazines or talking to people or where?" The results have shown television ahead of newspapers and the other sources since the 1960s with the 1987 figures showing television with 66% compared to newspapers at 36%, radio at 14%, magazines and people at 4% each, and don't know at 1%. Responses add up to more than 100% because multiple responses were allowed. The results also showed that the majority of people (50%) cite television as their only source of news. This percentage has increased steadily from near 20% in 1959. The percentage selecting newspapers only as a response has hovered around the 20% mark consistently since 1959.

Comments: The findings that show television coming out far ahead of newspapers and the other mass media seem somewhat surprising. Generally, other studies of media consumption habits that have gone beyond the results of just a few questions have shown that other news media seem to occupy considerable amounts of daily time, especially when compared to television news viewing. Further, weekly and annual ratings data gathered from a number of services show that in a given week, 60% or more (usually 2 out of every three households) does not watch any of the three network newscasts. For more regionally oriented news, the percentage of households watching local newscasts is higher than for network news, but, again, a sizable percentage (it varies from city to city) does not watch at all. Finally, circulation figures and readership studies of newspapers shows that more than 8 of every 10 households read a daily newspaper. Yet, television garners most of the responses. Why?

We don't know, although one of the present authors did study the question systematically. He found that he could control which medium would be selected as the "most used source" by varying the wording of the question (Anderson, 1971). The whole issue of "most used source" seems to involve judgments we don't ordinarily make. Try listing the specifics of what you know about any news story, and from where you learned each one. Finding this difficult or next to impossible? If so, you see the problems inherent with merely asking someone where they perceive they get most of their information from. We may answer "television" because it may have made a more vivid impression on our memory from time to time. But there is no everyday way that we would be able to know with any degree of accuracy which source acted in which particular way as a general rule.

The Roper survey associates the reliance on television as the major and/or only source of news to the superior credibility of television. In the survey report's own words: "Why is television increasing its lead as the primary source of news relied upon by most Americans? Because it is the news source most trusted by them." This conclusion stems from the responses to a single question asked of respondents since the first survey in 1959: "If you got conflicting or different reports of the same news story from radio, television, magazines, and the newspapers, which of the four versions would you be most inclined to believe—the one on radio, or television, or magazines, or newspapers?" Television (55%) leads newspapers (21%), magazines (7%) and radio (6%) in the latest survey results. Television's lead over newspapers and the other media has been widening since it took over the top spot in 1961.

Comments: The question as asked poses a purely hypothetical situation and a generally implausible one at that. Out of all of the news and information that you are exposed to on a daily basis, how many of the items present conflicting versions that you are aware of? And, for those rare items for which you perceive a conflict or major difference (not just a matter of degree of details), how many had different versions in each of the four media, that is, each of the media having a different version from the other three? Even when there was a discrepancy between just two of the four media, did the two media involved present their conflicting versions at roughly the same time? Or, was there one media account followed in time by another media account that perhaps updated or clarified or even changed the earlier version? The facts in many news stories often change as an event unfolds over time. And, with different media having different deadlines for their news presentations, it would follow that new versions would arise. For example, a major story might break just before the local newspaper goes to press. The paper would report as much of the story as it had at press time. The late news on television would presumably present a different account from the newspaper version because it would have had more time to collect information prior to its evening air time. Such circumstances, however, are not only rare occurrences, they are not really conflicting reports like the hypothetical ones alluded to in the survey question.

In spite of its implausibility, it does not seem difficult to answer the question, but it is a puzzle as to what is being answered. How can a measuring instrument tap into a respondent's sense of whether one particular medium is more "believable" than others? And how would we know when it has? Few social scientists would be satisfied with a single question that would supposedly measure the comparative believability of the media. Anderson (1971), in that same study on news sources, showed that respondents gave media different credibility ratings across different types of stories. His finding suggests that people are far more sophisticated in media judgments than the Roper question would give them credit for.

THEORY AND THE ROPER STUDIES

In social science, survey methods are used in conjunction with theory. Researchers, as is the case with experimental protocols, develop theoretical perspective from which hypotheses or research questions are advanced for empirical observation or testing. The point of collecting data is to demonstrate support for and increase our understanding of some set of mechanisms that evoke the features we measure. From this point of view, the Roper studies are atheoretical. They do not inform us about the processes of information seeking or about the dimensions of media credibility. The studies involve the application of technical methods to collect data that are then used by an advocacy agency (TIO) to advance a particular cause (the television industry). This practice comes out of a well-established tradition, but it isn't science.

While the Roper surveys were conducted and continue to be conducted without theory or hypotheses, the data from these surveys have been used with coherent theoretical perspectives and research questions/hypotheses. Steiner (1963) and Bower (1973) have used the Roper data, plus data collected in their own studies, to assess the public's attitudes toward television and the other mass media. Roper's data should not, therefore, be disregarded because it appears to be nonscientific in design and application.

Theory in social science is the foundation for research questions and/or hypotheses that in turn dictate the formulation of an appropriate measuring instrument. Data are then collected with the measuring instrument and the findings analyzed with an eye to whether or not the theory has been supported or not supported and why (or why not). Theories consistently supported gain stature and credibility in that the explanations advanced for the relationships among variables seem to hold up; the hypothesized relationships hold up when tested; predictions are confirmed.

What theory could we advance for television's reported advantage in media credibility? It could be because television news has an immediacy and unique visual impact not available to newspapers, radio, and magazines. Television may well give viewers the sense that they are seeing an event as it happened (seeing is believing?), not merely reading or hearing about it. Thus the medium that enables you to see as well as hear could be perceived by some people as being more believable than the other nonvisual media accounts.

Whether true or not, posing the argument of immediacy and impact allows us to get "inside" the data to determine if we actually have tapped into some credibility dimension with the Roper findings. If it is credibility and if it is related to our theory, then other questions can be asked based on these implications. If these questions are answered as our theory would predict, then our confidence in the original findings is supported. Without this theoretical analysis, however, findings, even repeated findings like Roper's, remain unexplained events about which nearly anything can be claimed.

SUMMARY

It is difficult to plot a conclusive evaluation of the Roper study as reported by TIO. As far as the sample is concerned, on the one hand, we can be assured that it does not truly represent "all non-institutionalized individuals 18 years old or older." On the other, it represents a substantially more systematic method of discovery than is usually practiced by most academic studies. Our acceptance of the claims of satisfaction are tempered by realizing that satisfaction is relative to the alternatives and contingent on particular circumstances. Are we happy that we get what we get? Perhaps so. There is good evidence from several sources that the claims about news are not as they are made. If network news programs are America's primary source of news, then, given attendance figures, news is not very important to us. Finally, without a theory of what credibility is and how it operates, one cannot judge the evidence presented there.

Without impugning any motive, the Television Information Office has a clear purpose in wanting us to believe that television is the superior medium—well-loved for its entertainment and well-respected for its news. It presents the Roper studies as "telling it like it is." It is not an uncommon stance. But their claims add up to a possible description in which we might find ourselves or be missing.

CENTRAL IDEAS OF SECTION II: A CRITICAL ANALYSIS OF A MEDIA USES AND IMPACT SURVEY

1. The voluntary character of most respondent surveys creates an intractable biasing condition that must be accounted for in the appraisal of the research findings.
2. Questions posed by surveys can be responded to honestly but in an unqualified manner. The answers may be without deception but still false. The questions themselves must be evaluated for the likelihood of this problem. Reports that do not provide the questions cannot be properly evaluated.
3. Exploratory surveys, such as Roper's news survey, are common but an insufficient basis for advancing an understanding of mediated communication. Most useful surveys illuminate an explanation of effects by garnering evidence for a theory.

SECTION III: NATURALISTIC INQUIRY

In the preceding chapter and thus far in this chapter, we have looked at the uses, strengths, and limitations of the most dominant research methods in mediated communication effects research—experiments and surveys. We have tried to emphasize the circumstances or conditions under which the use of these major procedures are appropriate or inappropriate. In the past decade or so, some media researchers have begun to adopt anthropological methods in their studies. These procedures have coalesced into a form of inquiry known by many different titles; the one we have chosen is naturalistic inquiry. In this section, we will look at the principle characteristics of naturalistic inquiry methods, how they differ from other research methods, and how they offer both advantages and disadvantages in assessing the impact of media on audiences. We will depart from presenting an evaluation of an exemplar study. The recency of these methods precludes a "classic" example and their present diversity makes comparison difficult.

CHARACTERISTICS OF NATURALISTIC INQUIRY METHODS

Naturalistic inquiry is often referred to as a qualitative research method. Qualitative research methods are distinguished from quantitative methods in that they do not rest their evidence on the logic of mathematics, the principle of numbers, or the methods of statistical analysis. While qualitative research, in its many different forms, frequently makes use of numbers and counting, it does not use the numerical values in the same ways as they are used in the collection and analysis of data in experiments and surveys. Qualitative methods may be critical or empirical. Naturalistic inquiry is an empirical method in that it finds its evidence in what can be experienced rather than in formal or analytic reasoning. (As you will remember, we are concerned only with empirical methods in this review.)

Lindlof and Meyer (1987) refer to all naturalistic inquiry under the term *interpretive paradigm*. Varieties include such theory and procedures known as: ethnography, phenomenology, ethnomethodology, symbolic interactionism, ecological psychology, semiotic analysis, and case studies. Lindlof and Meyer tell us that the interpretive paradigm:

> takes its subject to be the fields of meaning that pervade the projects of human life. Precisely because people cognize their graspable and imagined environments in symbolic schemes, continually developing future courses of action and revising past acts, the phenomena of social life are fundamentally self-referential and require different paths of inquiry than the exact sciences. (p. 4)

They elaborate further ("Thank goodness!" you're probably saying):

> For all the varieties of the interpretive paradigm, human behavior becomes a topic of investigation when it signifies a person's intentional orientation to the world, or when observing others attribute significance to it. The behaviors constituting social relations are in turn derived from intersubjective constructs of the social actors, and can be understood (or critiqued) only through some "insider" knowledge of those constructs. The work of the interpretive researcher is directed toward ontological concerns about the organization of human experience, namely, under

> what conditions communicative acts occur, how it is that people account for their acts, what versions of the world are proposed and negotiated through communication. (pp. 5-6)

Anderson (1987) describes the essence of interpretive methods in the following manner:

> The causes and consequences of human behavior are not in objectified attributes but in the meanings that are held by individuals. It is the purpose of the social scientist to make explicit those meanings by interpreting the social action of others. All experience, including the experience of the scientist, is meaningful in constitutive acts of interpretation. These acts segment the continuum of experience to create "sequences of action" which are infused with purpose and cause. These interpretations . . . result in the taken-for-granted facts of everyday life. The natural person practicing the natural attitude in everyday life creates and maintains the world "as we know it." It is the purpose of science to explicate these taken-for-granted facts.
>
> The scientist must approach the lifeworld within the natural attitude first as a naive participant and then as a critical observer because socially constructed meanings become most apparent when we participate in their construction and reflect on those constitutive acts. (pp. 244-245)

Naturalistic inquiry thus involves the researcher not as an objective observer (as in the natural and physical sciences) but as an active participant, an interpreter of "what is going on out there." Rather than observe at a safe, objective distance, naturalistic inquiry takes its researchers and immerses them in the midst of the particular environment of interest in which those social actions are being carried out by people (known as "actors"). For example, if a researcher wanted to know about the impact of televised commercials aimed at young children, the first presumption would be that whatever impact occurs, it occurs within some ongoing social action. Several different procedures might be used to illuminate that impact within the contexts of the social action: Extensive interviews with children and parents could be analyzed for the ways in which people interpret commercials in everyday decision making. Informants have kept activity diaries to record their routines and comment on the place of television's texts. Or, the researcher might select a household with young children and spend an extended period of time "living" with the family and observing how the children interact with television, their siblings, their parents, and so on. This researcher would then prepare a narrative (detailed description) of what was learned from the participative experience and what can be said about the influence of television, including the commercials, on the these children. The conclusions reached via the different methods would likely be different, but that would be expected, given different goals, different research approaches, and different kinds of information from which inferences would be made. The important thing about naturalistic inquiry at this preliminary point in our discussion is that the researcher looks for meanings to emerge from those being studied in their own environments. But naturalistic inquiry—as we define it here (following Anderson, 1987)—is much more than this focus. It differs from traditional modes of social scientific inquiry in many other important ways. These characteristics and differences are described in the following paragraphs.

INDUCTIVE PROCESS The first important distinguishing characteristic of naturalistic inquiry is that it is **inductive** in nature. By this we mean that the researcher either entertains no preconceived ideas of what is going on "out there" (the research setting of interest) or clearly identifies those preconceptions and sets them aside, assuming that what is going on out there will define itself in its own unique way. Traditional **hypothetic/deductive** science theorizes about the relationship among variables, forms specific hypotheses about the existence of these relationships, tests the hypotheses, and integrates the findings with its theory, noting when the theory has been confirmed (and if so, to what degree) or not confirmed. Naturalistic inquiry demands that the researcher formulate descriptions of variables and their interrelationships based on what is discovered during field work and analysis; there are no hypotheses or specific predictions of what will occur or be found. What is going on emerges during and after the inquiry.

The "meanings" for the social actions and actors being studied rest with the actors, not with the researcher, and they are not embedded in the research instruments that structure responses to fit the researcher's preconceived meanings. Think back to the earlier parts in this chapter where survey procedures were criticized for assuming that what was called for in the answers to a question(s) was uniformly understood by all respondents. In naturalistic inquiry, the researcher begins with the single, general question: "What is going on out there?" What is learned from the objects of study forms the basis for inductive inferences, moving from the specific to the general. And while qualitative researchers do in fact engage in the process of deduction, it is not used in the same manner as traditional scientific inquiry. Following the inductive process, the **ethnographer,** for example, might use what was learned (inferred) in a particular case to predict how those individuals will respond given the presence of certain conditions in the future. Such a procedure in fact helps to validate the accuracy of the researcher's inferences when the predictions are confirmed. But such deduction occurs in naturalistic inquiry much later in the research process.

REFLEXIVE ANALYSIS Naturalistic inquiry is also reflexive, in that the researcher is an integral part of the phenomena being studied. In a sense, the researcher is the research instrument because it rests on his or her skills in observing, inferring, explaining, and describing. This characteristic holds true to one substantial degree or another in the application of any one or a combination of the following: participant observation, the life history interview, the depth interview, the "informant" interview, and the so-called unobtrusive measures—for example, the examination of personal or institutional documents and artifacts, maps, diaries, audio recordings, and film/videotape records.

For example, in an informant interview, the researcher is able to elicit valuable information from a person who is an experienced participant in the social process being studied. This informant must also be articulate and able to describe the nature of the process engaged in by him- or herself and the other participants in the social setting; thus not every participant will make a good informant. But the researcher is still "involved" in such a process because he or she must be able to ask the right questions and know enough to be able to interpret and make sense of the answers. He or she must also be able to probe the informant to elicit as full a picture of what is going on as possible. A researcher interested in the process used by a managing editor to select which stories would appear and where in a newspaper may well combine periods of observation of an editor and intersperse some in-depth informant interviews as the research proceeded and the investigator learned more and more about the process. The interpretation of the observations and the informant interviews both require the active role of the researcher. The narrative written by the researcher represents one of the visible end products of the research instrument—the researcher.

CONTEXTUALIZED Naturalistic inquiry is also characterized by its attention to context. As mentioned previously in this and the preceding chapter, surveys and experiments presume that effects can be decontextualized, studied independently of the social contexts in which actions take place. In naturalistic inquiry, understanding the meanings for participants in what is going on relies heavily on a simultaneous grasp of the context(s) in which those actions take place. For example, the meanings ascribed to violent television content by a child growing up in an environment in which violent behavior is prevalent within the family structure would need to be interpreted within the framework of this particular context. Interpreting this child's reactions to televised violence would be a risky enterprise if contextual knowledge were not available.

Context is also an important part of understanding a process. As we have mentioned many times, mediated communication involves a series of interrelated processes that are enormously complex. Experiments and surveys, even panel studies in which the same sample is measured periodically over a period of time, usually fall short in their ability to account adequately for and describe the processes of which what was measured is a part. Knowledge of context considerably enhances the ability of the researcher to understand and explain what was observed and how it meshes with the overall context in which the phenomena are embedded.

HISTORICIZED EXPLANATIONS While achieving a detailed understanding of what is going on in a particular situation is a (if not the) major goal in naturalistic inquiry, the explanations that result from such inquiry are subjective or historicized (claims are attributed to the person making them). Of course it can be argued that all knowledge acquisitions and expressions are subjective and that there is no such thing as objective knowledge (true for all peoples and all times), but it is best to think of the hypothetic/deductive methods and qualitative methods on a continuum anchored on opposite ends by subjective and objective. Traditional scientific methods strive for and make claims of objectivity; naturalistic inquiry is subjective by its very nature. Naturalistic inquiry looks for the meanings ascribed to social actions by the actors (those people being studied) themselves.

Meaning operates at various levels. These layers of meaning are uncovered by the researcher as the inquiry progresses. Thus the level of meaning described by the researcher will be tied to the context of the study, including who the actors are, where and how they operate, and with what consequences. The medium of television, what it represents as technology, a taken-for-granted appliance in the household, the content it presents, the issues that the content or its presence raises, and so on, provides an excellent example of how different researchers or the same researcher could seek to uncover the meaning(s) that "television" has for a given individual or a given household or a sample of different individuals or households. In thinking about it, you probably realize that *television* means many different things to you, once you consider it in a number of different contexts, those contexts in which the medium presents itself and is used by you. A researcher studying those meanings might seek one or a number of levels, depending upon the general aim of the study.

EVERYDAY LIFE AS THE RESEARCH SITE Naturalistic inquiry examines the mundane. While the extraordinary, clearly idiosyncratic, or outrageous case is also subjected to scientific study, naturalistic inquiry operates to explain ongoing everyday life. Much of our day-to-day behavior is efficiently and conveniently arranged in patterns and is displayed in ordinary fashion. Think about the daily practices you engage in every day. You probably have a number of them for each day—a weekday wake-up-and-get-going practice in the morning, a going-to-class-to-coffee-to-class-to-lunch sequence that follows, a method for studying and/or leisure time pursuits. These practices are organized in routines that, as noted, are the social action signs by which we know what it is we are doing. Audience uses of mediated communication content are almost always embedded in a routine and a complex routine at that. By studying such routines, qualitative researchers are able to describe the routine and the meanings that are part of those routines for the people who enact them.

Almost by definition, behaviors that occur as part of a taken-for-granted pattern are done without conscious thought on the part of the individual. These patterns characterize so much of our behavior because they enable us to avoid directed thought, a process that demands effort, expends energy, and can be literally painful at times. And, because the process is so common to people everywhere, these behaviors escape our serious attention. When people engage in the process of monitoring how much television they watch and what they watch and when, many are surprised at what this monitoring process reveals. Their comments are prefaced with the words "You know, I never realized . . ." Yet, they are talking about their very own behavioral patterns, and patterns that have been in operation for some time. Naturalistic inquiry seeks to reveal the meanings of mundane social actions and to understand fully the nature of such actions.

THE RESEARCHER IS FULLY PRESENT Given that qualitative research studies social actions and actors and that the researcher is the research instrument, at some point (if not at many), the qualitative researcher must interact with the actors and/or in the environment in which the social actions occur. Naturalistic inquiry is interactive. Traditional science methods demand that the investigator stay "at arms length" or more away from the processes being examined so as to not bias what is observed or measured. Naturalistic inquiry demands that the researcher become immersed at least to some degree in the research setting. While completely unobtrusive methods (e.g., a hidden video camera and microphone) may be used to observe the action, analysis of the records will be substantially impaired without at least some first-hand knowledge of who the actors are, what the social actions mean to the actors, and, often, just what is and is not going on "out there."

If you were to view a tape of a Japanese tea ceremony for the first time and without any previous knowledge of the culture, you would be extremely hard pressed to understand or explain what it was you were "seeing." By learning about the ceremony and by interacting, you would be able to write a much more informed account of what was "on" this tape. In a similar manner, having a videotaped record of a room with people in it, interacting over a period of time, including some media behaviors, would present an equally difficult challenge to observers to describe what they were "seeing." You, of course, would be in a much more informed position to interpret some of what you observed in this case because you have experience yourself with the cultural setting shown on the tape. But your "informed" state of mind could lead you completely away from what was going on in the videotape household in that you would be tempted to interpret what you saw from what you knew from your perspective, informed by your experiences. These interpretations run directly counter to the goal of naturalistic inquiry, which is to understand the social actions and actors from their point of view; it is their interpretations that matter. To get at these interpretations, the researcher must have the opportunity to interact with those being studied, preferably as part of the same social setting(s). Such interaction seems essential to increase the chances that the narrative resulting from the study will be faithful to those who were studied and that the descriptions therein will be accurate and defensible.

Many qualitative researchers use multiple procedures to uncover as much as possible of what is going on for social actors in a particular arena of action. Many become members themselves to gain an appreciation of what it is like for those being studied. The actions and interactions of the researcher do have an impact on those being studied, especially if they are aware that a study is taking place. Any changes in behavior brought about by the awareness that the researcher is not an ordinary member would, it is hoped, revert to their natural state in due time as the researcher becomes absorbed into the group and its attendant rituals. When the researcher becomes a member, it can serve to provide not only valuable insights but, unfortunately, to bias the observations to the extent that what the researcher experiences is assumed to be operating for original members. As a result, researchers must abstract themselves at some point and be more of an observer than a participant. This gives researchers the enormous advantage of seeing the action from the outside looking in and with some inside knowledge of what the actors are experiencing.

MEMBER KNOWLEDGE Media researchers engaging in qualitative procedures frequently spend great amounts of time with a family or several families that serve as the focal point of the study. The researcher often feels like and becomes like another member of the family; he or she interacts freely with family members as a member and as a researcher, going back and forth, often quickly, from one role to the other. These interactions will provide the basis from which a richly detailed and sensibly constructed account/narrative can be developed that will not only do justice to those observed but will be meaningful to readers of the narrative account. One key prerequisite to useful narratives is the researcher's level and quality of interaction. Member knowledge, as it is called, is an important criterion of excellence in these studies.

SUMMARY

At this point in our discussion of naturalistic inquiry, you should have a good grasp of how qualitative methods differ from the hypothetic/deductive methods of traditional science. You should also be able to characterize naturalistic inquiry by its most significant features. Naturalistic inquiry is inductive, reflexive, contextual, subjective, mundane, and interactive. Naturalistic inquiry seems to at least hold the potential to assess mediated communication effects in ways that are unique from those that have dominated the research to date: experimental and survey/questionnaire methods. It seems well-suited to getting at many of the complex processes that comprise mediated communication, it seems to provide procedures that can capture the many nuances of audiences' interactions with media and mediated content, it seems to allow or even accommodate a number of different procedures and alternative interpretations and perspectives.

Naturalistic inquiry has all of this potential and undoubtedly more, but as we have learned by now, all research methods have their own inherent limitations as well as strengths. These strengths and limitations, discussed in the upcoming section of this chapter, will reveal a picture of as yet unrealized potential and perhaps in some areas, a potential that cannot be realized.

LIMITATIONS OF NATURALISTIC INQUIRY

On the surface, qualitative research sounds as if it provides the set of procedures that are so desperately needed to assess the impact of mediated communication. Yet a survey of the communication literature by Anderson (1984) showed that of more than 1,100 articles published in a five-year period, only 16 were qualitative studies (see Anderson, 1987, p. 237). In part, this scarcity is a result of communication scholars having been only recently trained in and exposed to naturalistic inquiry theories and procedures. It is also a result of some inherent problems in doing the research and in reporting it. These limitations will undoubtedly continue to account for a limited output of qualitative research in the future.

METHODS VERSUS STRATEGIES The first limitation of naturalistic inquiry is the relative absence of clear and easily understood research procedures. How does one go about doing a piece of ethnographic research? Where does the researcher go, having asked the question about what is going on out there? Qualitative procedures are strategies of engagement rather than recipes. They require the researcher to be tactically innovative in social action and at the same time, to record carefully each innovation and the action itself. Because the study is contextualized within natural action, prospective scholars must necessarily come to grips with many different ways of proceeding, depending upon the topic of interest, who is being studied and where, how unusual the people and/or circumstances are, what particular type of inquiry is undertaken, and so on, but only as potential approaches and not actual methods. How one goes about doing qualitative research is much harder to explain and demonstrate than the methods of experiments or surveys. (Do not, however, confuse the ease of documenting research methods with the ease of actually implementing the methods; learning to conduct experiments and surveys properly is not a quick or easy process.)

Having waded through the "how do I do this kind of thing" part of qualitative research, the second limiting hurdle is how to deal with yourself and your skills as an observer and researcher. Remember, in naturalistic inquiry, the researcher is the research instrument "par excellence." Are you going to be a sophisticated, elegant and smoothly operating instrument, the proverbial "well-oiled machine?" Or are you going to be an inept and obtrusive participant/observer who is incapable of seeing the forest because of the trees? Probably, you will start out like the latter and, perhaps, if you stick with it over time, end up closer to the former.

BEING THERE Naturalistic inquiry involves the identification of evidence that the researcher uses to support and arrive at inferences made about what is going on in the research environment. Out of the myriad of events observed over a period of time, several ought to emerge as particularly meaningful. These occurrences are known as "critical incidents." Critical incidents are those events that represent a significant part of what is going on, they enlighten first the researcher and later the reader regarding an important aspect of the social actions/actors being studied. A narrative developed from naturalistic inquiry must be edited; the goal of the narrative, after all, is not merely to write up all of the field notes. The narrative provides an overall structure that ultimately describes in appropriate detail and with appropriate examples and supporting material what was learned from the study. Critical incidents, therefore, provide evidence for major aspects that will help to shape the final form of the narrative. But, critical incidents depend upon the observational skills of the researcher, who must first be there and then be able to cull out the significant from the insignificant. The observer also must be able and willing to set aside any preconceptions and to seek validation in the field for preliminary inferences. Such observational and inferential skills do not come easily (or even, we suspect, naturally); they must be developed and perfected. Observational skills are one key link to meaningful qualitative research.

One of the authors recalls reading a narrative from a doctoral student in a graduate seminar in qualitative research methods that was richly detailed and went on page after page as the fascinating narrative unfolded about the roles played by television in a typical four-person (two adults and two children) household. The critical incidents were there, thoroughly documented, as the author described how the children used television and how they interacted while watching television and in play and other daily activities when not watching. It was only when the researcher described the observational schedule that it became clear that this marvelous piece of work, some 35-40 pages long, was based on a single two-hour observation period. Although the researcher knew the parents, his first and only in-person contact with the children occurred during this rather brief period. He had interviewed the mother and father in some depth, but he had talked with the children, observed their behavior and interactions, noted their nontelevision behaviors, and so on all during the two-hour block. This researcher had not accomplished the task of "being there." As readers of qualitative research, we need to look for evidence of serious commitment to studying the social actions and actors in the field.

QUALITY OF THE NARRATIVE As readers or potential users of the products made available to us by qualitative investigators, we are dependent upon the researcher as our only available link between us and the social actions and actors being observed. If I want to know about what it is like to be a managing news editor, my insights will be dependent upon the quality of the narrative provided by the researcher who has studied such a person in action on the job; and, the narrative, of course, will be dependent in part upon the observational skills of the researcher, his or her ability to be able to understand what is going on and what it means, and significantly, his or her ability to present those observations and understandings in the **ethnographic narrative.**

A third limitation of naturalistic inquiry, then, is its heavy dependence on the writing abilities of the researcher. Developing the narrative demands some creativity (not creativity in the sense of "making something up"). You can be a keen observer, having spent a great deal of time in the field, faithfully logging events, documenting critical incidents, and so on. But, when it comes time to make and present your case in a way that will be understood by others and to present the significance of your research in the best possible way, you must be up to the writing demands that will be placed upon you. Although sophisticated writing skills are no substitute for rigorous research, poor writing skills can leave the researcher with a great deal to say but only a limited opportunity to make his or her work known to others. If your interpretations are either poorly expressed or too limiting, or if you err in the opposite direction and "make something out of nothing," you will be presenting a narrative that is not as faithful to what you observed and learned about as it could be.

A similar problem presents itself when researchers elect to present their narrative in a fictional form (e.g., a novel). While the narrative account does indeed represent the sum of inferences and interpretations of the researcher, the line between fact and fiction can pose problems for the reader of the narrative. In the novel or fiction form, the operation of "dramatic license" cannot be gauged. When the author is taking liberties with what occurred to make the social actions and actor fit into some prototype or ideal pattern and when what is presented closely adheres to what was observed remains problematic for the reader. This situation is really no different than the one that occurs when a television or movie script or novel is "based on a true story," but is still presented as a fictional work. Where the basis in truth begins and ends is usually difficult for the reader to surmise, even with some guidance from the author. And the writing skills of the author become even more critical when the format for presentation is a fictional work.

RESEARCHER OBTRUSIONS A fourth limitation of naturalistic inquiry is the obtrusiveness of the researcher. While all research involves a certain amount of obtrusiveness, qualitative research (with the possible exception of covert or secret observations) involving social actors in their milieu is obtrusive by design. Thus such research procedures simultaneously dictate a strength and a weakness. When the researcher "becomes one of them," he or she gains invaluable insights through the experience of participant; observations, therefore, are informed and guided by such experiences. But being present and interacting as a participant/observer is not the same thing as being a conventional member of the group. Members are, of course, aware of what they do, but as we have pointed out, when there are patterned behaviors involved, what we do and why we do it usually escape self-examination. Researchers, on the other hand, have to juggle the dual role of participant and observer. Their presence may cause a considerable disruption in the normal course of social action for the group being studied.

When researchers gain access to an environment, they intrude on the people in that environment. People who are aware that they are being "studied" may over time become accustomed to the researcher's presence, but they may alter their behavior when the observer is present and/or they may remain guarded or noncommunicative on certain topics because they are just not comfortable sharing their thoughts and feelings with the researcher.

The uses of media by individuals and families lend themselves well to study via qualitative methods, especially because the rituals involving media are so commonplace. But mediated behaviors also involve intimacy and privacy that ordinarily would not be accessible to outsiders. As Lindlof and Meyer (1987) noted:

> Some aspects that may be part of the ritual may never be displayed at all or even verbally alluded to, escaping the researcher's awareness. Obvious examples would include activities such as drug use, intimate sexual behavior, more romantic moments than members may be used to sharing (e.g., a couple watching a favorite movie together), or more emotional or emotion-arousing uses. And, if such uses are referred to only by participants in verbal accounts, the ability of the researcher to observe the ritual and interpret it is quite obviously jeopardized (in any valid sense, at least). (pp. 14-15)

While obtrusiveness is an essential part of the participant observation process, the disadvantages can be minimized to a degree by the strength of commitment of the researcher. If the researcher is willing to spend a great deal of time in the household, his or her presence and its effects on those being observed will be eased. But this commitment demands spending large blocks of time and over an extended period. In a study of the media behaviors of a middle-aged, childless couple, Wolf et al. (1982) report that two researchers lived with the couple for extended blocks of time over a period of more than a year. Their impressions of "what was going on there" were the products of the kind of familiarity that has the potential for producing insightful and useful narratives. The authors validate their acceptance in the household when they were referred to by the couple as "their kids." Naturalistic inquiry without solid commitment by the researchers to be a part of the social setting is on shaky ground and may be only marginally useful to readers.

TIME DEMANDS The fifth and last limitation of naturalistic inquiry that we will discuss is the fact that such research is time consuming. An experimenter or survey researcher can design a series of studies, carefully develop and pretest the research instruments and then proceed to the field (or into the lab) to collect the data. Data collection proceeds rather quickly (in comparison to qualitative methods). Data analysis is also efficient and rapid; data files are created and validated to eliminate entry errors and analyzed by computer. The computer uses one of several statistical analysis packages to provide the researcher with results. While a large data set can be examined and reexamined in a nearly infinite number of ways, the researcher is supposed to have a clear sense of what interrelationships are predicted and how those relationships will be tested before the data are collected.

Such efficiency and speed are not available to qualitative researchers. The extensive period of field work—Sanday (1979) suggests at least a year—results in a veritable wealth of data. Now the researcher must make sense of all this data, organize it, catalogue it, interpret it, and then set out to draft a narrative. The preparation of the narrative, though informed by some general guidelines and standards, also means a unique task confronts the researcher—there are no templates here. The directions taken by the narrative will vary from study to study.

The most convincing reason that explains the lack of naturalistic inquiry in mediated communication is the huge amount of time demanded by such investigations. While some of the naturalistic studies of media audience members have been insightful and useful for understanding some aspects of mediated communication processes, many scholars remain unwilling to undertake such investigations. With the demand for producing published research being felt in nearly all academic institutions, this unwillingness is completely understandable. Time constraints, unfortunately, present a practical limitation that prevents the judgment of how far naturalistic inquiry can go in informing the field about the nature of mediated communication behaviors and rituals.

SUMMARY

At this point you should have at least a "feel" for naturalistic inquiry—its assumptions, procedures, characteristics, strengths, and limitations. In the preceding section, we have learned that while naturalistic inquiry seems to offer the potential for overcoming the limitations of traditional scientific methods and for offering informative insights into the complexities of mediated communication processes, the limitations of this type of research have to date prevented the potential from being realized. These limitations include: the absence of clear and easily understood research procedures; the reliance on the observational and inferential skills of the researcher; the dependence on the writing ability of the researcher; the obtrusiveness of the researcher; and, the commitment of extended periods of time to conduct and complete the research.

In evaluating a work of naturalistic inquiry, the reader must first attend to the central purpose of this type of research—the illumination of the meanings held by the actors of a social scene. It is not the discovery of decontextualized, determinate forces that predict human behavior. Given that intent, the criteria of evaluation concern the opportunity to observe and participate in the meaning process and the success of translating them to others. The researcher must show an openness to the scene by setting aside his or her own predispositions, a commitment to the action through an extended series of contacts, skill, and insight in observation, a respect for the action in thorough documentation, and a grasp of the understandings of both the actors and the readers in the research narrative. Our own evaluation of the research literature is that the struggle is more apparent than the success.

CENTRAL IDEAS OF SECTION III: NATURALISTIC INQUIRY

1. Naturalistic inquiry is a form of study from the empirical branch of qualitative methods whose evidence rests on documented experience, but is not dependent on the logic and methods of quantitative measurement and analysis.
2. Naturalistic inquiry has had more promise than performance, accounting for less than 2% of the communication research literature. Current exemplars are not necessarily reliable indicators of the approach.
3. Naturalistic inquiry differs from traditional hypothetic/deductive approaches by being inductive, reflexive, contextual, subjective, mundane, and interactive.
4. The limitations that naturalistic inquiry imposes by its nature or present development are the absence of clear and easily understood research procedures, the reliance on the observational and inferential skills of the researcher, the dependence on the writing ability of the researcher, the obtrusiveness of the researcher, and the commitment of extended periods of time to conduct and complete the research.
5. The limitations shown in practice have been primarily concerned with the lack of a committed engagement with the membership of study over an extended period of time. Most studies involve short visitations and limited association that cast their claims of understanding the social processes of the membership in doubt.

SECTION IV: THE PLACE OF SOCIAL SCIENCE

The last two chapters have provided a critical analysis of procedures that characterize the practice of the social sciences. It is easy after the seemingly unrelenting stream of problems and complaints to throw up one's hands and walk away from either the criticism or the science. Neither is helpful in the long run. What is helpful both to the practice of science and to the society that makes use of its claims is the recognition of the place the social sciences occupy as one struggling agent in the reality constituting practices of that society.

Science has long claimed a special hold on the truth and privileged itself to speak for all of us. Many now believe that what we held as truth has actually been a record of success in accomplishing human purposes. While we have been successful in approaching the problems humans face in their physical environment, we have been mostly unsuccessful in solving the social problems that beset the human condition. Now that lack of success can be understood in at least two different ways: Our science may be imperfect or we may lack the will to implement what we know demonstrating that political action is outside the realm of science.

As good academicians we find some truth in both alternatives. There is nothing more satisfying in the practice of science than making a general claim and having it be shown true in a series of specific instances. We believe that an honest appraisal of science's claims concerning media would find that satisfaction missing. We cannot understand the forces of violence in society by examining mediated content; we cannot predict elections in the character of campaign messages; we cannot manage pornography to limit crimes against women.

On the other hand, a genuine test of those issues in society would require us to grant social science far more power and resources than we have shown any inclination to do. It some respects, it is as if we fear our own understanding with perhaps some justification. Human knowledge does not transcend the human condition. It is used for human purposes, and we humans have taken up some mighty frightful goals. But the major point here is that we do have the ability to accomplish much more in the social sciences. We have not because as a society we have declined the opportunity. Many of the complaints about methods that we have voiced surround practices developed in response to long-term impoverishment. (Total public funding of the social sciences is considerably less than the cost of a single attack submarine.) We have had to abandon our elegance to survive. The shame of us scientists has been the pretense of our glory.

As it now stands, social science research is a rather weak voice often heard as a scold and largely ignored. Because of its limitations—limitations in no small part imposed by other sources of power—its claims must be viewed with justifiable skepticism. But the claim bounded in endless qualification emasculates action, which is why we have often pushed our claims beyond their legitimate support—a point to which we will return when we consider instrumentality in the chapter that follows.

This comment on place appears partly to prepare for Chapter 8 and partly to understand how the claims and practices of social science can be readily brought into question and still be delivered to its students with few qualifications. It is important for all of us as students of this science realistically to appraise what we can do and the place that is given us to do it.

CHAPTER SUMMARY

In this chapter, survey and qualitative research methods have been described and analyzed as they apply to our understanding of media communication. Survey/questionnaire methods are useful for documenting the presence of certain events or variables and for identifying the presence of relationships among variables, although claims concerning the nature of those relationships are usually not appropriate when using such methods. Surveys are limited in the study of mediated communication processes because they do not lend themselves to the examination of complex processes, nor do they lend themselves to providing valid descriptions of embedded social routines of which many mediated behaviors are a part. Naturalistic inquiry offers some potential for overcoming some limitations of traditional methods in the study of mediated communication. But, it, too, has limitations that have prevented it to date from being very informative or useful. And, because of its exorbitant time constraints, naturalistic inquiry may not make much of a contribution in the future given the economic realities of research.

With the significance and number of limitations associated with the research procedures available to social scientists interested in studying mediated communication phenomena, how can the claims generated by such methods be used to make sense of these complex processes? The answer, we suspect, rests in the need to be guarded in how much you accept and are willing to be guided by any particular study or series of studies. Given these critical limitations, any findings and conclusions must always be treated as highly tentative. Moreover, research that presents one method or another should not be rejected because of its choice of method. Each study needs to be judged in light of what it has to say and how it is limited. By using research that spans many different methods and theoretical perspectives, you can begin to make sense out of how media work and what the consequences are for audiences that use media content. Look at a study for what it presents and doesn't present; if it holds up under careful scrutiny and makes sense to you in the life that you live, you have gained some valuable insight into mediated communication.

In the chapter that follows, we will continue our investigation into our knowledge of media process and effects by examining the manner in which both theory and method produce claim. With some understanding of the nature of claim, we will then examine its instrumentalities for knowledge, society, and the research community. Despite all of the studies of media effects, you will discover that there is little certainty about what the effects of the media are, who is affected in what ways and when. What we know for sure remains only a very small part of what we suspect is an area fraught with enormous complexity and perhaps, at the present, insurmountable magnitude.

RELATED READINGS

Anderson, J. A. (1987). *Communication Research: Issues and methods.* New York: McGraw-Hill.

The material in Chapters 4-8 will be particularly useful for understanding survey methods in an overall context of quantitative research. The chapter on sampling is especially useful in this regard in that it lays out the rigors of sampling and assumptions behind the procedures that make up the backbone of survey methods.

Section Three deals exclusively with naturalistic inquiry methods. Included are an overview of the methodologies, research designs, the methods of participant observation from start-up to writing up the final outcomes, and the standards for evaluating qualitative research.

Babbie, E. (1986). *The practice of social research* (4th ed.). Belmont, CA: Wadsworth.

This well-accepted text provides useful background material on sampling, survey procedures, and the logic of causality. Babbie is a survey researcher by trade and training; he presents a forceful case for the circumstances when surveys are valuable sources of data and when their limitations preclude them from studying certain kinds of phenomena.

Hammersly, M., & Atkinson, P. (1983). *Ethnography: Principles in practice.* London: Tavistock.

An excellent overview of the underlying principles of naturalistic inquiry and the procedures used in engaging such study. The book promotes ethnographic research but is sketchy in laying out the most serious shortcomings of these procedures. The book is clearly written and well-supported with examples from sociological research.

Lindlof, T. (Ed.). (1987). *Natural audiences: Qualitative research of media uses and effects.* Norwood, NJ: Ablex.

While there are not many published pieces of media research employing qualitative methods to study media impact or effects, this book provides some excellent examples of such research. The studies themselves are further enhanced by perceptive commentaries following each section (Children, Families, Subcultures, and Institutions). A comprehensive, well-documented chapter introduces the book and critically examines the strengths and weakness of naturalistic inquiry in and of itself and in comparison with traditional hypothetic/deductive research.

8

Claims and Evidence

ANY SCHOLAR OF mediated communication is faced with the pause-giving task of coming to grips with the burgeoning body of claims that surrounds our understanding of media in society. As part of our preparation for this chapter we surveyed six journals (*Journal of Communication, Human Communication Research, Communication Research, Journal of Broadcasting and Electronic Media, Journalism Quarterly,* and *Critical Studies in Mass Communication*) over the years 1982-1986. We chose these journals because they are generally considered in the mainstream of media studies.

We selected 259 articles from these journals as being directly or indirectly connected with the content of this book. A sampling from this selection is listed at the end of this chapter. There were, of course, several other journals[1] and many more years that we could have added. Our intent was not to be exhaustive (an impossibility as the literature reproduces faster than it can be read), but to provide a specific resource for this chapter that examines the nature of claims about mediated communication typically—and currently—made. In this chapter, we will dissect (*deconstruct* is the current term of choice) these claims to show how they arise from a theoretical perspective, are supported by evidence that appears in a methodological approach, and are used for epistemological, societal, ideological, and professional ends.

The purpose of this effort is to complete the final leg of our search for effects. In the preceding three chapters we have considered the major lines of theory and methods of analysis. Theory and method provide the warrant and evidence for claim. To understand the claims made by researchers—from whence we get our notions of effects—we need to examine this relationship. The chapter is divided into six sections: The first examines the nature of claim; the second its relation to theory; the third its relation to method; the fourth explores the instrumentality of claim; the fifth concludes our search for effects; and the final section provides a resource of recent studies.

SECTION I: THE NATURE OF CLAIM

A claim is any arguable proposition. Any competently crafted article is essentially an argument that marshals evidence in support of a claim or set of claims. As we have seen in Chapters 6 and 7, the notion of claim comes in very early in the argument. Scientists are often perceived as working solely from the facts of their observations. The hard facts of most scientific studies in communication, however, involve whether a respondent put a pencil mark in this position or that. Those facts are neither very interesting nor informative. It is the claim about what those facts represent, which is both. The preceding chapters on methodology have investigated the nature of claims at that level. In this chapter we want to move to the level of substantive claim in which a supported assertion is made about the nature, practice, or process of mediated communication. Here are some recent examples:

> Heavy [more frequent] viewers of television often hold beliefs about the world that are more televisionlike or television-implied than the beliefs of light [less frequent] viewers (Hawkins, Pingree, & Alder, 1987, p. 572).

> This [discourse] analysis of the news has suggested that television does, indeed, advocate a particular vision of society. The distribution of economic and political powers to separate spheres is taken to be legitimate and natural. The private sector should, and normally does, work in and of itself; the state is meant to ensure a stable framework by monetary regulation and law enforcement; and the public sphere of political institutions can then work out the exact terms of their cooperation. (Jensen, 1987, p. 24)

> The major finding of this study was that inner-city subjects were significantly more aroused than a college sample by viewing ten types of violence. . . . The significantly higher arousal levels experienced by inner-city subjects is consistent with the concept of resonance. These findings support the theory that when media content is generally congruent with the real-life experiences of the audience, the result is a marked amplification of the reality of media messages. (Frost & Stauffer, 1987, p. 41)

> The results of this study illustrate that numerous social, psychological, economic, and political factors, intertwined in complex but coherent ways, act in concert to influence media usage and consumption. Configured in different ways, these factors give rise to certain clearly identifiable lifestyles whose adherents incorporate different types of media consumption for different purposes. It is clear from this study that media

> use indeed has multiple origins, and that need for activation [the production of a necessary, base level of arousal] interacts with political and social activities to produce different lifestyle requirements for information and other gratifications, many of which can be met via media consumption. (Donohew, Palmgreen, & Rayburn, 1987, p. 274)

> This study set out to show that an important part of voting, viewed as a cognitive process, is how people think in arriving at their choices. This runs counter to most of the literature that is focused on what—that is, the content of political cognitions. As an alternative approach, the concept of cognitive strategies should be useful for describing how cognition influences communication behavior. (Donohew, Palmgreen, & Rayburn, 1987, p. 53)

> The prospect that voters change their cognitive strategies during the campaign has an interesting practical implication, It suggests that the same voter will process information differently at different times during the campaign. Thus static notions that, for example, some voters are "issue oriented" and others "personality oriented" may miss the mark. All, or most, voters may process information in these ways but at different times. (Stamm, 1987, pp. 53-55)

These quotations give a good representation of the spectrum of claim that can be found in the empirical literature on media. They arise from separate theoretical stances (or variants thereof), use different methodologies, and have different rhetorical and social purposes or instrumentalities. The rest of this chapter will be organized around a "close reading" of these five quotations to examine how claim arises in and can be properly understood only in relation to its embedded theory, method, and instrumentality.

SECTION II: CLAIM AND THEORY

Our analysis in Chapter 5 has shown that the effects of mediated communication appear only when viewed from some theoretical perspective. That perspective sets the assumptions about media, content, audiences, the individual, the nature of meaning: its production and interpretation, behavior and action; in short, all of the necessary assumptions for the questions and answers of research to make sense.

In our selected review, we found seven separable perspectives: cultural studies, cultivation analysis, the exposure model, the interpretive model, Lippmann effects, social action, and uses and gratifications. While the particular journals selected greatly affect the relative proportion of the appearance of each of these perspectives, we were surprised by the overwhelming percentage of studies emanating from the exposure model (61%) nearly three times more than the appearance of the interpretive model as the next highest. For most researchers (publishing in these journals), then, content is still being viewed as a "meaning-delivery system" that works its effects in "mindless" (Zillmann & Bryant, 1985) ways.

Studies centrally located in this model presented content to a respondent group with no allowance for differential effects by individual type (e.g., Acker, 1983; Atkin, 1983; Donohue, Henke, & Meyer, 1983; Drew & Reese, 1984; or Miller, 1985). Studies that begin to slide toward the interpretive model differentiate respondents, but on the basis of states, conditions, or qualities that are beyond the control of the individual, such as gender, age, race, developmental stage, and the like (e.g., Cantor & Wilson, 1984; Collins & Wellman, 1982; McCombs & Poindexter, 1983, or Carlson, 1983).

Studies typical of the interpretive model (as we defined it) looked for differential effects of content over variables that could conceivably be under local control. Variables such as parental guidance, family communication style, media choice, selective exposure to content, and (sometimes) affective state appeared to meet this definition. (For examples, see Meadowcroft, 1986; Fallis, Fitzpatrick, & Friestad, 1985; Singer, Singer, & Rapaczynski, 1984; McIlwraith & Josephson, 1985; or McLeod & McDonald, 1985). It was often difficult for us to make this decision in sorting the studies as these variables were most often treated as constant characteristics of the individuals so classified.

Family interaction styles, for example, were almost always treated as environmental conditions for children (e.g., Meadowcroft, 1986; Singer et al., 1984). Children were never described as coconstructors of family life. This theoretical stance, however, was probably equally related to the cross-sectional methodologies (analysis at one point in time) generally used as to a principled position. Such methodologies do not permit the observation of choice, and consequently characteristics have to be viewed as fixed.

As a result, the interpretive model (which accounted for 21 of the total) is still uncertain as a theoretical position. It does not necessarily imply that interpretation is an achievement of a situated individual. Interpretation can still be seen as inevitable (exposure is sufficient) with a predictable outcome once the determining forces are known. In this conceptualization, there is no genuine interpretive work being done by the individual.

The uses and gratifications perspective accounted for half of the remaining studies (nine of the total), and nearly half of those appeared in a single journal (which clearly states the importance of reading broadly). The other 9% was distributed among the cultural, cultivation analysis, Lippmann effects (agenda-setting), and social action perspectives. In the sections that follow, we begin the promised "close reading" of our five exemplar studies with an analysis of the effect of the theoretical stance taken by the researchers on the claims that are produced. The analyses in this section are done study by study.

THE THEORY OF "TELEVISION BELIEFS"

The theory that drives the study from which our first quotation was taken is usually called cultivation analysis. Cultivation analysis views the media (though its practitioners focus almost entirely on television) as a centripetal force—one that draws a society's members toward a center and creates a level of homogeneity. It ordinarily does not consider the centrifugal forces of selective exposure in audiences or content specialization in media. The meaning of content is seen as fixed: It makes no sense to identify worldviews implied or expressed in television unless that view is there for all to see. Contrasting with that worldview, there is a genuine reality knowable in some ways (often through analysis of the uniform crime reports) to which we are all accountable.

Given that meaning is fixed in content, exposure to that content by a large, passively accepting audience is all that is necessary for those centripetal forces to work. The individual in that audience is seen as caught in the web of meaning spun by the media, pulled to a common, albeit distorted, understanding.

Hawkins, Pingree, and Adler, the authors we have quoted, were calling into question the passive audience tenet of cultivation analysis. It was their belief that cultivation goes through a construction process in which the worldview is extracted by (rather than presented to) individuals in the audience. The counterposition demonstrates another important aspect of theory in that a theoretical statement always provides the opportunity of opposition. The question of Hawkins et al. is facilitated by the presence of the opposing claim. It provides a context for understanding what Hawkins et al. are about.

THEORY AND THE "IDEOLOGY OF THE NEWS"

Klaus Bruhn Jensen writes from the European tradition of cultural studies and **discourse analysis.** This analysis is typically motivated by an interest in the semiotic means of controlling the distribution of power. It is a Marxist position in that it views society and its power as both stratified and closed, held in place by a structural ideology (system of beliefs) that is rehearsed again and again in the primary modes of communication. Media, therefore, are agents (in some views collusive, in others without choice) of this ideology providing for its expression and continuance. This conceptualization of the media places a premium interest on the content of the media as that content is the primary ideological resource. (Most media scholars using discourse analysis discount or ignore interpersonal networks.) The content is, of course, a system of delivered meaning that justifies its close analysis. As few as five years ago, the audience was almost always missing in these textual analyses and was presumed to be monolithic, typified, and passive. Now the audience is more likely to be seen as organized in different interpretive communities—those ideologically framing memberships that modify the consequences of exposure.

Discourse analysis fits very well with cultivation analysis (which explains its alignment here). Cultivation analysis attempts to show the audience mirroring the beliefs identified through some content study approach of which discourse analysis is a sophisticated variant. Discourse analysis, for its part, provides cultivation theories with a heightened social significance in that the analyst is no longer examining some potentially minor distortion but the very bond of society.

For Jensen, discourse analysis "shows how reality may be constructed in a textual form" (p. 13). When he goes on to argue that his analysis of 49 news stories from ABC and CBS network news shows a common ideology (see the exemplar quote), he uses the presumptions of his theory to demonstrate the significance of the factual commonalities discovered in his discourse analysis. It is only of passing interest that ABC and CBS cover news events in much the same way, but when that similarity is understood as the reproduction of the dominant ideology that crafts the reality in which we live, the importance of the finding is clear.

The reader should not be misled. It is not our purpose to debunk Jensen. Theories make sense out of otherwise meaningless facts. Eileen Meehan, who writes on the market forces that shape content might, for example, take Jensen's facts and use them as evidence for her own economic arguments. We might use those facts to demonstrate the standards of practice as developed within the news community. (Note that all three arguments would fail had the commonalities not been found.) That a theory predicts or explains an outcome does not preclude a different, even a competing theory to do the same.

We are led from that paragraph to comment on the ideological significance of theory itself: Theory as a set of reality statements empowers and disempowers research questions, modes of analysis, and, consequently, research practitioners. If one holds a "crackpot theory" one practices "crackpot science" and is ordinarily barred from society's resources. One's science is inevitably connected to its power in society. This notion of theory helps us to understand why any study emanating from a given theory is important to that theory: Its presence works to legitimate the theory, to revalidate its premises and, given limited publication resources,[2] to prevent the appearance of studies that do the same work for a competing theory.

THEORY AND "INNER-CITY SUBJECTS"

Richard Frost and John Stauffer begin their study with the question "Do . . . levels of arousal vary according to a person's social class, gender, or personality?" The question implies a particular view of the individual: The individual is seen as the composite of independent traits that develop as the result of the forces of environment, socialization, enculturation, and so on. (For a more thorough explanation of this model of the individual, see Anderson, 1987.) Typically, the individual is considered to exercise minimal control over the consequences of being marked by a given trait. Each of us, therefore, is the determinate product of the collection of traits that describe us. By accumulating our knowledge of the consequence of each separate trait, the complete individual can (one day) be explained.

Frost and Stauffer's question about social class is investigated by comparing a group of college student's physiological reactions to those of a group of inner-city inhabitants. It is in this comparison that we come to know the researchers' empirical definition of social class. It is a mixture of differences in race, income, education level, place of dwelling, and occupation, among others. The significance of this comparison, as pointed out by Frost and Stauffer, lies in the fact that inner city residents are more at risk as victims of physical violence as more physical violence is practiced in the inner city than in the white, suburban areas of the college group (p. 30). It is assumed that the conditions that describe the environment would have a consistent effect across all inhabitants and that any set of residents volunteering would show those consequences.

The research protocol is derived from an exposure model in which content delivers its meaning in atomistic parts that can be separated from the narrative without change and the audience is composed of autonomous individuals whose response is a reaction to the decontextualized content alone. This protocol is a standard protocol that has been used in most of the studies on violence in the media and its relationship to aggression in social behavior.

The protocol connection makes obvious the extended reasoning that underlies this study. If inner-city residents are more aroused by violent fare, then the higher rates of violence in the inner-city may well be explained by the increased levels of arousal evidenced by inner-city viewers.

There is a sinister side to this reasoning—undoubtedly not intended by Frost and Stauffer—that inner city folks get what they deserve. Perhaps, it is the effect of genetics or parenting or one's own failures that predict both social class and levels of arousal. If so, then we are where we rightfully belong and so are they. As a young, middle-class woman remarked on the beggars at Mazatlan, "They probably deserve to be poor." We are, however, ahead of ourselves as such is not a part of the theory of a study but of its **instrumentality.**

At any rate, Frost and Stauffer claim that the differences they found were explained by social class and were important because of it. From this theoretical perspective we now know that one of the characteristics of social class is a higher physiological response level to violent visual material. Those findings are significant because—again within this theory—such levels have been associated with increased measures of aggression in laboratory studies.

THEORY OF "INFORMATION LIFE-STYLES"

In this study, Lewis Donohew, more associated with motivation theory, joins Palmgreen and Rayburn, who are scholars, from the "uses and gratification" school. Uses and gratifications theory, as we have seen, is a derivation of reinforcement theory (which simply states that acts are repeated because they bring pleasure or prevent punishment) that adds the dimension of cognitive recognition of those gratifications. Media use, therefore, is a pattern of attendance (or avoidance); media gratification, the reinforcement for that pattern; and cognitive recognition is the ability to describe—and consequently, to some extent control—that gratification. Scholars within the uses and gratifications school of thought, therefore, seek to find patterns in everyday media usage, ask respondents to identify the utility of those patterns, and explain the patterns found with the reasons given.

Uses and gratifications theory is clearly on the active, controlling audience side of the ledger, but Donohew et al. add an interesting fillip to their study by investigating the effect of a physiological (and thereby unconscious) need for arousal. The need for arousal has been used to explain why, for example, we doodle, drum our fingers, or click a ballpoint pen during a boring lecture. The lecture is lowering the arousal level we need for activity. As with all physiological needs, the need for arousal is considered beyond normal choice. At least, special techniques of recognition are necessary for an individual consciously to manipulate these needs.

By joining interests, Donohew et al. provide a connection between uses and gratifications theory and another realm of theory—motivation theory—one ordinarily considered in opposition to uses and gratifications theory. Motivation theory sees the human organism organized by primary and secondary needs. Primary needs are the consequence of genetics and secondary needs the consequence of environment. In either case, being driven by our needs is what motivates (and explains) action. The opposition to uses and gratifications is found in that motivation theory does not grant cognitive recognition of needs to the ordinary person. Only the extraordinarily educated individual (such as a motivation theorist) can generally monitor his or her own need states.

As is typical in such joint ventures, Donohew et al. submerge the conflict with almost no comment and bring these two lines of thought together. In this study, we now have a theoretical individual who is driven (and explained) by sets of given, inculcated, and personally crafted needs, some under cognitive control some not, but each element making its own independent contribution to the patterns of media use. This is a more sophisticated model than either of the two from which it springs (and a multivariate statistician's dream).

As Donohew et al. point out, it is our understanding of these needs that is the primary contribution of analyses along these lines. The overwhelming complexity produced by the performing individual can be reduced to a set of (albeit also complex) standardized motives that explain the human condition.

THEORY AND "COGNITIVE STRATEGIES"

To begin with the notion of cognitive strategies is somewhat misleading. Stamm's work is based on measures two or three steps removed from any cognitive workings. His "cognitive strategies" are actually patterns in judgment measures that he attributes to different cognitive strategies. There is, of course, no necessary provision that different outcome patterns require different cognitive strategies or that a given outcome pattern is connected to one and only one strategy. It is, however, a common graciousness to ignore this kind of slippage in research arguments, and, though we will examine the problem more generally in the methodology section, for the moment, we will grant it.

Cognitive theories have followed along the course of the as yet unresolved body/mind, nature/nurture fracture with individual theories more or less working on one side or the other. Physiological theories tend to seek the limits of sensation, perception, memory, information processing, and the like and psychological theories the motives of cognitions, their symbolic organization (cognitive maps, schemata, value structures), and processing performances (types of thinkers, cognitive strategies, and tactics).

We can locate Stamm very quickly as coming from a psychological performance perspective. Following traditional reductionistic reasoning, this perspective seeks the relatively few number of standardized strategies (five seems like an outside number) that can explain the individual differences one finds in performance outcomes. Stamm provides the theoretical opportunity—not often given—for individuals to select different strategies at different times. This opportunity, of course, raises the question of another set of strategies to determine the selection of most proximate set. That is, how does one strategize the choice of strategy? By providing the opportunity, Stamm actually weakens the contribution of his study by suggesting that there is a more important level of analysis to be investigated. (Choice in Western science theory is always a problem. It smacks of a prior metaphysics and has to be explained by some determining agent, which, in turn, is always the proper and more elegant target of analysis.)

When evaluating theories of cognitive strategies, two questions are useful: What is the source of the strategy, and where is it located? Stamm is silent on both of these, which is not unusual. Given his other positioning, we can assume that the source is exogenous—some cultural or educational practice. Its location is clearly endogenous as a decontextualized cognitive reaction or characteristic of the individual. (As Stamm permits change of strategy, the reaction label is better.) There are other sources: Individual creativity or the cognitive processing itself in an ad hoc rather than a priori strategy, to name two. There are other locations: The research protocol itself and the social action relationship seem to spring readily to mind.

Stamm's work links or alludes to two other lines of thought, voting behavior and decision making. His two strategies "hedging" and "wedging" are indistinguishable from the 40-year-old voting behavior concepts of **assimilation effect** and **contrast effect** (Lazarsfeld, Berelsen,

& Gaudet, 1948).[3] In the past five years, decision-making research has moved whole-hog into strategies mostly from formalist-researcher-defined, like Stamm's—rather than strategy-in-use-action-defined perspectives. Voting behavior studies typically have been motivated by the concerns of candidates not those of voters. Decision-making studies have been concerned with right decision making rather than understanding its practice. Stamm reports little exploration in either of these literatures. They are important to us because they transmit the image of the good voter deciding well in the privacy of his or her own cognitions. They suggest nothing of the cultural, social, or ritualistic character of campaigning, voting, and decision making. These perspectives also ignore—something that Stamm, to his credit, does not—the nonvoter, the individual who dominates American elections.

The sum of Stamm's theoretical components places him inside the "limited effects" camp. Limited effects theorists grant varying degrees of control to the individual and "limit" the direct influence of content. For Stamm, the limits of influence are created in the cognitive activity of the voter. These limits are defined by and located in the cognitive strategies used.

SUMMARY

In this section, we have considered how theoretical perspectives and not facts motivate and justify substantive claim. We have seen that it is through theory that reality statements become television-inspired, commonalities in coverage become an ideology, differences in physiological measures are explained by a construct called social class, differences in choice statements are described as different life-styles springing from constellations of motives, and responses on evaluative statements are seen as cognitive strategies. In each case, there is nothing in the facts that requires the claim. Facts are permissive, allowing a variety of substantive claims. Facts become evidence within a theoretical context. Their power as evidence depends on the meaningful interpretation gained by that context.

Our evaluation of claim, then, requires a prior evaluation of theory. To what extent is the theory competent, coherent, inclusive? Can you find yourself (and the theorist) within it or does it speak to a class of people "out there"? Who and what does it empower? What purposes does it serve? Media theories are more cosmological than not. There are few small purposes in their attempt to tell the story of us.

CENTRAL IDEAS OF SECTION I: THE NATURE OF CLAIM SECTION II: CLAIM AND THEORY

1. Any competent research study makes knowledge claims (generally the findings or conclusions of the study), which are arguable propositions about what we know. The skeptical stance of science requires claim to be held in doubt.

2. Seven perspectives—cultural studies, cultivation analysis, the exposure model, the interpretive model, Lippmann effects, social action, and uses and gratifications—appeared in our journal review. The exposure model dominated recent research in communication journals.
3. Cultivation analysis emphasizes the centripetal and ignores the centrifugal forces of media and media use.
4. Discourse analysis in media studies usually involves the application of critical methods to a carefully collected assemblage of texts generally representing some genre. The purpose of discourse analysis is to discover the "underlying messages" of, say, power, gender, or, as shown here, economic ideology.
5. Theory is an empowering ideological framework in which evidence is made sensible.
6. Cognitive structures when used in theory are generally considered beyond the direct control of the individual who harbors them. They are the "unseen motivators" of action.

SECTION III: CLAIM AND METHOD

Method and claim are related in two ways: (1) The way the researcher goes about studying a question determines the facts that will be discovered or created. (2) The methods used establish the bases for the validity of the facts as evidence for a claim. Let's bring the materials we have been working on into focus on these two points.

FACTS FROM METHOD

Presume with us that we want to study the differences across gender on the viewing of news programs. We ask this question because we suspect that one gender uses news in ways that are different from another gender's. We have two theoretical questions to answer: What is gender and what is it about gender that comes into relationship with the viewing of news? We could define gender as the presence or absence of a set of physical characteristics or as levels of certain hormones or as the choice by the respondent from among listed genders or according to some catalogue of social characteristics or something else.

It is the theory of **gender** that we hold that would determine this definition. Let's presume that our theory states that gender is a social construction involving the individual's practices and performances of others toward those practices. We might argue that gender is a continuous variable passing through three points: feminine, **androgynous,** and masculine. The importance of gender in this formulation is that it creates a semiotic frame into which news programs enter.

Moving quickly, we go into the field with questions about news watching and the following gender questions: "Would you describe yourself as 'masculine,' 'feminine,' or a 'mixture of both'?"

Place a mark where you think you fall on this dimension:

Masculine— — — — — — — Both— — — — — — — Feminine

Whatever appears in the analysis of news and gender the facts that we will classify as facts of gender are wholly contained in the marks on that scale. "The respondent made this mark" is the only factual statement. Every statement beyond that is claim. Ask a different question or questions; get different facts, although the same claims might be made from and about them.

We hope this example hasn't been tedious. Its purpose was to demonstrate that if you don't know the method, you don't know the facts. That fact poses some difficulties in evaluating claims about the media. The best evaluation begins with the questions that were asked—information that is quite often missing.[4] The worst condition for evaluating claim is when only the claim itself is present, as is often the case in the popular press or in textbooks on media effects. The truth-value of a claim is not present in the claim itself. It is derived from the theory that permits it, as we have seen, and finds its expression in the methods used to materialize it, as we shall see in the next section.

METHODOLOGICAL VALIDITY

Truth (or validity for the squeamish) in claim arises through three levels of questioning of method. The three levels are called (a) internal validity, (b) construct validity, and (c) external validity (Anderson, 1987).

INTERNAL VALIDITY Internal validity asks, simply, will the measure do what you want it to do? In the gender example there are two criteria for the answer: (a) Does the measure classify individuals in a consistent and reliable manner? (b) Will it support the hypothesis? Measures fail the first criterion in two possible ways. The trait intended to be measured may not exist, so no measurement device will ever work. The measurement device may not be adequate. Notice that this is a pernicious relationship as are most in validity. In this case, because the adequacy of the measurement is always in question, the researcher can never discover the true absence of a trait. He or she may become exhausted and discouraged but never sure.

The second criterion of internal validity involves the prediction made by the researcher as to the outcome of the analysis. If that prediction—sometimes called a research hypothesis or research question—is not supported, the only supported move of evaluation is to call the validity of method into question. Again the hypothesis cannot be directly falsified, only not supported in some methodological frame. To return to our example, if we fail to distinguish news watching over gender (if individuals classified in different genders do not also exhibit different patterns in news watching), then our measures have failed the test of internal validity. The reason for this failure may be the hypothesis itself (being false), but it is method that we have to call into question because the possibility always exists that better methods would bring the relationship to light.

Generally, the issue of internal validity is not a problem in reading research results. Few studies that are considered completely to have failed this criterion are published, although in any given study both success and failure are purely judgment calls. Quite often, however, the reader is faced with deciphering studies that have mixed results. In our exemplar set, the cognitive processing hypothesis of Hawkins et al. was so contrary to the data that they claimed support for the reverse prediction (p. 573). There is no true evidentiary support in this case, only an empirical finding as this research team, of course, knows. It does sound as if they are rethinking their position, nonetheless.

Stauffer and Frost also report mixed results. Although they found differences across their measure of social class, they did not find it across their measure of gender (male/female) or across the personality measures used. It is quite clear that these failures do not rule out finding differences across a better measure of gender or a different personality test. On the other hand, it is possible that masculine and feminine responses to filmed violence are indeed similar.

In the face of mixed results, what conclusions can the reader draw? Is one out of three not bad or does it suggest that there is a different theoretical model that will give a better fit to the effect suspected? Hawkins et al. appear to be holding their model suspect; Frost and Stauffer seem to suggest the limitations of their measures. We readers have to make the same judgments for ourselves.

CONSTRUCT VALIDITY Construct validity asks the question, does the measure address what we say it does? Do categories of male/female or masculine/androgynous/feminine really address the reality of gender? This would seem to be a most important question. Unfortunately, we have only the most indirect evidence for an answer. Measures of reliability (can you get the same measurement results more than once) offer negative evidence. Low reliability scores under some circumstances indicate poor construct validity, but high reliability scores simply allow the question to remain. The most often used argument for construct validity is the face value of the measure: Male/female sure seems like it's gender-related.[5] Evidence for construct validity can also come from a showing of the relationship between two measures that claim to address the same trait. It's sort of a safety in numbers argument as both could be wrong; there is no increasing probability of being right, rather just infinite variations of being wrong.

To apply the question of construct validity to our examples, we can consider Jensen's claim about ideology in the news. Jensen finds a predicted similarity between the coverage of ABC and CBS in their national news programs. His study has passed the test of internal validity. His claim, however, is that the measures that he used to identify the commonalities (actors, agents, coherence, and presuppositions) are the stuff of ideology. To evaluate his claim, we must first have an understanding of what ideology is. It is not necessary to have his understanding as he is claiming that ideology exists as a material practice accessible to us all. Our suspicion would be that a lot of us don't have a clear notion of what the material practice of ideology might look like. Our choice, then, is to accept Jensen's claim on authority or reject it from ignorance.

On the other hand, who cares? If society requires ideological practices to function, then we should find traces of them in nearly every legitimized public display. It is not surprising that the way our society reports its reality represents its ideology. It is easy to accept Jensen's claim, particularly if that claim has a utility for media bashing or political empowerment. Please notice that this is no criticism of Jensen. It is a comment on the degree of skepticism and our own intellectual preparation that we as readers must have in place in our evaluation of the construct validity of a work. The system will not do that work for us.

EXTERNAL VALIDITY External validity, sometimes called mundane realism or, as we have often done, ecological validity, raises the question of transferability of the findings of a research study to a statement about conditions in the lived world. It is the last of the validity questions and is approached only after there is reasonable assurance that the issues of internal and construct validity have been solved. There are a couple of rules of thumb that help guide the inquiry:

The first is *the map is not the territory*. Surveys and ethnographic descriptions are maps of the traits, features, and actions within some human territory. Like a map, we are concerned with the accuracy, amount of detail, order and arrangement of relationships, datedness, and significance of the features in representing the topography. No one doubts that in the 1988 New Hampshire primary, respondents to the polls put Dole in the lead the night before the election. Bush won the primary, however, by a considerable margin. We have seen how this can happen: A biased sample is drawn either through poorly designed procedures or even the chance selection of too many Dole supporters (accuracy) or the volatility of the situation is such that voters moved to a different position after the poll was taken (datedness).

In election polling, we have the luxury of a real world event demonstrating the validity of the pollster's claim. In nearly every other situation, we do not have that luxury. Hawkins et al., Donohew et al., Jensen, and Stamm of our exemplar set all attempt to map some territory of human endeavor. Of all the things that can go wrong, as pointed out in Chapter 7, we will have no evidence that any did go wrong. The easiest and, unfortunately, the most dangerous, assumption to make is that nothing went wrong. After all, these researchers worked as carefully as they could, followed standard procedures, and now believe in their work. Who are we, in the absence of evidence, to question?

Perhaps Stamm gives us an example of why we should question. Stamm's work is based on a technique called **cohort sampling.** It involves taking different successive samples from what is presumed to be the same population. Stamm took four different samples of voters to test for cognitive strategies. He states simply that they were presumed to be the same (p. 44). His major finding, remember, was that cognitive strategies changed during the course of the campaign with individuals of given types. The problem, of course, is that he doesn't have the same individuals over the course of his study. Could the differences he found be a sampling artifact? Most certainly. Are they? Nobody knows. So now what?

You deserve an answer but we can't give you one. Stamm is following the tenets of sampling theory that also happen to justify his claim. Now for us, Stamm's claims fit right in with our notions of the contingent individual adjusting to the contextual demands of interpretation. Stamm's work is useful and, therefore, true. All right, we don't deny that we are pushing the point here. Nonetheless, this conclusion—dressed up in academic language—is the way validity claims often get resolved because we have no corroborating real-world event against which to test those claims. This move—accepting a work because it is useful—is the main doctrine of American pragmatism and is the center of the next section on instrumentality.

For now, we turn to the second rule of thumb: *Good laboratory experiments show what can happen, not necessarily what does happen (bad ones show nothing at all).* This rule states that a study can be both valid and irrelevant at the same time. Brannigan and Goldenberg (1987) provide an interesting critique of the aggressive pornography studies that illustrates this rule. The aggressive pornography studies (e.g., Donnerstein, 1980; Malamuth & Donnerstein, 1982; Zillmann & Bryant 1982) have shown that males exposed to massive doses of pornography, particularly violent pornography, are more likely to be sexually aggressive toward women. Brannigan and Goldenberg (1987) can grant the findings and then dismiss them because

> in our view, the relationships discovered in the laboratories are so far removed from the circumstances about which we legitimately are worried and the results so qualified in terms of their equivalence to existing social circumstances as to be politically irrelevant. (p. 277)

If the researchers' claims are politically irrelevant, they have nothing to say to us as we manage the lives that we live. They fail the test of external validity. Note that in this conclusion Brannigan and Goldenberg have not raised questions of whether a difference was found (internal validity) or whether the surrogate measure tapped into aggression toward women (construct validity). They can accept both of those levels of validity and still cast the studies aside. In short, if one wanted to produce aggression toward women (unthinkable as that is), the laboratory protocol might be a good way to do it. That protocol, according to Brannigan and Goldenberg, however, does not help us to understand the circumstances in society that lead to aggression toward women or the role pornography plays in them.

Where do Brannigan and Goldenberg find their evidence for the rejection of the pornography studies? In exactly the same place that we found the difficulties with the study by Bandura and associates in Chapter 6—the compromises, presumptions, and incredulities that permit the study in the first place. The analysis is neither pleasant nor pretty. It does not provide new evidence. It works because it holds the Emperor's new clothes up to ridicule. This type of analysis is very irritating to practitioners because it shifts the grounds under which the studies were conducted. In essence, it challenges accepted practices and holds the research to a different, albeit higher, standard.

Given this analysis and granted the power of this text, we can apply the rule to our example in the study by Frost and Stauffer. Does the showing of 10 segments of filmed violence in a community recreation center under the conditions of an experiment relate to how people watch films? Does the finding of increased arousal levels for inner-city respondents explain the levels of violence in those locales? If they don't, what is the value of the study?

WHAT'S OUT THERE We found five methodologies accounting for 92% of our journal sample. The survey method was most prevalent (46) followed by content analysis (15), analytical (14), experimental (14), and ethnographic (3). Content analysis is a descriptive method akin to surveys that examines the characteristics of units of (surprise) content that may be conversations, journal articles, television programs, popular music lyrics and so on. (For examples, see Soley & Reid, 1985; Selnow, 1986; or Kepplinger, 1982.) Analytical methods follow the rules of reasoned discourse and are generally synthetic arguments rather than empirical studies. They chart the implications of other studies or do theory development work among other tasks. (Exemplars are Hall, 1985; Bryant, 1986; Adoni & Mane, 1984, and this chapter.)

These findings give us some cause for concern: So many of our knowledge claims are apparently being generated within a single descriptive methodology (the sum of surveys and content analysis is 61). Current thought in empirical methods recommends an extended program of research focusing on a problem from multiple methodological angles. The majority of our literature—with notable exceptions—is characterized by single-effort, single-method studies. Our knowledge may be significantly tainted by the bias and artifacts of an overly present method of analysis.

SUMMARY

The methodology used to translate questions about reality into scientific studies are responsible to three levels of validity analysis. The method must first give an interpretable answer. In general, this requirement is met if the hypothesis is supported. Second, the method must produce measurements and conditions that do what the researcher claims they do. Opinion questions must measure preexisting opinions, not create them, and so forth. Finally, the results must make sense in the world in which we live.

Though not quite funny hats, methods are the accepted practices of an intellectual community of analysts. They are not guarantees of valid claims. As accepted practices and not guarantees, they are both vulnerable to attack by calling into question their presumptions and resistant to that same attack by invoking the protection of the communal fortress.

Unfortunately, there are few genuine answers to the three questions of validity. It is rare that studies will predict a directly observable phenomenon in the real world. We do not build bridges in the social sciences or construct societies. Our accomplishments are part of the very world we try to understand. In the next section, we examine this relationship by exploring the instrumentality or social action consequences of research.

CENTRAL IDEAS OF SECTION III: CLAIM AND METHOD

1. Methods of sampling, measurement, and analysis uncover (or create) the facts that will be used in evidence to warrant a claim. If one does not know the method, one cannot evaluate the facts.
2. There are three validity questions in any research study: The questions of internal validity—is the study competent, construct validity—does it study what it claims, and external validity—can it generalize to the mundane.
3. Studies that fail internal or construct validity call their methods not their hypotheses into question.
4. The major difficulty in determining external validity is the lack of an opportunity to corroborate research findings in real-world tests.
5. Survey methods are the most common found in our survey representing some cause for concern of bias owing to a single approach.

SECTION IV: INSTRUMENTALITY

Instrumentality in research refers to the entire scope of utilities that research has for the practitioner, for the research profession, the society in which it is located, and for human knowledge. These utilities can be explored across a number of interpretive categories. We will choose four: epistemic, economic, ideological, and professional.

EPISTEMIC UTILITIES OF RESEARCH

Epistemology is broadly understood as the theory of human knowledge. The epistemic utilities of research begin, of course, with its aim at producing knowledge claims. The simple evaluative question is what do we know now, that we didn't know before? The answer to the question is not quite so straightforward for it involves the manner in which we know and the value we attach to the claim. That leaves us with three qualities by which to evaluate a knowledge claim: its content, character, and value. We have explored the content characteristics of claims in the previous sections of this chapter and found that content had to be understood within theory and method. Now we can turn to character and value.

CHARACTER To understand the character of a knowledge claim, presume that we tell you that our research demonstrates that children can learn both good and bad behaviors by watching television. Our guess is that you probably wouldn't be surprised. You may have already come to accept that claim from your own experience. The difference is that what you knew as a claim in commonsense knowledge has now risen to be a claim in scientific knowledge. The truth value of that claim has not changed—it is either true or false in both knowledges—but the character of its evidence has moved from native to expert. With expert evidence, our knowledge claim ceases to be a local understanding only and is capable of becoming a distributed one. As a distributed claim, it enters into a professional body of discourse concerning the nature and effects of mediated communication. There it is open to acceptance, attack, and/or exploitation by various intellectual communities (e.g., academicians, clinicians, politicians, and so on). Until it attains the expert character that permits distribution, however, the claim normally lacks this communal utility. That is, it is an impropriety to grant it notice.

Examples of statements like these are found in nearly every study: "Analysis revealed the strongly interpretive nature of sibling interaction during television viewing. Typically, an older sibling interpreted for the younger" (Alexander, Ryan, & Munoz, 1984, p. 359). "The major finding of this study is that young people are able to differentiate between social reality and television reality" (Adoni, Cohen, & Mane, 1984, p. 47). "Specifically, cognitive skills are likely to be learned by the adolescent from his parents, by observing consumer behaviors, and from newspaper and television contact" (Moore & Moschis, 1983, p. 73).

Much of what we read in the effects literature—children learn, people get aroused, individuals gain information—is principally charged with creating a body of professional discourse with a consistent expert character, rather than telling us something we did not already know at the commonsense level. This understanding does not trivialize the work, but it does explain our lack of surprise.

VALUE The value question is the pragmatic "so what?" What has the researcher accomplished by making the claim? The answer is going to depend on your level of attack. Certainly in achieving the status of a distributed claim the researcher's work has made a contribution to a body of discourse that permits the community to address that claim.[6] That alone is of genuine value. There are, however, wider demands. We alluded to these demands in our analysis of the content of the claims by Frost and Stauffer. At a primitive level, Frost and Stauffer found differences in certain physiological measures between an aggregate of college students and an aggregate of inner-city respondents. These findings were brought up through the assumptions of theory and method to be interpreted as meaning that inner-city residents (as a social class) experience higher levels of arousal from the viewing of violent cinematic content. If arousal potentiates action, then the inner-city respondents' "higher arousal levels may be connected to their real-life surroundings" (p. 41). The value of the claim has now been extended to the possibility of control of a dysfunctional condition in society.

This extension is an important justification of the place social science research has in society and the privileges it garners. If it cannot be made regularly in the whole of research, then both place and privileges become suspect and the charge of professionalism, that we write only for ourselves, can be raised. Researchers, then, are motivated to make that extension. It becomes a design consideration and provides a direction for the arguments crafted from the evidence. Socially significant claims, therefore, are a prior intent not the inevitable consequence of the evidence.

ECONOMIC UTILITIES OF RESEARCH

At the sociological level of the individual, research is everyday work. It's a job. We researchers get paid for our productivity that most often is measured in the number of publications, grants, and so on. The evaluation of quality, of course occurs, but it is less clear, less certain a measure of productivity than quantity.

At a higher sociological level, research can be seen as a marketable commodity "sold" to funding agents of education, government, and private enterprise. We have seen how research in mediated communication has been characterized by an agenda in violence and politics set not simply by the theoretical developments of researchers but by the availability of research monies. The term *administrative research* has been applied by oppositional writers to this corpus of work. The term is meant to imply research in the service of government and industry managers designed for their purposes rather than higher epistemological goals. There is no question of the presence of "hired guns" in our industry. But there is also no question that research is an industry, and oppositional writing—from any direction—seeks access to the table of resources.

For our purposes, the import of the view of research as an industry is that the demands of the research market emphasize the appearance of certain topics and certain methods of research. The complex of forces involves the political climate, the ideology of funding agents, the requirements of the publishing industry, the criteria of academic meritocracy, and so on. The result is what we see: the short journal or chapter-sized report presenting a hypothetic/deductive argument using quantitative evidence drawn from relatively small, volunteer samples.

Recognizing these market forces helps to understand the continuing presence of this research form in the face of widespread, but obviously ineffectual, criticism. We certainly want to be careful here. Our point is no more than the realization that research is bound to a market and, therefore, not free to follow only epistemic avenues. We do believe that the contemporary production of research (in any given era) is the result of those market characteristics and that epistemological values appear in the winnowing processes of time.

IDEOLOGICAL UTILITIES OF RESEARCH

If ideology is the set of beliefs that promotes the way we live, then research claims must both emanate from and reflexively maintain the tenets of that ideology. It is not difficult to find the embedded ideological statements in the research of our exemplar set. Donohew et al. (1987) imply an accepted version of the order of things in their description of the life-style types. Their description of Type 1—"The Disengaged Homemaker" reads as women who "like to try the latest hairstyles and are heavy credit card users, but they dislike sports, ballet, art galleries, and concert-going. They have few interests outside the home" (p. 266).

The ideological components are referenced in the selection of the traits recognized by the researchers as distinguishing individuals in important ways. What work gets done in identifying a class of individuals who like the "latest hairstyle" but "have few interests outside the home?" Part of that work is the continuation of the socially useful typification of women. Our society clearly has a meaningful stance on people who like the latest hairstyles, shopping, and little else. That meaningfulness is why Donohew et al. selected those items for their questionnaire in the first place. (Again don't read this as an attack. Whatever choices these respected researchers would make would be ideologically loaded. If they were not, the findings would have little significance and interest.)

The proper condition of class gets easily referenced in Frost and Stauffer's (1987) assumption that "the environment of the the inner-city residents is indeed more violent than that of the college students" (p. 41). The characterization of "more violent" depends on a particular set of criteria (to which most of us would readily agree), apparently accepted by the researchers as the only way one would arrive at the definition.

The unquestioned (and necessary) acceptance of some stance is, of course, what makes the force of ideology interesting to examine. Jensen's (1987) "discovery" in his news analysis "that television does, indeed, advocate a particular vision of society" (p. 24) gains its value from the ideological assumption that an "objective" presentation of news is possible. (Many would argue that any narrative of events must be either establishment or oppositional, that objectivity can be described but not performed.) Jensen uses the fact that the press claims objectivity to power the importance of his finding.

The ideological positioning of critiques (including our own) also raise some interesting questions. Brannigan and Goldenberg (1987) continue the statement we quoted earlier with this remark:

> In addition, the introduction of this type of research into considerations of censorship even may be dangerous since this research seems to underwrite the belief that the censorship of pornography will make the streets safe for women, thus creating a misplaced sense of security. A similar mentality might abolish bridges in the hope of eradicating suicide. (p. 277)

Certain ideological words and phrases seem to be highlighted, "censorship," "streets safe for women," and the metaphor of "abolishing bridges." The whole of the quotation brings to mind the National Rifle Association's arguments against gun control: "Guns don't kill people; people kill people." Perhaps for Brannigan and Goldenberg, "Pornography doesn't rape women; men rape women."[7] (Both arguments conveniently forget that guns and pornography may create opportunities for people to kill and to rape.)

The quotation has a clear utility for preserving the status quo. It moves to disempower those who would use the experimental findings on pornography to mount an attack on the pornography industry. It associates them with the forces of censorship and imbues them with both a dangerous and a foolish mentality. Do we believe that Brannigan and Goldenberg are the hirelings of the triple-X video crowd? Not in the least. We presume they are arguing from a traditional liberal stance that accepts pornography as a cost of free speech and assumes that the causes of violence against women are larger than a given piece of content. Certainly, their argument can be located in that stance.

Given their analysis, could Brannigan and Goldenberg have concluded differently? They might have concluded that indeed the experimental studies lack ecological validity and do not of themselves justify the control of pornography. The studies do, however, have sufficient force to offer the opportunity to take some action clearly identified as society's reflection of violence against women. We might not abolish bridges, but we could build fences along their edges.

We have noted that the ideological positioning of research and comment is necessary. One must stand somewhere in order to speak. Our analysis of the ideological components of these examples is not drawn from a belief that the authors should have done otherwise. The purpose is to demonstrate the work accomplished by these texts in the larger social arenas. Research not only provides for various social positions, it also provides for itself. It would seem clear that the practices of social science are inadequate to provide an incontrovertible argument on the several issues of content effects. Science, however, does have a record of claiming that purpose for its own, separating itself from commonsense reasoning, political processes, and questions of value. Science is presented as the voice of reason. This mythic voice of reason, of course, is performed by individuals like ourselves who are using common sense, are deeply involved in political processes at all levels, and readily assert our values. The ideology of science as the caretaker of reason provides conditions for the creation of an intellectual elite.

One consequence of that creation is that it encourages techniques to separate the elite from the ordinary. There is a clear survival value in technical language and arcane methods. In some part, research is difficult to read and understand by the nonscientist because the nonscientist is not supposed to be privy to the writing. It is written for and by members of a technical community who are justified by an ideological privileging of certain kinds of evidence, even if that evidence has done little more than provide for its own community.

We are led to a final comment in this section on ideology. The comment is recognizably gratuitous but useful to us and perhaps to others. Our science is now governed by an ideology of determinism that sees human life as the product of inevitable and irresistible forces. That ideology traps us in interesting ways. It essentially removes science's contribution to the solution of social problems by placing them outside the arena of social action—the only place where we as individuals can exercise any semblance of choice and control. Look again at the pornography argument. Let's grant the causal relationship between that content and crimes against women and ignore any problem or objection. In a stroke of brilliance, the senators from Wisconsin and Utah write an enforceable bill that is passed into law. Does pornography disappear? No, the pressures of consumer demand will create an illegal market for bootleg pornography, with the industry turning to management by machine gun. Predicting these outcomes, science is placed in the ultraconservative position of arguing for doing nothing at all.

It is the authors' belief that we need a different way of understanding the intertwining of force and creativity in human life. The determining forces of our physical and social environment are imprecise; they offer space for free play that grants the opportunity to redirect their outcomes. We need a scientific ideology that recognizes environmental determinants but also permits us to revel in that free play space rather than seeing ourselves as the crushed masses of the inevitable. Both ideologies make use of the same facts of our existence, but one suppresses action and the other offers hope.

PROFESSIONAL UTILITIES OF RESEARCH

We have commented that a body of discourse is a necessary component of any academic discipline and that contributing to that corpus is an epistemic endowment in that it brings claims into communal view. Contributing to the discipline's discourse is also an important method of demonstrating one's membership in that discipline. Doing research, then, is an accepted and expected practice of belonging. The point here is that motives of membership are often sufficient reasons for doing this work and are sub-rosa but recognized criteria of publication. Such motives do not necessarily affect the epistemic value of the work. The dark side of these motives, however, is the practice of careerism, in which individuals in old-boy/old-girl networks follow research fads and manage the exchange of gifts. Topics that are currently "hot" tend to be victimized by careerism attracting work that can be more chaff than wheat.

Finally, there are the personal reasons leading us to research and write. They are a mixed lot, ranging from the aesthetic delight of solving some problem to struggling to maintain a protected life-style to doing it because one knows how. They include compulsions and creative urges. In short, all the reasons why people do one thing rather than another.

SUMMARY

This examination of the instrumentalities of research has looked at the content, character, and value of claim within epistemic, economic, ideologic, and professional utilities. Research is a human endeavor embedded in its society. Its practice is naturalized within that environment. Any research claim, therefore, finds some place within all of society's instrumentalities. The evaluative task for the reader is to determine which utility predominates. From the perspective of validity, of course, we want epistemic utilities to be in the forefront and to be of greater value than simply the discipline's ends. These evaluations are not easy. A researcher's motives may be clearly in the service of epistemology but the consequences of the claim may be more economic or ideological. For example, will Frost and Stauffer's claims be useful for understanding inner-city violence, or will they perpetuate an ideological stance that these are lesser folk who are victims of themselves? It would certainly seem easier for an elite to believe the latter than to seek the redistribution of power and wealth. What we do know is that Frost and Stauffer's claims are not facts but are statements of varying utility.

The multiple utilities of research, particularly in the absence of demonstrable problem solving, coupled with our expanded technology of distribution, result in the chaotic literature of any social science discipline, including that directed toward mediated communication. It is certainly possible to read in narrow communities within a discipline and to get the feeling of orderly progress. Every expansion of one's scope, however, brings confusion, contradiction, and complaint. This condition does not absolve us of our reading, but does encourage a skeptical, evaluative attitude.

CENTRAL IDEAS OF SECTION IV: INSTRUMENTALITY

1. Research is charged with the epistemic duty of creating new knowledge, generally in an orderly fashion.
2. Claim can be evaluated by its qualities of content, character, and value. One trait of the character of a research claim is its expertness that permits it to be distributed in a body of professional discourse. Value in research claim usually appeals to social, economic, or political consequences.
3. Research is an industry whose practitioners do real work for the same reasons that others work in their industries. The research product is subject to market influences as any product is.
4. Research as an element of society supports the ideological constructs of that society.
5. To do research requires membership in the community of researchers. The work of research must also do the work of maintaining that community.

SECTION V: IN SEARCH OF EFFECTS—HAVE WE FOUND THEM YET?

Over 100 pages ago we started a quest in the beginning of Chapter 5 for the effects of mediated communication. What we found is that the business of studying effects is carried on in several different research communities that each have their own way of constituting the nature of an effect. It was a little like shopping for an automobile and discovering that all the manufacturers had a different idea of what a car would look like and do. If that wasn't confusing enough, we discovered that the different methods of research resulted in incomparable facts because they were a mixture of method and substance. Finally, we discovered that the facts were not very useful in themselves but made sense only as evidence for claim. Claims, we found, did not arise directly from the facts of data but were X interpretations of the data from some (or multiple) perspective(s) of theory, methodology, and instrumentality. It was in claim, however, that we found the effects of our search.

What then are the effects of the media? Tell us first how you organize your world. It has been our contention that media effects are the product of the interpenetration of text and action. We have also argued that any given site of an effect is the improvisational performance of self and other—a performance under local control and presenting a partial representation of cultural themes.

Given this view of the world, an experiment is a particular site of an effect. That is, the protocol with its research and respondent actors, the various layers of understanding and social contracts in place, the constraints on media use and subsequent behavior, and so on is the stage on which the effects performance can be given. Given a competent job, we probably would not deny the claims of the research. We can accept that the researcher did a fine job of demonstrating an effect for given conditions.

In a similar manner, we would examine the administration of and the response to a survey as a bit of social action. It is a performance in which the respondent can come to make sense of that task by fitting or developing descriptions to accommodate the research instrument. The aggregation and analysis of those responses is an interpretation of those descriptions.

And last, we see the ethnographic study as the sense-making narrative of a traveler to a community unknown to us. In each case, the research claims are themselves interpretive constructions of the social constructions of reality located in theory and serving multiple utilities.

But what are the effects of the media? Tell us first of the site of the effect. What are the cultural themes relevant to the actors? What communal understandings are in place? What routine is being performed? Who are the referenced others? What is the character of the relationship? What are the rehearsed and naturalized practices of that relationship? What is its institutionalized status and local history? What are the opportunities for supervision? What materials of performance are available? What are the improvisational skills of the actor? How will an effect be recognized?

The most effective epistemological contribution of our research to date has been to demonstrate what can happen in the interweaving of media texts and social action. People believe, buy, vote, speak, act, and accommodate media in the process. It is a fundamental error, however, to hold that people cannot believe, buy, vote, speak, or act without the media. Most descriptions of media effects are similar to attributing a 75-73 basketball win to the last bucket scored. The total performance of both teams constitutes the outcome.

Nevertheless, we do have an ever-growing professional corpus of claim about the effects of the media. In the section that follows we present the category scheme that we used to sort the 259 articles we selected as our resource and examples from each category. This display gives you a sense of the complexity of the literature and of the futility of expecting that a particular claim will be generally held. Keep in mind that this selection is just that—a selection, not an exhaustive representation.

SECTION VI: RECENT STUDIES

The presentation of these recent studies is ordered alphabetically by theory. (Descriptions of the theoretical perspective have been presented in Chapter 5.) Under each theory are the methodologies that appeared in our selection for that theoretical stance. The exemplars that are presented are simply convenient selections—we have not chosen for what we think are the best or worst examples, though we enjoyed reading all that appear. We have tried not to duplicate examples used elsewhere. An asterisk (*) indicates that the example(s) exhausts the category. Note that all 259 studies are listed in our reference section along with the other works we used in the preparation of this text.

CULTURAL STUDIES

ANALYTICAL STUDIES

Becker, S. L. (1984). Marxist approaches to media studies: The British experience. *Critical Studies in Mass Communication, 1,* 66-80.

Cawelti, J. G. (1985). With the benefit of hindsight: Popular culture criticism. *Critical Studies in Mass Communication, 2,* 363-379.

Grossberg, L. (1984). Strategies of Marxist cultural interpretation. *Critical Studies in Mass Communication, 1,* 392-421.

*ECONOMIC ANALYSIS**

Meehan, E. R. (1986). Conceptualizing culture as a commodity: The problem of television. *Critical Studies in Mass Communication, 3,* 448-457.

*SURVEY**

Sigman, S. J., & Fry, D. L. (1985). Differential ideology and language use: Readers' reconstructions and descriptions of news events. *Critical Studies in Mass Communication, 2,* 307-322.

CULTIVATION ANALYSIS

*ANALYTICAL STUDY**

Bryant, J. (1986). The road most traveled: Yet another cultivation critique. *Journal of Broadcasting and Electronic Media, 30,* 231-244.

*SURVEY**

Morgan, M. (1986). Television and the erosion of regional diversity. *Journal of Broadcasting and Electronic Media, 30,* 123-139.

Perse, E. M. (1986). Soap opera viewing patterns of college students and cultivation. *Journal of Broadcasting and Electronic Media, 30,* 175-193.

Potter, W. J. (1986). Perceived reality and the cultivation hypothesis. *Journal of Broadcasting and Electronic Media, 30,* 159-174.

EXPOSURE MODEL

*ANALYTICAL STUDIES**

Gaziano, C., & McGrath, K. (1986). Measuring the concept of credibility. *Journalism Quarterly, 63,* 451-462.

Meadowcroft, J. M., & McDonald, D. G. (1986). Meta analysis of research on children in the media: Atypical development? *Journalism Quarterly, 63,* 474-480.

Gumpert, G., & Cathcart, R. (1985). Media grammars, generations and media gaps. *Critical Studies in Mass Communication, 2,* 23-35.

CONTENT ANALYSES

Adams, W. C. (1986). Whose lives count?: TV coverage of natural disasters. *Journal of Communication, 36,* 113-122.

Luttbeg, N. (1983). News consensus: Do US newspapers mirror society's happenings? *Journalism Quarterly, 60,* 484-488, 578.

Greenberg, B. S., D'Alessio, D. (1985). Quantity and quality of sex in the soaps. *Journal of Broadcasting and Electronic Media, 29,* 309-321.

*CASE STUDY**

Breed, W., & DeFoe, J. R. (1982). Effecting media change: The role of cooperative consultation on alcohol topics. *Journal of Communication, 32,* 88-99.

EXPERIMENTS

Wakshlag, J., Vial, V., & Tamborini, R. (1983). Selecting crime drama and apprehension about crime. *Human Communication Research, 10,* 227-242.
Lemert, J. B., Elliott, W. R., Nestbold, C. J., & Rarick, G. R. (1983). Effects of hearing a presidential primary debate: An experiment. *Communication Research, 10,* 155-173.
Rothschild, M. L., Thorson, E., Reeves, B., Hirsch, J. E., & Goldstein R. (1986). EEG activity and the processing of television commercials. *Communication Research, 13,* 182-220.
Silverman-Watkins, T., Levi, S. C., & Klein, M. A. (1986). Sex stereotyping as factor in children's comprehension of television news. *Journalism Quarterly, 63,* 311.
Christ, W. G., & Medoff, N. J. (1984). Affective state and the selective exposure to and use of television. *Journal of Broadcasting, 28,* 51-63.

*ETHNOGRAPHIES**

Bourgault, L. M. (1985). "PTL Club" and protestant viewers: An ethnographic study. *Journal of Communication, 35,* 132-148.

*FIELD EXPERIMENTS**

Winett, R. A., Lichter, I. N., Chinn, D. E., & Stahl, B. (1984). Reducing energy consumption: The long-term effects of a single TV program. *Journal of Communication, 34,* 37-51.
Rucker, B. W. (1982). Magazine and teenage reading skills: Two controlled field experiments. *Journalism Quarterly, 59,* 28-33.

SURVEYS

Christensen, P. G., & DeBenedittis, P. (1986). Eavesdropping on the FM band: Children's use of radio. *Journal of Communication, 36,* 27-38.
Levy, M., & Fink, E. L. (1984). Home video recorders and the transience of television broadcasts. *Journal of Communication, 34,* 56-71.
Reeves, B., & Garramone, G. M. (1982). Children's person perception: The generalization from television people to real people. *Human Communication Research, 8,* 317-326.
Carlson, J. M. (1983). Crime shows and viewing by preadults, the impact on attitudes towards civil liberties. *Communication Research, 10,* 529-552.
Durkin, K. (1984). Children's accounts of sex roles stereotypes in television. *Communication Research, 11,* 341-362.
Andreason, M. (1986). Attentional penchants and recall of information from background radio. *Journalism Quarterly, 63,* 24-30, 37.
Izard, R. S. (1985). Public confidence in the news media. *Journalism Quarterly, 62,* 247-255.
Davis, R. H., & Westbrook, G. J. (1985). Television in the lives of the elderly: Attitudes and opinions. *Journal of Broadcasting and Electronic Media, 29,* 209-214.
Henke, L. L. (1985). Perceptions and use of news media by college students. *Journal of Broadcasting and Electronic Media, 29,* 431-436.

INDUSTRY CHARACTERISTICS AND PRACTICES

ANALYTICAL STUDIES

Compaigne, B. J. (1985). The expanding base of media competition. *Journal of Communication, 35,* 81-96.
Dimmick, J., & Rothenbuhler, E. (1984). The theory of the niche: Quantifying competition among media industries. *Journal of Communication, 34,* 103-119.

Cantor, M. G., & Cantor, J. M. (1986). American television in the international marketplace. *Communication Research, 13,* 509-520.

SURVEYS

Docherty, D., Morrison, D. E., & Tracey, M. (1986). The British film industry and the declining audience: Demythologizing the technological threat. *Journal of Communication, 36,* 27-39.

Howard, H. H. (1986). An update on cable ownership: 1985. *Journalism Quarterly, 63,* 706-709, 781.

Lain, L. B. (1986). Steps toward a comprehensive model of newspaper readership. *Journalism Quarterly, 63,* 67-74, 121.

INTERPRETIVE MODEL

ANALYTICAL STUDIES

Webster, J. T., & Wakshlag, J. J. (1983). The theory of television program choice. *Communication Research, 10,* 430-446.

Chesebro, J. W. (1984). The media reality: Epistemological functions of media in cultural systems. *Critical Studies in Mass Communication, 1,* 111-130.

Copeland, G. A., & Slater, D. (1985). Television, fantasy and vicarious catharsis. *Critical Studies in Mass Communication, 2,* 352-362.

Watkins, B. (1985). Television viewing as a dominant activity of childhood: A developmental theory of television effects. *Critical Studies in Mass Communication, 2,* 323-337.

EXPERIMENTS*

Garramone, G. M. (1983). Issues versus image orientation and effects of political advertising. *Communication Research, 10,* 59-76.

Garramone, G. M. (1985). Motivation and selective attention to political information formats. *Journalism Quarterly, 62,* 37-44.

Cantor, J., Ziemke, D., & Sparks, G. G. (1984). Effects of forewarning on emotional responses to a horror film. *Journal of Broadcasting and Electronic Media, 28,* 21-31.

ETHNOGRAPHIES*

Lull, J. (1982). A rules approach to the study of television and society. *Human Communication Research, 9,* 3-16.

James, N. C., & McCain, T. (1982). Television games preschool children play: Patterns, themes and uses. *Journal of Broadcasting, 26,* 783-800.

Lull, J. (1982). How families select televisions programs: A mass observational study. *Journal of Broadcasting, 26,* 801-812.

Wolf, M. A., Meyer, T. P., & White, C. (1982). A rules-based study of television's role in the construction of social reality. *Journal of Broadcasting, 26,* 813-829.

SURVEYS

Kubey, R. W. (1986). Television news in everyday life: Coping with unstructured time. *Journal of Communication, 36,* 108-123.

Sun, S., & Lull, J. (1986). The adolescent audience for music videos and why they watch. *Journal of Communication, 36,* 115-125.

Messaris, P., & Kerr, D. (1983). Mothers comments about TV relation to family communication patterns. *Communication Research, 10,* 175-194.

Roberts, D. F., Machen, C. M., Hornby, L. C., & Hernandez-Ramos, P. (1984). Reading and television, predictors of reading achievement at different age levels. *Communication Research, 11,* 9-49.

Becker, L. B., & Dunwoody, S. (1982). Media use, public affairs knowledge, and voting in a local election. *Journalism Quarterly, 59,* 212-218, 255.
Johnson, C., & Gross, L. (1985). Mass media use by women in decision-making positions. *Journalism Quarterly, 62,* 850-854, 950.
Wober, J. M., & Gunter, B. (1986). Television audience research at Britain's Independent Broadcasting Authority, 1974-1984. *Journal of Broadcasting and Electronic Media, 30,* 15-31.
Zemach, T., & Cohen, A. (1986). Perception of gender equality on television and in social reality. *Journal of Broadcasting and Electronic Media, 30,* 427-444.

LIPPMANN EFFECTS

*SURVEYS**

Williams, W., Jr., Shapiro, M., & Cutberth, C. (1983). The impact of campaign agendas on perceptions of issues in 1980 campaign. *Journalism Quarterly, 60,* 1983, 226-231.
Hofstetter, C. R., & Strand, P. J. (1983). Mass media and political issue perceptions. *Journal of Broadcasting, 27,* 345-358.

SOCIAL ACTION

*ETHNOGRAPHIES**

Lemish, D. (1982). The rules of viewing television in public places. *Journal of Broadcasting, 26,* 757-782.
Lemish, D. (1985). Soap opera viewing in college: A naturalistic inquiry. *Journal of Broadcasting and Electronic Media, 29,* 275-293.
Pacanowsky, M. E., & Anderson, J. A. (1982). Cop talk and media use. *Journal of Broadcasting, 26,* 741-756.
Alexander, A., Ryan, M. S., & Munoz, P. (1984). Creating a learning context: Investigations on the interaction of siblings during television viewing. *Critical Studies in Mass Communication, 1,* 345-364.

USES AND GRATIFICATIONS

ANALYTICAL STUDIES

Levy, M. R., & Windahl, S. (1984). Audience activity and gratifications: A conceptual clarification and exploration. *Communication Research, 11,* 51-78.
Lichtenstein, A., & Rosenfeld, L. B. (1983). Uses and misuses of gratifications research: An explication of media functions. *Communication Research, 10,* 97-109.
Rubin, A. M. (1982). Directions in television and aging research. *Journal of Broadcasting, 26,* 537-551.
McQuail, D. (1984). With the benefit of hindsight: Reflections on uses and gratifications research. *Critical Studies in Mass Communication, 1,* 177-193.

SURVEYS

Rubin, A. M. (1984). Ritualized and instrumental viewing. *Journal of Communication, 34,* 67-77.
Bantz, C. H. (1982). Exploring uses and gratifications: A comparison of reported uses of television and reported uses of favorite program type. *Communication Research, 9,* 352-379.
Lichtenstein, A., & Rosenfeld, L. (1984). Normative expectations and individual decisions concerning media gratification choices. *Communication Research, 11,* 393-413.
Rayburn, J. D. II, & Palmgreen, P. (1984). Merging uses and gratifications and expectancy value theory. *Communication Research, 11,* 537-562.

Wenner, L. A. (1982). Gratifications sought and obtained in program dependency: A study of network evening news programs and Sixty Minutes. *Communication Research, 9,* 539-560.

McLeod, J. M., Bybee, C. R., & Durall, G. A. (1982). Evaluating media performance by gratifications sought and received. *Journalism Quarterly, 59,* 312, 359.

CHAPTER SUMMARY

This chapter brought to a close our search for the effects of mediated communication. We found those effects in the claims that are advanced by researchers as they punctuate, describe, and explain the lives we lead.

Claim, we discovered, is first made sensible from some theoretical perspective. That is, it is theory that makes fact observable and provides the warrants that allow the facts to stand as evidence. It is this evidence, visible from theory, that makes a claim possible. Because theory makes claim possible, before we can evaluate a claim, we must evaluate the wellspring theory. And because that theory intends to make sense of the way we—each of us—live, it has to make sense in our lives. We must be able to find ourselves and our practices within it.

It is method that generates the facts that become evidence within theory. There are three requirements by which we can evaluate the worth of those facts: The method must first generate facts that are interpretable—understandable within the theoretical frame in place. Generally, this requirement means that the facts make sense within the research hypotheses. This requirement is known as internal validity.

Second, the facts must be about the concepts of interest. If the study is about aggression, then the facts must well meet our understanding of what aggression is. When facts meet this requirement, they have construct validity.

Third, the facts must move into the world in which we live. If they do not—if they reference something that does not occur in the natural world, we say they lack external or ecological validity.

In the third major section of the chapter we considered the notion of instrumentality. Instrumentality concerns itself with the utilities of research—the place of research in the formation of knowledge, the maintenance of society, the production of the community of researchers, and the personal gratifications of researchers. We examined the epistemological, economic, ideological, and professional utilities of the process and the product of research.

We then considered whether we had found the effects of the media—that goal we had set for ourselves in Chapter 5. We determined that we both had and had not. We had in the sense that we now knew how an effect would become apparent to us within some theoretical perspective, through some method of evoking facts, and for a multitude of purposes. We had not in the sense that we had not found a set of knowledge claims generally accepted by both the research community and the larger society in which it resides. The current state of knowledge about effects is that any claim is controversial and vulnerable.

As the last bit of work in this chapter, we examined the variety of research studies that is currently being generated in the field of mediated communication.

In the next chapter, we take a specific look at the theoretical stance we believe grants a better promise of understanding mediated communication, that of accommodation theory. We consider its presumptions, premises, requirements, and implications.

NOTES

1. *Communication Monographs, Communication Quarterly, Communication Yearbook, American Sociological Review, Public Opinion Quarterly, Journal of Personality, Journal of Social Psychology,* among others, regularly publish articles of interest. They arise from a theoretical perspective, are supported by evidence that appears in a methodological approach, and are used for epistemological, societal, ideological, and professional ends.

2. Without getting breathless, it is interesting to muse about the potential of computerized scholar networks (such as Comserve) in which distribution is automatic. Such networks may fail because they do not discriminate and thereby legitimate.

3. The Lazarsfeld et al. study was listed in the references, but we could not find a citation in the text. Assuming we didn't just miss it over several readings, the citation could have been edited out, the article seemed "stripped," or the reference added in response to a reviewer's complaint.

4. Of the five studies we are examining, none provides the questions asked, although Donohew et al. give a partial listing and Frost and Stauffer give a standardized description of their physiological measures.

5. This is also an argument from ridicule: How could you not believe that male/female is gender? Once a measurement practice has been accepted (or not rejected) by the research community, the argument from ridicule is very powerful. We don't entertain questions that play on our basic insecurities.

6. A body of professional discourse also serves to create and maintain an academic discipline. Communities of study must have textbooks, journals, conventions in order to become present as a recognizable entity.

7. Brannigan and Goldenberg appear to characterize the problem as crimes by men against women although pornography can be indicted more generally.

RELATED READINGS

Morgan, G. (1983). *Beyond method.* Newbury Park, CA: Sage.

A reader that attempts a broad look at social science and the conflicts that beset it. Morgan has assembled a group of writers who collectively consider "how else we might play this game called research." Reading the opening pages of the several chapters gives a good idea of the other things going on in social science today.

Rowland, W. D. (1985). *The politics of TV violence.* Newbury Park, CA: Sage.

The author examines the influence of politics and the various, often competing, political agendas as they affected the funding of media violence research and the interpretation of the research findings. This book provides a carefully documented behind-the-scenes account of how media effects issues become tools to advance policy initiatives and how legitimate scientific issues are poorly understood or dismissed because of their complexity and/or uncertainty of resolution. Provides good examples of political and economic instrumentalities of research.

Part III

An Organizing Theory

9

Accommodation Theory

IN THE PRECEDING CHAPTERS, we have been concerned with the nature and processes of communication especially those involving mediated communication, the concept of an "effect" of mediated communication, the sources of evidence for effects, and the claims about effects that are drawn from that evidence. In this chapter, we want to bring together the terms and concepts of the explanation of the place and performance of mediated communication. We call this explanation Accommodation Theory. Because most of the terms and concepts of this theory have been presented in earlier chapters, this chapter is by way of summary and review from which the implications for research practices and our own understanding will be drawn.

The chapter is divided into three sections: The first takes up a review of the two axiomatic principles of this theory; the second presents a comparison of the reality premises of the traditional, cultural and social action theories; and the final section examines the implications of Accommodation Theory for the research practitioner, the teacher of mediated communication studies, and the individual.

SECTION I: TWO AXIOMS OF ACCOMMODATION

Two principles form the foundation of Accommodation Theory: First, we hold that any human life is a coconstruction between self and other. Second, we posit that meaning is an achievement of interpretation historicized in its accomplishment and not something that is delivered by content. In the two major headings that follow, we consider the reasoning that supports these axioms and their implications.

HUMAN LIFE FOUND IN SOCIAL ACTION

To begin with, Accommodation Theory acknowledges that the primary characteristic of human life is its performance in social action. In its broadest conceptualization, social action is the expenditure of energy by one in reference to another. Social action, therefore, is implicated in any shared semiotic system of symbols and/or performances. What is not given to social action is the primarily unknown set of autonomic functions by which we are a material entity and have direct experience of the world. While it is certainly true that these functions get interpreted in social action, it is also certainly true that they exist independent of that action. The argument that we are tapping into here is an ancient one and fundamentally unresolved. The argument in Western thought is, of course, the **mind/body duality** celebrated by Descartes, submerged by American Behaviorism, and restored most recently by European scholars. We cannot solve the argument but we can—and must—position ourselves within it. (We are, admittedly, a long way from the TV set or newspaper, but we need this work to make sense of that action.)

THE ARGUMENT OF THE MIND

The modern statement of the "mind" part of the argument holds that our knowledge of reality is born within a historicized system of interpretation driven primarily by language, but with the involvement of other semiotics. The concept of interpretation is in direct opposition to traditional empiricism that would hold that we have direct contact with an objective reality and its experience is written on our soul. The word *historicized* implies that there are no transcendent truths. Such truths that are passed from generation to generation are re-created (produced anew) in each era in the terms of that time. In a fairly simply said but exceedingly deep example, this argument states that the fundamental truths of, say, Newtonian physics are not the same now as they were in Newton's time, and they will not be the same in the future. It is even argued that our explanation for this change—that we have a continuously *improving* (rather than just *changing*) understanding—is simply a device to maintain the concept of absolute truth.

Before you throw your high school physics book at us, let's consider what Accommodation Theory has to take from this argument. It essentially takes two concepts: First, it takes the idea that any understanding (knowledge) is an achievement of interpretation. And second, the achieved interpretation is governed by the semiotic systems implicated in its accomplishment. Our understanding, therefore, is neither revealed nor given to us. It is a referenced practice located in time and place (historicized). What one knows at any moment depends on who is present (cognitively) and the semiotic systems[1] in place.

THE ARGUMENT OF THE BODY

The argument from the body points out that we all are subject to the same physical forces and have the same mechanisms for contacting the energies (sound, light, heat, and so on) of those forces. These communalities allow us to recognize the culturally based differences in the response to dropping a three pound rock on the toe. Some are more expressive than others, but we assume some common response of flesh and bone. Just what those communalities are, however, is open to considerable question. Studies in neurophysiology have shown that significant brain structures, which are genetically possible but not determined, and relationships among these and other structures of the brain are formed after birth. Arguments from these studies claim that functional structures of cognitive performance are thereby developed in response to the organism in its environment. These functional structures are called the physical traces of culture. (That cultural imprint is not the consequence of Culture writ large but of its partial representation, on site, in local performance.) Finally, there is strong neurological evidence that what we don't use in cognitive capacity, we lose, and conversely what we do use, gets better.

So where are we? We end up with the machinery of cognitive performance being both open to its environment and modifiable in practice and, therefore, unique and having fixed characteristics common to all individuals. Such is the most recent compromise in the nature/nurture controversy.

The implications of this understanding of the features of the brain for Accommodation Theory are considerable. For one thing it demonstrates that the very materiality of our individuality is dependent on others—those who raised us, teach us, and interact with us on a daily basis. For another it implies that no matter how variable the cultural components of interpretation, there are some elements that we all share. *It is, therefore, possible for us both to participate in the "same experience" and to achieve radically different interpretations of it.*

It also points out the significance of institutionalized practices in child rearing, education, and the workplace. The community has claim over what it is to be a child, a parent, a student, and a worker because these practices influence the character of the individual. We have already argued that it is the communality of experience that is the basis for communication. Here is good physiological evidence for that claim.

OUR POSITION

The set of arguments that continue to swirl around mind versus body in the nature of human knowledge is implicitly a set of arguments concerning the nature of the human individual. The position used in Accommodation Theory is that the individual is incomplete and dependent on the other so that the self is always in the state of becoming what is realized moment-by-moment in the course of action. We hold that understanding is an achievement of a local performance of interpretation in which the social action semiotics of language and practice are heavily implicated but that also involve generic elements of sensation and perception. What this view rejects is the various notions of the individual as an essentially predetermined mechanism, as a self-contained microcosm of society, as an element independent of its locality, as a prisoner of a linguistic community, or as the agent of cause or the place of consequence in the processes of communication. We are a communal creation within broad genetic limits, realize our self in the presence of others, live local performances, know more than what can be spoken, and find cause and consequence in the processes of communication in the enabling relationship. We will gradually unpack the implications of these claims as we work the other terms of this theory. For now, a useful summarizing statement is that what creates human life is not the individual but the community. It is the focus of self in relation to other that will help us understand communication.

TERMS OF SOCIAL ACTION

Social action is a referenced activity that is cooriented and coordinated with an other and appears in mutually supervised, improvisational performances under local control that are partial representations of communal themes of action. Disassembling that sentence: The concept of referenced activity has to do with autonomy. Autonomy is the question of the power of evaluation. When an entity has the power to establish the criteria of its own evaluation, it is said to have autonomy. In social action, the individual is referenced within a relationship. The relationship may be autonomous (though most likely it is referenced within higher order relationships), but the individual is not.

That social action is cooriented and coordinated with another can be seen over the whole sociological spectrum. For example, academics have the privilege of contemplation because the efficiency of production labor provides the space. The author in Chapter 4 has to be granted the right of the terms of his performance before a single word can be written. It does not take two persons to push the keys of the word processor but it takes a host of others before what is written is a book. For a college student to go to class requires the societal institution of education, in which students and teachers live off the backs of the primary workforce; the development of a curriculum, the presentation of a course within that curriculum; the assemblage of the classroom scene; and finally the local tasks of particular individuals appearing in the same place accepting the premises of the same performance. That one's classroom neighbor does not scream incessantly, but sleeps quietly, is significant proof of coorientation and coordination in the classroom.

The notion of mutual supervision reinforces the relational setting of social action. Whatever the terms of the relationship, each has particular responsibilities to the other that are demanded by the relationship and for which each is held accountable by the other. For example, when we step into our automobile we enter into a relationship with the other drivers and users of the right of way. In a number of actions, we supervise each other's driving—with our horn, lights, driving maneuvers, and so on. Even the anonymity of most driving situations does not release us from this supervision. In more personal situations, people comment on nearly everything in performance. In the strategic management of this supervision, we often form cliques in order to provide the criteria of evaluation and predictable supervisory routines.

Improvisational performances are part of the solution to the problem of human behavior being understandable in its purpose yet highly variable in its performance. The improvisational nature of a performance allows us to see it as arising on-site, in response to local conditions. As an improvisation, it is an improvisation of something within a higher level of order—the communal theme of action. As an improvisation, it is also under local control, performed by particular individuals in historic time and place. The particular individuals, time, and place all matter in the nature of its performance.

The relationship between the locally controlled improvisation and the communal theme of action of which the improvisation is a partial representation is an important one. The improvisation is both a re-creation and an innovation of the theme. It reproduces our understanding of the theme and at the same time extends that understanding by showing yet another possibility of performance within it. The communal theme for its part allows us to understand what it is that we are doing. The theme is the set of premises by which we make sense of the innovations that the improvisation contains. The demands for performance are such that an individual must find a way to express the theme within the site of the performance according to the criteria held by the community and supervised locally.

If it had to be done alone, the demands of performance would invoke a potentially disabling level of uncertainty: The site must be read, the premises of action accounted for, the community of evaluation referenced, the nature of supervision noted, and so on. This is work, however, that we do together both through time and in time. One's culture and community provide templates of performances through time. All of us have gone to school but none of us had to invent the role of student, although we each performed it in our own way. As we each came to that fateful first day, we came into the presence of a living archive of exemplars of how to perform "student." The tools and technology of the classroom and the staging of the education process further embodied the terms of our performance: "Here is our room. This is your desk."

At the moment that we became a student, we were surrounded by people who shaped and supervised our performance—peers, teachers, administrators, parents, family, acquaintances, all those who made it possible for us to be students participated in our student life. By the end of the fourth month, we had given more than 100 performances of being a student, each one unique but all within the premises of that role. Most of us in that short period became well-practiced though not necessarily "good" students.

The circumstances of our entrance into student life are repeated more or less in each entrance we make. And in almost every life move, it is an entrance into an ongoing continuity of social action. Within that framework, performances are practiced; evaluation is strategically managed within and through membership; and supervision is a set of tactics by which performances are empowered (or disabled) within the premises of the theme.

THE LIMITS OF SOCIAL ACTION

There are two pernicious extremes that can be taken in an evaluation of social action theory: that social action involves the presence of another or that everything involves social action. We have already spoken extensively about the falsity of the first position. Social action is invoked in any activity that *references another in some relationship*. It is the relationship that governs the appearance of social action not the presence of someone other than self.

As to the second, once adopted, the social action view is somewhat difficult to contain. Anderson writes:

> As I backpack in the mountains I am continuously and overwhelmingly alone. Yet, in every action, I am forced to conform to the presence of others. I follow the trails that others have made, cook my meals in their fire rings, sleep where they slept, conduct myself according to the rules of the Park Service. I am also governed by the technology of my equipment—the material product of the efforts of others. If I were to be endangered by injury or whatever, dozens of people are committed to my rescue. I employ good safety practices just for that reason—sort of the "clean underwear" code of the wilderness. No one wants to be a jerk.

Though Anderson can readily find the social action components of even very solitary activities, his experiences on the mountain trails are qualitatively different on the dimension of social action from his experiences in the office, in his home, or even at other forms of play. On the trail, he recovers a level of autonomy not ordinarily available. No one will comment on the fires that he makes, the meals that he cooks, or the pitch of his tent (other than the voices he carries with him). His work has no lasting product and his performances are beyond supervision. This space of separateness has been granted by his communities; it is, in common language, "a chance to get away," verifying its different state.

The crucial components of social action identified in this difference is (a) the degree of presence and force of the relationship between self and other; (b) the move of autonomy from the communal relationship to the individual; (c) the reduced potential for supervision of performance, and (d) lessened accountability for its results. Because, according to our claim, the self is incomplete, one never steps out of the relationship between self and other. Even in backpacking that relationship continues in photographs taken, stories prepared, and in the activity itself, as noted previously. In these circumstances of isolation however, the relationship has less presence and force—the individual has fewer immediate responsibilities for it. With fewer relational responsibilities, judgments about oneself move closer to the present, more under individual control. The absence of other coupled with the immediate disappearance of performance traces reinforces the individual's sense of autonomy. Such circumstances are unusual, not ordinary. While there are autonomous moments in all of our lives, the prevailing characteristic of human life is the relationship between self and other.

INTERPRETATION

We are doing some tough work here: We have first asked you to give up the notion of the autonomous self—a notion widely represented in fable and myth. Now we will move against one's natural sense of the world presenting itself to us in meaningful ways. We stated the doctrine of interpretation a few paragraphs earlier when we claimed that understanding is an achievement of a local performance of interpretation. The concept of "achievement" is clearly an important one and deserves some additional attention.

UNDERSTANDING AS ACHIEVEMENT

The idea of understanding as achievement is a direct countermove to naive **empiricism.** Naive empiricism—a central tenet of Western, commonsense argument—holds that world *presents* itself to us and is *re*-presented in our understanding of it. That is, there is an isomorphic relationship between the properties of the world and the properties of our cognitive understanding of it. This position further states that while our understanding may be distorted or incomplete at any point in time, it is ultimately correctable through the primacy of experience. The opposing position is that the world is, say, a continuous stream of energy (including matter) the properties of which are constructed in human understanding to accomplish human purposes.[2] The validation of human understanding is in its instrumentality.

THE ROLE OF LANGUAGE

In the abstract, human understanding begins with its contact with the energy of the world; it moves from the particular in the immediate present through the capacity of signification—the ability to punctuate that energy into separate properties, embeds itself in social action through the linguistic sign, and validates itself in human performances. In the lives we actually lead, human understanding has little opportunity for private practice but leaps within hours of birth into icon, symbol, and sign. A particular significance of the socialization of a child within a linguistic community is that the learning of the sign motivates the formation of the signified punctuation of the world. Learning the "names of things" creates them as elements of our knowledge. Our language indeed shapes the world, rather than the world giving rise to our language.

We are born into and spend a lifetime practicing a system of understanding called language. Doing so, however, does not eliminate our linguistically independent contact with the world (there can be experience independent of language) or our ability to signify—even if it cannot be said—its energy (the claim that all that is known cannot be said). The doctrine of interpretation does not deny the presence of the world outside human understanding nor does it deny human understanding outside language. It simply says that the claims we make about the properties of the world are human claims derived from the particular characteristics of human ways of knowing. It also states that signification—the punctuation of reality—is a given of human cognition, and that language is a human invention that directs the signifying act but does not possess it.

INSTRUMENTALITY What we have done so far in this discussion of interpretation is to move us away from a concept of an objective reality to a human construction of reality that is invoked primarily in language and that both motivates (enables) and is validated in instrumental action. What remains is a discussion of the implications of the final phrase of that sentence—that one that refers to the instrumentality of understanding. We begin with the argument that the production of knowledge is a communal activity. This is an obvious move once one abandons the idea of knowledge as discovery. By communal, we mean that the questions we ask, the explanations we construct, and the truths we hold arise within a historicized, sociopolitical system. Consider the difference between a technological and a contemplative society. The technological society will believe it more important to have computers than mantras and will develop a computer science. The contemplative one will use its resources perfecting the inner self through, perhaps, the science of meditation. Each will consider the other primitive. We are not attempting a real comparison here but working to permit the observation that "who we are" is an important component of "what we know." Knowledge is a product of the social world through society's determination of which problems shall be prior, the manner in which it provides for the knowledge maker, and the processes of acceptance and dissemination.

The instrumentality of understanding, then, does not suggest a forward-looking decision process in which we decide what we want to be and then pursue knowledge to create that state. Rather, it claims that knowledge is used to accomplish who we are. That understanding, embedded in an ongoing social system, illuminates why we know what we know. The instrumentality of understanding has equally important implications for the local performance of interpretation. Once again, understanding is an achievement embedded in social processes. Its instrumentality arises within those processes as part of their accomplishment. What we know depends on who we are in the company we keep. What we know, therefore, is not a fixed state—an individual does not have all of his or her knowledge equally available in any one context. Understanding appears in the relationship between self and other. A friend writes:

> I don't know algebra anymore. I used to know algebra quite well. That was when I was both taking math classes and teaching basic statistics. I would perform the algebraic manipulations with a flourish at the board. But now my course work is long since done and others teach statistics. I cannot create and maintain the space in my life to perform that knowledge. They won't let me know algebra anymore.

Our friend is not alone. In fact, great bodies of knowledge have been lost to humankind because the communities of their performance were destroyed. That knowledge became extinct.

THE PERFORMANCE OF INTERPRETATION

We have been examining the implications of the claim of understanding as an achievement of a local performance of interpretation. We discovered the initial performance of interpretation at the instant of separation from the particular and immediate to the essential and general. That act of signification is, of course, the foundation of language, but the invention of a language irrevocably changes the course of signifying for the members of that linguistic community. We further argued that interpretation is performed in the relationship between self and other and that knowledge, consequently, is a social product. All of this work has been in the basement of our argument to be constructed on top of it concerning the interpretation of media texts.

In these more public spaces we will find components that analogue to those in the foundation. The fundamental contact with texts of any sort is a semiotic one. That contact however, is not point-to-point with each sign connecting to one and only one signified and each signified being independent of all others. Semiotic connections are in layered webs of significance permitting considerable connected, interpretive movement. Although none of us would disagree as to the words contained herein, there are many legitimate interpretations of this paragraph. There is, therefore, no single interpretation that this combination of signs must invoke.[3]

In conversations, classrooms, literary criticism, research, we deal with this openness by privileging particular interpretations—the cocommunicant, the teacher, the author, the researcher. That privileging is practiced, naturalized, and part of the understanding of having a conversation, being in class, doing criticism and research. It is, nevertheless, part of the performance of interpretation in these locales and not a cognitive reflex. We run into considerable difficulty when we assume that performance constraints in one arena transfer to others. In particular, we err if we assume that the audience of media texts must privilege, or even does privilege, the interpretation of the media practitioner, the media critic, or media researcher.

We have argued for multiple interpretations of media texts. We have argued for an initial interpretation within the constraints of the social action of reception. Our ethnographic studies have shown that the potential for meaning does not end with that interpretation. Rather, some of the openness of the text is preserved for transport into other action contexts. New interpretations, whether anticipated or not, can arise within those contexts.

THE INTERPRETIVE IMPORTANCE OF ROUTINES If interpretation appears in the context of social action, then the character of social action has special significance for the character of interpretation. Social action, as we have seen, is not an ad hoc adventure—something to be invented each day. It is organized into routines that are the product of cultural and communal forces and are locally performed. In this manner, self and other know what is being done and how to interpret the events and texts within the performance. Consequently, the sense made of media texts will be appropriate to the premises of the action in place.

How is it that space and time become available for an interlude of media use? Certainly our definitions of work and leisure and the allowances of our friends and family will participate in the conditions of that interlude and the sense we make of it. Whether for pleasure or gain, whether granted solitude or engaged in a shared space, and whether other circumstances are implied, all create the context for the interpretations achieved in that interlude.

We can also easily see that the same mediated text can achieve different interpretations in the activities of shopping, lunch discussion, political decision making, and the like, not because the text changes but because the premises of interpretation change.

THE PLACE OF TEXT IN ACTION: THE ACCOMMODATION METAPHOR Routines make performance demands. They also establish the constraints of performance. Our routines both empower and disable texts. On the other hand, any performance reinvents the premises of the routine, by locating them in time and place within an improvised achievement. It is within the space of improvisation that innovation occurs. Texts, therefore, can clarify, confound, reaffirm, modify, enlarge, contract, affect, or effect the premises of action through improvised innovations that are, nonetheless, true to the premises in the first place. In short, mediated texts are accommodated within the routines of social action. The notion of accommodation is that there is some larger activity (here, the routine) that has slack that can be taken up. That is, the understandings in place are not so precise or inelastic that there is no room for movement. In taking up and giving up the slack, an accommodation will be made most likely toward the larger activity, but perhaps not always and certainly not only. Nevertheless, it is the ordinary practice of incorporating media into our lives that seeks to achieve the routines that exist prior to and independent of their texts.

SUMMARY

We have made two important moves in this section. In the first, we imposed an active process of interpretation first, at the fundamental level, between human understanding and the world, and in the second, we imposed that interpretive process at a more recognizable level between media texts and human behavior. Interpretation at the fundamental level is marked first by signification and second by language. As humans, we punctuate the energy of the world and derive its properties from that punctuation. The human capacity to signify is prior to language, but language invokes the manner of our signification. All that can be known, therefore, cannot be said, but understanding is clearly located in language.

It is our membership in a language community that raises the seeming paradox of texts: The fact that we can agree on the content and disagree on its interpretation. The reference system of language has been called the "webs of significance" to distinguish it from some point-to-point isomorphism. Texts potentiate interpretation but do not evoke a particular interpretation. The achievement of interpretation is a performance of social action directed by the premises of that action.

This last claim leads us to the second move of this section in the discussion of the notion of accommodation. That notion begins with the claim that social life is organized into meaningful routines that contain the premises of interpretation of what is being done. Social life is culturally and communally organized prior to, but makes use of mediated texts in its performance. Any performance is a localized reinvention of that social life as an improvisation on the themes of the social action in place. In the process of reinvention, the premises of action are vulnerable to innovation—an innovation that, nonetheless, will be true to the premises. *There is, therefore, an accommodation in which texts are interpreted according to the premises of action and the premises of action are reinvented using, in part, the texts at hand.*

Prior effects theory has valorized the text—located the explanation for effects in textual characteristics. Such theories use our ready agreement on the facts of content to create an objective source for effect. There are good, practical reasons for this kind of theory. A text is available, has good definition, can be captured, archived, transported, manipulated, in short, is factual.

Accommodation Theory privileges social action as the premises and site of interpretation that is ongoing, emergent, localized, and historical. Effects are created and performed in the routines of everyday life. There are genuine, practical difficulties for the analyst in this theoretical stance. The most obvious is that the object of inquiry is no longer the physical object of the text but the premises and performances of social action. The analyst is sent out to become a member of the community and to achieve its communal understanding. The shade is drawn on the Olympian view.

CENTRAL IDEAS OF SECTION I: TWO AXIOMS OF ACCOMMODATION

1. As humans, we find our self in relation to other and live our lives in a system of understanding called language. Nonetheless, we also contact the world as a material element and have knowledge beyond what can be spoken.
2. Studying the individual, therefore, is only partially helpful in understanding the human condition; the more potent site is the community.
3. Social action is cooriented, coordinated, mutually supervised, improvisational, under local control, and a partial representation of the cultural theme in place.
4. The terms of the cultural themes and performances of social action are carried in the ongoing performances of others, the staging of the action (site, setting, properties, and so on), the technologies in place, and the accomplishments anticipated.
5. Individual autonomy is a struggle and mostly a fiction.
6. Meaning is not the product of a cognitive reflex but an achievement locatable—and, therefore, contextualized—in time and place.
7. Interpretation is surrounded by language and works to maintain the context of its performance.
8. A most important part of that context is the instantiated routine.
9. The work of most interpretive acts is to maintain the understandings in place. Those understandings, nonetheless, are not rigidly fixed, but have free play and elasticity. They can accommodate texts that redefine them.

SECTION II: ACCOMMODATION THEORY—IN COMPARISON

The next two headings attempt to place Accommodation Theory within the realm of communication theory by considering the reality premises, the evidence of their arguments, and the methods of study of the major lines of theoretical thought.

ACCOMMODATION THEORY: A COMPARISON OF REALITY PREMISES

One way of locating Accommodation Theory within the realm of social science inquiry is to conduct a comparison of its reality premises with those of other effects theories. To do this comparison, let's regroup the various models of effects discussed in Chapter 5 into three sets: a traditional set, an interpretive set, and a social action set.

The traditional set of models or theories uses exposure to known content to predict behavioral outcomes. As we have seen, there are several variations and elaborations on this form—direct effects, Lippmann effects, and uses and gratifications studies, for example. We call this set "traditional" because it most closely resembles classical cause and effect reasoning, and while not the first, its exemplars have certainly been the most frequent. (For exemplar studies conducted under variants of this mode understanding, see Snow, in press; Berkowitz & Geen, 1966; Becker, 1976; Katz, Gurevitch, & Haas, 1973; Palmgreen & Rayburn, 1982; Zillmann & Bryant, 1982.)

Before the rise of **behaviorism,** early forms of interpretive theories directed research in message effects (e.g., symbolic interactionism, Gestalt psychology, Wundt's introspective psychology). Today, the center of the interpretive model is simply the achievement of an understanding—often called meaning or sense making—concerning the content. Interpretivists vary as to where that achievement is located—the semiotic, the culture, the individual—and the manner of its practice, but agree that the source of any effect is in the interpretation accomplished rather than the content delivered. (Exemplars are found in Carey, 1975; Deming, 1988; Grossberg, 1986; Hall, 1980; Brunsdon & Morley, 1978; Peterson, 1987.)

Social action theorists continue on where most interpretivists end, to work the re-creation of meaning in the social action routines that fill everyday life. The major contribution of social action theorists, then, is to complete the cycle that interpretivists begin to study, by examining the conditions in which an effect can emerge. Social action theorists agree that the source of any effect is in the interpretation achieved, but add that the effect itself is an accomplishment of cooriented human endeavor. (For examples, see Alexander, Ryan, & Munoz, 1984; Becker, 1982; Lindlof, 1988; Wolf, 1987; Pacanowsky & Anderson, 1982. Wolf and Pacanowsky & Anderson are two of several exemplars in their respective references.)

We will examine these theoretical perspectives first in an analysis of nature of explanation that is consitituted in each set and then as an application of this analysis, in a consideration of the implications for a theory of the audience.

NATURE OF EXPLANATION FOR THE THREE SETS

Each of the three sets of theories has to make claims about the ontology of (1) the cause, (2) the agent of action, and (3) the effect in order to produce explanation about the role of media in society. We explore these claims in what follows:

TRADITIONAL THEORIES Traditional theories locate the cause of effects in the mediated text, establish the agent of action in the individual responding to the text and find the effect in the behavioral acts attributed to the individual acting under the influence of the text. The following assumptions about the text, the individual, and behavior are required to accomplish this explanation.

A text is typically posited with known (and, therefore, fixed) semiotic and semantic properties that are delivered in its presentation. The conditions of presentation—medium, setting, and so on—are part of these known properties. This text has the capacity to induce functionally equivalent (common-valued) cognitive and physiological states in individuals. Only exposure through attendance is required of the audience.

Texts, competently prepared, are considered semantically complete. ("Competent" is a qualifier necessary to make the obvious exclusion.) A semantically complete text is a theoretically useful concept that posits texts that contain all of the necessary information needed for their proper decoding. Proper decoding, in this theoretical stance, will follow a set of rules that are part of the semiotic or language system in use. Good languages have good rules for interpretation that result in an understanding of the meaning of the text that has high intersubjectivity. Generally, proper decoding is responsible for the intent of the author. The author's intent becomes the meaning of the text. Authors of competent texts are assumed to be always guided by intents whether explicit, implicit, conscious, unconscious, clear, difficult, complex, conflicted, or ambiguous, and so on. (A claim to a conflicted meaning, for example, is evidenced by the text.) In this way, researchers can talk about distortion, decoding errors, and the like. Further, texts can be categorized across meaning properties rather than just content properties. A text deemed violent because it portrays a fist of one hitting the face of another (content property) instigates aggression (meaning property). Content properties are equated with meaning properties because the text is semantically complete.

The individual is considered the site of behavioral acts that can be influenced by cognitive and physiological states that themselves can be modified by exogenous conditions (the text). The external control of internal states can be mediated by both internal and external conditions. Cognitive traits, interpretive practices and context of reception are part of these mediating conditions. Mediating conditions, however, mediate in functionally equivalent ways over those individuals affected. There is dismissible freedom in the performance of a response (little or no invention, innovation, or improvisation). Once controlling and mediating conditions are known, the response is predictable, or, at least, such individual differences that do occur do not significantly affect the character of the criterion behavior but distribute around that norm.

The theory of the individual used by traditional effects theories contains no notion of a central self. In fact, such a notion is often disparaged with the term **homunculus.** The individual is explained through a series of possibly independent cognitive structures, such as attitudes, values, motives, schemata, maps, scripts, and so on. Such structures are symbol-based and developed through learning processes called socialization, enculturation, maturation, development, and the like. A child is considered to be relatively open to these processes (and therefore vulnerable); an adult relatively closed (and therefore categorically predictable). These cognitive structures are called upon to conduct different operations but always to direct the character of behavior. The cognitive structures of the mind, therefore, explain acts of behavior. Within common practices of socialization—most broadly Western societies—the same sets of structures develop, and it is the nature of these structures, not the performing individual, that is of interest. (Liberals can be French, British, Canadian, or American but they are still liberals. For later comparisons, we will call this an interest in the categorical individual.)

For a particular cognitive structure to come into play, it must be cued—often by a semantically complete text for the purpose of the author. The interplay of these last two principles means that the individual is the single site for understanding behavior (cognitive structures explain behavioral acts) but the behavior of the individual is open to modification by another through the process of cueing. At this point cognitive structure reasoning breaks down (as all theories do) because this description, while perhaps adequate for common folk, will not do for the researcher who is obviously above having his or her buttons pushed.

Behavior for traditional effects theorists has objective properties of meaning that are displayed in its performance and of consequence for the larger entities of society and culture. Behavior, therefore, can be categorized and the categories related to one another. The meaning of the behavior held by the respondent is irrelevant or assumed to be the same as that specified by the researcher. Further, the categories are such that elements in a superset can represent elements in a subset. (Laboratory criterion measures can represent, say, a street crime.)

INTERPRETIVE THEORIES The jumble of analytical writing that is often grouped into what is called the interpretive stance is distinguished by its move to empower the audience. Traditional effects models require only exposure for the text to work its effect; interpretive models add some decoding performance under the control of the audience or individual. These interpretive models have the following requirements:

Texts are semantically incomplete or polysemic. There is an important distinction between these two constructs that has implications for the entire structure of the analysis of effects. The concept of semantically incomplete texts is used to motivate the claim for the necessity of an interpretive act on the part of the receiver for meaning to emerge. The text no longer delivers its meaning but is the site of an interpretation to be constructed. With the notion of incomplete texts, *Meaning is a local production and effects cannot be predicted from content properties.*

Polysemic texts on the other hand are conglomerate texts—usually media texts—that have layers of semantically complete texts running through them. The text becomes a site of contested interpretation with different audience communities producing different sense-making achievements. However, because the texts are semantically complete, the possible meanings can be specified and the probable meanings claimed by the critic. Further, *meaning is a cultural production* as one's cultural ideologies determine how the mix of texts will be read by the individual. Ideology, you will remember (or not), is the set of understandings achieved by virtue of membership in a cultural/social/economic structure. Ideology is the individual's tool of interpretation.

Both constructionists and culturists (you're going to need a program to keep these folks straight) move away from the notion of the text as cause. In both cases, the text is a site of action—interpretation. The causal agent will be located within that interpretation.

In their formulation of the individual, interpretivists using either type of text concept make a radical break with the traditional effects theorists because they liberate the individual from content. The explanatory agent is no longer content properties cueing cognitive structures developed across individuals through common socialization practices. The explanatory agent, here, is some interpretive act. For constructionists, who as a group have done far less work in developing theory, this act is sometimes partially explained through cognitive structures sometimes unexplained. Regardless of how interpretation is explained, it is the individual as an interpreting actor that is of interest.

Culturists, though politically estranged from traditional effects research, are theoretically closer to traditionals than to constructionists. Culturists represent a more sophisticated critical attack on content and on the mediation of culture than traditionals but basically rely on traditional, mentalist notions for explaining differences in interpretation. For their part, these notions are class or gender or race ideologies rather than attitudes or values or schemata, but the consequence for theory at this point is the same. Constructionists are likely to grant considerably more free play to the individual, and some have recovered the concept of choice.

Culturists do make one move quite different from the traditionals and constructionists: Individuals are liberated from content, but are trapped in ideology. The premises and logic of different ideologies become the explanatory agents for effects. (Connections can be made here to traditional studies that make use of mediating cultural variables; it is the next step that is significant.) While individuals "perform effects," the site of the effect is the ideology. That is, it is the ideologically situated individual who can be affected. The individual of interest is in his or her ideology(ies) (or the ideological individual).

Constructionists follow the traditional line in seeing an objective behavior—historicized certainly, but not local. Behavior is culturally interpretable. It is interesting that behavior is not a text for most constructionists. Culturists are not interested in individual behavior.

They are interested in collective behavior. The collective is not the sum of individual acts: Individual acts cannot be aggregated to understand social forces. Generally, it is the behavior of the collective as directed by the premises of its ideology that has value for their analysis.

SOCIAL ACTION THEORIES The most recent interest in ethnographic methods has intermixed with interpretive ideas to provide a third perspective on effects: Social action models—the location of our very own Accommodation Theory. The distinguishing characteristic of these models is the emphasis placed on social routines as the site of effects. Using our same format, the assumptions of these models are as follows:

Texts are semantically open. Social action theorists are more constructionist than not. The difference is in the social action claim that sense making is an ongoing, emerging performance. There is never a single understanding of the meaning of a text but a continual re-creation of meaning as the text is accommodated within everyday life. Even when an understanding is "archived" in discourse, that archived text simply becomes a reference point in the continuous spiral of sense making. The distinction between open and incomplete texts is that the open concept includes the idea of incompleteness and extends the interpretive act to multiple performances. Interpretation, then, is itself a performance, residing in some social action context through which meaning is accomplished. Meaning is an achievement of social action with clear empirical traces in what people do. The agents of cause and the consequences of texts arise within this social action context. Texts, as we have noted, are empowered or disabled by the social action in which they are brought forward for interpretation.

The individual is incomplete. Social action theory breaks off most decisively from the mainstream of American social science by (mostly implicitly) claiming that the individual is made whole only in reference to an other. Pointing out that the semiotic is a sociological achievement that creates a community of intellect, these theorists argue that no individual is ever permitted to be solely responsible for his or her cognitions. An individual's knowledge, beliefs, attitudes, values, and so on, are always framed within the alternatives presented by the social action. Studying an individual without reference to the protocol of study, as is traditionally done, moves the location of effect to an imaginary, objectified force. The individual lives in mutually supervised, face-to-face relationships that provide the reality of effect.

Behavior itself is a text. Act is the content of action, which is behavior made meaningful within some social action context. Making check marks on a questionnaire is first made sensible within the context of the survey administration, then again in the research report, and then again in its applications. Each move is a re-creation of the meaning of that initial act. How one understands, therefore, what another does, depends on the place of its interpretation.

Social action theorists hold that we are born into a preexisting framework of social action routines that provide the alternatives of our behavior and the meaning of our acts. To understand the effect of violent content on an individual requires the study of where and how aggression is manifested within the routines of the community in which that individual participates to discover how such violent content is accommodated within them. To understand the effect of violent content on a society requires the study of how that society creates and reproduces the routines of aggression and the study of the everyday performance of aggression. Being a criminal, in this perspective, is as much a way of life as being a college professor. Society creates both of these lives.[4] Violent content most likely appears in both but is accommodated in different ways. It may even be that the criminal considers the depiction of violence on television to be childish and naive.

IMPLICATIONS FOR A DEFINITION OF A MEDIUM

The theoretical and methodological analysis that we have done to this point allows us to attempt a reconceptualization of the notion of a medium, both to describe better what a medium is and to capture its significance in society. Previous definitions of a medium have focused on the devices of technology (radio, film, television), on various industries (broadcast television versus cable television), on the residual rather than living texts produced (residual texts have been fixed for analysis like a mounted insect), or on the distribution characteristics (mass versus personal media). While these characteristics are certainly part of the concept, each fails to emphasize the central nature of mediation—a medium mediates. As an initial effort to centralize the definition, we offer the following.

A medium is a recognizable human activity that organizes reality into readable texts for engagement.[5] This activity is recognizable by the following:

A. Its *standing,* which is manifested by its place as an institution or element of society supported by an industry and its practices (see Chapter 2) and by its character in mundane usage—the manner in which it is made sensible in the routines of social action (see Chapter 4). The concept of standing emphasizes the fact that media exist in two different orders—within the apparatuses of society and within the practices of social action. An understanding of its presence in our lives, then, requires an analysis within both orders.

B. Its *technology,* which we have found in the devices, practices, codes (texts) that regulate and define these devices and practices and the knowledge we claim about all three.

C. Its *manner of organizing,* which are the formats, logics, forms, and conventions we discussed in Chapter 3.

D. Its *texts,* which are the ongoing objects of our attendance, the subjects of discourse and other action, and a common base of experience (see Chapters 3 and 4). We insist that the texts used to distinguish a medium are those that are actually engaged by auditors in the practice of reception. These practices are not represented by those of media analysts who capture and make special texts that are embedded, ordinary, plastic, and disposable.

E. Its *enacting performances,* which occur with a good measure of independence in the community of practitioners and within the context of reception/interpretation (see Chapters 1 and 4). The study of enacting performances is the areas of greatest neglect in media analysis. Enacting performances, however, are the site of the production of meaning.

We think each of the terms of this definition is problematic (arguable), which, for us, increases its value as a perspective upon media. Several examples come to mind—the school, the church, the organization, our system of transportation. (Our system of transportation organizes the reality of space through direction, distance, practices of travel, and so on, and produces many readable texts, including the highways laid down upon the face of the earth.) Our concern with radio, television, film, newspapers, and the like, is not that they produce signs and symbols in syntactic relationships but that they are reality agents. The value of the enlarged scope of our definition is that it lets us come to an understanding of the multiplicity of agents with standing in both the societal and social action orders that are involved in the mediation/construction of the reality in which we live.

We also believe that this scope works to eliminate the error of referring to "the media" as a monolithic collective with the same characteristic operations and outcomes. Media organize reality in substantively different ways and among them present both complementary and competitive views. This differentiation is true even among the narrative media such as television, newspapers, and film.

Finally, our definition allows us to distinguish the process of communication from both media and texts. *Communication,* as we have defined it, is the achievement of a common understanding between two or more individuals. It is not simply the interpretive analysis of text or the participation in media technology. It is, as the root of the term implies, an active "coming together." Media texts do not necessarily communicate, but they are always a resource for interpretation. It is the particular contribution of social action theory and its accompanying ethnographic methodology that this distinction can be made and evidenced.

IMPLICATIONS FOR A THEORY OF AN AUDIENCE

A common gloss in the study of media is the term audience. While all theories demand particular characteristics of the concept, few theorists and almost no researchers specify the elements of the construct and consider their implications. Having set ourselves up to right this wrong, we are now ready to consider the traditional, interpretive, and social action positions on the audience.

The concept of audience is first burdened with a classic heritage of individuals coming together both physically and socially to create the motive and site for public presentations. Classic audiences were not aggregates of isolates but were interacting, interconnected social memberships. In the classic audience, the achievements of interpretation were located in the membership that had the immediate and practical means of mutual accomplishment. We call this classic heritage a burden because its traces appear as default assumptions in many claims, even in the relative absence or neglect of empirical support.

For example, traditionals often claim that some categorical aggregate (such as Frost & Stauffer's social class) that can be distinguished from some other categorical aggregate on a measure of content effect is an audience without bothering to discover the mechanisms of common interpretation or the manner of common engagement of the media. Similarly the community branch of the interpretivists more often than not lay claim to interpretive communities that give no evidence of interaction. It is our classical understanding of audience that permits such claims.

We can avoid this easy slippage by examining the manner in which the construct of audience is reconstructed in most research. We have already seen that traditionals and interpretivists of the critical issue and hegemony branches use the notion of audience as the site of exposure to content. Content is viewed as either a causal or catalytic agent[6] that initiates the effects cycle. In these formulations, the concept of audience is built up out of the terms of location, presence, frequency, duration, fixed meaning, common engagement, and overdetermination of interpretation.

The concept of location accomplishes two tasks: (a) It establishes the place of the operating agent of content—on television, in the newspaper, at the movies; (b) by setting the place, it requires the process of attendance that becomes the explanation for the actions of watching television, reading the newspaper, going to the movies. Attendance is required for exposure to occur as content is in a location.

As exposure—the required condition of media effect—requires attendance, the terms of presence, frequency, and duration come into the research purview. Individuals are considered audience members by their presence and differences among audience elements are cited by virtue of their duration or frequency.

Any approach that includes an analysis of content necessitates some belief in fixed meaning that can be addressed in the characteristics of content in order that the researcher's "read" be the basis of audience response. Even the liberating or audience-empowering claims of polysemy or openness provide for the audience's interpretive moves by virtue of content characteristics—it is, of course, the text that is open or polysemic.

Audience surveys and the global claims of critics clearly assume that the methods of engagement of mediated content practiced by the explained individuals will have no or, at least, trivial impact on the relationship between content and interpretation. The simplest way to accomplish this assumption is to presume that the content/medium presentation requires certain practices of engagement for exposure to be authentic.

Interpretation stands as a prime difficulty for all audience analyses. Traditional approaches deny interpretation by ignoring the possibility; critical studies generally recognize interpretation but then do not account for its local performance. Silverman (1983) sets the dilemma for us by describing "readerly" and "writerly" interpretations: Readerly interpretations are overdetermined by the text. Meaning is invoked as a cognitive reflex in response to the text. Writerly interpretations view the text as a resource to be assembled and reassembled in accordance with the interpretive achievements of the auditor. Most analytical frameworks grant writerly interpretations to the analyst and assume readerly responses from the audience.

We can contrast the traditionals, critical issue, and hegemonists with social action theorists and the more ethnographic of the intepretivists along these terms. To start, remember that both of the latter theorists would organize their analysis around the situated relationship—individuals situated in time, place, and reference. Generally, they assume a social constructed reality that is the product of local achievements within a linguocultural semiotic frame. Their analyses have as their explanatory objects the accomplishments of meaning that empower that reality. Neither would necessarily deny any of the audience terms useful to describe traditional and most critical approaches. They would, however, hold them as problematics for which there will be local solutions with recognizable empirical traces.

For example, in social action theory, the study of media effects is not dependent on location, although location can be important. In these theories, media texts are both objects found in locations and subjects dispersed throughout social discourse. One does not have to go to a *Rambo* film to be encouraged or appalled by the figure of Rambo. Rambo (at least in the U.S.) is a sign (one of many) of our times in the full semiotic sense. Our "exposure" to it is not specifically located; we can constitute what it signifies without that exposure; and we can use the sign in any isotopic fashion, well beyond the limits of the initial artistic invention.

By questioning exposure and location, the givens of attendance, frequency, and duration also come into question. It may be that "heavy" users of media are different from "light" users. But until we know what the practices of heavy and light use are and how they constitute the differences we observe, the distinction is of little explanatory value.

Meaning, methods of engagement, and interpretation are, of course, the center of study of social action research. An audience is constituted in the social action that accommodates mediated texts both as objects and subjects. Assumptions concerning meaning, engagement, and interpretation in the absence of empirical evidence would be recognized as an incomplete effort. While content may be analyzed, content is never the entry point into analysis.

What we have seen in this investigation of audience terms is that for traditionals, with their emphasis on content, the audience is often a neglected site of analysis. Social action theorists, on the other hand, center their analysis on the practices by which an audience comes into being (and perhaps neglect content). When a claim is made that an audience exists and that common interpretations result in its members, both text and audience explanations need to be present. As readers we should expect them.

ACCOMMODATION THEORY: A COMPARISON OF EVIDENCE AND METHODS OF STUDY

One's theory of the world establishes the questions one asks of it, the evidence that will be accepted as answers, and motivates an affinity toward certain methods of study. In the paragraphs that follow we consider these consequences as they appear in the traditional, interpretive, and social action theory sets.

TRADITIONAL Traditional effects theories move to objectify and, therefore, to separate both cause and effect from the circumstance of performance. This separation permits the study of classes of causes and effects. For example, learning can be considered a class of effects. If it can be demonstrated that learning (effect) occurs following exposure to content (cause) in a particular research protocol (context), the effect of learning can be generalized to any condition of exposure because traditional theories do not consider the context of performance as a significant element in explanation. As a result, evidence for the claim of a learning effect can be generated in any readily available situation—usually some controlled setting such as a classroom or laboratory.

Traditional theories, consequently, show an affinity toward survey and experimental methods of study. Surveys, as we have seen, examine the penetration of media into society, the frequency of attendance to media and their content, the distribution of content categories over types of individuals, and motives for, consequences of, and gratifications from attendance as dominant interests. Note that media, content, categories, types, motives, consequences, and gratification are all objectified, meaning that, say, the presence of a newspaper in a home of a given type has the same significance as its presence in any other home of that type.

We know that experimental methods manipulate controlled settings to determine if the presence of one variable in one configuration will have a different effect from its absence in another, presumably, in-all-other-ways equal configuration. This move is not nearly so difficult for critics as the next one in which the researcher claims that the experimental setting generalizes to all conditions (of interest) in which the variable is present (ecological validity). Traditional researchers make this claim on the belief that (1) content has a fixed value as a causal agent that transcends its location; (2) the criterion measure of the protocol is an element in a class of effects, elements of which also appear in the mundane setting of concern; and (3) the relationship between content as cause and behavior as effect is stable across context.

Because content and effects are objectified, traditional theories motivate little ethnographic analysis. Such analysis, in this perspective, is considered prescientific, helpful in developing good hypotheses and proper measures, but not in generating hard evidence.

INTERPRETIVE Most interpretive studies in media have developed out of a course of inquiry called cultural studies. This form of inquiry comes from critical traditions that hold that the object of inquiry is not simply discovery *but also direction toward the good.* The interpretive analyst gains position because of a superior insight into the text of our lives and a firm grasp of what ought to be—both to be demonstrated in the quality of the argument crafted. Inherent in this frame of analysis is rejection of the status quo or, at least, insistence on its modification for the better.

Critical methods, as the good mind reasoning well, have placed less emphasis on the process of or the collection of observations. The critical analyst typically draws observations from the surrounding territory, the scientist, or other "factual" sources and applies critical methods to the reasoning about these observations. Nonetheless, the last half-decade has seen a growing relationship between ethnography and criticism. Ethnography creates a text that must then be critically analyzed. Ethnography can also supply the observations from which social criticism can proceed. When they appear, ethnographic methods are most common in studies that make use of the concept of **interpretive communities** as the object of explanation. These communities, which may be the audience of a content genre, fellow ideologues and/or members of an organization, family, or other social grouping, provide the frame of interpretation by which members achieve a common interpretation that distinguishes them from nonmembers. Cultural studies generally, however, have not demonstrated a felt need for participant ethnography as the foundation of their argument.

Interpretive theories not of the cultural studies genre have generally arisen in response to felt defects of the "direct effects" viewpoint. As noted, these interpretive theories place an "active audience" within the relationship between content and effect. Both content and effect are still objectified and, therefore, can move across location, but the relationship between them is modified by the cognitive states, knowledge, skills, or intentions of the audience. These mediating cognitions are themselves considered objectively rather than historically. Questions asked from this stance then are similar to "What has to be known to properly interpret the given content?" or "How does this intention modify the interpretation of X content?" As you can see, this reasoning would have the same methodological affinities as the traditional.

Active audience theories offer a positive stance for the researcher concerned with the effects of media. By arguing that cognitive states can be interposed between content and effect, the consequences of exposure can be modified by inducing the proper cognitive state. One avenue for action, then, is to provide the necessary knowledge, skills, and attitudes through instruction in media literacy. Children can be taught the proper use of the media and, therefore, avoid their deleterious effects.

SOCIAL ACTION THEORIES Social action theories are concerned with the explanation of the relationship between self and other. While not everything of human interest, the scope of this concern is not inconsiderable, ranging over the fundamentals of language, all social relationships or referenced behavior. As we noted, social action will not explain the neuronic synapsis, but will deal with that concept as explanation. Questions of meaning are at the center of social action theories as meaning is a situated coproduction of text and action not the spasm of a cognitive reflex. When social action theories are turned to mediated communication, the questions addressed concern the empowerment of texts in action and the processes of reinvention of the premises of action that include the application of texts. Such questions would include the achievement of meaning, the manner in which mediated texts become significant in our lives, and the incorporation of mediated texts in the premises of action.

Accommodation Theory takes a particular stance in addressing these and similar questions by privileging an ongoing and organizing semiotic of social action in which we participate in mutually supervised, face-to-face relationships, locally improvising on cultural and communal themes of performance. Mediated texts are accommodated within these social action routines that are, in the main, both prior to and extant after the appearance of given texts. For Accommodation Theory, the organizing principle is not the text but the social action—the performance of the relationship between self and other as a valid expression of the mutually held theme(s) of performance; the focus can be on the relationship or the themes of performance but is often on the individual as a relating member, achieving understanding in interpretive performances; and the examination of effect is taken from the premises of the action in place.

Social action theories generally and Accommodation Theory especially adopt a phenomenological/ethnographic approach to the study of human interests. **Phenomenology** is an epistemological philosophy that claims that knowledge is an act of human consciousness, not a revelation or a discovery (see Traudt, Anderson, & Meyer, 1988). Modern phenomenologists have argued that knowledge claims are historicized human accomplishments produced for human purposes—that our understanding is in the grasp of human interpretation for the here and now. In moving these axioms to the study of social action, analysts claim that social reality is constructed and empowered by a set of partial, fragmented, often conflicted truths that arise in the action itself. A culture and the communities within it are the creators and keepers of their own truths. As these truths arise in the improvisations of members, the premises of social action are emergent, ongoing, and evolutionary.

The conclusion of this line of reasoning is that individual human behavior can be understood as a local production that is both a representation and improvisation of partial, fragmented, conflicted, emergent, ongoing, and evolutionary premises of action. Our understanding of human behavior will, therefore, be partial, fragmented, conflicted, emergent, ongoing, and evolutionary. In short, there will be no final statements on the progress of social reality as that reality is always in the process of becoming in one view and dissolving from another. This argument may appear to be disabling to the researcher, but there is a great deal of work to be done in the middle of things—work that will necessarily be done again and again as the premises of action evolve.

These phenomenological arguments generate two specific requirements for the study of social action: (1) Given that social action premises are the product of human endeavor, the proper site of study is everyday life. (2) Because the premises of social action are re-created in quotidian performances of relational members, we come to understand the premises by understanding how performances become valid expressions of them. These requirements invoke ethnographic methods as the primary means of study.

Phenomenologically based ethnography holds that the proper explanatory targets are the premises of action; the proper object of study is the performing individual situated within these premises; and the manner of accomplishment is through the achievement of a member's understanding. In practical terms, these suppositions state: (1) Premises of action arise only in true communities. (They do not arise in scientific aggregates like voters, children, romance readers, economic classes.) The first task of research is the identification of the membership of interest. (2) Our expertise extends only to the memberships we hold. (Without specific and systematic involvement, the academic elite cannot speak the truths of an underclass community.) The second task of research, then, is to gain access to and accomplish the terms of that membership. (3) The claims that can be made from any systematic study are themselves as partial, fractionated, conflicted as any member's performance would be and are—a characteristic most often ignored—infected by their academic context. (Science itself is a human practice.) The third task of research is to analyze reflexively its own text of claim. The well-done social action ethnography will show the research analyst in the field site for an extended period during which a substantial archive of field notes would be created. This archive would be used to develop a member's account of the premises of action that as a text of interpretation would be the object of critical analysis.

For social action theories, ethnography is the methodological center. Survey and experimental methods are used inside of or in support of the ethnographic claims (nearly the reverse of traditional approaches).[7] They are, nonetheless, used. For example, a study being conducted at the University of Utah hopes to show how mediated texts are used as utilities in the achievement of valid respondent performances in experimental protocols. This experiment uses the same computer animated text across its conditions but varies the premises of the context of response to show how text and context interpenetrate in interpretive performances. The purpose of the study is to support the social action argument that interpretive performances meanings do not transport across locations. If true, one would be cautioned against applying laboratory results to settings other than the laboratory.

Evidence for social action theories comes from the practices of self and other in the community of their jointly produced lives. For the empirical, social action analyst, the prime source of this evidence is the phenomenological ethnography. These methods require the analyst to become a member and report the terms of performance as a member to those of us who are not.

SUMMARY

In this investigation of evidence and methods, we have found that the perspective of any particular theoretical standpoint extends a view over far more than the scientific issues at hand. As we so clearly saw in Chapter 8, any theory also involves a worldview, an embedded set of notions that organize reality and determine what counts as evidence of claim. For the traditional theorist, the social world is organized around a set of social forces or influences that transcend time and place. Once these forces have been discovered and catalogued, their operation can be tracked in any communication situation.

For the interpretive as well as the social action theorist, the social world is a creation of human endeavor. That world is a historical world fully understandable only in its location. For most interpretivists, communication involves interpretation predictable along ideological lines. For the social action theorist, the practice of communication is organized around sets of premises that arise in social action and are re-created in local performances of interpretation. These premises are the property of communities (memberships) located in time and place.

Traditionals, therefore, direct their research toward the discovery of the "fixed" influences of communication; interpretivists, the critical examination of the ideological components of culture; and social action theorists, the community-owned premises of social action. Traditionals use experimental and survey methods in their search for discovery, interpretivists apply critical methods in their study of the cultural text, and social action theorists center ethnography as the method of illuminating premise from performance.

CENTRAL IDEAS OF SECTION II: ACCOMMODATION THEORY—IN COMPARISON

1. Traditionals require an objective text with fixed meaning characteristics to establish a causal agent. They avoid the idea of choice in order to create the individual as a set of reacting (rather than interpreting) components. These components constitute the self.
2. Interpretivists use different formulations of the nature of content to arrive at a condition that allows interpretive work to be conducted upon the text. Where that work gets done—locally or culturally—is a distinguishing mark. Constructionists empower the self to a greater degree than culturalists.
3. Social action theorists view text as an impetus for interpretation but the site is the localized social action performance. That interpretation is an improvisation directed by the routines under accomplishment. The self is discovered in relation to other.
4. The concept of audience gives a clear indication of the implications of the epistemic differences among these theories. Traditionals and most critical approaches use the terms of exposure, location, presence, duration, frequency, content meaning characteristics, common modes of engagement, and overdetermined interpretation to constitute the audience concept. Social action theorists see the audience as locally constituted in the methods by which mediated texts are accommodated in social action.
5. It is the traditionals move to separate cause from effect that creates the demand for an objective text and a reacting individual. That separation also invokes the use of experimental and survey methodologies.
6. Interpretive theories are of two separate branches: one arising out of cultural studies, the other in opposition to direct effects notions and in support of the active audience formulation. The first branch takes a critical approach directing inquiry toward the good. The second makes use of the entire spectrum of empirical methodologies in causal or descriptive explanations depending on their particular emphases.
7. Social action theorists locate interpretation in the social action in place and consequently hold that the community in everyday life is the site of analysis that privileges ethnographic methods.

SECTION III: ACCOMMODATION THEORY—SO WHAT?

This final section was motivated by a conversation overheard while walking across campus. A fellow was exclaiming to a woman walking by his side, "I'm so tired of theory! I've spent four years mired in theory—I want something real." This section, then, considers the "real" or at least practical implications of Accommodation Theory for the researcher, teacher, and citizen.

IMPLICATIONS FOR THE RESEARCHER

Accommodation Theory moves the causal agent of any effect from the characteristics of content to the local performance of interpretation in which meaning is achieved. Further, it holds that the effect, itself, is a product of the social action in which the mediated text is accommodated. This position has implications for the manner in which we interpret the claims attributed to the mediated communication literature and the methods we use in future studies.

REINTERPRETING THE LITERATURE The initial practical consequence of this theoretical stance is that much of the existing survey and experimental literature on effects has to be read with a new interpretation. For most experimental studies, the claim of external validity is never simply granted but involves the major burden of evidence. External validity in experimentation, remember, involves the belief that the protocol of the experiment can stand for—or provide information about—real world situations. Accommodation Theory, of course, would not support such a belief. An experiment is a "real world situation" all on its own for the respondents and experimenter alike. It is not a neutralized, invisible context that can be ignored. The protocol locates the performance. The effect measured is a product of that performance within that context.

Surveys are brought into question in two ways: First, the argument that the *statistical utility* of categorical aggregates (voters, college graduates, and the like) implies an *explanatory utility* is generally rejected. Explanatory utility is found in true memberships that involve relational systems of exchange rather than the exposure to a presumed set of common influences.[8] The different implications for explanation between memberships and categorical aggregates are as follows: With memberships, explanation is rooted in the observable practices of the relationship; with aggregate categories, explanation is based on the invisible influences created in the interaction between elements of the class and their social/physical environment. We are concerned with the practicing individual, not the individual as the vortex of swirling influences.

Second, the assumption that classes of action can be decontextualized and produce useful explanation is rejected. For example, the question, "How many hours do you spend watching television?" assumes that the hours so classified can be accumulated as belonging to the same class of activity. As we have argued, a given behavior such as watching television, can have radically different meanings in action. Treating each incidence of a behavior as the same denies or ignores the truth of the social action claim.

The net of these reinterpretations is that experimental studies demonstrate the possibilities of performance within social action, not the inevitable consequences of exposure to a particular content. It is certainly true that findings from some experimental studies are a matter of genuine concern. We have seen the findings of Zillmann and Bryant (1982) that exposure of undergraduate males to massive, concentrated doses of pornography in a setting in which degrading statements about women are permitted and accepted leads to an apparent lessened sensitivity to the crime of rape. What remains to be seen is whether the ordinary practice of the use of pornography supports the conditions that lead to this consequence. (Of course, if the goal is to ban pornography, then the Zillmann & Bryant findings may be enough for the campaign.) Experimental studies must be held in doubt until the boundaries of their application—their mundanity—can be determined in ethnographic analysis.

The "so what" directed toward survey literature is considerably more insistent. The most useful surveys are those conducted across a membership, coupled with an understanding of that membership's relevant premises of action. Most surveys are not of this sort. For example, survey studies have shown that television viewing peaks at about age 12, goes into rapid decline during the teens and twenties, and then begins a slow recovery to peak again in the fifties and sixties. It is, of course, not age that determines these changes but that the cultural practices for that age happen to serve as a marker. The survey has told hing about these but does offer suggestions of interesting points of entry into them. We now have thousands of such suggestions. It is, perhaps, time to get on with the real work of explanation.

METHODS OF STUDY For Accommodation Theory, media use is a practice nested inside the routines of everyday life. These routines are the consequence of the coordination of our jointly produced lives. Any performance is a local production by self in relation to other as improvised in accordance with the terms of performance held by the community, where the community of greatest import is that membership with supervisory ability.[9] An understanding of media use—its character, methods, causes, and consequences—requires the study of the improvisations as accountable to the communal premises. It is clear from this restatement that the most profitable methods of study are those that permit us to contact the improvisations of local performances in order to illuminate the premises of action. As we noted, the center is clearly held by ethnographic methods (see, Anderson, 1987), but surveys and experimentation have their place. The traditional literature has given us a full agenda of study. What are the practices of aggression within the memberships that support antisocial violence?[10] How are mediated texts accommodated within those practices? How do communities create the sex offender? How is pornography used within legitimated relationships? The list is long and interesting.

RE-CREATING THE INDIVIDUAL A final, and probably most difficult implication, is the need for a construction of a new conception of the individual to guide the understanding of human behavior. This is a call to move away from the concept of the autonomous, decontextualized individual that populates the majority of our research theories. This is not a new call. It is repeated here to underscore our woefully inadequate understanding of the force of relationship. It is always in relationship that the situated individual performs, and all individuals are situated in relationship. The pretense of our theories is to ignore the fundamental character of our nature.

IMPLICATIONS FOR THE TEACHER

More than anything, we have to come to a more sophisticated presentation of science and its claims in the classroom. Science is a practice of ordinary human endeavor; its claims, the historicized texts of cultural, economic, ideological, professional, and so on, instrumentality. To valorize the practice as apolitical (more precious than human) and to present its claims without the analysis of the unquestioned suppositions that enable those claims is simply irresponsible. Researchers—those of us who make our living off the practice of scientific study—should not be the sole proprietors of scientific education. We all need exposure to a philosopher and critic of science as well.

The elitist perspective of the common presentation of the "mass media" literature needs to be abandoned. Most of Meyer's and Anderson's students believe *both* that televised violence causes aggression and that the effect never happens to them. Most likely because it doesn't. What permits us to maintain the claims of the literature in ordinary fashion is that the claims refer to someone else—in fact, someone less, the young, the disadvantaged, the poor. A friend writes:

> I'm sitting in the audience of a prestigious telecommunications policy seminar. A handsome black woman sits next to me. The speakers are going on about how we must control the presentation of commercials for sugared-cereals because the poor spend their meager resources on these nutritionally inadequate foods. I turned to the woman and asked if that meant that we didn't fall for the commercial's pitch. She said, "It means, honey, that there aren't any poor in this place. Given what they have, the poor manage their lives very well, thank you."

The political character of the claim of effects must be addressed. The claims of science are just that: partial, fragmented, contested claims, infested with power, purpose, and politics.

We must also present the overwhelming value of these claims to the media themselves. Media managers approach the issue of effects in Januslike fashion. To the media regulators they present the face of "no harm." To their client advertisers and in the promotion of their programs to the audience, they present the face of great power. Advertisers are promised "customer results" and audiences "programs of gripping intensity" that in congressional hearings have no "measurable social consequences." Their temporizing in the view of regulators notwithstanding, the media claim for themselves great social power. For example, Anderson writes:

> My media effects class will meet at the television studio tonight. I have been asked to be a guest on another talk program exploring the effects of television. This guest shot is the third in six months in this market. The format is always the same: The host introduces the topic by working up a frenzy over the powerful effects of the medium. This night, the host claims that television was the primary reason that the civil rights campaign succeeded and that he is very proud of that success. I am outraged. In a single statement, this man had trivialized the years of effort and sacrifice by civil rights workers that made it possible to present the final drama on the air. For him, television discovered the injustice of racism and righted the wrong. But in truth, television presented the civil rights "wars" because it had to. It was forced to present them by the civil rights movement. The moth discovered the flame.

We, of course, are aware of similar claims being made about the Vietnam war, the Iran hostage episode, and the like. What these claims do is to position the media as powerful influences in society. What these claims ignore is the manner in which other elites influence both the content and the manner of presentation through economic and political power.

IMPLICATIONS FOR THE CITIZEN

Media enter our lives through the preexisting routines of social action. We will find media effects by examining the performances of those routines. The effects will occur when the claims of a commercial are used to justify some action; when the news reinforces our notions of what is right or wrong; when we use a television character as a way of describing an acquaintance; when our expectations of people, places, or things yet unexperienced are based on what we have seen, heard, or read; and when we use the signs or symbols of media to identify ourselves or others. The list of effects is potentially endless, limited only by our improvisational creativity.

Are there scenarios in which we are vulnerable to manipulation by mediated texts? Certainly, but the vulnerability is brought about by the social action routine, not the text itself. Our vulnerability appears in performance. Consider this: Consumer capitalism evokes Christmas shopping and the torrent of Christmas advertising, not the other way around. Successful Christmas products that are hard to obtain become a superior way for some to perform gifting—that complex contract of altruism and competition. For others, deliberately not giving that product is the more successful way. The performance of one or the other depends on the local relationship involved. Both choices, however, depend on the presence of a widely popular product and, therefore, both reveal their vulnerability to media texts. The stance of opposition often surrenders as much freedom as that of compliance.

News provides another example of this vulnerability. Technology's collapse of time and distance has permitted democratic governments to move many of their actions beyond the accounting of the voter. Complex arms transfers can be accomplished in a few days, but it may be years before voters can express themselves. The U.S. political system appears to have developed the "political scandal" as the method by which the myth of voter participation is continued. As the soap opera of news reports—perhaps, managed in the theater of congressional hearings—plays before us, appeals by opposing groups of political elites are made to what the public demands. Public opinion polls are brought into play as evidence of what the public wants. In truth, the public never speaks. One elite group or the other gains an advantage, and we—the audience—are declared the winners. We demonstrate our vulnerability to this myth when we congratulate ourselves.

Is this vulnerability a legitimate concern? Clearly, but the focus of our concern must not be on the media and their texts prematurely. Our vulnerability arises in our own practices, not through the force of an objectified media power or the inevitable persuasiveness of a text. The problem of young men trivializing crimes against women will not be solved by removing pornographic texts from distribution. The solution lies in our performance of gender. Censoring pornography may have its benefits, but the failure to understand the overarching control of social action has led most censorious efforts—on pornography, violence, materialism—to be dangerous deflections from the path of true reform. We are better seen as perpetrators than as victims.

CENTRAL IDEAS OF SECTION III: ACCOMMODATION THEORY—SO WHAT?

1. In considering research methodologies from the perspective of Accommodation Theory, experimental studies become places for the performance of a recognizable social action—the laboratory experiment. The consequences attributed to the conditions of the experiment have to be understood as a product of the protocol.
2. From the same perspective, surveys that cannot be located within a membership and the meanings held by that membership have little explanatory utility for the social action at hand.
3. Critical studies are the texts of a particular membership.
4. To grasp social action properly means to enter the field of everyday life and the communities that constitute the social realities in which we live.
5. The typical practice of the presentation of social science and its claims is deceptive.
6. Because we poorly understand the social action of audience communities, we also poorly understand the place of media within those communities.
7. We must be able to find ourselves—our performing, social selves—in our scientific explanations if they are to provide us with information of practical value.

CHAPTER SUMMARY

In examining the structure of Accommodation Theory, this chapter began with a review of the foundational assumptions about human life.

Human life was found in social action, defined as the expenditure of energy by one in relation to another. For social action theory, the individual is incomplete, realized in relational performance. Human life, therefore, arises in the community.

Attention was then turned to the terms of social action. Social action was defined as a referenced activity that is cooriented and coordinated with an other and appears in mutually supervised, improvisational performances that are under local control and are partial representations of communal themes. Social action is identified by the power of the relationship, the location of autonomy, the potential of supervision, and the accountability of performance. Social action is organized and understood in the routines of everyday life.

Human understanding was identified as an achievement within social action in which language plays the major role to punctuate the energy of the world. As an achievement, understanding has a location in a historical instrumentality.

The interpretation of mediated texts was seen as a performance of sense making, not the delivery of meaning. Sense making is, therefore, a situated action not a cognitive reflex.

The metaphor of accommodation of media and their texts was explained by positing overarching and preexisting routines of social action into which the media and their texts are incorporated. In the practices of media use and the adaptation of media texts, the routines are partially reinvented and an accommodation emerges.

The character of Accommodation Theory was then considered in relation to the pool of existing theories in the study of effects. The assumptions about cause and consequence, meaning, behavior, and the self of these theories as organized into three sets—traditional, interpretive, and social action—were considered.

We first applied our analysis of these theories to a consideration of their implications for a reconceptualization of the definition of a medium. We defined a medium as any recognizable human activity that organizes reality into readable texts for engagement. We identified the points of recognition as the medium's standing, technology, manner of organizing, texts, and enacting performances.

We then investigated the implications for a theory of the audience. We examined the classical heritage of the term as part of the physical and social site for public performance. We found its modern-day counterpart for critical approaches and traditionals to be built up out of the terms of exposure, location, presence, duration, frequency, content characteristics of meaning, common methods of engagement, and overdetermined interpretation. On the other hand, we found that social action theorists constitute the audience in the local practices of accommodation.

In the next section, the implications of the differing epistemic assumptions for the nature of evidence and the proper methods of study within theory were discussed. It was shown that traditionals use survey and experimental methods to discover the fixed influences of communication, interpretivists are concerned with the critical examination of the ideological components of media texts, and social action theorists seek the community-owned premises of local performances through ethnographic analysis.

In the final section, the implications for the researcher, the teacher, and the citizen were explored. For the researcher, Accommodation Theory directs a reinterpretation of the existing literature, generally, a change in the method of study, and a reconceptualization of the nature of the individual. For the teacher, Accommodation Theory implies a situated explanation of the practices of science and of the academy revealing the partial, fragmented, and contested claims of both. Finally, for the citizen, Accommodation Theory warns that reform of the media will require a reformation of our practices. The problems of our society are ours to own. Change for the better will inevitably mean change for all.

NOTES

1. We have been careful to use the plural in referring to the semiotics of interpretation. It is certainly true that language is the preeminent semiotic. Language, however, may not always be necessary and it certainly is not sufficient. Along with language, we have, at least, sensory imagery and the practiced performances of coordinated activity.

2. Metaphors for a propertyless world are difficult. We use the concept of energy because it is in the exchange of energy that we contact the world.

3. Consider, for example, how the paragraph might be positively read (not in opposition) by a social scientist, a semiotician, or an analyst from reader's criticism.

4. For the traditional, criminality is a state of mind induced through socialization processes or even preordained by genetics. The criminal mind—the cause of criminality—can be studied wherever it is handy, such as prison. For the social action theorist, criminality is a practice supported by society at large (typically identified as a necessary evil, like the poor) and locally performed within some community. Trying to understand the performance of criminal lives in society by studying incarcerated individuals, so the argument goes, is akin to an attempt to understand the natural lives of a species by its members in a zoo.

5. *Readable, texts,* and *engagement* are used in their most generic sense (e.g., *readable* means in some way interpretive).

6. The idea of a catalytic agent is one in which media content can evoke interpretive processes, themselves dependent upon agents other than content (ideology, social memberships, mutual accomplishments, and so on), and yet the content itself remains unchanged. This conceptualization allows the analyst to specify the evoking characteristics of the content from a position outside the social action field of interpretation.

7. For the social action theorist, laboratories are settings where effects are created (not discovered) in the same way as any other social action site. That a given laboratory protocol invokes a particular response is a demonstration of how to invoke that response (potentially a finding of great value), but not evidence of imaginary, determining forces.

8. We use the concept of membership to indicate any collection of individuals who reference one another and practice communicative exchange. Thus memberships include lovers, friends, families, clubs, churches, work organizations, and social groups, but ordinarily not cohorts of age, gender, class, or education.

9. In the analysis of the domestic media, this membership is the family for most individuals. The growing number of young adults who live alone are still supervised in even their solitary performances by friends and family through conversation and other performance demands.

10. The answer to the question of what is antisocial violence is itself a social action.

Glossary

ACHIEVEMENT: A term that recognizes that meanings, understandings, interpretations are all cognitive work in performance and not reflex.

AGENDA SETTING: The conceptualization of the media as a mechanism by which society has a common set of topics to act upon. The name given to the research on this mechanism.

AGGREGATE: To bring together a collection of elements with some common characteristic or characteristics in order to study the effects of the common trait(s). The collection itself.

ANDROGYNOUS: In the study of gender, the term refers to those who show both male and female characteristics of behavior.

ARTIFACT: The product of some process. In research, an artifact refers to outcomes that are explained by the research methods rather than the relationship between variables. Artifacts fail construct and external validity tests.

ASSIMILATION EFFECT: Arises in attitude studies of campaigns that look at positions of self and some candidate over a period of time. The assimilation effect is noted when the candidate's position is brought closer to the self-position. See also *contrast effect.*"

AUDITOR: The general term for an individual engaging a mediated text. A member of an audience.

BEHAVIORISM: A set of older theories in social science that focuses on observable, outcome behaviors and avoids explanations that involve cognitive processes. Directly opposite interpretive theories.

CANONICAL AUDIENCE: The audience as defined by a community of practitioners—the audience as it is presumed (ought to) be.

CASE STUDY: The study of a particular instance. Case studies differ from ethnographies in that they are generally considered preliminary descriptive work in support of later experimental work.

CAUSAL RELATIONSHIP: A relationship in which one condition is required for another condition to appear. The antecedent (or agent) must be sufficient and necessary for the consequent (outcome) to appear. See also *conditional relationship*.

CIRCULATION AUDIT: An analysis of the distribution of a newspaper or magazine sometimes coupled with the study of its readership.

CLOSED ENDED ITEMS: A standard measurement procedure that couples questions with possible answers. Respondents must select one of the offered answers as their own. See also *open-ended items*.

CLOSED TEXTS: Texts whose positioning in a context overdetermines their interpretation so that one or only a limited number of interpretations are sensible. See also *open texts, polysemic texts,* and *plasticity*.

CODES OF WORKMANSHIP: The understandings of how a job should be done. The set of expectations for what it means to do something.

COHORT SAMPLE: A sampling technique in which more than one sample is taken from the same population usually over time. Each sample is considered to vary from one another only in regard to the changes that have occurred in the population over the time span.

COMMODITY AUDIENCE: The product that is sold to advertisers in access sales systems. The commodity audience is made visible through some system of circulation measurement.

COMMODITY CONTENT: The product of a media industry.

COMMUNICANTS: Individuals engaged in communication—the mutual achievement of meaning.

COMMUNITY OF PRACTITIONERS: A membership that coconstructs and maintains a system of understandings of their performance and products.

CONDITIONAL RELATIONSHIP: A relationship that associates the appearance of one element with another. The first variable (the independent variable) may be a cause, a facilitator, or an index of the second (the dependent variable). See also *causal relationship*.

CONTENT ANALYSIS: A set of research procedures that codify the characteristics of a text, usually for quantitative analysis.

CONTRAST EFFECT: Arises in attitude studies of campaigns that look at positions of self and some candidate over a period of time. The contrast effect is noted when the candidate's position is pushed further away from the self-position. See also *assimilation effect*.

CONVENTION: A standardized presentation or characteristic of content.

CORRELATION: A statistical procedure in which two or more observations are collected on each element under study (e.g., time spent with television and time spent in reading). The observations are correlated when the place of one observation relative to its class is similar to the place of the other relative to its class. For example, television time and reading time would be positively correlated if individuals who spent a lot of time watching television also spent a lot of time reading. They would be negatively correlated if individuals who spent a lot of time watching television spent little time reading. They would show no correlation if those who spent a lot of time watching television showed no pattern (spent little or a lot of time) in reading.

COSMOLOGICAL: The grand scale. Cosmological explanations encompass the largest scope (e.g., astronomy and some branches of sociology).

CRITERION MEASURE: The measure of interest in a research protocol.

DETERMINED: An idea, generally in contradistinction to improvisation, which, as fully developed, states that any human behavior is fully explainable by exogenous and endogenous agents.

DISCOURSE ANALYSIS: The equivalent from critical methodologies of content analysis.

ECOLOGICAL VALIDITY: Along with *mundane realism,* one of the terms used for external validity that refers to the applicability of research outcomes to "real world" situations.

ECOLOGY: A set of relationships among animate and inanimate elements. In the study of mediated communication it is the the set of relationships among practitioners, consumers, technology, and so on.

EGALITARIAN STRUCTURE: A market structure in which there are few barriers to entry allowing a diversity of owners and ownership characteristics.

EMPIRICAL: Pertaining to that which can be experienced. Empirical methods are those that privilege direct observation.

EMPOWERMENT: The understandings that order action.

EMPIRICISM: A form of argument that bases its arguments in experience.

ENACTMENT: A term used to recognize characteristics of society that are the product of human work rather than the environment.

EPISTEMOLOGY: The study of our knowledge most often located in causal relationships.

ETHNOGRAPHER: One who studies the understandings and performances of members of a community.

ETHNOGRAPHIC NARRATIVE: The most common product of ethnography is the ethnographic narrative, which is the story of the coconstructed understandings and performances of community members.

ETHNOGRAPHY: The study that creates a written interpretation of the understandings and performances of a community.

FAIR TEST: One in which the relationship claimed for two or more variables can possibly fail.

FEDERAL COMMUNICATIONS COMMISSION: The regulatory agency of the broadcast and cable industries.

FEDERAL TRADE COMMISSION: A government regulatory agency of interest here because of its concern for advertising and trade practices.

FEMINISM: A body of writings and sociopolitical practices that see society as a sex/gender system that subjugates women and works for change.

FUNCTION: A word of multiple definitions in science but most often used in mediated communication to refer to purpose of some societal structure or personal act.

GENDER: The social practices by which the masculine and feminine domains are defined.

GENRE: A classification of texts that have common logics, conventions, and formats.

GRATIFICATIONS OBTAINED: In the uses and gratifications perspectives, they are the recognized outcomes of some episode of media use.

GRATIFICATIONS SOUGHT: In the uses and gratifications perspective, they are the recognized intentions of some episode of media use.

HEGEMONY: The relationship of power among elements in a social structure.

HISTORICIZED: The move to locate a concept in a time and place. The requirement that any human action must be in a context that becomes part of that action. The denial of the utility of decontextualizing such action in analysis.

HOMUNCULUS: The imaginary person inside the person who governs cognitive operations used to point out the weakness of such theorizing.

HORIZONTAL CONTROL: Pertaining to control of a product by the consumers.

HYPOTHETIC/DEDUCTIVE: A traditional form of research in which a general relationship is posed (hypothesized) and a particular instance deduced from it.

ICON: A type of sign that represents at least some characteristics of the signified.

IMITATION: In mediated communication, the behavioral response of mimicry or its approximation; the concern that individuals will mimic what they attend to in content.

IMPROVISATION: The idea that any performance of social action is accomplished in particular setting with local materials and cannot, therefore, be overdetermined. Improvisation allows for innovation and invention in performance.

IMPROVISATIONAL SPACE: The slack or free play allowed for local performances by the understandings of what is being done.

INDEXICAL: The term used to describe texts or performances that depend on and reference some larger domain of understanding for their own sensibility (e.g., "Nothing says lovin' like something from the oven.").

INDUCTIVE: A form of reasoning that moves from the particular to the general. Ethnography is inductive because it makes claims about general understandings from the specific practices of a community.

INNOVATION: As used here, it refers to development of modified social action understandings through performance.

INSTRUMENTALITY: The accomplishment, intended or not, of an understanding, performance, and so on, generally in reference to a larger social structure.

INTERPRETIVE COMMUNITY: A concept of interpretive theory that places individual interpretation inside the understandings held by some larger community. The community may be created in joint practice (as a membership) or by social forces (as a class). Social action theorists claim only the former as an interpretive community, critical theorists accept the latter.

LANGUAGE: A human invention that provides a recognizable system of interpretation.

LITERAL MEANING: A "conventional" meaning privileged by a community.

LOCAL CONTROL: A reference to the improvisations of particular actors in a performance of social action. Because of its improvisational manner, the course and outcome of these performances are found in the performances themselves.

MACROFUNCTIONAL: The instrumentality that accounts for and explains some societal (macro) structure.

MARXISM: A body of texts and social practices that sees society as a class structure (traditionally based on the control of the means of production) that results in the subjugation of those lower in the structure. As a critical study it works to relieve the harm of this economic subjugation.

MASTER IDENTITY: An understanding of the domain of some text or performance that governs or participates in the interpretation of the particular text or practice.

MATRIX TEXT: The term used to describe the larger view of the content of the media; the recognition that each element in the flow of content can be brought into relationship with one another.

MEDIATING FACTOR: In a research protocol or a theory, it is a construct that can modify or promote the outcome of a relationship between variables.

MICROFUNCTIONAL: The instrumentality that accounts for and explains some individual (micro) performance.

MIND/BODY DUALITY: The traditional (Judaic/Christian) separation of the physical from the cognitive (spiritual).

MULTISTAGED, STRATIFIED, AREA PROBABILITY SAMPLE: A procedure in which a sample is drawn in several steps (multistaged) based on physical locations (addresses) according to the relative proportion of such locations (probabilities) in the divisions of a geographical domain (stratified area).

NATURAL ATTITUDE: The transparent understandings that empower our actions. A term used by writers in ethnography and phenomenology.

NICHE: A location in an ecology that will support and protect its inhabitants. The metaphor for the creation of place for an element of an industry in its market.

OLIGOPOLY: A market structure in which restrictions on ownership create the conditions for all elements of an industry to be in the hands of a few owners. This structure usually results in direct competition and little diversity of product.

ONTOLOGY: The study of the nature of things.

OPEN-ENDED ITEMS: Questions in a survey that place few restrictions on the possible answers. See *closed-ended items.*

OPEN TEXTS: Texts that can participate in a number of contexts and therefore interpretations. See also *plasticity, closed texts,* and *polysemic texts.*

PARTIAL REPRESENTATION: A recognition that a performance is made sensible under broad cultural themes and is there for a partial representation of those themes.

PHENOMENA: Anything signified.

PHENOMENOLOGY: A philosophy describing the nature of human knowledge. The study of human life from this perspective.

PLASTICITY: A characteristic of texts that permits their participation in different contexts and interpretive performances. See also *open texts, closed texts,* and *polysemic texts.*

POLYSEMIC TEXTS: Texts that can be addressed on a multitude of levels because they are composites of different subtexts. See also *open texts, closed texts,* and *plasticity.*

POWER: Here, the ability to effect an outcome.

PRAGMATICS: The branch of semiotics that deals with the relationships between the sign and the interpreter. In communication, the branch of study that deals with the instrumentality (what can be done with or accomplished by) of communication.

PRAXIOLOGY: The study of performance.

PRODUCT DIFFERENTIATION: The separation of products of the same class by traits other than their primary performance (color, image, packaging, and the like).

PROTOCOL: The entire set of conditions surrounding a research study.

QUOTIDIAN: Everyday, ordinary. (Because of the perspective of this text we need many ways to call up the mundane.)

RATING: A value calculated in broadcast and cable circulation studies by taking the ratio of the actual measured audience over the possible audience.

RATIONALITY OF THE MARKET PLACE: The extent to which the performance of the market place can be predicted; its stability and lack of volatility.

READERSHIP AUDIT: An analysis of selected characteristics of an aggregate of consumers of a newspaper or magazine.

REDUCTIONISM: A line of reasoning prevalent in science that holds that the traits and characteristics of individual elements can be reduced to a smaller number of conditions that explain all of them (e.g., an individual's behavior can be explained by the his or her socialization history).

REFLEXIVE: The term used to describe the instrumentality of text or performance in maintaining the understanding that permitted the text or performance in the first place (e.g., any performance of a routine is a recognition and reinforcement of that understandings of that routine).

REPRESENTATIVE SAMPLE: A selection of elements from a population that shows all the characteristics of the population in the same proportion as the population.

REPRESENTATIVENESS: A quality of a sample or a simulation to stand for a population or mundane performance.

RULE: An understanding that governs performance.

RULES THEORY: A perspective that explains human behavior from the notion of a rule rather than fixed forces or cognitive reflexes.

SCALE: The size or scope of one domain relative to another.

SCENE: A term commonly used in ethnographic study to reference the recognized components of the setting, its properties and action.

SCHEMATA: Devices of cognition generally organized in some structure (e.g., schemata for interpreting televised texts).

SELF-REPORTS: A common device of survey measurement that relies on the statement of the respondent for the evidence of some variable rather than observation of it.

SEMANTIC FRAME: The constraints imposed by the circumstances of sense making on the interpretive process.

SEMIOTIC COMMUNITY: A membership that coconstructs and maintains common means of understanding.

SEMIOTIC SYSTEM: A system of knowledge that engages the world and makes sense of it.

SEMIOTICS: The study of the sign and signification in its semantic (the relation of the sign to its signifieds); syntactic (the relationships among signs) and pragmatic (the relationship of the sign to the interpreter) elements.

SENSE MAKING: An accomplishment of interpretation by which experience is in some way ordered and made coherent.

SIGN: Something that stands for something else to a cognizing entity.

SIGN SYSTEM: Signs that carry syntactic rules governing the relationships between them.

SIGNIFICATION: In communication, the fundamental cognitive process by which the experienced world is punctuated and referenced.

SIMPLE RANDOM SAMPLE: A sample drawn from a known population using methods that give all members an equal chance of being selected.

SIMULATION: The creation of a performative context to represent some mundane performance.

SOCIAL ACTION: The general term for the process of accomplishment of what is sensible to one and other.

SOCIOLOGICAL SCALE: The order of human interrelations from the individual to community to society to global village and beyond.

STAKEHOLDER: An individual or societal element with an interest in the performance of an industry.

STRUCTURATION: A term from Giddens (1985) that refers to the institutionalized interconnections enacted among elements in a system that reproduce that system. The methods by which a society provides for its good continuation.

SURROGATE: A substitute that represents the qualities of interest in a research study.

TECHNOLOGY: The knowledge, practices, devices, and texts that constitute the understanding of a domain of human action as seen from the perspective of the device itself.

TEXT: The term used to describe the bounded set of signs presented for interpretation.

THE OTHER: The generalized term for the individuals the self references in social action.

VERTICAL CONTROL: The condition in which use of a product is governed by the producer rather than the consumer. See *horizontal control*.

VERTICAL INTEGRATION: The condition in an industry in which the total process from resource to product is under the control of that industry or company.

VICARIOUS LEARNING: The technique of learning an action by watching another be rewarded for its performance.

Bibliography

Acker, S. R. (1983). Viewers perceptions of velocity and distance in televised events. *Human Communication Research, 9,* 335-348.

Adams, W. C. (1986). Whose lives count? TV coverage of natural disasters. *Journal of Communication, 36,* 113-122.

Adoni, A., & Mane, S. (1984). Media and the social construction of reality toward an integration of theory and research. *Communication Research, 11,* 323-340.

Adoni, H., Cohen, A., & Mane, S. (1984). Social reality and television news: Perceptual dimensions of social conflict in selected life areas. *Journal of Broadcasting, 28,* 33-49.

Alexander, A. (1985). Adolescents' soap opera viewing and relational perceptions. *Journal of Broadcasting and Electronic Media, 29,* 295-308.

Alexander, A., Ryan, M. S., & Munoz, P. (1984). Creating a learning context: Investigations on the interaction of siblings during television viewing. *Critical Studies in Mass Communication, 1,* 345-364.

Allen, R. (Ed.). (1987). *Channels of discourse: Television and contemporary criticism.* Chapel Hill: University of North Carolina Press.

Allen, R., & Hatchett, S. (1985). The media and social reality effects self- and system-orientation of blacks. *Communication Research,* 13, 97-123.

Altheide, D. L. (1985). Impact of format and ideology on TV news coverage of Iran. *Journalism Quarterly, 62,* 346-351.

Altheide, D. L., & Snow, R. P. (1979). *Media logic.* Beverly Hills, CA: Sage.

Altheide, D. L., & Snow, R. P. (1988). Toward a theory of mediation. In J. A. Anderson (Ed.), *Communication yearbook 11* (pp. 194-223). Newbury Park, CA: Sage.

Althusser, L. (1971). *Ideology and ideological state apparatuses. Lenin and philosophy and other essays* (T. B. Brewster, Trans.). New York: Monthly Review Press.

Althusser, L. (1979). *For Marx.* London: Verso.

Anderson, D. R., & Lorch, E. P. (1983). Looking at television: action or reaction. In J. Bryant & D. R. Anderson (Eds.), *Children's understanding of television* (p. 133). Hillsdale, NJ: Lawrence Erlbaum.

Anderson, J. A. (1971). *An analysis of the methodologies used in media credibility studies.* Paper presented at the International Communication Association convention, Phoenix.

Anderson, J. A. (1980). The theoretical lineages of critical viewing curricula. *Journal of Communication, 30,* 64-71.

Anderson, J. A. (1983). Television literacy and the critical viewer. In J. Bryant & D. R. Anderson (Eds.), *Children's understanding of television* (pp. 297-330). Hillsdale, N. J.: Lawrence Erlbaum.

Anderson J. A. (1984, May). *Forms of argument in naturalistic inquiry in communications.* Paper presented at the International Communication Association convention, San Francisco.

Anderson, J. A. (1987). *Communication research: Methods and issues.* New York: McGraw-Hill.

Anderson, J. A., & Avery, R. K. (1978). An analysis of changes in voter perceptions of candidates positions. *Communication Monographs, 45,* 354-361.

Anderson, J. A., & Avery, R. K. (1983). *The influence of cognitive styles on voter perceptions of presidential candidates.* Paper presented at the International Communication Association convention, Dallas.

Anderson, J. A., & Avery, R. K. (1988). *Reconceptualizing the audience: Media's rituals in the life of the audience: An ethnographic approach.* Paper presented at the Western Speech Communication Association convention, San Diego.

Anderson, J. A., Avery, R. K., Burnett Pettus, A., Dipaolo Congalton, J., & Eastman, S. T. (1985). *Voter rationales for candidate preferences: An analysis of conversational data.* Paper presented at the Speech Communication Association convention, Chicago.

Anderson, J. A., Avery, R. K., Burnett Pettus, A., Dipaolo Congalton, J., & Eastman, S. T. (1986). *Ideology and history in campaign conversations.* Paper presented at the International Communication Association convention, Chicago.

Anderson, J. A. & Meyer, T. P. (1973). *Man and communication.* Washington, DC: University Press of America.

Anderson, J. A., & Meyer, T. P. (1975). Functionalism and the mass media. *Journal of Broadcasting, 10,* 11-22.

Andreason, M. (1986). Attentional penchants and recall of information from background radio. *Journalism Quarterly, 63,* 24-30, 37.

Atkin, C. K. (1983). Effects of realistic TV violence versus fictional violence on aggression. *Journalism Quarterly, 60,* 615-621.

Atkin, C. K., & Greenberg, B. S. (1983). The portrayal of driving on television, 1975-80. *Journal of Communication, 33,* 44-55.

Atkin, C., K., Greenberg, B. S., & McDermott, S. (1983). Television and race role socialization. *Journalism Quarterly, 60,* 407-414.

Atkin, C., Hocking, J., & Block, M. (1984). Teenage drinking: Does advertising make a difference. *Journal of Communication, 34,* 157-167.

Atkin, D., & Littman, B. (1986). Network TV programming: Economics, audiences, and the ratings game, 1971-1986. *Journal of Communication, 36,* 32-50.

Atkin, C. L., Murray, J. P., & Nayman, O. B. (1971). *Televison and social behavior.* Washington DC: U.S. Government Printing Office.

Attalah, P. (1984). The unworthy discourse: Situation comedy in television. In W. D. Rowland, Jr., & B. Watkins (Eds.), *Interpreting television* (pp. 222-249). Newbury Park, CA: Sage.

Atwood, R. A., Zahn, S. B., & Webber, G. (1986). Perceptions of the traits of women on television. *Journal of Broadcasting and Electronic Media, 30,* 95-101.

Austin, B. A. (1984). Portrait of a film audience. *Journal of Communication, 34,* 74-87.

Austin, B. A., & Myers, J. W. (1984). Hearing impaired viewers of prime time television. *Journal of Communication, 34,* 60-71.

Babbie, E. R. (1979). *The practice of social research* (2nd ed.). Belmont, CA: Wadsworth.

Bakhtin, M. (1981). *The dialogic imagination.* Austin: University of Texas Press.

Bakhtin, M. (1986). The problems of speech genres. In C. Emerson & M. Holquist (Eds.), *Speech genres and other late essays* (V. W. McGee, Trans., pp. 60-102). Austin: University of Texas Press.

Ball-Rokeach, S. J. (1985). The origins of individual media-system dependency: A sociological framework. *Communication Research, 12,* 485-510.

Ball-Rokeach, S. J., & DeFleur, M. (1976). A dependency model of mass media effects. *Communication Research, 3,* 3-21.

Bandura, A. (1965). Influence of models' reinforcement contingencies on the acquisition of imitative responses. *Journal of Personality and Social Psychology, 1,* 589-595.

Bandura, A. (1969). *Principles of behavior modification.* New York: Holt, Rinehart, Winston.

Bandura, A. (1973). *Aggression: A social learning analysis.* Englewood Cliffs, NJ: Prentice-Hall.

Bandura, A. (1978). Social learning theory of aggression. *Journal of Communication, 28*(3), 12-29.

Bandura, A., Ross, D., & Ross, S. A. (1961). Transmission of aggression through imitation of aggressive models. *Journal of Abnormal and Social Psychology, 63,* 575-582.

Bandura, A., Ross, D., & Ross, S. A. (1963). Imitation of film-mediated aggressive models. *Journal of Abnormal and Social Psychology, 66,* 3-11.

Bantz, C. H. (1982). Exploring uses and gratifications: A comparison of reported uses of television and reported uses of favorite program type. *Communication Research, 9,* 352-379.

Baran, S. J., & Blasko, V. J. (1984). Social perceptions and the byproducts of advertising. *Journal of Communication, 34,* 12-20.

Baron, J. N., & Reiss, P. C. (1985a). Same time, next year: Aggregate analyses of the mass media and violent behavior. *American Sociological Review, 50,* 347-363.

Baron, J. N., & Reiss, P. C. (1985b). Reply to Phillips and Bollen. *American Sociological Review, 50,* 372-376.

Barthes, R. (1968a). *Elements of semiology* (A. Lavers & C. Smith, Trans.). New York: Hill & Wang.

Barthes, R. (1968b). *Writing degree zero* (A. Lavers & C. Smith, Trans.). New York: Hill & Wang.

Barthes, R. (1972). *Mythologies* (A. Lavers, Trans.). New York: Hill & Wang.

Barthes, R. (1974). *S/Z* (R. Miller, Trans.). New York: Hill & Wang.

Barthes, R. (1975). *Pleasure of the text* (R. Miller, Trans.). New York: Hill & Wang.

Barthes, R. (1977a). *Image-music-text* (S. Heath, Ed. & Trans.). London: Fontana.

Barthes, R. (1977b). An introduction to the structural analysis of narratives. In R. Barthes *Image-music-text* (S. Heath, Ed. & Trans., pp. 79-124). London: Fontana.

Barton, J. L., & Gregg, R. B. (1982). The Mid-East conflict as a TV news scenario: A formal analysis. *Journal of Communication, 32,* 172-185.

Barwise, T. P., Ahrenberg, A.S.C., & Goodhardt, G. J. (1982). Glued to the box?: Patterns of TV repeat viewing. *Journal of Communication, 32,* 22-29.

Baudrillard, J. (1975). *The mirror of production* (M. Poster, Trans.). St. Louis, MO: Telos.

Baudrillard, J. (1981). *For a critique of the political economy of the sign* (with an introduction by C. Levin, Trans.). St. Louis, MO: Telos.

Bauer, R. A. (1963). The initiative of the audience. *Journal of Advertising Research, 3,* 2-7.

Bauer, R. A. (1964). The obstinate audience. *American Psychologist, 19,* 319-328.

Bechtel R. B., Achelpohl, C., & Akers, R. (1971). Correlates between observed behavior and questionnaire responses on television viewing. In E. A. Rubinstein, G. A. Comstock, & J. P. Murray (Eds.), *Television and Social Behavior* (Vol. 4). Washington, DC: U.S. Government Printing Office.

Becker, H. S. (1982). *Art worlds.* Berkeley: University of California Press.

Becker, L. B. (1976). Two tests of media gratifications: Watergate and the 1974 election. *Journalism Quarterly, 53,* 28-33.

Becker, L. B., & Dunwoody, S. (1982). Media use, public affairs knowledge, and voting in a local election. *Journalism Quarterly, 59,* 212-218, 255.

Becker, L. B., & McLeod, J. M. (1976). Political consequences of agenda-setting. *Mass Communication Research. 3,* 8-15.

Becker, S. L. (1984). Marxist approaches to media studies: The British experience. *Critical Studies in Mass Communication, 1,* 66-80.

Bellah, R. N., Madsen, R., Sullivan, W. M., Swidler, A., & Tipton, S. M. (1985). *Habits of the heart.* Berkeley: University of California Press.

Belson, W. (1987). *Television violence and the adolescent boy*. London: Saxon House.
Bennett, L., Gressett, L. A., & Halton, W. (1985). Repairing the news: A case study of the news paradigm. *Journal of Communication, 35,* 50-68.
Bennett, W. L. (1983). *News: The politics of illusion.* New York: Longman.
Benton, M., & Frazier, P. J. (1976). The agenda-setting function of mass media at three levels of "information holding." *Communication Research, 3*(3), 261-274.
Berelson, B. (1959). The state of communication research. *Public Opinion Quarterly, 23,* 1-6.
Berger, A. A. (1981). Semiotics and TV. In R. P. Adler (Ed.), *Understanding television* (pp. 91-114). New York: Praeger.
Berger, P., & Luckmann, T. (1967). *The social construction of reality.* Garden City, NY: Anchor.
Berkowitz, L. (1962). Aggressions: A social learning analysis. New York: McGraw-Hill.
Berkowitz, L. (1965). The concept of aggressive drive: Some additional considerations. In L. Berkowitz (Ed.), *Advances in experimental social psychology 2* (pp. 301-330). New York: Academic Press.
Berkowitz, L. (1974). Some determinants of impulsive aggression: Role of mediated associations with reinforcements for aggression. *Psychological Review, 81,* 165-176.
Berkowitz, L. (1984). Some effects of thoughts on anti- and prosocial influences of media events: A cognitive-neoassociationist analysis. *Psychological Bulletin, 95,* 410-427.
Berkowitz, L. (1986). Situational influences on reactions to observed violence. *Journal of Social Issues, 43*(3), 93-106.
Berkowitz, L., & Alioto, J. (1973). The meaning of an observed event as a determinant of its aggressive consequences. *Journal of Personality and Social Psychology, 28,* 206-217.
Berkowitz, L., & Geen, R. G. (1966). Film and violence and the cue properties of available targets. *Journal of Personality and Social Psychology, 3,* 525-530.
Berkowitz, L., & Geen, R. G. (1967). Stimulus qualities of the target of aggression: A further study. *Journal of Personality and Social Psychology, 5,* 364-368.
Berkowitz, L., & Rawlings, E. (1963). Effects of film violence on inhibitions against subsequent aggression. *Journal of Abnormal and Social Psychology, 66,* 405-412.
Blumer, H. (1933). *Movies and conduct.* New York: Macmillan.
Blumer, H. (1969). *Symbolic interactionism.* Englewood Cliffs, NJ: Prentice-Hall.
Blumler, J. G. (1979). The role of theory in uses and gratifications studies. *Communication Research, 6,* 9-36.
Blumler, J. G. (1985). The social character of media gratifications. In K. E. Rosengren, L. A. Wenner, & P. Palmgreen (Eds.), *Media gratifications research: Current perspectives* (pp. 41-59). Beverly Hills, CA: Sage.
Blumler, J. G., Gurevitch, M., & Katz, E. (1985). Reaching out: A future for gratifications research. In K. E. Rosengren, L. A. Wenner, & P. Palmgreen (Eds.), *Media gratifications research: Current perspectives* (pp. 255-273). Beverly Hills, CA: Sage.
Blumler, J. G., & Katz, E. (Eds.). (1974). *The uses of mass communication: current perspectives on gratifications research.* Beverly Hills, CA: Sage.
Bogart, L. (1972). *Silent politics: Polls and the awareness of public opinion.* New York: Wiley-Interscience.
Bogart, L. (1985). How U.S. newspaper content is changing. *Journal of Communication, 35,* 82-90.
Bollen, K. A., & Phillips, D. P. (1982). Imitative suicides: A national study of the effects of television news stories. *American Sociological Review, 47,* 802-809.
Bourdieu, P. (1977). *Outline of a theory of practice* (R. Nice, Trans.). Cambridge: Cambridge University Press.
Bourgault, L. M. (1985). PTL Club and protestant viewers: An ethnographic study. *Journal of Communication, 35,* 132-148.
Bower, R. T. (1973). *Television and the public.* New York: Holt, Rinehart & Winston.
Bowers, T. A. (1973). Newspaper political advertising and the agenda-setting function. *Journalism Quarterly, 50,* 552-556.
Brannigan, A. (1987). Pornography and behavior: Alternative explanations. *Journal of Communication, 37,* 185-189.

Brannigan, A., & Goldenberg, S. (1987). The study of aggressive pornography: The vicissitudes of relevance. *Critical Studies in Mass Communication, 4,* 262-283.
Breed, W., & DeFoe, J. R. (1982). Effecting media change: The role of cooperative consultation on alcohol topics. *Journal of Communication, 32,* 88-99.
Breed, W., & Kitsanes, T. (1961). Pluralistic ignorance in the process of opinion formation. *Public Opinion Quarterly, 25,* 382-392.
Brooks, P. (1976). *The melodramatic imagination: Balzac, Henry James melodrama, and the mode of excess.* New Haven, CT: Yale University Press.
Brown, J. D., & Campbell, K. (1986). Race and gender in music videos: The same beat but a different drummer. *Journal of Communication, 36,* 94-106.
Brown, R. (Ed.). (1976). *Children and television.* Beverly Hills, CA: Sage.
Brunk, G. G., & Fiskin, J. A. (1982). Media coverage of presidential candidates: A study of popularity prior to the 1976 national nominating conventions. *Communication Research, 9,* 525-538.
Brunsdon, C. (1981). Crossroads: Notes on soap opera. *Screen 22, 4,* 32-7.
Brunsdon, C., & Morley, D. (1978). *Everyday television: Nationwide.* London: British Film Institute.
Bryant, J. (1986). The road most travelled: Yet another cultivation critique. *Journal of Broadcasting and Electronic Media, 30,* 231-244.
Bryant, J., & Anderson, D. R. (Eds.). (1983). *Children's understanding of television: Research on attention and comprehension.* New York: Academic Press.
Bryant, J., Brown, D., Parks, S., & Zillmann, D. (1983). Children's imitation of a ridiculed model. *Human Communication Research, 10,* 243-255.
Bryant, J., Carveth, R. A., & Brown, D. (1981). Television viewing and anxiety: An experimental examination: *Journal of Communication, 31,* 106-119.
Bryant, J., & Zillmann, D. (1984). Using television to alleviate boredom and stress: Selective exposure as a function of induced excitational states. *Journal of Broadcasting, 28,* 1-20.
Bryce, J. W., & Leichter, H. J. (1983). The family and television: Forms of mediation. *Journal of Family Issues, 4,* 309-328.
Buerkel-Rothfuss, N. L., Greenberg, B. S., Atkin, C. K., & Neuendorf, K. (1982). Learning about the family from television. *Journal of Communication, 32,* 191-201.
Burt, M. R. (1980). Cultural myths and support for rape. *Journal of Personality and Social Psychology, 38,* 217-230.
Bybee, C. R. (1982). Mobilizing information and reader involvement: An empirical test. *Journalism Quarterly, 59,* 399-405, 413.
Bybee, C., Robinson, D., & Turow, J. (1982). Determinants of parental guidance of children's television viewing for a special subgroup: Mass media scholars. *Journal of Broadcasting, 26,* 697-710.
Cantor, J., & Reilly, S. (1982). Adolescents' fright reactions to television and films. *Journal of Communication, 32,* 87-99.
Cantor, J., & Sparks, G. G. (1984). Children's fear responses to mass media: Testing some Piagetian predictions. *Journal of Communication, 34,* 90-103.
Cantor, J., & Wilson, B. J. (1984). Modifying fear responses to mass media in preschool and elementary school children. *Journal of Broadcasting, 28,* 431-433.
Cantor, J., Wilson, B. J., & Hoffnar, C. (1986). Emotional responses to a televised nuclear holocaust film. *Communication Research, 13,* 257-277.
Cantor, J., Ziemke, D., & Sparks, G. G. (1984). Effects of forewarning on emotional responses to a horror film. *Journal of Broadcasting and Electronic Media, 28,* 21-31.
Cantor, M. G., & Cantor, J. M. (1986). American television in the international marketplace. *Communication Research, 13,* 509-520.
Cantril, H., Gaudet, H., & Hertzog, R. (1940). *The invasion from Mars.* Princeton: Princeton University Press.
Carey, J. (1975). Communication and culture. *Communication Research, 2,* 173-191.
Carey, J. (1976). How media shape campaigns. *Journal of Communication, 26,* 50-57.

Carey, J. (1985). Overcoming resistance in cultural studies. *Mass communications review yearbook 5* (pp. 27-40). Beverly Hills: Sage.
Carey, J., & Jreiling, A. (1974). Popular culture and uses and gratifications: Notes toward an accommodation. In J. Blumler & E. Katz (Eds.), *The uses of mass communications: Current perspectives on gratifications research* (pp. 225-248). Beverly Hills, CA: Sage.
Carlson, J. M. (1983). Crime shows and viewing by preadults, the impact on attitudes towards civil liberties. *Communication Research, 10,* 529-552.
Carveth, R., & Alexander, A. (1985). Soap opera viewing motivations and the cultivation process. *Journal of Broadcasting and Electronic Media, 29,* 259-273.
Cater, D., & Strickland, S. (1975). *TV violence and the child: The evolution and fate of the Surgeon General's report.* New York: Russell Sage Foundation.
Caughie, J. (1984). Television criticism: A discourse in search of an object. *Screen 25,* 4/5, 109-120.
Cawelti, J. G. (1985). With the benefit of hindsight: Popular culture criticism. *Critical Studies in Mass Communication, 2,* 363-379.
Chaffee, S. H., & Hocheimer, J. L. (1985). The beginnings of political communication research in the United States: Origins of the "limited effects" model. In M. Gurevitch & M. R. Levy (Eds.), *Mass communication review yearbook 5* (pp. 75-104). Beverly Hills, CA: Sage.
Chaffee, S. H., & Miyo, Y. (1983). Selective exposure and the reinforcement hypothesis: An intergenerational panel study of the 1980 campaign. *Communication Research, 10,* 3-36.
Chaffee, S. H., & Wilson, D. G. (1977). Media rich, media poor: Two studies of diversity in agenda holding. *Journalism Quarterly, 54,* 466-476.
Chatman, S. (1978). *Story and discourse: Narrative structure in fiction and film.* Ithaca, NY: Cornell University Press.
Chesebro, J. W. (1984). The media reality: Epistemological functions of media in cultural systems. *Critical Studies in Mass Communication, 1,* 111-130.
Christ, W. G., & Medoff, N. J. (1984). Affective state and the selective exposure to and use of television. *Journal of Broadcasting, 28,* 51-63.
Christensen, F. (1987). Effects of pornography: The debate continues. *Journal of Communication, 37,* 186-187.
Christenson, P. G. (1982). Children's perceptions of TV commercials and products, the effect of PSAs. *Communication Research, 9,* 491-524.
Christenson, P. G., & DeBeneditis, P. (1986). Eavesdropping on the FM band: Children's use of radio. *Journal of Communication, 36,* 27-38.
Christenson, P. G., DeBeneditis, P., & Lindlof, T. R. (1985). Children's use of audio media. *Communication Research, 12,* 327-343.
Clancy-Hepburn, K., Hickey, A., & Nevill, G. (1974). Children's behavior responses to TV food advertisements. *Journal of Nutrition Education, 6,* 93-96.
Cline, V. B., Croft, R. G., & Courrier, S. (1973). Desensitization of children to television violence. *Journal of Personality and Social Psychology, 27,* 360-365.
Cobb, C. J. (1986). Patterns of newspaper readership among teenagers. *Communication Research, 13,* 299-326.
Cobb, R. W., & Elder, C. D. (1983). *Participation in American politics: The dynamics of agenda building* (2nd ed.). Baltimore: Johns Hopkins University Press.
Cohen, A., Adoni, H., & Drori, G. (1983). Adolescence perceptions of social conflicts in television news and social reality. *Human Communication Research, 10,* 203-225.
Collins, J., & Abel, J. D. (1985). Activation as news exposure predictor. *Journalism Quarterly, 62,* 316-320.
Collins, R., Curran, J., Garnham, N., Scannell, P., Schlesinger, P., & Sparks, C. (Eds.). (1986). *Media, culture and society: A critical reader.* Beverly Hills, CA: Sage.
Collins, W. A. (1973). Effect of temporal separation between motivation, aggression, and consequences: A developmental study. *Developmental Psychology, 8,* 215-221.
Collins, W. A. (1981). Recent advances in research on cognitive processing television viewing. *Journal of Broadcasting, 25,* 327-334.

Collins, W. A., & Wellman, H. M. (1982). Social scripts and developmental patterns in comprehension of televised narratives. *Communication Research, 9,* 380-398.

Compaigne, B. J. (1985). The expanding base of media competition. *Journal of Communication, 35,* 81-96.

Comstock, G. (1974). Review of S. Milgram and R. L. Shotland, *Television and antisocial behavior. Journal of Communication, 24*(3), 155-158.

Comstock, G. (1977). Types of portrayal and aggressive behavior. *Journal of Communication, 27*(3), 189-198.

Comstock, G. (1980a). New emphases in research on the effects of television and film violence. In E. L. Palmer & A. Dorr (Eds.), *Children and the faces of television: Teaching, violence, selling.* New York: Academic Press.

Comstock, G. (1980b). *Television in America.* Newbury Park, CA: Sage.

Comstock, G., Chaffee, S., Katzman, N., McCombs, M., & Roberts, D. (1978). *Television and human behavior.* New York: Columbia University Press.

Comstock, G. A., & Fisher, M. (1975). *Television and human behavior: A guide to the pertinent scientific literature.* Santa Monica, CA: Rand.

Cook, F. L., Tyler, T. R., Goetz, E. G., Gordon, M. T., Protess, D., Leff, D. R., & Molotch, H. L. (1983). Media and agenda-setting: Effects on the public, interest group leaders, policy makers, and policy. *Public Opinion Quarterly, 47,* 16-35.

Copeland, G. A., & Slater, D. (1985). Television, fantasy and vicarious catharsis. *Critical Studies in Mass Communication, 2,* 352-362.

Culbertson, H. M., & Stemple, G. H. III (1985). Media malaise: Explaining personal optimism and societal pessimism about health care. *Journal of Communication, 35,* 180-190.

Culbertson, H. M., & Stemple, G. H. III (1986). A media use and reliance affect knowledge level. *Communication Research, 13,* 579-602.

Cushman, D. (1977). The rules perspective as a theoretical basis for the study of human communication. *Communication Quarterly, 25,* 30-45.

Danowski, J. A., & Ruchinskas, J. E. (1983). Period, covert, and aging effects: A study of television exposure in presidential election campaigns, 1952-1980. *Communication Research, 10,* 77-96.

Davis, R. H., & Westbrook, G. J. (1985). Television in the lives of the elderly: Attitudes and opinions. *Journal of Broadcasting and Electronic Media, 29,* 209-214.

Davison, W. P. (1983). The third person effect in communication. *Public Opinion Quarterly, 47,* 1-15.

de Certeau, M. (1984). *The practice of everyday life* (S. F. Rendall, Trans.). Berkeley: University of California Press.

Dee, J. L. (1987). Media accountability for real-life violence: A case of negligence or free speech? *Journal of Communication, 37,* 106-138.

DeFleur, M. L. (1970). Theories of mass communication (2nd ed.). New York: David McKay.

DeFleur, M., & Ball-Rokeach, S. (1975). *Theories of mass communication.* New York: David McKay.

DeFleur, M. L., & Dennis, E. E. (1985). *Understanding mass communication* (2nd ed.). Boston: Houghton Mifflin.

Delia, J. (1977). Constructivism and the study of human communication. *Quarterly Journal of Speech, 63,* 66-83.

Deming, C. J. (1985). *Hill Street Blues* as narrative. *Critical Studies in Mass Communication, 2,* 1-22.

Deming, C. J. (1988). Toward a television-centered, television criticism: Lessons from feminism. In J. A. Anderson (Ed.), *Communication yearbook 11* (pp. 148-176). Newbury Park, CA: Sage.

Denisoff, R. S., & Bridges, J. (1982). Popular music: Who are the recording artists. *Journal of Communication, 32,* 132-142.

Dennis, J. (1986). Preadult learning of political independence: Media and family communication effects. *Communication Research, 13,* 401-433.

Derrida, J. (1978). *Writing and difference* (A. Bass, Trans.). Chicago: University of Chicago Press.
Dervin, B. (1987). The potential contribution of feminist scholarship to the field of communication. *Journal of Communication, 37,* 107-120.
Desmond, R. J., Singer, J. L., Singer, D. G., Kalam, R., & Colimore, K. (1985). Family mediation patterns and television viewing: Young children's use and grasp of the medium. *Human Communication Research, 11,* 461-480.
Diener, E., & DeFour, D. (1978). Does television violence enhance program popularity? *Journal of Personality and Social Psychology, 36,* 333-341.
Dienstbier, R. A. (1977). Sex and violence: Can research have it both ways? *Journal of Communication, 27*(3), 176-188.
Dimmick, J., & Rothenbuhler, E. (1984). The theory of the niche: Quantifying competition among media industries. *Journal of Communication, 34,* 103-119.
Dixon, N. F. (1981). *Preconscious processing.* Chichester, England: John Wiley.
Docherty, D., Morrison, D. E., & Tracey, M. (1986). The British film industry and the declining audience: Demythologizing the technological threat. *Journal of Communication, 36,* 27-39.
Dominick, J. R. (1984). Video games, television balance, and aggression in teenagers. *Journal of Communication, 34,* 136-147.
Donnerstein, E. (1980). Aggressive erotica and violence against women. *Journal of Personality and Social Psychology, 39*(2), 269-277.
Donnerstein, E., Donnerstein, M., & Barrett, G. (1976). Where is the facilitation of media violence? The effects of nonexposure and placement of anger arousal. *Journal of Research in Personality, 10,* 386-398.
Donohew, L., Palmgreen, P., & Rayburn, J. D. II (1987). Social and psychological origins of media use: A lifestyle analysis. *Journal of Broadcasting and Electronic Media, 31,* 255-278.
Donohue, T. R., Henke, L. L., & Meyer, T. P. (1983). Learning about television commercials: The impact of instructional units on children's perceptions of motive and intent. *Journal of Broadcasting, 27,* 251-261.
Doob, A. W., & MacDonald, G. E. (1979). Television viewing and fear of victimization: Is the relationship causal? *Journal of Personality and Social Psychology, 37,* 170-179.
Dorr, A. (1986). *Television and children: A special medium for a special audience.* Beverly Hills, CA: Sage.
Dorr, A., Graves, S. B., & Phelps, E. (1980). Television literacy for young children. *Journal of Communication, 30*(3), 71-83.
Drabman, R. A., Robertson, S. J., Patterson, J. N., Jarvie, G. J., Hammer, D. D., & Cordua, G. (1981). Children's perception of media portrayed sex roles. *Sex Roles, 7,* 379-389.
Drabman, R. S., & Thomas, M. H. (1977). Children's imitation of aggressive and prosocial behavior when viewing alone and in pairs. *Journal of Communication, 27*(3), 199-205.
Drew, D. G., & Reese, S. D. (1984). Children's learning from a television newscast. *Journalism Quarterly, 61,* 83-88.
Dubanoskiu, R. A., & Parton, D. A. (1971). Imitative aggression in children as a function of observing a human model. *Developmental Psychology, 4,* 489.
Dunwoody, S., & Ryan, M. (1985). Scientific barriers to the popularization of science and the mass media. *Journal of Communication, 35,* 26-42.
Durkin, K. (1984). Children's accounts of sex roles stereotypes in television. *Communication Research, 11,* 341-362.
Eco, U. (1979). *The role of the reader: Explorations in the semiotics of texts.* Bloomington: Indiana University Press.
Edelstein, A. (1973). Decision making and mass communication: A conceptual and methodological approach to public opinion. In P. Clarke (Ed.), *New models for communication research* (Vol. 2). Beverly Hills, CA: Sage.
Einsiedel, E. F., Salomone, K. L., & Schneider, F. P. (1984). Crime: Effects of media exposure and personal experience on issue salience. *Journalism Quarterly, 61,* 131-136.
Einstein, H. (1983). *Contemporary feminist thought.* Boston: G. K. Hall.

Elliott, W. R., & Slater, D. (1980). Exposure, experience, and perceived TV reality for adolescents. *Journalism Quarterly, 57,* 409-414, 431.
Epstein, E. J. (1973). *News from nowhere.* New York: Random House.
Eron, L. D. (1986). Interventions to mitigate the psychological effects of media violence on aggressive behavior. *Journal of Social Issues. 43*(3), 155-169.
Esserman, J. F. (Ed.). (1981). *Television advertising and children: Issues, research and findings.* New York: Child Research Service.
Faber, R. J., Meyer, T. P., & Miller, M. M. (1984). The effectiveness of health disclosures within children's television commercials. *Journal of Broadcasting, 28,* 463-476.
Faber, R. J., & O'Guinn, T. C. (1984). Effect of media advertising and other sources on movie selection. *Journalism Quarterly, 61,* 371-377.
Faber, R. J., Perloff, R. M., & Hawkins, R. P. (1982). Antecedents of children's comprehension of television advertising. *Journal of Broadcasting, 26,* 575-584.
Fallis, S. S., Fitzpatrick, M. A., & Friestad, M. S. (1985). Spouses discussion of television's portrayals of close relationships. *Communication Research, 12,* 59-81.
Feshbach, S. (1955). The drive reducing function of fantasy behavior. *Journal of Abnormal and Social Psychology, 50,* 3-11.
Feshbach, S. (1961). The stimulating versus cathartic effects of vicarious aggressive activity. *Journal of Abnormal and Social Psychology, 63,* 381-385.
Feshbach, S., & Singer, R. D. (1971). *Television and aggression.* San Francisco: Jossey-Bass.
Fetler, M. (1984). Television viewing and school achievement. *Journal of Communication, 34,* 104-118.
Fiske, J. (1986a). Television and popular culture: Reflections on British and Australian critical practice. *Critical Studies in Mass Communication, 3*(2), 200-216.
Fiske, J. (1986b). Television: Polysemy and popularity. *Critical Studies in Mass Communication, 3*(4), 391-408.
Fiske, J., & Hartley, J. (1978). *Reading television.* London: Methuen.
Foucault, M. (1972). *Archaeology of knowledge* (A. M. Sheridan-Smith, Trans.). New York: Pantheon.
Freedman, J. L. (1986). Television violence and aggression: A rejoinder. *Psychological Bulletin, 100*(3), 372-378.
Freimuth, V. A., Greenberg, R. H., De Witt, J., & Romano, R. (1984). Covering cancer: Newspapers and the public interest. *Journal of Communication, 34,* 62-73.
Friedrich-Cofer, L., Huston, A. C., & Huston, L. (1986). Television violence and aggression: The debate continues. *Psychological Bulletin, 100*(3), 364-371.
Frost, R., & Stauffer, J. (1987). The effects of social class, gender, and personality on physiological responses to filmed violence. *Journal of Communication, 37,* 29-45.
Fry, D. L., & Fry, V. H. (1985). Elements of a semiotic model for the study of mass communication. In M. McLaughlin (Ed.), *Communication yearbook 9.* Beverly Hills, CA: Sage.
Fry, D. L., & McCain, T. L. (1983). Community influentials' media dependence in dealing with a controversial local issue. *Journalism Quarterly, 60,* 458-463, 542.
Gaddy, G., & Pritchard, D. (1985). When watching religious TV is like attending church. *Journal of Communication, 35,* 123-131.
Gaddy, G. D., & Tanjong, N. (1986). Earthquake coverage by the Western press. *Journal of Communication, 36,* 105-112.
Gandy, O. H., Jr. (1982). *Beyond agenda-setting: Information subsidies and public policy.* Norwood, NJ: Ablex.
Gantz, W. (1983). The diffusion of news about the attempted Reagan assassination. *Journal of Communication, 33,* 56-66.
Gantz, W. (1985). Exploring the role of television in married life. *Journal of Broadcasting and Electronic Media, 29,* 65-78.
Gantz, W., Krendl, K., & Robertson, S. R. (1986). Diffusion of approximate news events. *Journalism Quarterly, 63,* 282-287.
Gantz, W., & Masland, J. (1986). Television as babysitter. *Journalism Quarterly, 63,* 530-536.

Gantz, W., & Razazahoori, A. (1982). The impact of television schedule changes on audience viewing behaviors. *Journalism Quarterly, 59,* 265-272.

Garramone, G. M. (1983). Issues versus image orientation and effects of political advertising. *Communication Research, 10,* 59-76.

Garramone, G. M. (1984). Audience motivation effects: More evidence. *Communication Research, 11,* 79-96.

Garramone, G. M. (1985). Motivation and selective attention to political information formats. *Journalism Quarterly, 62,* 37-44.

Gaziano, C., & McGrath, K. (1986). Measuring the concept of credibility. *Journalism Quarterly, 63,* 451-462.

Gazzaniga, M. S. (1985). *The social brain: Discovering the networks of the mind.* New York: Basic Books.

Geen, R. G. (1975). The meaning of observed violence: Real vs. fictional violence and consequent effects on aggression. *Journal of Research in Personality, 9,* 270-281.

Geen, R. G. (1976). Observing violence in the mass media: Implications of basic research. In R. G. Geen & E. C. O'Neal (Eds.), *Perspectives on aggression* (pp. 193-234). New York: Academic Press.

Geen, R. G. (1983). Aggression and television violence. In R. G. Geen & E. I. Donnerstein (Eds.), *Aggression: Theoretical and empirical reviews, issues in research* (Vol. 2, pp. 103-125). New York: Academic Press.

Geen, R. G., & Berkowitz, L. (1967). Some conditions facilitating the occurrence of aggression after the observation of violence. *Journal of Personality, 35,* 666-676.

Geen, R. G., & Stonner, D. (1973). Context effects in observed violence. *Journal of Personality and Social Psychology, 25,* 145-150.

Geen, R. G., & Stonner, D. (1974). The meaning of observed violence: effects on arousal and aggressive behavior. *Journal of Research in Personality, 8,* 55-63.

Geen, R. G., & Thomas, S. L. (1986). The immediate effects of media violence on behavior. *Journal of Social Issues, 42*(3), 7-27.

Geis, F. L., Brown, V., Jennings, J., & Corrado Taylor, D. (1984). Sex vs. status in sex associated stereotypes. *Sex Roles, 11,* 771-785.

Geis, F. L., Brown, V., Jennings, J. W., & Porter, N. (1984). TV commercials as achievement scripts for women. *Sex Roles, 10,* 513-525.

Gerbner, G., & Gross, L. (1976). Living with television. *Journal of Communication, 26,* 173-199.

Gerbner, G., Gross, L., Beeck, M. J., Jeffries-Fox, S., & Signorielli, N. (1978). Cultural indicators: Violence profile No. 11. *Journal of Communication, 28,* 176-207.

Gerbner, G., Gross, L., Eleey, M., Jackson-Beeck, M., Jeffries-Fox, S., & Signorielli, N. (1977). TV violence profile No. 8: The highlights. *Journal of Communication, 27*(3), 171-180.

Gerbner, G., Gross, L., Morgan, M., & Signorielli, N. (1980). The mainstreaming of America. *Journal of Communication, 30*(3), 10-29.

Gerbner, G., Gross, L., Signorielli, N., Morgan, M., & Jackson-Beeck, M. (1979). The demonstration of power: Violence profile No. 10. *Journal of Communication, 29*(3), 177-196.

Giddens, A. (1984). *The constitution of society: Outline of the theory of structuration.* Berkeley: University of California Press.

Gitlin, T. (1983). *Inside prime time.* New York: Pantheon.

Glynn, C. J., & McLeod, J. (1981). Implications of the spiral of silence theory for communication and public opinion research. In D. D. Nimmo & K. R. Sanders (Eds.), *Handbook of political communication.* Beverly Hills, CA: Sage.

Goldstein, A. (Ed.). (1983). *Prevention and control of aggression.* New York: Pergamon.

Goranson, R. E. (1970). Media violence and aggressive behavior: A review of experimental research. In L. Berkowitz (Ed.), *Advances in experimental social psychology* (Vol. 5, p. 131). New York: Academic Press.

Gordon, T. F., & Verna, M. E. (1978). *Mass communication effects and process: A comprehensive bibliography, 1950-1975.* Beverly Hills, CA: Sage.

Gormley, W. T., Jr. (1975). Newspaper agendas and political elites. *Journalism Quarterly, 52*, 304-308.

Graber, D. A. (1984). *Processing the news: How people tame the information tide.* New York: Longman.

Gramsci, A. (1971). *Prison notebooks.* London: Lawrence Wishart. (Original work published in 1927.)

Granzberg, G. (1982). Television, the story teller: The Algonquin Indians of central Canada. *Journal of Communication, 32*, 43-52.

Greenberg, B. S., & D'Alessio, D. (1985). Quantity and quality of sex in the soaps. *Journal of Broadcasting and Electronic Media, 29*, 309-321.

Greenberg, B. S., & Dominick, J. R. (1969). Racial and social class differences in teenagers' use of television. *Journal of Broadcasting, 13*, 331-344.

Greenberg, B. S., Neuendorf, K., Buerkel Rothfuss, N., & Henderson, L. (1982). The soaps: What's on and who cares? *Journal of Broadcasting, 26*, 519-535.

Gronbeck, B. E. (1984). *Writing television criticism.* Chicago: Science Research Associates.

Grossberg, L. (1984). Strategies of Marxist cultural interpretation. *Critical Studies in Mass Communication, 1*, 392-421.

Grossberg, L. (1986). Is there rock after punk? *Critical Studies in Mass Communication, 3*, 50-74.

Grotta, G. L., & Newsome, D. (1982). How does cable television in the home relate to other media use patterns? *Journalism Quarterly, 59*, 588-591, 609.

Guback, T. (1987). The evolution of the motion picture theater business in the 1980s. *Journal of Communication, 37*, 60-77.

Gumpert, G., & Cathcart, R. (1985). Media grammars, generations and media gaps. *Critical Studies in Mass Communication, 2*, 23-35.

Gunter, B. (1981). Measuring television violence: A review and suggestions for a new analytical perspective. *Current Psychological Reviews, 1*, 91-112.

Gunter, B., & Furnham, A. (1984). Perceptions of television violence: Effects of programme genre and physical form of violence. *British Journal of Social Psychology, 23*, 155-184.

Gunter, B., & Wober, M. (1982). Television viewing and perceptions of women on TV and in real life. *Current Psychological Research, 2*, 277-288.

Gurevitch, M., Bennett, T., Curran, J., & Woollacott, J. (Eds.). (1982). *Culture, society and media.* London: Methuen.

Habermas, J. (1984). *Theory of communicative action* (T. McCarthy, Trans.). Boston: Beacon.

Hackett, R. A. (1985). The hierarchy of access: Aspects of source bias in Canadian TV news. *Journalism Quarterly, 62*, 256-265, 277.

Hall, S. (1980). Encoding/decoding. In S. Hall, D. Hobson, A. Lowe, & P. Willis (Eds.), *Culture, media, language* (pp. 128-139). London: Hutchinson.

Hall, S. (1985). Signification, representation, ideology: Althusser and the poststructuralist debates. *Critical Studies in Mass Communication, 2*, 91-114.

Halloran, J. D. (1964). *The effects of mass communication.* Leicester: Leicester University Press.

Halmos, P. (Ed.). (1969). The sociology of mass media communicators. *Sociological Review Monographs, 13.*

Hardt, H. (in press). The return of the critical and the challenge of radical dissent: Critical theory, cultural studies, and American mass communication research. In J. A. Anderson (Ed.), *Communication Yearbook 12.* Newbury Park, CA: Sage.

Hartley, J. (1982). *Understanding news.* London: Methuen.

Hawkins, R. P. (1977). The dimensional structure of children's perceptions of television reality. *Communication Research, 4*, 299-320.

Hawkins, R. P., & Pingree, S. (1980). Some processes in the cultivation effect. *Communication Research, 7*, 193-226.

Hawkins, R. P., & Pingree, S. (1986). Activity in the effects of television on children. In J. Bryant & D. Zillmann (Eds.), *Perspectives on media effects.* Hillsdale, NJ: Lawrence Erlbaum.

Hawkins, R. P., Pingree, S., & Adler, I. (1987). Searching for cognitive processes in the cultivation effect: Adult and adolescent samples in the United States and Australia. *Human Communication Research, 13,* 553-577.

Hawkins, R., & Pingree, S. (1982). Television influence on social reality. In D. Pearl, L. Bouthilet, & J. Lazar (Eds.), *Television and behavior.* Rockville, MD: National Institute of Mental Health.

Heller, M. A. (1982). Semiology: A context for television criticism. *Journal of Broadcasting, 26,* 847-854.

Heller, M. S., & Polsky, S. (1975). *Studies in violence and television.* New York: American Broadcasting Company.

Henke, L. L. (1985). Perceptions and use of news media by college students. *Journal of Broadcasting and Electronic Media, 29,* 431-436.

Hennigan, K. M., DelRosario, M. L., Heath, L., Cook, T. D., Wharton, J. D., & Calder, B. J. (1982). Impact of the introduction of television crime in the United States: Empirical findings and theoretical implications. *Journal of Personality and Social Psychology, 42,* 461-477.

Herman, E. S. (1985). Diversity of news: "Marginalizing" the opposition. *Journal of Communication, 35,* 135-146.

Himmelweit, H. T., Vince, P., & Oppenheim, A. N. (1958). *Television and the child: An empirical study of the effects of television on the young.* London: Oxford University Press.

Hirsch, P. M. (1980). The "scary world" of the nonviewer and other anomalies: A reanalysis of Gerbner et al.'s findings on cultivation analysis. Part I. *Communication Research, 7,* 403-456.

Hirsch, P. M. (1985). U.S. cultural productions: The impact of ownership. *Journal of Communication, 35,* 110-121.

Hocking, J. G. (1982). Sports and spectators: Intraaudience effects. *Journal of Communication, 32,* 100-108.

Hodge, R., & Tripp, D. (1986). *Children and television: A semiotic approach.* Stanford, CA: Stanford University Press.

Hofstetter, C. R., & Strand, P. J. (1983). Mass media and political issue perceptions. *Journal of Broadcasting, 27,* 345-358.

Hölmlov, P. G. (1982). Motivation for reading different content domains. *Communication Research 9,* 314-320.

Hopple, G. W. (1982). International news coverage in two elite newspapers. *Journal of Communication, 32,* 61-74.

Houlberg, R. (1984). Local television news audience and the parasocial interaction. *Journal of Broadcasting, 28,* 423-429.

Hoveland, C., Lumsdane, A., & Sheffield, F. (1949). *Experiments on mass communications.* Princeton, NJ: Princeton University Press.

Howard, H. H. (1986). An update on cable ownership: 1985. *Journalism Quarterly, 63,* 706-709, 781.

Howitt, D., & Cumberbatch, G. (1974). Audience perceptions of violent television content. *Communications Research, 1,* 204-227.

Howitt, D., & Cumberbatch, G. (1975). *Mass media, violence and society.* London: Elek Science.

Hoyt, J. L. (1970). Effect of media violence "justification"on aggression. *Journal of Broadcasting, 14,* 455-464.

Huesmann, L. R. (1986). Psychological processes promoting the relation between exposure to media violence and aggressive behavior by the viewer. *Journal of Social Issues, 42*(3), 125-139.

Huesmann, L. R., & Eron, L. D. (Eds.). (1986). *Television and the aggressive child: A cross-national comparison.* Hillsdale, NJ: Lawrence Erlbaum.

Huesmann, L. R., Eron, L. D., Klein, R., Brice, P., & Fischer, P. (1983). Mitigating the imitation of aggressive behaviors by changing children's attitudes about media violence. *Journal of Personality and Social Psychology, 44,* 899-910.

Hughes, M. (1980). The fruits of cultivation analysis: A reexamination of the effects of television in fear of victimization, alienation and approval of violence. *Public Opinion Quarterly, 44,* 287-302.

Hur, K. K., & Robinson, J. P. (1981). A uses and gratifications analysis of viewing "Roots" in Britain. *Journalism Quarterly, 58,* 582-588.

Husson, W. (1982). Theoretical issues in the study of children's attention to television. *Communication Research, 9,* 323-351.

Huston, A. C., & Wright, J. C. (1983). Children's processing of television: The informative functions of formal features. In J. Bryant & D. R. Anderson (Eds.), *Children's understanding of television: Research on attention and comprehension* (pp. 35-68). New York: Academic Press.

Innis, R. E. (1985). *Semiotics: An introductory anthology.* Bloomington: University of Indiana Press.

Iwao, S., de Sola Pool, I., & Hagiwara, S. (1981). Japanese and U.S. media: Some cross-cultural insights into TV violence. *Journal of Communication, 31,* 28-36.

Iyengar, S. (1979). Television news and issue salience: A reexamination of the agenda-setting hypothesis. *American Politics Quarterly, 7,* 395-416.

Iyengar, S., & Kinder, D. R. (1987). *News that matters: Agenda-setting and priming in a television age.* Chicago: University of Chicago Press.

Izard, R. S. (1985). Public confidence in the news media. *Journalism Quarterly, 62,* 247-255.

Jackson-Beeck, M. (1979). Interpersonal and mass communication in children's political socialization. *Journalism Quarterly, 56,* 48-53.

James, N. C., & McCain, T. (1982). Television games preschool children play: Patterns, themes and uses. *Journal of Broadcasting, 26,* 783-800.

Jameson, F. (1981). *The political unconscious: Narrative as a socially symbolic act.* Ithaca, NY: Cornell University Press.

Jassem, H., & Glasser, T. L. (1983). Children, indecency and the perils of broadcasting: The "scared straight" case. *Journalism Quarterly, 60,* 509-512, 578.

Jensen, K. B. (1987). News as ideology: Economic statistics and political ritual in television network news. *Journal of Communication, 37,* 827.

Jhally, S., & Livant, B. (1986). Watching as working: The valorization of audience consciousness. *Journal of Communication, 36,* 124-143.

Johnson, C., & Gross, L. (1985). Mass media use by women in decision-making positions. *Journalism Quarterly, 62,* 850-854, 950.

Jowett, G. S. (1987). Propaganda and communication: The reemergence of a research tradition. *Journal of Communication, 37,* 97-114.

Kaid, L. L., Hale, K., & Williams, J. (1977). Media agenda-setting of a specific political event. *Journalism Quarterly, 54,* 584-587.

Kaiser, S. B., & Chandler, J. L. (1985). Older consumers' use of media for fashion information. *Journal of Broadcasting and Electronic Media, 29,* 201-207.

Kaminsky, S. M., & Mahan, J. H. (1985). *American television genres.* Chicago: Nelson Hall.

Kaplan, E. A. (Ed.). (1983). *Regarding television.* Los Angeles: American Film Institute/University Publications of America.

Katz, E., Gurevitch, M., & Hass, H. (1973). On the use of mass media for important things. *American Sociological Review, 38,* 164-181.

Katz, E., & Szecsko, T. (Eds.). (1980). *Mass media and social change.* Beverly Hills, CA: Sage.

Kellermann, K. (1985). Memory processes in media effects. *Communication Research, 12,* 83-131.

Kenny, D. A. (1984). The NBC study and television violence. *Journal of Communication, 34*(1), 176-182.

Kenrick, D. T., Stringfield, D. O., Wagenhals, W. L., Dahl, R. H., & Ransdell, H. J. (1980). Sex differences, androgyny, and approach responses to erotica: A new variation on the old volunteer problem. *Journal of Personality and Social Psychology, 38,* 517-524.

Kepplinger, H. M. (1982). Visual bias in television campaign coverage. *Communication Research, 9,* 432-446.

Kepplinger, H. M., & Ruth, H. (1979). Creating a crisis: German mass media and oil supply in 1973-74. *Public Opinion Quarterly, 43,* 285-296.

Klapper, J. T. (1960). *The effects of mass communication.* New York: Free Press.

Knight, G., & Dean, T. (1982). Myth in the structure of news. *Journal of Communication, 32,* 144-161.

Knutson, J. F. (Ed.). (1973). *Control of aggression: Implications from basic research.* Chicago: Aldine-Atherton.

Kraus, S., & Davis, D. K. (1976). *The effects of mass communication on political behavior.* University Park: Pennsylvania State University Press.

Kubey, R. W. (1986). Television news in everyday life: Coping with unstructured time. *Journal of Communication, 36,* 108-123.

Lacan, J. (1968). *The language of the self: The function of language in psychoanalysis* (A. Wilden, Trans.). New York: Dell.

Lain, L. B. (1986). Steps toward a comprehensive model of newspaper readership. *Journalism Quarterly, 63,* 67-74, 121.

Lang, G. E., & Lang, K. (1981). Watergate: An exploration of the agenda-building process. In G. C. Wilhoit & H. DeBock (Eds.), *Mass communication review yearbook 2* (pp. 447-468). Beverly Hills, CA: Sage.

Latimer, M. K., & Cotter, P. R. (1985). Effects of news measure on selection of state government news sources. *Journalism Quarterly, 62,* 31-36.

Lavine, G. F. (1986). Learned helplessness in local TV news. *Journalism Quarterly, 63,* 12-18, 23.

Lazersfeld, P. F., Berelson, B., & Gaudet, H. (1948). *The people's choice.* New York: Columbia University Press.

LeBon, G. (1893). *The crowd: A study of the popular mind.* London: Ernest Benn.

Lemert, J. B., & Ashman, M. J. (1983). Extent of mobilizing information in opinion and news magazines. *Journalism Quarterly, 60,* 657-662.

Lemert, J. B., Elliott, W. R., Nestbold, C. J., & Rarick, G. R. (1983). Effects of hearing a presidential primary debate: An experiment. *Communication Research, 10,* 155-173.

Lemish, D. (1982). The rules of viewing television in public places. *Journal of Broadcasting, 26,* 757-782.

Lemish, D. (1985). Soap opera viewing in college: A naturalistic inquiry. *Journal of Broadcasting and Electronic Media, 29,* 275-293.

Levy, M. (1983). Conceptualizing and measuring aspects of audience "activity." *Journalism Quarterly, 60,* 109-115.

Levy, M., & Fink, E. L. (1984). Home video recorders and the transience of television broadcasts. *Journal of Communication, 34,* 56-71.

Levy, M., & Windahl, S. (1984). Audience activity and gratifications: A conceptual clarification and exploration. *Communication Research, 11,* 51-78.

Leyens, J. P., Herman, G., & Dunand, M. (1982). The influence of an audience upon the reactions to filmed violence. *European Journal of Social Psychology, 12,* 131-142.

Leyens, J. P., & Parke, R. D. (1975). Aggressive slides can induce a weapons effect. *European Journal of Social Psychology, 5,* 229-236.

Lichtenstein, A., & Rosenfeld, L. B. (1983). Uses and misuses of gratifications research: An explication of media functions. *Communication Research, 10,* 97-109.

Lichtenstein, A., & Rosenfeld, L. B. (1984). Normative expectations and individual decisions concerning media gratification choices. *Communication Research, 11,* 393-413.

Liebert, D., Sprafkin, J., Liebert, R., & Rubinstein, E. (1977). Effects of television commercial disclaimers on the product expectations of children. *Journal of Communication, 27*(1), 118-124.

Liebert, R. M., & Baron, R. A. (1971). Short term effects of televised aggression on children's aggressive behavior. In J. P. Murray, E. A. Rubenstein, & G. A. Comstock (Eds.), *Television and Social behavior* (Vol. 2). Washington, DC: U.S. Government Printing Office.

Liebert, R., Cohen, L. A., Joyce, C., Murrel, S., Nisonoff, L., & Sonnenschein, S. (1977). Predispositions revisited. *Journal of Communication, 27*(3), 217-221.

Lindlof, T. R. (Ed.). (1987). *Natural audiences.* Norwood: NJ: Ablex.

Lindlof, T. R. (1988). Media audiences as interpretive communities. In J. A. Anderson (Ed.), *Communication Yearbook 11,* Newbury Park, CA: Sage.

Lindlof, T. R., & Meyer, T. P. (1987). Mediated communication as ways of seeing, acting and constructing culture: Its tools and foundations of qualitative research. In T. R. Lindloff (Ed.). *Natural audiences.* Norwood, NJ: Ablex.

Linz, D., Donnerstein, E., & Penrod, S. (1984). The effects of multiple exposures to film violence against women. *Journal of Communication, 34,* 130-147.

Lippmann, W. (1922). *Public opinion.* New York, Harcourt Brace.

Litman, B. R. (1982). The influence of the TV market. *Journal of Communication, 32,* 33-52. London: Sage.

Livingstone, S. M. (1987). The implicit representation of characters in Dallas. *Human Communication Research, 13,* 399-420.

Lowery, S., & DeFleur, M. L. (1987). *Milestones in mass communication research: Media effects* (2nd ed.). New York: Longman.

Loye, D., Gorney, R., & Steele, G. (1977). Effects of television: An experimental field study. *Journal of Communication, 27*(3), 206-216.

Lull, J. (1980a). Family communication patterns and the social uses of television. *Communication Research, 7,* 319-339.

Lull, J. (1980b). The social uses of television. *Human Communication Research, 6,* 197-209.

Lull, J. (1982a). A rules approach to the study of television and society. *Human Communication Research, 9,* 3-16.

Lull, J. (1982b). How families select televisions programs: A mass observational study. *Journal of Broadcasting, 26,* 801-812.

Lull, J. (1982c). Popular music: Resistance to new wave. *Journal of Communication, 32,* 121-131.

Luttbeg, N. (1983). News consensus: Do U.S. newspapers mirror society's happenings? *Journalism Quarterly, 60,* 484-488, 578.

Maccoby, E. E., Levin, H., & Selya, B. M. (1956). The effects of emotional arousal on the retention of film content: A failure to replicate. *Journal of Abnormal and Social Psychology, 53,* 373-374.

Mailloux, S. (1982). *Interpretive conventions.* Ithaca, NY: Cornell University Press.

Malamuth, N. M. (1983). Factors associated with rape as predictors of laboratory aggression against women. *Journal of Personality and Social Psychology, 45,* 432-442.

Malamuth, N. M., & Briere, J. (1986). Sexual violence in the media: Indirect effects on aggression against women. *Journal of Social Issues, 42*(3), 75-92.

Malamuth, N. M., & Check, J.V.P. (1981). The effects of mass media exposure on acceptance of violence against women: A field experiment. *Journal of Research in Personality, 15,* 436-446.

Malamuth, N. M., Haber, S., & Feshbach, S. (1980). Testing hypotheses regarding rape: Exposure to sexual violence, sex differences, and the "normality" of rapists. *Journal of Research in Personality, 14,* 121-137.

Malamuth, N. M., Heim, M., & Feshbach, S. (1980). Sexual responsiveness of college students to rape depictions: Inhibitory and disinhibitory effects. *Journal of Personality and Social Psychology, 38,* 399-408.

Mann, J., Berkowitz, L., Sidman, J., Starr, S., & West, S. (1974). Satiation of the transient stimulating effect of erotic films. *Journal of Personality and Social Psychology, 30,* 729-735.

Manning, S. A., & Taylor, D. A. (1975). The effects of viewed violence and aggression: Stimulation and catharsis. *Journal of Personality and Social Psychology, 31,* 180-188.

Marx, K., & Engels, F. (1970). *The German ideology* (C. J. Arthur, Ed. & Trans.). New York: International Publishers.

Mattes, J., & Cantor, J. (1982). Enhancing responses to television advertisements via the transfer of residual arousal from prior programming. *Journal of Broadcasting, 26,* 553-566.

McCall, G. J., & Simmons, J. L. (1978). *Identities and interactions.* New York: Free Press.

McCombs, M. E. (1976). Agenda-setting research: A bibliographic essay. *Political Communication Review, 1,* 1-7.

McCombs, M. E. (1977). Newspapers versus television: Mass communication effects across time. In D. L. Shaw & M. E. McCombs (Eds.), *The emergence of American political issues: The agenda-setting function of the press* (pp. 89-105). St. Paul, MN: West.

McCombs, M. E. (1981). The agenda-setting approach. In D. D. Nimmo & K. R. Sanders (Eds.), *Mass communication review yearbook 2* (pp. 219-224). Newbury Park, CA: Sage.

McCombs, M. E., & Gilbert (1986). News influences on our pictures of the world. In J. Bryant & D. Zillmann (Eds.), *Perspectives on media effects* (p. 115). Hillsdale, NJ: Lawrence Erlbaum.

McCombs, M. E., & Masel Waters, L. (1976). Agenda-setting: A perspective on mass communication. *Mass Communication Review, 3,* 3-7.

McCombs, M., & Poindexter, P. (1983). The duty to keep informed: News exposure and civic obligation. *Journal of Communication, 33,* 88-96.

McCombs, M. E., & Weaver, D. H. (1985). Toward a merger of gratifications and agenda-setting research. In K. E. Rosengren, L. A. Wenner, & P. Palmgreen (Eds.), *Media gratification research* (pp. 95-108). Beverly Hills, CA: Sage.

McDonald, D. G. (1983). Investigating assumptions of media dependency research. *Communication Research, 10,* 509-528.

McDonald, D. G. (1986). Generational aspects of television coviewing. *Journal of Broadcasting and Electronic Media, 30,* 75-85.

McIlwraith, R. D., & Josephson, W. L. (1985). Movies, books, music, and adult fantasy life. *Journal of Communication, 35,* 167-179.

McIlwraith, R. D., & Schalow, J. R. (1983). Adult fantasy life and patterns of media use. *Journal of Communication, 33,* 78-91.

McLeod, J. M., Bybee, C. R., & Durall, G. A. (1982). Evaluating media performance by gratifications sought and received. *Journalism Quarterly, 59,* 3-12, 59.

McLeod, J. M., Glynn, C. J., & McDonald, D. G. (1983). Issues and images: The influence of media reliance in voting decisions. *Communication Research, 10,* 37-58.

McLeod, J. M., & McDonald, D. G. (1985). Beyond simple exposure: Media orientations and their impact on political processes. *Communication Research, 12,* 3-33.

McQuail, D. (1969). *Towards a sociology of mass communication.* London: Collier-Macmillan.

McQuail, D. (Ed.). (1972). *Sociology of mass communications.* Harmondsworth: Penguin.

McQuail, D. (1983). *Mass communication theory.* Beverly Hills, CA: Sage.

McQuail, D. (1984). With the benefit of hindsight: Reflections on uses and gratifications research. *Critical Studies in Mass Communication, 1,* 177-193.

McQuail, D., & Windhahl, S. (1981). *Communication models for the study of mass communication.* New York: Longman.

Meadowcroft, J. M. (1986). Family communication patterns and political development: The child's role. *Communication Research, 13,* 603-624.

Meadowcroft, J. M., & McDonald, D. G. (1986). Meta analysis of research on children in the media: Atypical development? *Journalism Quarterly, 63,* 474-480.

Meehan, E. R. (1986). Conceptualizing culture as a commodity: The problem of television. *Critical Studies in Mass Communication, 3,* 448-457.

Mendelsohn, H. A. (1974). Comments on media violence research. *Public Opinion, 38,* 183-198.

Messaris, P., & Kerr, D. (1983). Mothers' comments about TV relation to family communication patterns. *Communication Research, 10,* 175-194.

Messaris, P., & Sarett, C. (1981). On the consequences of television-related parent-child interaction. *Human Communication Research, 7,* 226-244.

Meyer, M., & Nissen, U. (1981). *Effects and functions of television children and adolescents: A bibliography of selected research literature, 1970-1978.* Hamden, CT: Linnet Books.

Meyer, T. P. (1971). Some effects of real news film violence on the behavior of viewers. *Journal of Broadcasting, 15*(3), 275-285.

Meyer, T. P. (1972). Effects of viewing justified and unjustified real film violence on aggressive behavior. *Journal of Personality and Social Psychology, 23,* 21-29.

Meyer, T. P., Traudt, P. J., & Anderson, J. A. (1980). Nontraditional mass communication research methods: An overview of observational case studies of media use in natural settings. In D. Nimmo (Ed.), *Communication yearbook 4.* New Brunswick, NJ: Transaction Books.

Milgram, S., & Shotland, R. L. (1973). *Television and antisocial behavior: Field experiments.* New York: Academic Press.

Miller, M. M., & Reese, S. D. (1982). Media dependency as interaction, effects of exposure and a reliance on political activity and efficacy. *Communication Research, 9,* 227-248.

Miller, W. (1985). A view from the inside: Brain waves and television viewing. *Journalism Quarterly, 62,* 508-514.

Modleski, T. (1982). *Loving with a vengeance: Mass produced fantasies for women.* London: Methuen.

Modleski, T. (Ed.). (1986). *Studies in entertainment: Critical Approaches to mass culture.* Bloomington: Indiana University Press.

Moore, R. L., & Moschis, G. P. (1983). Role of mass media and the family and development of consumption norms. *Journalism Quarterly, 60,* 67-73.

Morgan, M. (1982). Television and adolescents' sex role stereotypes: A longitudinal study. *Journal of Personality and Social Psychology, 55,* 76-87.

Morgan, M. (1986a). Television and adults' verbal intelligence. *Journalism Quarterly, 63,* 537-541.

Morgan, M. (1986b). Television and the erosion of regional diversity. *Journal of Broadcasting and Electronic Media, 30,* 123-139.

Moriarity, S. F., & McGann, A. F. (1983). Nostalgia and consumer sentiment. *Journalism Quarterly, 60,* 81-86.

Morley, D. (1980). *The nationwide audience: Structure and decoding.* London: British Film Institute.

Morley, D. (1981). The nationwide audience—a critical postscript. *Screen Education, 39,* 3-14.

Morley, D. (1986). *Family television: Cultural power and domestic leisure.* London: Comedia.

Mosher, D. L., & Anderson, R. D. (1986). Macho personality, sexual aggression, and reactions to guided imagery of realistic rape. *Journal of Research in Personality, 20,* 77-94.

Mulac, A., Bradac, J. J., & Mann S. K. (1985). Male/female language differences and attributional consequences in children's television. *Human Communication Research, 11,* 481-506.

Muller, W., & Meyer, M. (Eds.). (1985). *Children and families watching television: A bibliography of research on viewing processes.* New York: K. G. Saur.

Mumby, D., & Spitzack, C. (1985). Ideology and television news: A metaphoric analysis of political stories. *Central States Speech Journal, 34*(3), 162-171.

Murray, J. P. (1980). *Television and youth: 25 years of research and controversy.* Boys' Town, NE: Boys' Town Center for the Study of Youth Development.

Nelson, C., & Grossberg, L. (Eds.). (1988). *Marxism and the interpretation of culture.* Urbana, IL: University of Chicago Press.

Newcomb, H. (1984). On the dialogic of aspects of mass communication. *Critical Studies in Mass Communication, 1*(1), 34-50.

Newcomb, H., & Alley, R. S. (1983). *The producer's medium: Conversations with creators of American TV.* New York: Oxford University Press.

Nimmo, D., & Combs, J. E. (1983). *Mediated political realities.* New York: Longman.

Noble, G. (1975). *Children in front of the small screen.* Beverly Hills and London: Sage.

Noelle-Neumann, E. (1974). The spiral of silence: A theory of public opinion. *Journal of Communication, 24,* 43-51.

Noelle-Neumann, E. (1977). Turbulences in the climate of opinion: Methodological applications of the spiral of silence theory. *Public Opinion Quarterly, 41,* 143-158.

Noelle-Neumann, E. (1979). Public opinion and the classical tradition: A reevaluation. *Public Opinion Quarterly, 43,* 143-156.

Noelle-Neumann, E. (1984a). The spiral of silence: A response. In K. R. Sanders, L. L. Kaid, & D. D. Nimmo (Eds.), *Political communication yearbook 1* (pp. 66-94). Carbondale: Southern Illinois University Press.

Noelle-Neumann, E. (1984b). *The spiral of silence: Public opinion our social skin.* Chicago: University of Chicago Press.

O'Gorman, H. J. (1975). Pluralistic ignorance and white estimates of white support for racial segregation. *Public Opinion Quarterly, 39,* 313-330.

O'Gorman, H. J. (1979). White and black perceptions of racial values. *Public Opinion Quarterly, 43,* 48-59.

O'Gorman, H. J., & Gary, S. L. (1976). Pluralistic ignorance: A replication and extension. *Public Opinion Quarterly, 40,* 449-458.

Pacanowsky, M. E., & Anderson, J. A. (1982). Cop talk and media use. *Journal of Broadcasting, 26,* 741-756.

Paine, D., & Caron, A. (1982). Anglophone Canadian and American mass media, use and effects on Quebecois adults. *Communication Research, 9,* 113-144.

Paletz, D. L., & Entman, R. M. (1981). *Media, power, politics.* New York: Free Press.

Palmgreen, P., & Clark, P. (1977). Agenda-setting with local and national issues. *Communication Research, 4,* 435-452.

Palmgreen, P., & Rayburn J. D. II (1982). Gratifications sought and media exposure and expectancy value model. *Communication Research, 9,* 561-580.

Parke, R. D., Berkowitz, L., Leyens, J. P., West, S. G., & Sebastian, R. J. (1977). Some effects of violent and nonviolent movies on the behavior of juvenile delinquents. In L. Berkowitz (Ed.), *Advances in experimental social psychology* (Vol. 10, pp. 135-171). New York: Academic Press.

Peirce, K. (1983). Relation between time spent viewing television and children's writing skills. *Journalism Quarterly, 60,* 445-448.

Perry, D. G., & Perry, L. C. (1976). Identification with film characters, covert aggressive verbalization, and reactions to film violence. *Journal of Research in Personality, 10,* 399-409.

Perse, E. M. (1986). Soap opera viewing patterns of college students and cultivation. *Journal of Broadcasting and Electronic Media, 30,* 175-193.

Peters, J. D. (1986). Institutional sources of intellectual poverty in communication research. *Communication Research, 13,* 527-559.

Peterson, E. E. (1987). Media consumption and girls who want to have fun. *Critical Studies in Mass Communication, 4,* 37-50.

Phillips, D. P. (1974). The influence of suggestions on suicide: Substantive and theoretical implications of the Werther effect. *American Sociological Review, 39,* 340-354.

Phillips, D. P. (1979). Suicide, motor vehicle fatalities, and the mass media: Evidence toward a theory of suggestion. *American Journal of Sociology, 84,* 1150-1174.

Phillips, D. P. (1982). The impact of fictional television stories on U.S. adult fatalities: New evidence on the effect of the mass media on violence. *American Journal of Sociology, 87,* 1340-1359.

Phillips, D. P. (1983). The impact of mass media violence on U.S. homicides. *American Sociological Review, 48,* 560-568.

Phillips, D. P., & Bollen, K. (1985). Same time, last year: Selective data dredging for negative findings. *American Sociological Review, 50,* 364-371.

Phillips, D. P., & Hensley, J. E. (1984). When violence is rewarded or punished: The impact of mass media stories on homicide. *Journal of Communication, 34*(3). 101-116.

Piccirillo, M. C. (1986). On the authenticity of televisual experience: A critical exploration of parasocial closure. *Critical Studies in Mass Communication, 3,* 337-355.

Pingree, S. (1983). Children's cognitive processing in constructing social reality. *Journalism Quarterly, 60,* 415-422.

Pingree, S. (1986). Children's activity and television comprehensibility. *Communication Research, 13,* 239-256.

Pingree, S., & Hawkins, R. P. (1982). What children do with television: Implications for communications research. In B. Dervin & M. Voight (Eds.), Progress in communication sciences (Vol. 3, pp. 225-244). New York: Ablex.

Pingree, S., with Hawkins, R. P., Rouner, D., Burns, J., Gikonyo, W., & Neuwirth, C. (1984). Another look at children's comprehension of television. *Communication Research, 11,* 477-496.

Pollay, R. W. (1984). The languishing of "Lydiametrics": The ineffectiveness of econometric research on advertising effects. *Journal of Communication, 34,* 8-23.

Potter, W. J. (1986). Perceived reality and the cultivation hypothesis. *Journal of Broadcasting and Electronic Media, 30,* 159-174.

Prasad, V. K., Rao, T. R., & Sheikh, A. A. (1978). Mother vs. commercial. *Journal of Communication, 28*(1), 91-96.

Pritchard, D. (1985). Race, homicide and newspapers. *Journalism Quarterly, 62,* 500-507.

Purloff, R. M., Wartella, E. A., & Becker, L. B. (1982). Increasing learning from TV news. *Journalism Quarterly, 59,* 83-86.

Radway, J. (1984). *Reading the romance: Feminism and the representation of women in popular culture.* Chapel Hill: University of North Carolina Press.

Radway, J. A. (1986). Identifying ideological seams: Mass culture, analytical method, and political practice. *Communication, 9,* 93-123.

Rayburn, J. D. II, & Palmgreen, P. (1984). Merging uses and gratifications and expectancy value theory. *Communication Research, 11,* 537-562.

Rayburn, J. D. II, Palmgreen, P., & Acker, T. (1984). Media gratifications and choosing the morning news program. *Journalism Quarterly, 61,* 149-156.

Reagan, J. (1984). Effects of cable television on news use. *Journalism Quarterly, 61,* 317-324.

Reeves, B., & Garramone, G. M. (1982). Children's person perception: The generalization from television people to real people. *Human Communication Research, 8,* 317-326.

Reeves, B., & Garramone, G. M. (1983). Television's influence on children's encoding of person information. *Human Communication Research, 10,* 257-268.

Reeves, B., & Thorson, E. (1986). Watching television: Experiments on the viewing process. *Communication Research, 13,* 343-361.

Reid, L. N., & Soley, L. C. (1982). Effects of imagery eliciting on recognition and recall for radio commercials. *Journal of Broadcasting, 26,* 567-574.

Reno, R. (1986, September 15). *The Salt Lake Tribune.* p. B-10.

Reynolds, P. D. (1979). *Ethical dilemmas and social science research.* San Francisco: Jossey-Bass.

Rimmer, T. (1986). Visual form complexity and TV news. *Communication Research, 13,* 221-238.

Roberts, D. F., Machen, C. M., Hornby, L. C., & Hernandez-Ramos, P. (1984). Reading and television, predictors of reading achievement at different age levels. *Communication Research, 11,* 9-49.

Rogers, E. M., & Chaffee, S. H. (1983). *Communications as an academic discipline: A dialogue. Journal of Communication, 3*(3), 18-30.

Roper, B. W. (1986). Evaluating polls with poll data. *Public Opinion Quarterly, 50,* 10-16.

Rosengren, K. E. (1983). Communication research: One paradigm, or four? *Journal of Communication, 33,* 185-207.

Rosengren, K. E. (1985). Growth of a research tradition: Some concluding remarks. In K. E. Rosengren, L. A. Wenner, & P. Palmgreen (Eds.), *Media gratifications research: Current perspectives* (pp. 275-285). Beverly Hills, CA: Sage.

Rosenthal, R. (1986). Media violence, antisocial behavior and the social consequences of small effects. *Journal of Social Issues, 42*(3), 141-154.

Rothenbuhler, E. W. (1986b, May). *The saliency of genre in identifications of television programs: Comparing college students and television critics.* Paper presented at the meeting of the International Communication Association, Chicago.

Rothenbuhler, E., & Dimmick, J. (1982). Popular music: Concentration and diversity in the industry 1974-1980. *Journal of Communication, 32,* 143-149.

Rothschild, M. L., Thorson, E., Reeves, B., Hirsch, J. E., & Goldstein R. (1986). EEG activity and the processing of television commercials. *Communication Research, 13,* 182-220.

Rowe, K. (1985). Swedish youth and music: Listening patterns and motivations. *Communication Research, 12,* 353-362.

Rowland, W., & Watkins, B. (Eds.). (1984). *Interpreting television: Current research perspectives.* Beverly Hills: Sage.

Rowland, W. D., Jr. (1983). *The politics of TV violence.* Beverly Hills, CA: Sage.

Rubin, A. M. (1979). Television use by children and adolescents. *Human Communication Research, 5,* 109-120.

Rubin, A. M. (1982). Directions in television and aging research. *Journal of Broadcasting, 26,* 537-551.

Rubin, A. M. (1983). Television uses and gratifications: The interaction of viewing patterns and motivations. *Journal of Broadcasting, 27,* 37-51.

Rubin, A. M. (1984). Ritualized and instrumental viewing. *Journal of Communication, 34,* 67-77.

Rubin, A. M. (1985). Media gratifications through the life cycle. In K. E. Rosengren, L. A. Wenner, & P. Palmgreen (Eds.). *Media gratifications research: Current perspectives* (pp. 195-208). Beverly Hills, CA: Sage.

Rubin, A. M. (1985). Use of daytime television soap operas by college students. *Journal of Broadcasting and Electronic Media, 29,* 241-258.

Rubin, A. M. (1986). Uses, gratifications, and media effects research. In J. Bryant & D. Zillmann (Eds.). *Perspectives on media effects* (pp. 281-302). Hillsdale, NJ: Lawrence Erlbaum.

Rubin, A. M., & Perse, E. M. (1987). Audience activity and soap opera involvement. *Human Communication Research, 14,* 246-268.

Rubin, A. M., Perse, E. M., & Powell, R. A. (1985). Loneliness, parasocial interaction, and local television news viewing. *Human Communication Research, 12,* 155-180.

Rubin, A. M., & Rubin, R. B. (1982a). Contextual age and television use. Human *Communication Research, 8,* 228-244.

Rubin, A. M., & Rubin, R. B. (1982b). Older persons TV viewing patterns and motivations. *Communication Research, 9,* 287-313.

Rubin, A. M., & Rubin, R. B. (1985). Interface of personal and mediated communication: A research agenda. *Critical Studies in Mass Communication, 2,* 36-53.

Rubin, R. B., Rubin, A. M., Perse, E. M., Armstrong, C., McQue, M., & Fiax, N. (1986). Media use and meaning of music video. *Journalism Quarterly, 63,* 353-359.

Rucker, B. W. (1982). Magazine and teenage reading skills: Two controlled field experiments. *Journalism Quarterly, 59,* 28-33.

Rule, B. G., Bisanz, G. L., & Kohn, M. (1985). Anatomy of a persuasion schema: Targets, goals and strategies. *Journal of Personality and Social Psychology, 48,* 1127-1140.

Rule, B. G., & Ferguson, T. J. (1986). The effects of media violence on attitudes, emotions, and cognitions. *Journal of Social Issues, 42*(3), 29-50.

Runco, M. A., & Bezdek, K. (1984). The effect of television and radio on children's creativity. *Human Communication Research, 11,* 109-120.

Ryan, M. (1982). Evaluating scholarly manuscripts in journalism and communications. *Journal of Broadcasting, 59,* 273-285.

Said, E. (1984). *The world, the text and the critic.* Cambridge, MA: Harvard University Press.

Salmon, C. T., & Kline, F. G. (1984). The spiral of silence ten years later: An examination and evaluation. In K. A. Sanders, L. L. Kaid, & D. D. Nimmo (Eds.), *Political communication yearbook 1* (pp. 331). Carbondale: Southern Illinois University Press.

Salomon, G. (1979). *Interaction of media, cognition, and learning.* San Francisco: Jossey-Bass.

Salomon, G., & Leigh, T. (1984). Predispositions about learning from print and television. *Journal of Communication, 34,* 119-135.

Sanday, P. R. (1979). The ethnographic paradigm(s). *Administrative Science Quarterly, 24,* 527-538.

Schiller, H. (1969). *Mass communication and the American empire.* New York: Augustus M. Kelly.

Schleifer, S. (1986). Trends in attitudes toward and participation in survey research. *Public Opinion Quarterly, 50,* 17-26.

Schmid, A. P., & De Graaf, J. (1982). *Violence as communication.* Beverly Hills, CA: Sage.

Schramm, W., & Chien, G. C. (1968). *Learning from television: What the research says.* Washington, DC: National Society of Professionals in Telecommunications.

Schramm, W., Lyle, J., & Parker, E. (1961). *Television in the lives of our children.* Stanford, CA: Stanford University Press.

Schudson, M. (1984). *Advertising, the uneasy persuasion: Its dubious impact on American society.* New York: Basic Books.

Schwichtenberg, C. (1987). Sensual surfaces and stylistic excess: The pleasure and politics of Miami Vice. *Journal of Communication Inquiry, 10*(3), 45-65.

Selnow, G. W. (1984). Playing video games: The electronic friend. *Journal of Communication, 34,* 148-156.

Selnow, G. W. (1986). Solving problems on prime time television. *Journal of Communication, 36,* 63-72.

Selnow, G. W., & Bettinghaus, E. P. (1982). Television exposure and language development. *Journal of Broadcasting, 26,* 469-479.

Selnow, G. W., & Reynolds, H. (1984). Some opportunity costs of television viewing. *Journal of Broadcasting, 28,* 315-322.

Sharits, N., & Lammers, B. H. (1983). Perceived attributes of models in prime-time and daytime television commercials: A person perception approach. *Journal of Marketing Research, 20,* 64-73.

Shatzer, M. J., Korzenny, F., & Griffiths-Korzenny, M. A. (1985). Adolescent viewing "Shogun": Cognitive and attitudinal effects. *Journal of Broadcasting and Electronic Media, 29,* 341-346.

Shaw, D. L., & McCombs, M. E. (Eds.). (1977). *The emergence of American political issues: The agenda-setting function of the press.* St. Paul, MN: West.

Sherman, B. L., & Dominick, J. R. (1986). Mix in music videos: TV and rock "n" roll. *Journal of Communication, 36,* 79-93.

Shimanoff, S. (1980). *Communication rules.* Beverly Hills, CA: Sage.

Shoemaker, P. J. (1982). The perceived legitimacy of deviant political groups: Two experiments on media effects. *Communication Research, 9,* 249-286.

Shoemaker, P. J. (1987). Mass communication by the book: A review of 31 texts. *Journal of Communication, 37,* 109-131.

Showalter, E. (1985). *The new feminist criticism: Essays on women, literature and theory.* New York: Pantheon.

Sigman, S. (1980). On communication rules from a social perspective. *Human Communication Research, 7,* 37-51.

Sigman, S. J., & Fry, D. L. (1985). Differential ideology and language use: Readers' reconstructions and descriptions of news events. *Critical Studies in Mass Communication, 2,* 307-322.

Signorielli, N. (1982). Marital status and television drama: A case of reduced options. *Journal of Broadcasting, 26,* 585-597.

Signorielli, N. (1986). Selective television viewing: A limited possibility. *Journal of Communication, 36,* 64-76.

Silverman, K. (1983). The subject of semiotics. Oxford: Oxford University Press.

Silverman-Watkins, T., Levi, S. C., & Klein, M. A. (1986). Sex stereotyping as factor in children's comprehension of television news. *Journalism Quarterly, 63,* 311.

Singer, B. D. (1973). Feedback and society: A study of the uses of mass channels for coping. Lexington, MA: Heath.

Singer, J. L., & Singer, D. G. (1981). *Television, imagination, and aggression: A study of preschoolers.* Hillsdale, NJ: Lawrence Erlbaum.

Singer, J. L., Singer, D. G., & Rapaczynski, W. S. (1984). Family patterns and television viewing as predictors of children's beliefs and aggression. *Journal of Communication, 34*(3), 73-89.

Slater, D., & Elliott, W. R. (1982). Television's influence on social reality. *Quarterly Journal of Speech, 68,* 69-79.

Soley, L. C., & Reed, L. N. (1985). Baiting viewers: Violence and sex in television program advertisements. *Journalism Quarterly, 62,* 105-110, 131.

Sommer, R., & Pilisuk, T. (1982). Pesticide advertising in farm journals. *Journal of Communication, 32,* 37-42.

Sontag, S. (Ed.). (1983). *Barthes: Selected writings.* London: Fontana/Collins.

Sparks, G. J., & Cantor, J. (1986). Developmental differences in fright responses to a television program depicting a character transformation. *Journal of Broadcasting and Electronic Media, 30,* 309-323.

Sparks, G. L., & Fehlner, C. L. (1986). Faces in the news: Gender comparison of magazine photographs. *Journal of Communication, 36,* 70-79.

Sprafkin, J. N., Liebert, R. M., & Poulos, R. W. (1975). Effects of prosocial televised example on children's helping. *Journal of Experimental Child Psychology, 20*(1), 119-126.

Sreberny-Mohammadi, A. (1984). The "world of news" study. *Journal of Communication, 34,* 121-133.

Stamm, K. R. (1987). Cognitive strategies and communication during a presidential campaign. *Communication Research, 14,* 35-57.

Stanford, S. W. (1984). Predicting favorite TV program gratifications from general orientations. *Communication Research, 11,* 419-536.

Stanford, S., & Riccomini, B. (1984). Linking TV program orientations and gratifications: An experimental approach. *Journalism Quarterly, 61,* 76-82.

Stauffer, J., Frost, R., & Rybolt, W. (1983). The attention factor in recalling network television news. *Journal of Communication, 33,* 29-37.

Steiner, G. (1963). *The people look at television: A study of audience attitudes.* New York: Knopf.

Steuer, F. B., Applefield, J. M., & Smith, R. (1971). Televised aggression and the interpersonal aggression of preschool children. *Journal of Experimental Child Psychology, 11,* 442-447.

Streeter, T. (1986, May). *Polysemy, plurality, and media studies.* Paper presented at the meting of the International Communication Association, Chicago.

Strodthoff, G. C., Hawkins, R. P., & Schoenfeld, A. C. (1985). Media roles in a social movement: A model of ideology diffusion. *Journal of Communication, 35,* 134-153.

Stroman, C. A. Television viewing and self-concept among black children. *Journal of Broadcasting and Electronic Media, 30,* 87-93.

Stroman, C. A., & Seltzer, R. (1985). Media use and perceptions of crime. *Journalism Quarterly, 62,* 340-345.

Sun, S., & Lull, J. (1986). The adolescent audience for music videos and why they watch. *Journal of Communication, 36,* 115-125.

Surette, R. (1985). Television viewing in support of punitive criminal justice policy. *Journalism Quarterly, 62,* 373-377, 450.

Surgeon General's Scientific Advisory Committee on Television and Social Behavior. (1971). *Television and growing up: The impact of televised violence.* Washington, DC: U.S. Government Printing Office.

Sutherland, J. C., & Siniasky, S. J. (1982). The treatment and resolution of moral violations on soap operas. *Journal of Communication, 32,* 67-74.

Swanson, D. L. (1981). A constructivist approach. In D. D. Nimmo & K. R. Sanders (Eds.). *Handbook of political communication.* Beverly Hills, CA: Sage.

Swanson, L. L., & Swanson, D. L. (1978). The agenda-setting function of the first Ford-Carter debate. *Communication Monographs, 45,* 330-353.

Tamborini, R., Zillmann, D., & Bryant, J. (1984). Fear and victimization: Exposure to television and perceptions of crime and fear. In R. N. Bostrom (Ed.), *Communication yearbook 8* (pp. 492-513). Beverly Hills, CA: Sage.

Tan, A. S., & Tan, G. (1986). Television news and mental health. *Journalism Quarterly, 63,* 106-113.

Tanker, J. W., Jr., Chang, T., & Tsang, K. (1984). Citation networks as indicators of journalism research activity. *Journalism Quarterly, 61,* 89-96, 124.

Tarde, G. D. (1969). *On communication and social influence: Selected papers* (T. N. Clark, Ed.). Chicago: University of Chicago Press.

Taylor, D. G. (1982). Pluralistic ignorance and the spiral of silence: A formal analysis. *Public Opinion Quarterly, 46,* 311-335.

Thomas, M. H. (1982). Physiological arousal, exposure to a relatively lengthy aggressive film and aggressive behavior. *Journal of Research in Personality, 16,* 72-81.

Thomas, M. H., Horton, R. W., Lippincott, E. C., & Drabman, R. S. (1977). Desensitization to portrayal of real-life aggression as a function of exposure to television violence. *Journal of Personality and Social Psychology, 35,* 450-458.

Thomas, M. H., & Tell, P. M. (1974). Effects of viewing real versus fantasy violence upon interpersonal aggression. *Journal of Research in Personality, 8,* 153-160.

Thomas, S. (1985). The route to redemption: Religion and social class. *Journal of Communication, 35,* 111-122.

Thomas, S., & Callahan, B. P. (1982). Allocating happiness: TV families and social class. *Journal of Communication, 32,* 184-190.

Thorburn, D. (1981). Television melodrama. In R. P. Adler (Ed.), *Understanding television* (pp. 73-90). New York: Praeger.

Thorburn, D. (1982). Television melodrama. In H. Newcomb (Ed.), *Television: The critical view* (3rd ed.; pp. 529-546, original work published in 1976). New York: Oxford University Press.

Tichenor, P. J., & Wackman, D. B. (1973). Mass media and community public opinion. *American Behavioral Scientist, 16,* 593-606.

Tiedge, J. T., & Ksobiech, K. (1986). The "lead-in" strategy for prime time TV: Does it increase the audience? *Journal of Communication, 36,* 51-63.

Traudt, P. J., Anderson, J. A., & Meyer, T. P. (1987). Phenomenology, empiricism, and media experience. *Critical Studies in Mass Communication, 4,* 302-310.

Turner, C. W., & Berkowitz, L. (1972). Identification with film aggressor (covert role taking) and reactions to film violence. *Journal of Personality and Social Psychology, 21,* 256-264.

Turner, C. W., Hesse, B. W., & Peterson Lewis, S. (1986). Naturalistic studies of the long-term effects of television violence. *Journal of Social Issues, 42*(3), 51-73.

Turow, J. (1983). Local television: Producing soft news. *Journal of Communication, 33,* 111-123.

Turow, J. (1984). *Media industries.* New York: Longman.

Turow, J., & Coe, L. (1984). Curing television's ills: The portrayal of health care. *Journal of Communication, 34,* 36-51.

Tyler, T. M., & Cook, F. L. (1984). The mass media and judgments of risk: Distinguishing impact on personal and societal level judgments. *Journal of Personality and Social Psychology, 47,* 693-708.

Van der Voort, T.H.A. (1986). *Television Violence: A child's eye view.* Amsterdam, Holland: Elsevier Science.

van Dijk, T. A. (1983). Discourse analysis: Its development and application to the structure of news. *Journal of Communication, 33,* 20-43.

Varis, T. (1984). The international flow of television programs. *Journal of Communication, 34,* 143-152.

Vidmar, N., & Flaherty, D. H. (1985). Concern of personal privacy in an electronic age. *Journal of Communication, 35,* 91-103.

Vidmar, N., & Rokeach, M. (1974). Archie Bunker's bigotry: A study in selective perception and exposure. *Journal of Communication, 24*(1), 36-47.

Virts, P. H. (1984). Information processing in television program decision making. *Journal of Broadcasting, 28,* 65-78.

Volosinov, V. N. (1973). *Marxism and the philosophy of language* (L. Matejka & I. R. Titunik, Trans., original work published in 1929). New York: Seminar.

Wahl, O. F., & Roth, R. (1982). Television images of mental illness: Results of a metropolitan Washington media watch. *Journal of Broadcasting, 26,* 599-605.

Wakshlag, J. J., Bart, L., Dudley, J., Growth, G., McCutchen, J., & Rola, R. (1983). Viewer apprehension about victimization and crime drama programs. *Communication Research, 10,* 195-217.

Wakshlag, J., Vial, V., & Tamborini, R. (1983). Selecting crime drama and apprehension about crime. *Human Communication Research, 10,* 227-242.

Wartella, E. (1979a). Children and television: The development of the child's understanding of the medium. In C. Wilhoit & H. de Bock (Eds.), *Mass communication review yearbook 1* (pp. 516-554). Beverly Hills, CA: Sage.

Wartella, E. (Ed.). (1979b). *Children communicating: Media development of thought, speech, and understanding.* Beverly Hills, CA: Sage.

Wartella, E., & Reeves, B. (1985). Historical trends in research on children in the media: 1900-1960. *Journal of Communication, 35,* 118-133.

Watkins, B. (1985). Television viewing as a dominant activity of childhood: A developmental theory of television effects. *Critical Studies in Mass Communication, 2,* 323-337.

Watkins, B., Calvert, S., Huston Stein, A., & Wright, J. C. (1980). Children's recall of television material: Effects of presentation mode and adult labeling. *Developmental Psychology, 16,* 672-674.

Weaver, D. (1980). Audience need for orientation and media effects. *Communication Research, 7,* 361-376.

Weaver, D. (1984). Media agenda-setting and public opinion: Is there a link? In R. N. Bostrom (Ed.), *Communication yearbook 8.* Beverly Hills, CA: Sage.

Weaver, D. H., Buddenbaum, J. M., & Ellenfair, J. (1985). Press freedom, media freedom, and development, 1950-1979: The study of 134 nations. *Journal of Communication, 35,* 104-117.

Weaver, D., & Elliott, S. N. (1985). Who sets the agenda for the media? A study of local agenda building. *Journalism Quarterly, 62,* 87-94.

Weaver, J., & Wakshlag, J. J. (1986). Perceived vulnerability to crime, criminal victimization experience, and television viewing. *Journal of Broadcasting and Electronic Media, 30,* 141-158.

Webb, E. J., Campbell, D. T., Schwartz, R. D., & Sechrest, L. (1966). *Unobtrusive measures, nonreactive research in the social sciences.* Chicago: Rand McNally.

Webster, J. G. (1986). Audience behavior in the new media environment. *Journal of Communication, 36,* 77-91.

Webster, J. G., & Wakshlag, J. J. (1982). The impact of group viewing on patterns of television choice. *Journal of Broadcasting, 26,* 445-456.

Webster, J. T., & Wakshlag, J. J. (1983). The theory of television program choice. *Communication Research, 10,* 430-446.

Weimann, G. (1983). The theater of terror: Effects of press coverage. *Journal of Communication, 33,* 38-45.

Welsch, A. J., & Watt, J. H., Jr. (1982). Visual complexity in young children's learning from television. *Human Communication Research, 8,* 133-145.

Wenner, L. A. (1982). Gratifications sought and obtained in program dependency: A study of network evening news programs and Sixty Minutes. *Communication Research, 9,* 539-560.

Wertham, F. (1954). *Seduction of the innocent.* New York: Holt, Rinehart.

Wigand, R. T., Shipley, C., & Shipley, D. (1984). Transborder data flow, informatics, and national policies. *Journal of Communication, 34,* 153-175.

Wilhoit, G. C., & Weaver, D. (1983). Foreign news coverage and two U.S. wire services: An update. *Journal of Communication, 33,* 132-148.

Williams, R. (1974). *Television: technology and cultural form.* London: Fontana.

Williams, W., Jr., & Semlak, W. D. (1978). Structural effects of TV coverage on political agendas. *Journal of Communication, 28,* 114-119.
Williams, W., Jr., Shapiro, M., & Cutberth, C. (1983). The impact of campaign agendas on perceptions of issues in 1980 campaign. *Journalism Quarterly, 60,* 226-231.
Windahl, S., Hojerback, I., & Hedinsson, E. (1986). Adolescents without television: A study in media deprivation. *Journal of Broadcasting and Electronic Media, 30,* 47-63.
Winett, R. A. (1986). *Information and behavior: Systems of influence.* Hillsdale, NJ: Lawrence Erlbaum.
Winett, R. A., Lichter, I. N., Chinn, D. E., & Stahl, B. (1984). Reducing energy consumption: The long-term effects of a single TV program. *Journal of Communication, 34,* 37-51.
Winter, J. P., & Eyal, C. H. (1981). Agenda-setting for the civil rights issue. *Public Opinion Quarterly, 45,* 376-383.
Withey, S. B., & Abeles, R. P. (Eds.). (1980). *Television and social behavior: Beyond violence and children, a report of the committee on television and social behavior.* Hillsdale, NJ: Lawrence Erlbaum.
Wober, J. M., & Gunter, B. (1986). Television audience research at Britain's Independent Broadcasting Authority, 1974-1984. *Journal of Broadcasting and Electronic Media, 30,* 15-31.
Wolf, M. A. (1987). How children negotiate television. In T. R. Lindlof (Ed.), *Natural audiences.* Norwood, NJ: Ablex.
Wolf, M. A., Meyer, T. P., & White, C. (1982). A rules-based study of television's role in the construction of social reality. *Journal of Broadcasting, 26,* 813-829.
Worchel, S., Hardy, T. W., & Hurley, R. (1976). The effects of commercial interruptions of violent and nonviolent films on viewers' subsequent aggression. *Journal of Experimental Social Psychology, 12,* 220-232.
Worth, S., & Adair, J. (1972). *Through Navajo eyes: An exploration in anthropology and film communication.* Bloomington: Indiana University Press.
Wright, C. R. (1965). *Mass communication: A sociological perspective.* New York: Random House.
Wright, J. W. II, & Hosman, L. A. (1986). Listenership perceptions of radio news. *Journalism Quarterly, 63,* 802-808, 814.
Wulfemeyer, K. T. (1983). The interests and preferences of audience for local television news. *Journalism Quarterly, 60,* 323-328.
Yaffe, M. (1982). *The influence of pornography on behavior.* London: Academic Press.
Zemach, T., & Cohen, A. (1986). Perception of gender equality on television and in social reality. *Journal of Broadcasting and Electronic Media, 30,* 427-444.
Zillmann, D. (1979). *Hostility and aggression.* Hillsdale, NJ: Lawrence Erlbaum.
Zillmann, D., & Bryant, J. (1982). Pornography, sexual callousness, and the trivialization of rape. *Journal of Communication, 32,* 10-21.
Zillmann, D., & Bryant, J. (1985a). Affect, mood, and emotion as determinants of selective exposure. In D. Zillmann & J. Bryant (Eds.), *Selective exposure to communication* (pp. 157-190). Hillsdale, NJ: Lawrence Erlbaum.
Zillmann, D., & Bryant, J. (Eds.). (1985b). *Selective exposure to communication.* Hillsdale: Lawrence Erlbaum.
Zillmann, D., & Bryant, J. (1986). Shifting preferences in pornography consumption. *Communication Research, 13,* 560-578.
Zillmann, D., & Bryant, J. (1987a). Effects of pornography: The debate continues: A response. *Journal of Communication, 37,* 187-188.
Zillmann, D., & Bryant, J. (1987b). Pornography and behavior: Alternative explanations: A response. *Journal of Communication, 37,* 189-192.
Zillmann, D., & Johnson, R. C. (1973). Motivated aggressiveness perpetuated by exposure to aggressive films and reduced by exposure to nonaggressive films. *Journal of Research in Personality, 7,* 261-276.

Index

About the Authors

JAMES A. ANDERSON (Ph.D., University of Iowa, 1965) is Professor of Communication at the University of Utah. His scholarly writing concerns the relationship between theory and method in science, an area he most recently explored in *Communication Research: Issues and Methods* (1987). His research interests focus on the communication structures and practices of social action routines, political campaigns, media literacy, and family ethnographies.

TIMOTHY P. MEYER (Ph.D., Ohio University, 1970) is the Ben J. and Joyce Rosenberg Professor at the University of Wisconsin, Green Bay, where he teaches courses in mediated and interpersonal communication. He was formerly on the faculty of Communication Studies at the University of Massachusetts, Amherst, and was Professor of Radio/Television/Film at the University of Texas at Austin.

His research includes more than 200 books, book chapters, journal articles, and scholarly papers, and has been featured in publications outside and in the field of communication, including the *Journal of Personality & Social Psychology, Journal of International Cultural Studies, Journal of Advertising, Journal of Marketing, Journal of Advertising Research, Journalism Quarterly, Journal of Communication, Journal of Broadcasting, Critical Studies in Mass Communication,* and elsewhere. His research has focused on the impact of mediated communication, most notably on children and adolescents, advertising and marketing communication, traditional and nontraditional research methods, and communication theory.

He is also a research consultant and has done work in media and in management communications for clients in the entertainment industry, network news, and major corporations in the Midwest and the East and West coasts. His clients have included NBC, ABC, Lorimar, Allstate Insurance, and General Motors.

NOTES